HR MANAGER'S GUIDE TO ATTENDANCE MANAGEMENT

Hugh Secord, B.A., M.B.A., C.H.R.P.

THOMSON
CARSWELL

Includes Index.

ISBN 978-0-7798-1452-7

A cataloguing record for this publication is available from Library and Archives Canada.

THOMSON CARSWELL

One Corporate Plaza
2075 Kennedy Road
Toronto, Ontario
M1T 3V4

Customer Relations
Toronto 1-416-609-3800
Elsewhere in Canada/U.S. 1-800-387-5164
Fax 1-416-298-5082
World Wide Web: http://www.carswell.com
E-mail: carswell.orders@thomsonreuters.com

About the Author

Hugh Secord, B.A., M.B.A., C.H.R.P. has his Masters of Business Administration (Finance) from York University and an Honours Bachelor of Arts (Sociology, Economics) from the University of Toronto. Hugh Secord has twenty-three years of experience in Labour Relations and Human Resources Management, the majority of which has been at the executive level. Hugh has extensive experience in the manufacturing and distribution industries where he has acted as chief spokesman in over one hundred collective agreements and has been involved in resolving hundreds of grievances and employment disputes. He is engaged in an active practice as a Management Consultant specializing in labour-management relations, employee relations, and transforming organizational culture. His clients are primarily in the private sector engaged in a variety of activities including primary industries, manufacturing, financial services, real estate development, and distribution/logistics.

Hugh authored *Implementing Best Practices in Human Resources Management* and is the author of the Carswell publications, *Best Practices: Communication Issues in Human Resources Management*, *Best Practices: Strategic Human Resources Management*, and *Best Practices: Termination.* Hugh has written over one hundred and fifty articles on Labour Relations and Human Resources topics. In addition, he has taught Employment Law and Organizational Behaviour and has spoken on labour topics in various forums.

TABLE OF CONTENTS

GUIDE TO ATTENDANCE MANAGEMENT

Chapter 1 — The Importance of Attendance Management

1.1 — What is Attendance Management?

One of the fundamental bases for the employment relationship is the implicit understanding that the employee will report for work regularly. In exchange for an agreed-upon wage and other considerations the employee agrees to attend work when scheduled to do so. Some employment contracts may offer flexible schedules whereby the individual agrees to work a given number of hours over a period of time, but the premise remains the same. The essential understanding is that the employee will provide the services he was contracted for during a set period of time.

If we consider this at its extreme, the underlying assumption is that the individual will report to work one each day he is scheduled to work. However, given the enduring nature of the employment relationship, employers accept that the occasional absence due to illness, injury, or family emergency, would not be enough to repudiate the contract. Employers who can afford to will provide income protection coverage for employees who become disabled and cannot perform their regular duties for a period of time. It is taken as a given that not all employees will be able to attend work each and every time they are scheduled to do so.

Given the understanding that from time to time some employees will be absent from work, employers ought to be able to expect a normal pattern of absenteeism. For any given population of employees there should be a normal rate of absenteeism. Unfortunately there is not much consensus as to what a normal rate of absenteeism is.

Arbitrators, for example, tend to subscribe to the belief that the level of absenteeism will differ depending on the organization, working conditions and industry standards. This notion has a certain intuitive appeal. One would assume that people working in physical demanding occupations or who toiled under harsh conditions would likely have higher absenteeism rates than those who work in more sedentary roles in less taxing environments. However, empirical evidence does not necessarily support these assumptions.

Companies that actively manage employee attendance will have significantly lower rates of absenteeism then those in the same industry that do not. Regardless of the industry an organization can maintain regular attendance amongst all its employees by proactively addressing the issues that cause excessive absenteeism. Regardless of the industry, attendance at work is not so much dependant on the nature of the work and the physical working conditions as it is on the overall culture of the organization.

Attendance Management is about stating the organization's expectations regarding reporting to work regularly and on time, proactively addressing the root causes of excessive absenteeism, and ensuring employees understand the consequences of not attending at work.

In this book we will cover all the various aspects of Attendance Management including:

- Monitoring Attendance and Measuring Absenteeism
- Identifying Attendance Abuse
- Dealing with Culpable Absenteeism
- Dealing with Innocent Absenteeism
- Identifying Pattern Absenteeism and its Root Causes
- Managing Lateness
- Managing Workplace Injuries and Occupational Illnesses
- Developing Policies for Family Emergencies
- Rewards and Recognition for Perfect Attendance

Attendance management is an extremely important part of human resources management. The measure of absenteeism is an effective measure of the efficacy of an organization's overall employee relations programming. If absenteeism is high then we can surmise that employee morale is low and that the employee relations efforts are not effective. On the other hand, if absenteeism is low we can surmise that employees are engaged and empowered and, therefore, the programming is effective.

Unfortunately there is no magic bullet that will end all the attendance issues an organization may face. Attendance Management is a complex undertaking that involves a variety of interlinked initiatives. It also requires front line supervisors to be skilled at dealing with employee issues in a balanced fashion. Nevertheless, an organization that has deployed the full suite of initiatives discussed in this book will undoubtedly succeed in maintaining above average attendance statistics (and a decisive competitive advantage); each initiative on its own will contribute to improving employee attendance. An organization does not have to implement every program discussed herein. In fact at the outset an organization should focus on the initiatives that will have the biggest initial return. As the programs gains momentum the organization can add other initiatives and reap additional gains.

1.2 — The Importance of Managing Attendance

Attendance is measured as a rate of absenteeism. There are a number of variations on how to measure absenteeism based on what is included or omitted from the measure. Typically we focus on short-term or casual absenteeism and do not include long-term absences in the measure. Therefore a typical absenteeism rate is defined as the number of days lost due to absences of three days or less as a proportion to the number of work days scheduled. This is usually expressed as a percentage.

$$\text{Casual Absenteeism \%} = \frac{\text{Days Lost Due to Absences of Less than Three Days}}{\text{Number of Scheduled Work Days}}$$

The numerator typically does not include long-term absences (where a single absence exceeds three days), bereavement leave, excused leaves of absence, jury duty or attendance in court as a witness, and in some cases absences due to workplace injuries or illnesses. The rationale for this is that these types of absences are beyond the immediate control of both the organization and the individual. In the case of an illness or injury that exceeds three days the assumption is that the absence is less controllable than casual absences of a day or two. We will discuss this point later. The denominator only includes scheduled days of work and thus excludes days not scheduled (e.g. weekends), statutory holidays, and vacation days.

While this is an adequate measure and will serve as an important tool in managing casual absenteeism it does not measure the true effect of absenteeism on the organization. The full absenteeism rate is the number of days lost due to all absences as a proportion of the work days scheduled. We will still exclude bereavement leave, excused leaves of absence, and jury duty or attendance in court as a witness. However, we would include all absences due to injury, illness, or family emergency regardless of the length of the absence or the cause.

$$\text{Full Absenteeism \%} = \frac{\text{Days Lost Due to Absences}}{\text{Number of Scheduled Work Days}}$$

We will discuss these measures at length later. However, we introduce them here so the reader will appreciate how the impact of absenteeism is determined.

1.3 — The Statistics Canada 1997 Labour Force Survey

The Statistics Canada 1997 Labour Force Survey showed that an average 7.4 days were missed by each full-time employee in 1997. For a company with 1,000 employees, with an average salary of $190 per day, this translated into $1,400 per employee, per year for incidental absenteeism or a total cost to the company of $1.4 million per year.

Statistics Canada reported in 2004 that the employee absenteeism rate jumped from 7.3 workdays in 1997 to more than 9 workdays. Across Canada for all employers this translated to a loss of 97.5 million workdays. With an average wage in 2004 of $18.50 the losses to the economy due to absenteeism was a staggering $1.8 billion. This amount only measures the wages for those days. The actual cost to the economy is significantly higher. Unfortunately there is no consensus as to what the cost actually is but we can safely presume that inflating the lost wages by a factor of ten to account for lost production, health care costs, replacement worker costs, and other related costs is a relatively conservative estimate. So absenteeism is costing the Canadian economy well in excess of $18 billion annually.

Absenteeism does differ between sectors of the economy (though the causal factors are speculative and exceptions to the patterns may indicate that the causes are cultural rather than related to the working environment).

Absenteeism By Industry[1]

Industry	Days Lost Per Annum
Health care and social services	14.4
Transportation and warehousing	11.1
Public administration	10.9
Utilities	10.2
Manufacturing	9.9
Industry	Days Lost Per Annum

[1]Source: Statistics Canada *Days Lost per Worker by Industry 1997 and 2007*. Version modified May 22, 2008. http://www40.statscan.ca/101/cst01/labor61a.htm?sdi=days lost per worker

Business, building and other support services	9.6	
All services-producing industries	9.2	
All goods-producing industries		9.1
Educational services	8.8	
Accommodation and food services	7.9	
Primary industries		7.9
Finance, insurance, real estate, and leasing	7.8	
Information, culture, and recreation	7.8	
Trade		7.6
Other services	7.6	
Construction	7.2	
Professional, scientific, and technical	5.6	

The latest StatsCan census data (2007) shows that absenteeism is generally increasing in all industries:

Industry	Days Lost Per Annum	
Health care and social services		14.3
Transportation and warehousing	12.2	
Public administration	11.2	
Utilities		10.2
Manufacturing	10.6	
Business, building and other support services	10.3	
All services-producing industries	9.8	
All goods-producing industries		10.6
Educational services	8.1	
Accommodation and food services	8.5	
Primary industries		8.9
Finance, insurance, real estate, and leasing	8.1	

Information, culture, and recreation	9.3	
Trade		9.3
Other services	9.5	
Construction	9.4	
Professional, scientific, and technical	6.6	

Notes:

* Includes days lost due to personal or family responsibilities

Highlights from the 2007 census data include the following observations:

- Estimates from the Labour Force Survey indicate that both the incidence and the number of days lost for personal reasons (illness or disability, and personal or family responsibilities) have shown a rising trend since 1997. Several factors have contributed: notably, an aging workforce; the growing share of women in the workforce, especially mothers with young children; high worker stress; and more generous sick- and family-related leave benefits.

- In an average week in 1997, excluding women on maternity leave, about 5.5% (484,000) of all full-time employees holding one job were absent from work for all or part of the week for personal reasons. By 2007, the figure had risen to 8.8% (969,000). Total work time missed also rose steadily, from 3.0% of the scheduled week in 1997 to 4.1% in 2007. Extrapolated over the full year, work time lost for personal reasons increased from the equivalent of 7.4 days per worker in 1997 to 10.2 days in 2007.

- Full-time employees in the public sector (more likely unionized or female) lost more work time in 2007 for personal reasons (about 12.8 days on average) than their private-sector counterparts (9.5 days).

Ernest B. Akyeampong noted in his analysis titled, "Trends and seasonality in absenteeism:"[2]

> The weekly number of employees failing to report for work because of an illness or disability has increased steadily over the past 10 years — from 431,000 in 1997 to 758,000 in 2006. Controlling for employment growth does not change the picture; the incidence rose consistently, climbing from 3.8% in 1997 to 5.4% in 2006. *Contributing factors include the aging of the workforce and improvements in sick-leave entitlements.* [Emphasis mine.]

[2]Statistics Canada, 2000-. *Perspectives on Labour and Income*, Statistics Canada Catalogue no. 75-001-XIE http://www.statcan.ca/english/freepub/75-001-XIE/75-001-XIE2007106.htm

> The trend for each type of illness-related absence has been generally upward, but much more pronounced for part-week absences. For example, while the number of employees reporting a full-week absence rose by almost one-third (from 199,000 in 1997 to 262,000 in 2006), part-week absences more than doubled (from 232,000 to 496,000). Similarly, the incidence of full-week absences rose marginally from 1.8% to 1.9% between 1997 and 2006, while that of part-week absences jumped from 2.0% to 3.5%. *Simply stated, part-week absences have been the major driving force for the increase in overall work absences due to illness or disability during the past decade.* [Emphasis mine.]

We can surmise that the rising trend is indicative of an increasing sense of entitlement amongst employees. The expectations that an employee is entitled to take time off regardless of the actual need is created by increasing disability benefits and by the perception that because of non-work related priorities for family matters the individual is entitled to take time away from work to address personal needs.

Interestingly Akyeampong also noted that absenteeism rates fluctuated seasonally, increasing during the winter months. While the incidence of the flu and colds likely increases during the colder months, people are also more likely to take vacation time during the summer. Perhaps this skews reporting because individuals may not be reporting illnesses while on vacation. It is also possible that there is less perceived need to use up sick leave entitlements when vacation credits are available to an employee.

In another analysis of absenteeism[3] trends Katherine Marshall noted: "The combination of two job-related factors — belonging to a union and having medical or disability insurance coverage — also significantly increased the likelihood (1.7 times) of a leave from work for personal illness when compared with workers who had neither benefit."

This observation again seems consistent with the notion of a developing culture of entitlement wherein employees fell they have the absolute right to take time off regardless of whether they have an illness that justifies the absence.

Marshall further observes:

> While unions may not directly encourage the use of long-term personal illness leave, they may have the power to protect against possible reprimand and hence may indirectly bolster its use. Furthermore, unionized settings tend to offer more generous sick leave policies. Indeed, almost half (47%) of unionized leave takers reported receiving full pay compensation compared with only one-quarter of the total not unionized. Therefore, non-unionized workers (with or without insurance coverage) may be more likely to continue working, despite not feeling well, if reprisal is feared

---

[3]Statistics Canada, 2000-. *Perspectives on Labour and Income*, Statistics Canada Catalogue no. 75-001-XIE. http://www.statcan.ca/english/freepub/75-001-XIE/1040675-001-XIE.html Monthly.

> or reduced pay is at stake. In reality, choosing to take an absence falls on a continuum, based on factors such as perceived consequences, degree of work attachment, and ability to attend.

Interestingly she also notes that while long-term absences are increasing in frequency absences due to work-related illness and injury has been dramatically declining. Quoting the Canadian Centre for Occupational Health and Safety,[4] she notes this reduction is due to many factors including: changing technologies, better educated workers, and industry initiatives together with occupational health and safety policies and programs.

We can hypothesize from these trends and analyses that given that the increase in absenteeism may be influenced by factors such as motivation, work attachment, and perceived consequences there is likely a degree of volition involved in high rates of absenteeism. Organizations that place a significant emphasis on attendance management controls, in a similar manner to how health and safety issues have been addressed, are likely to see significant decreases in their rates of absenteeism and substantial cost savings as a result.

Attendance management programs have been effective in reducing absenteeism rates by more than 50% regardless of the industry. It is not unheard of for companies to maintain absenteeism rates of less than 1%. They obviously enjoy a significant cost advantage over their competitors because of this. More importantly they also are likely to experience higher levels of productivity, improved product/service quality, and lower turnover as a result.

Readers should try to estimate the cost of absenteeism their organizations are incurring.

Let's use the example of a manufacturing firm with 500 employees and an average weighted straight time wage of $22.50. At the low range the organization can expect to lose 4,950 days of production. If we factor in the full payroll burden at 30% the cost of a loss day is $234 and the total cost for this organization is $1,158,300 per year. At the high range the loss is closer to $10 million.

For argument's sake let's assume the low end of the range. A 50% reduction would net the company of over $500k in savings. For an organization of 500 employees that buys a lot of human resources programming. In our experience solid Attendance management programs typically reduce absen-

[4]Canadian Centre for Occupational Health and Safety (CCOHS). 2003. Performance report for the period ending March 31, 2003. Ottawa: CCOHS. www.ccohs.ca/ccohs/reports/performance_03.html

teeism to between 2% and 4%; so a 50% reduction is well within the reach of any organization.

One of the problems that human resources practitioners face in dealing with absenteeism is that many organizations do not measure it at all, and when they do they tend to underestimate the costs. In some cases it is simply assumed that the hidden costs are part of doing business. Managers do not realize the significant gains that can be made in controlling absenteeism.

1.4 — Corporate Culture and Attendance Management

It is not relevant what industry an organization is in with respect to controlling absenteeism. Looking at the statistics above at first glance it would seem that this is a misguided notion. Many argue that health care workers and people employed in social services experience higher rates of absenteeism because of the nature of their professions. These workers tend to be more prone to social stressors that will impact on their health. We do not dispute this. However, this does not explain why people in public administration experience significantly higher rates of absenteeism then people employed in primary industries.

The full explanation of why rates differ between economic sectors has never been fully explored and likely never will be. There are a complex set of factors that influence absenteeism rates. One that is often overlooked is the correlation between absenteeism and the availability of income protection benefits. Another is that there tends to be higher rates of absenteeism amongst public sector employers then amongst private sector employers.

The organization's culture is the most significant determinant of absenteeism. Company culture has many factors including the specific industrial setting, the nature of the work, and the physical environment. However, an organization can develop a unique culture that sets it completely apart from its industry competitors and in this way can nullify any effects that are common amongst employers in that sector.

So while the statistics seem to indicate that the absenteeism rate will be dictated by the industry the organization operates it is better the reader ignores this and concentrates on developing a culture where regular attendance is the norm. The ideas in this book have been employed in a number of different contexts. In two separate companies in the pulp and paper industry the author worked with the human resources practitioners were able to maintain absenteeism levels of less than 1%. They would not have been able to do this if they had accepted that 7.9 days of absences per year per employee was the norm.

I do not intend to downplay the impact stress has on people in certain occupations. In developing a comprehensive program to deal with absenteeism the practitioner must identify root causes and establish specific approaches to deal with them.

A recurring theme in organizations that experience excessive rates of absenteeism (often exceeding the industry norms reported above) is evidence of a culture of entitlement. Employees believe that the income protection provided to them in the form of paid sick days is a benefit they are entitled to take regardless of whether or not they are sick. Moreover, they do not believe the organization has the right to question their use of these days. Couple this with employees who experience work-related stressors, and are not provided with alternative coping strategies and high absenteeism is bound to occur.

Alternatively organizations that have high degrees of employee engagement and empowerment typically have above-average attendance rates. Certainly one of the ultimate goals for any human resources practitioner is to implement initiatives, including a comprehensive attendance management strategy that will transform the corporate culture from one of *entitlement* to one of *engagement*. The initiatives described herein are intended to provide guidance and support to employees while at the same time raising the company's expectations. The objective is to create a common set of goals and a common value set to motivate the employee to be at work.

1.5 — The Relationship Between Attendance and Work-Life Balance

Each year our lives seem to become more complex. People are living longer. Families have come to depend on two incomes in order to maintain a reasonable standard of living. The demands placed on individuals at home and at work seem to be increasing and there appears to be an erosion of the traditional family support networks. Despite technological advances and increased levels of productivity most Canadians are working longer hours today than they did a decade ago.

These are some of the factors that have disrupted the work-life balance. Older workers are finding that because their parents are living longer, and they have chosen to have children of their own later in life, they are faced with the prospect of having to be caregivers to both at the same time. With both spouses working there often is no one immediately available to tend to a sick child or parent when an emergency arises. In single parent families the stress of these factors is compounded.

The cost of urban living has dramatically increased in Canada. Hence many workers must commute from the suburbs. The increased time going to and from work has significantly reduced the amount of time workers are able to spend with their families and to tend to their household responsibilities.

In the workplace itself there have been many changes. Dramatic shifts in technology put consistent pressure on employees to keep up or become obsolete. Through a number of economic corrections organizations have adopted a "lean and mean" approach which translates into fewer workers doing more things.

It is safe to assume that workers today face many more stressors than they did a few decades ago. We certainly see this as a correlation with rising absenteeism rates. However, we might hypothesize that while stressors are changing the root cause of increased worker distress, many workers do not have effective coping strategies to help them deal with stress.

Stress is the condition that results when a person experiences a perceived disruption in his environment that causes an imbalance between the demands of the situation and the resources available to the individual (biological, physiological, or social) to meet those demands. In biological terms stress is the disruption of homeostasis (the condition when all internal systems are in balance) through physical or psychological stimuli.

When we experience stress our bodies react. We experience a state of alarm during which hormones are released, we react, and then we rest. In other words we adapt to the situations to meet the demands and cope with the stressor (or external stimulus). In many situations we are able to cope and may even feel euphoric after having dealt with the stressor. This state is known as eustress and is a positive outcome. When we train for an athletic endeavour we put stress on our bodies then allow it to rest. This should create a sense of well-being and will strengthen our bodies to be able to cope with new stressors (more exercise).

However, in some situations we are not able to cope as well and the result is distress. If, for example, we are exposed to a stressor for a sustained period and cannot adapt an effective coping strategy then we will become distressed. This can become manifest in several different types of health problems.

In the absence of work-life balance, we need to seek coping strategies. These might involve removing ourselves from the stressful situation, changing our attitudes towards the stressor, or adapting a specific coping strategy to manage the stress. If we do not find a way to restore the balance then we will experience distress in any number of ways including health problems, substance abuse, or increased friction at work or at home.

Obviously for people in distress one coping strategy may be to absent themselves from work. While this may be effective in the very short term it is not an effective long-term strategy. So work-life stressors can have an impact on attendance simply because employees may experience anxiety and choose to take a mental health day.

However, the more problematic product of work-life imbalance is the long-term effects on an individual's health. People in distress can suffer from heart disease, ulcers, adaptation disorders, and substance abuse. They may also be prone to many transitory illnesses because of a reduced ability to ward off illnesses. All of these can lead to significant increases in absenteeism.

1.6 — Employee Engagement and Attendance

An engaged employee is an individual who actively subscribes to the objectives of the organization and is committed to the achievement of those goals. The engaged employee readily identifies with the mission and values of the organization and proactively acts to further them.

Engaged employees are enthusiastic about their work and are willing to invest discretionary effort into the enterprise. So, even if there are few negative consequences to calling in sick the engaged individual will choose to attend work unless she is physically unable to. Conversely a disengaged employee will direct discretionary effort towards other pursuits.

How does an organization take steps to engage employees? There are a number of factors that influence an individual's level of work commitment including:

- Job Importance: Employees want a sense that what they do is important and/or they are contributing to an important objective or undertaking.
- Role Clarity: If employees understand precisely what is expected of them they are able to make decisions about their work throughout the day and to take the initiative to ward off boredom or alienation.
- Opportunities: Employees are likely to be more committed if they see what's in it for them to make an effort. This could be opportunities for advancement, transfers to interesting assignments, or simply opportunities to learn new skills.
- Regular: One of the most overlooked performance management tools is supervisory feedback. Employees want to know how well they are performing from a reliable source they respect.

- Organizational Integrity: Employees want to identify with the mission and values of the organization and to be assured that they are working for an ethical company.
- Effective Communications: Employees need to know what is going on, particularly with respect to how organizational events will impact them and their roles.

1.7 — Understanding Behaviour: Why Employees Stay Away From Work

People stay away from work for a variety of reasons. When employees are sick or injured they will be absent until they have recovered. (Although, we all seem to know those people who despite being too ill insist on reporting to work and infecting others.) People stay away from work for other reasons. They may have outside demands on their time such as attending to a sick child or parent or dealing with a private matter.

An employee may experience a conflict in the demands on his time. In dealing with a dying relative the commitment to family will outweigh the commitment to the workplace and he will choose to be absent. For others the lack of commitment to their work or their employer results in their choosing not to attend at work due to relatively minor conflicts with their time or energy.

A disengaged employee will opt out of reporting to work if she experiences a problem starting her car in the morning. On a practical level she could take public transportation or ask a friend to drive her to work. However, because she is not committed to attending, and because her perceptions of the potential consequences are that nothing much negative will happen she will choose to take the day off.

If employees feel entitled to days off with pay they will actively seek opportunities to use them rather than losing the perceived benefit even though the consequences may be a lack of adequate income protection in the event of a real illness later in the year. Again this is a product of the individual weighing the consequences of his behaviour against the perceived benefits. It is also a product of the individual's level of engagement.

The employee who is not committed will perceive that to a certain extent he has the discretion as to whether or not he needs to report to work on a given day. In the absence of any consequences to deter absences an employee not committed to his work will at time use his discretion to absent himself from work to pursue other interests.

However, many organizations fail to understand that there are many different reasons why employees are unable to maintain regular attendance. They try to find a singular approach that will address people with problematic attendance records. Typically this involves applying a variation of progressive discipline. However, punishment will not be effective as a consequence of behaviour that is non-culpable. Punishing an employee who is sick, injured, or suffers from a chronic condition will not motivate the individual to make improvements. In fact, it may simply exasperate the problem. Punishment alone will also not yield lasting results. The approaches discussed in this book advocate mixed consequences. When an employee does something wrong you punish the individual. When he does something right, you reward him. In other cases you might withhold praise. In others you may need to provide coaching, counselling, or other forms of support.

The interesting thing about attendance management is that it calls upon supervisors and managers to use all the skills required to be a good people manager. If supervisory staff are able to master the skills discussed in this book, chances are they will be able to manage employees in all contingencies. So as a side benefit not only will implementing an effective attendance management process result in bottom-line savings and improved productivity, but the organization will gain a more confident and effective supervisory group who are able to handle all kinds of different situations.

Chapter 2 — Principles of Attendance Management

2.1 — The Legal Framework of Managing Attendance

One of the fundamental duties an employee has under a contract of employment is to regularly attend work. In exchange for a promised wage or salary, the individual agrees to report to work when scheduled to do so. It is the basis of the employment agreement. The obligation to attend work means that an employee is expected to be at work regularly, to be punctual, and to report in a condition fit to perform his prescribed duties. An exception to this rule is the call-casual employee who does not expect regularly scheduled hours and therefore is not obliged to report when called (though after repeated refusals the employer would be entitled to end the relationship without notice). In this instance the employer also has fewer obligations and is not obliged to provide work or compensation on a regular or scheduled basis, or at all.

With the exceptions of on-call/casual employees and employees hired on a fixed term, people are hired at a company with the expectation that the employment will continue indefinitely. Hence there is an expectation that considering the permanent nature of the work and the promise of compensation the individual will be at work performing the required duties when scheduled to do so.

The specific requirements of attendance may differ depending on the nature of the work or the individual's position in the organizational hierarchy. Whereas an executive may not be obliged to maintain a fixed schedule of hours, people lower in the chain of command will be expected to report to work at a specified time and to work a scheduled number of hours. In the former case of the executive the obligation to attend at work might be extended to include attendance at social events or conferences outside normal business hours or away from the normal place of business.

Attendance at work usually implies actually being present at the place of business or reporting to a given location to begin the workday. Again this requirement will vary depending on the nature of the employment. Executives are not necessarily required to report to a specific location on a scheduled basis, whereas an accounting clerk will be. With the advent of telecommunications technology, alternative arrangements can be made for people to work at home regularly or on an ad hoc basis and still be considered as having been in attendance on those days.

In an ideal world the expectations to report to work as scheduled means that an employee is expected to report to work every day he is scheduled to do so. Obviously over the course of years of employment events may occur that make it impossible for the person to report to work. People get sick, they may be injured in an accident, or they may have to take care of a family emergency. A temporary absence for legitimate reasons does not constitute a breach of the employment contract. Nor does a single incident of tardiness give cause to terminate an individual.

However, excessive absences, tardiness, or the permanent inability to attend work could constitute a breach of the employment contract and result in ending the employment relationship. The question for the employer is to define what constitutes excessive absences or tardiness, or alternatively to determine what constitutes a permanent disability that prevents the individual from performing the fundamental duties of his position.

An organization's tolerance for absenteeism will be determined by a number of different factors. Its culture may influence what is acceptable and what constitutes excessive absenteeism. Hence, excessive absenteeism is usually defined in relation to an organizational average or industrial norm. The organization may also tolerate different levels of absenteeism depending on the specific nature of the individual's work. Higher levels of absenteeism may be tolerated for production workers because the absence of an individual does not have a significant impact on the overall running of the business, whereas the continued absence of an executive could have a detrimental impact on the organization even if it persists only over a relatively short period of time.

2.2 — Culpable Absenteeism

An absence for reasons that are not legitimate may constitute just and sufficient cause for termination even if there is only one occurrence. The employee has an obligation to report any absence to the employer on a timely basis and to provide a reason for the absence. The employer is also entitled to require supporting evidence from the employee to justify the absence. An employer is entitled to end the employment relationship if the employee has not reported the absence in a timely manner or if the employee fails to provide a legitimate reason for the absence. However, the employer must provide the employee with an opportunity to provide an explanation for the absence and/or his failure to report it in a timely manner.

Employees are not entitled to take scheduled time off work unless they have a legitimate reason for not being able to attend or they have been authorized to take leave of their schedule. Employees who absent themselves for reasons that are not considered legitimate may be subject to disciplinary action and in some cases even a single incident may be considered a breach of the employment contract and just cause for dismissal without notice.

Culpable absenteeism is blameworthy absenteeism. Taking a day off sick when not actually sick is culpable behaviour worthy of some discipline. Other forms of culpable absenteeism may include absences due to self-inflicted illness such as a hangover brought on by overindulgence or injuries caused by extreme recreational activities. The common element being that the individual has direct control over the absence and therefore the employer is not obliged to excuse the absence.

Tardiness is also typically considered as being culpable behaviour. A single incidence of lateness due to oversleeping or car problems might be excused, if the individual otherwise has a clean record of attendance. However, repeated tardiness is considered to be a choice made by the employee not to take care of the underlying problem causing the tardiness. Again because the individual has control over her tardiness and there is an element of volition the employer does not have to tolerate or excuse the behaviour.

There are other examples of attendance-related behaviours that are culpable and in most cases should result in immediate termination. These include falsifying medical notes, making false claims for disability benefits, or faking an injury. These are serious offenses and can be considered as criminal or quasi-criminal. As such the employer bears a high standard of proof if it is relying on one of these causes to end the employment relationship.

2.3 — Innocent Absenteeism

Most employee absences are considered innocent or non-culpable. Individuals, through no direct fault of their own, may become ill, get injured, or have to face a family emergency. Innocent absenteeism includes:

- sickness
- injury (work-related or otherwise)
- family emergencies

Innocent absenteeism is not considered blameworthy, but in many respects it is considered to be within the control of the individual. As discipline has no effect in controlling or reducing innocent absenteeism, the individual's supervisor needs to counsel the individual instead on how to take steps to improve his attendance.

Innocent absenteeism may take many different forms and the management of each will differ. These include:

- excessive "casual" absenteeism: where the individual has a pattern of taking one or two days off sick and the total days absent exceed the company average
- chronic Absenteeism: where the individual has a high incidence of illnesses or injuries that cause him to be absent for significant periods of time
- pattern absenteeism: a form of excessive absenteeism where the days taken form an obvious pattern such as Fridays and Mondays
- long-term absences: were the individual is off for an extended period of time measured in months

Many organizations provide specific benefits to insure employees for any loss of income due to sickness or illness. Unfortunately this has lead to the belief amongst employees and supervisors alike, that the organization cannot question any absence covered under these benefits. In fact, because these absences are insured the company has the right to insist that the employee validate the need for the absence. As well high users of the benefits should be counselled on how to reduce their usage. The only distinction we draw is that if the behaviour is not directly culpable then a disciplinary response is inappropriate.

Family emergencies tend to be included as part of innocent absenteeism but are distinct. While the employee is not culpable she can take steps to mitigate the impact on her attendance and accommodate the needs of the employer (to have the individual at work).

2.4 — Approved Leaves

Employees may be absent, with or without pay, under an approved leave of absence covered under a company policy or collective agreement. Many employers establish policies that allow employees days off with pay for bereavement, jury duty, court appearances under subpoena, or for legitimate personal reasons. These days are typically not included as part of absenteeism as they are seen as being external to the individual and beyond their control.

While relatively rare some employees may abuse these leaves. Unfortunately a small minority of employees may be brazen enough to lie about the death of a family member in order to get an excused day off. Employees may claim more days off for jury duty then they were actually required to be in attendance at court. Obviously these are blameworthy behaviours that should be met with discipline or termination.

The unfortunate consequence of these rare examples of abuse is that the employer should, and has the right, to insist on some proof that the leave is required.

Other forms of approved leave of absence include formal extended leaves and sabbaticals, leaves for doctor or dentist appointments, and other approved reasons leave work early. These are in the complete authority of a supervisor to control and are therefore not normally considered as part of an absenteeism control program. However, in some organizations supervisors have been lax in managing these leaves. As a result the incidence of approved casual absences may have grown to problematic levels. As such these may be brought under the scope of the attendance management program and made part of the training supervisors receive to control overall absenteeism.

2.5 — Emergency Leave

Under the *Ontario Employment Standards Act, 2000*, employees working for organizations with 50 or more employees are entitled to take unpaid leaves of absence for up to ten days in a calendar year for any of the following reasons:

- personal illness, injury or medical emergency
- death, illness, injury, medical emergency of or urgent matters relating to:
    - a spouse
    - a parent, step-parent, foster parent, child, step-child, foster child, grandparent, step-grandparent, grandchild, or step-grandchild of the employee or the employee's spouse
    - the spouse of an employee's child
    - a brother or sister of the employee
    - a relative of the employee who is dependent on the employee for care or assistance.

For most employers these examples of emergency leave will be already covered under an existing company policy or under the terms of a collective agreement. The Act governs minimum standards and not an additional benefit.

2.6 — Frustration of Contract Defined

The frustration of contract stands for the proposition that where one party is unable to discharge his obligations under the contract the other party is entitled to sever the relationship without notice. In employment contracts this doctrine has been commonly applied to cases involving employee absences. When an employee becomes injured or ill and the condition interferes with his regular attendance at work the employment contract may be said to be frustrated. Certainly this is not the case when the absence is transitory or short-term. However, if an individual's injury or illness is of a chronic or permanent nature and is likely to continue to interfere with the regular discharge of his duties to the employer, including the duty to attend work regularly, then the employer may be entitled to deem the contract to be frustrated and to dismiss the employee without notice or severance.

This doctrine has become very controversial in recent years and may be less relevant in the employment context. Before an employer could claim that an employment contract had been frustrated due to illness or injury to the employee the employer would have to demonstrate that:

- The employee's pattern of past absences demonstrated her inability to attend at work regularly; or
- The nature of the individual's injury or illness was permanent and, therefore, it had become impossible for the individual to perform his duties to the employer including the duty to attend at work regularly; and
- The employer had attempted to discharge its duties to accommodate the individual to the point of undue hardship and found it impossible to do so.

A contract is said to be frustrated when one of the parties is unable to fulfill his obligations due to some unforeseen circumstances. In the employment context we usually use the term to refer to terminations resulting from long-term illnesses or injuries. An employer does not have just cause to summarily dismiss an employee simply because he has been absent from work. However in situations where the employee suffers from a permanent condition or injury that prevents her from fulfilling her obligations to the employer the employment contract may become frustrated.

2.7 — Time Theft

The term *time theft* is used in many different contexts. The implied meaning is where an employee is stealing time by doing something other than performing the work he is being paid to perform. Some observers cite the following examples of time theft:

- excessive socializing and personal telephone calls
- using Company time & facilities to operate another business
- handling personal business at work
- slowing down the work pace to create overtime
- taking long lunch hours and breaks

Unfortunately the term is far too dramatic in some cases. These are all examples of culpable behaviour worthy of a disciplinary response. However, the term "theft" implies a serious offense that gives cause to end the employment relationship. A single incident of taking an excessively long lunch break would hardly be just and reasonable cause for termination.

However, there is another form of time theft that does justify immediate dismissal. This occurs when an employee falsifies time records to claim pay for hours not actually worked. A common example of this is to have another employee "clock" the individual in and/or out so that she will get a full days' pay on a day she was absent or worked only part of the shift. In the absence of strong mitigating factors this conduct usually justifies termination for both the individual and the person who assisted them in the conspiracy.

2.8 — Progressive Discipline and Absenteeism

Progressive discipline is a widely accepted hierarchy of disciplinary measures wherein the penalty for misconduct becomes progressively more severe and culminates in the termination of employment. The idea is that penalties will serve as a warning that if immediate corrections in behaviour do not arise then the employee will move closer to the point of discharge.

A typical progression looks like this:

First Offense	—	Verbal Warning
Second Offense	—	Written Warning
Third Offense	—	One-Day Suspension
Fourth Offense	—	Three-Day Suspension
Fifth Offense	—	Termination of Employment

As stated above, discipline is only appropriate in the case of culpable absenteeism. Organizations can create complex and confusing attendance management systems because they mix disciplinary models and end up with employees who have two or three parallel streams of discipline. Supervisors can easily become frustrated by the system and as a result are often lax in the enforcement of policies because they find them to be burdensome and ineffective.

For example, the organization may actually apply discipline to attendance management but separate attendance-related actions from the other causes for discipline. On top of these two systems they might also run a third that only applies to tardiness and a fourth that applies to performance. The result is an unworkable mess.

Following the simple axiom that innocent absenteeism is not subject to discipline then all culpable absenteeism issues should be treated as misconduct and the appropriate level of discipline is determined by the severity of the behaviour and the employee's current record.

2.9 — Positive Discipline and Absenteeism

An alternative to progressive discipline that can be applied to innocent absenteeism is a system called *positive discipline*. Some organizations refer to this as employee counselling or coaching.

It differs from progressive discipline in that there is no penalty associated with each step of the process. However similar progressions and a failure to make substantial and sustained improvements could result in the termination of the employment relationship. While some find it difficult to accept, a termination in this case is not considered disciplinary.

Technically, the employment ends because the employee is unable to demonstrate that he can fulfill his obligations to attend work regularly.

The progressions may move from counselling with the frontline supervisor, to a meeting with the local manager to a penultimate meeting with the general manager and/or the human resources representative.

However, the important distinction is that the focus should be on problem solving. The employee's attendance record should be reviewed and the employee asked what he could do to improve upon it. Offers of assistance through the Employee assistance program may be made, but it is up to the employee to choose a course of action that suits his circumstances.

The key is to ensure that there is a scheduled follow-up and that in the interim period the employee's attendance is monitored. If there are improvements the next follow-up session may be scheduled covering a longer period of time. With continued improvements the employee will eventually have attendance review meeting once per year (in line with all employees under the program).

Scenario A:

The employee is called in to review his absenteeism record for the first time. The supervisor goes over the record and the plant averages and asks the employee if there are any specific reasons for his absenteeism the supervisor should be aware of. The employee does not offer any reasons.

The supervisor explains that apart from the problematic absenteeism record the employee performs well and he would like to see immediate improvements. He informs the employee that the company has a confidential Employee assistance program that he can access if he needs any help dealing with issues. The supervisor then informs the employee that he is scheduling a follow-up meeting in one month's time. The conversation is documented and a letter is sent to the employee covering the discussion.

During the month the employee is absent one day. However, that one day actually is a significant improvement over his previous record. The supervisor tells him at the one month follow-up meeting that the one day absent is an improvement and hopes for continued progress. A subsequent follow-up is scheduled for three months.

Scenario B:

The employee is called in to review her absenteeism record for the first time. The supervisor goes over the record and the plant averages and asks the employee if there are any specific reasons for her absenteeism the supervisor should be aware of. The employee does not offer any reasons.

The supervisor explains that apart from the problematic absenteeism record the employee performs well and he would like to see immediate improvements. He informs the employee that the company has a confidential Employee assistance program that she can access if she needs any help dealing with issues. The supervisor then informs the employee that he is scheduling a follow up meeting in one month's time. The conversation is documented and a letter is sent to the employee covering the discussion.

Over the one-month period the employee is absent three times and a total of five days, which does not represent an improvement at all. She is again asked if there are any specific issues the supervisor should be aware of and the employee remains unresponsive. The supervisor again reminds the employee that help is available and schedules a follow-up meeting in one month's time with the local manager.

You should see the pattern from these two short examples. If there are improvements the process intensity decreases but there still needs to be follow-up. If the employee in Scenario A falls back into an unacceptable pattern he will go back to monthly reviews.

The progressions are not automatic but depend on the circumstances and whether or not the individual is making an effort. When progress is noted the employee's reward is praise from the supervisor (which is documented) and the reduced threat of escalated meetings.

The meetings are short and to the point as the onus must be firmly placed on the shoulders of the employee to correct the problem.

In some cases the employee may simply refuse to acknowledge that there is a problem. There is no need for debate as the process is designed to progress the employee towards having to make a decision to take steps to improve or leave the organization.

However, in rare instances the employee may identify a chronic condition or other mitigating circumstances that will need to be taken into consideration. When this occurs the supervisor/manager should seek guidance from a human resources practitioner.

The progressions are not strictly linear under positive discipline because improvements can occur to change the stage or timing of each step. As well the steps will occur even if there are no triggering events. Under progressive discipline no action is taken unless the employee's actions trigger a response. Under this process meetings are scheduled regardless because positive improvements need to be acknowledged and reinforced in order for the system to work.

2.10 — Measuring Attendance

"That which gets measured gets managed." In order to effectively control absenteeism the first step is to measure it. Conceptually measuring absenteeism is relatively simple. In large organizations it can become more difficult because of the numerous different types of schedules employees may be working. For this reason the best measure is a relative measure of absences to scheduled shifts expressed as a percentage.

There are different ways to measure absenteeism rates depending on what gets included as absences and for what purpose. Typically an organization is going to want a measure of the overall impact of absenteeism on the cost of doing business. However, this measure is too inclusive to serve as a comparator for managing casual absenteeism. So a second measure excluding leaves of absence and long-term absence is calculated to arrive at an average for casual absenteeism. Separate measures can also be developed to isolate days lost due to workplace accidents or injuries (often called severity rates).

The calculation for casual absenteeism typically only includes absences of one to three days (though some organizations may include all absences from one to five days in length).We usually use days absent and days scheduled as opposed to hours in order to keep matters relatively simple.

The total absenteeism rate is the total number of days worked divided by the total number of days scheduled for each employee. For example an employee who is scheduled to work five days a week and has three weeks' vacation and ten statutory holidays is scheduled to work 235 days per year. If this employee is absent 12 days his absenteeism rate is (12/235) X 100 = 5.1%.

This can be compared to the simple average of all employees. If the individual exceeds the average then he is considered to be a high user.

One way to calculate the average might be to take the total number casual absences divided by the total number of scheduled days for all employees. If we had 25 employees all working five days a week with three weeks' vacation and ten statutory holidays the denominator would be 5875. If these 25 employees together were absent for 527 days the absenteeism rate would be (527/5875) X 100 = 9%.

2.11 — Setting Attendance Performance Objectives

In the absence of a formal attendance management program a supervisor may become frustrated with an employee she believes is excessively absent. In meeting with the employee the supervisor is apt to say something along the lines of "Your attendance is terrible. You're never here!" Of course this kind of vague accusation does little more than put the employee on the defensive and set up the potential for conflict.

Hence the measures of actual attendance are important in communicating expectations to the employee in concrete terms. Let's say the employee has been absent 16 times for a total of 26 days over the course of the past twelve months (or 11%). The supervisor can begin the discussion by saying that she wants to simply review the employee's attendance record. She can point out the facts. He may even bring a calendar showing exactly which days the employee missed (year-long attendance record cards are available from most office supply companies and provide an excellent tool for tracking attendance manually). The supervisor can then draw the comparison for the employee to the organization average.

By being objective the employee has little room to argue the facts. The supervisor can then explain that because the employee's absenteeism exceeds the average she would like to explore ways that the employee might improve. The only way the supervisor can actually influence behaviour is to try to get the employee to agree to improve. The most obvious goal is to get his absenteeism rate down to the plant average.

The interesting thing about setting the average as a goal is that if all the high users are able to achieve it the average will come down and they will have a new target to shoot for. Thus using averages in this instance is an easy way to build continuous improvement into the system.

Appendix A — Sample Attendance Management Policies and Procedures

Effective: May 2008

Purpose:

Our attendance management policy has been instituted in order to control absenteeism and provide counselling to employees who have attendance-related problems.

The following policies and procedures are effective May 14, 2007. The policies may be amended from time to time to ensure compliance with any governing legislation, and will be reviewed annually by the senior management team. Team members will be informed by their supervisors of any changes that have an impact on them.

It is our expectation that every team member will attend at work on a regular, timely, and consistent basis. We recognize and accept that team members may from time to time suffer illness or injury that prevents them from reporting to work. However, excessive absenteeism hurts all of us. It drives up the costs of our products, hurts profitability, and puts an added burden on the other employees who do come to work regularly. The intention of these policies and procedures are to provide guidelines so everyone understands how excessive absenteeism will be managed. The policies also establish the rules with respect to authorized absences. Team members should review these rules so that when they need time off they are aware of the processes they need to follow in order to gain authorization.

Authorized Leaves

Preapproved Leaves of Absence: Any team member may apply for a leave of absence of up to one month without pay in order to attend to personal business. Leaves of absence (except as described elsewhere in this policy) are granted only on an exceptional basis. Leaves of absence will only be granted provided there is no significant impact on production or if there is a compelling reason in the view of management to grant such a leave.

In order to be granted a leave of absence a team member must make a written request as far in advance as possible, and no less than one week prior to the anticipated beginning of the leave. The request must state when the leave is to commence, when it is to end, and what the purpose of the leave is. Management reserves the right to require proof of the need for any leave. No leave shall be granted to an employee for the purpose of pursuing gainful employment elsewhere.

Team members who use the leave of absence for a purpose other than the one for which it has been granted will be subject to termination. A team member who fails to return from leave on the anticipated date of return may be deemed to have abandoned his position and his employment may be terminated.

Preapproved leaves of absences do not include leave for family emergencies (see below), though may include compassionate leave under certain circumstances. Therefore management reserves the sole right and discretion to require an employee to use his vacation entitlement first before the leave is granted.

This policy shall also apply to a short-term leave to attend to a pre-booked medical or dental appointment. Given the seasonality of our work it is expected that team members will make every effort to book personal appointments on their own time and where possible to book appointments in the off-season. Where it is impossible for the employee to accommodate the needs of the business a leave of less than one day may be granted provided the company receives a written request at least one week in advance and proof of the appointment. Leave may not be granted if the request is made with less than one week's notice. If the team member requires a full day to attend to an appointment she will be required to use a vacation day rather than being granted a leave under this policy.

Approval to Leave Early: Team Members may request to leave early to attend a pre-booked appointment with a medical or dental practitioner as provided for above, with at least one week's written notice to the company. No other requests to leave early shall be granted.

Other Approved Leaves of Absence: Employees may also be granted authorized leave under other policies governing jury duty, witness duty, parental leave, or bereavement leave.

Sickness and Injury

Policy: Under most circumstances an absence due to personal sickness or injury will be considered an authorized leave. Team members with high absenteeism rates may be required to provide medical substantiation when they are unable to report to work because of an injury or illness, and in any case team members who are absent for a continuous period of more than three days will be required to provide a doctor's note substantiating the reason for the absence.

Casual Absenteeism and Pattern Absenteeism: While sickness or injury is considered a legitimate excuse for absences team members who have high absenteeism rates have a significant impact on the company and on their fellow team members. The company will track casual absenteeism rates (all absences of three days or less) and will counsel any team member whose absenteeism persistently exceeds the average for the business unit. In the event that a team member is unable to reduce his absenteeism rate after several counselling meetings, the company reserves the right to deem his contract of employment to be frustrated and to discharge them.

A specific program will be established for every team member who is considered to be a high user of absences. Team members are expected to cooperate fully in these efforts. Employees may be required to undergo physical exams or to provide medical examination if they continue to have high absenteeism rates or exhibit a pattern of absenteeism.

The company has an Employee assistance program that is available to all team members on a voluntary basis. Team members are encouraged to use this program to assist them in improving high absenteeism rates.

Family Emergencies: Legislation in Ontario provides for authorized leave to team members due to sickness (their own) or due to family emergencies which include having to tend to a sick or dying relative, or to deal with a personal emergency where their presence is required. The ten (10) days provided for under that legislation is inclusive and does not represent an addition to the leaves provided under our policies. There has been a high use of emergency leave in the past that has to be brought down. Hence it should be noted that authorization will only be granted for emergency leave under the definition provided under the *Employment Standards Act* that is substantiated with documented proof and falls within the ten (10) days inclusive of personal sick days.

Team members who have been absent for more than ten (10) days because for sickness, family emergency, and/or any other reason described under the Act, and who subsequently have a need for additional leave will be judged on an individual basis.

Leave will not be granted for "personal reasons." The company reserves the right to use its discretion when granting leave, however no authorization will be granted for emergency leave if the need is not substantiated with appropriate documentation deemed acceptable by the company.

Unauthorized Absences

Culpable Absences and Attendance Related Misconduct: Culpable absenteeism includes any abuse of the company policies or misuse of sick leave. Any use of sick leave or emergency leave other than for accommodating the employee when she is sick or has a true family emergency to deal with will be considered as misuse of the company policies. Any abuse or misuse of company policies in this regard will result in disciplinary measures up to and including the termination of employment.

Team members should also note that they are required to report absences one hour prior to the start of the shift. They are to speak directly with their supervisor whenever possible and provide a reason for the absence, an expected date and time of return, and provide information as to how they may be contacted while they are absent. In the event that the team member cannot reach his supervisor he must leave a message which provides the above mentioned information. Failure to call in one hour prior to the beginning of the shift or to provide the necessary information will be considered as a form of misconduct regardless of the underlying reason for the absence.

Tardiness: It is a reasonable expectation on the part of the company to require team members to report to work on time. This means being at their work stations ready to work when their schedule starts. A team member who reports late, i.e. is not at his work station when the schedule begins, will be consider to be tardy and will be dealt with accordingly.

We understand that on an exceptional basis a team member may be unable to report for work on time. However, team members with a pattern of tardiness will be subject to progressive discipline up to and including discharge. Tardiness, outside of exceptional or fortuitous circumstances, will be considered as a form of culpable absenteeism.

In the event that an employee is late by one hour or more he will not be permitted to work and the day will be recorded as an unexcused absence, and dealt with accordingly.

Gross Misconduct: Gross misconduct as it relates to attendance issues refers to any behaviour that seriously undermines the employment relationship or represents a breach of trust. For example, forging or altering a doctor's note is considered to be gross misconduct. The penalty for acts of gross misconduct is immediate termination of employment.

Chapter 3 — Absenteeism Prevention

3.1 — Managing For Better Attendance

Improving employee attendance pays enormous dividends for any organization. Not only will lower absenteeism reduce the direct costs associated with lost productivity and disability insurance premiums, but the culture of the organization will substantially improve. The morale of employees who do report to work regularly is dragged down by those who have attendance issues. The workload has to be picked up by others who feel the drain on their energy of having to do someone else's work.

Employees who pride themselves on their attendance records will lose respect for their supervisors and management because they see others as getting away with not reporting to work on a regular basis. People who otherwise might never think of skipping a day off work will be less hesitant if they perceive the work culture tolerates the occasional absence without question.

To turn this around the organization has to change expectations. Organizations that experience attendance-related problems may find that a culture of entitlement has been created amongst employees. Where an employer offers a set number of sick days at full pay employees may feel entitled to take those sick days even if they have no cause to use them. Under some sick days policies the employee is not allowed to accumulate days off with pay from year to year. Individuals believe that if they do not use the benefit they are effectively losing the beneficial rewards of it. If the individual sees others availing themselves of the benefit, and there is no downside consequences of doing so even if the benefit is being used frivolously, they will believe that they have to take the time off or they will experience a tangible loss.

In order to counteract the culture of entitlement an organization has to reset its expectations and change the perceptions of the employees. This is no easy task. To understand how this may be accomplished we need to understand what potentially motivates employees and how expectations can be managed for effect.

3.2 — The Hawthorne Effect

The term *Hawthorne effect* refers back to the results of a series of experiments on managing factory workers carried out between 1924 and 1933 by

Elton Mayo at the Hawthorne Works of the Western Electric Company in Chicago. The experiments attempted to determine the effect of lighting on the productivity of the workers. As expected when the lighting levels were increased productivity went up. However, the researchers were puzzled to find that when lighting levels were decreased to the original levels productivity continued to rise. The obvious implications were that some other variables were at play that affected productivity more than lighting levels.

The researchers concluded that the workers were reacting to the fact that they knew they were being observed. The change in working conditions signalled that the researchers expected a change in behaviour to occur. Thus we have come to refer to an experimental effect in the direction expected (e.g. increased productivity) for a reason other than expected (e.g. increased lighting levels) as the Hawthorne effect. In the case of the original experiment at Western Electric a significant positive effect (improved productivity) turned out to have no causal basis in the theoretical motivation for the intervention (improved lighting) but was apparently due to the effect on the participants of knowing themselves to be studied in connection with the outcomes measured. Through the entire series of experiments carried out, the manipulation of various conditions (pay, light levels, rest breaks etc.) resulted in productivity rising, including the eventual return to the original conditions. This held true for individual workers as well as for the group mean. The conclusion drawn by the researchers was that the important effect here was the feeling of being studied. This is now referred to as the Hawthorne effect.

The importance of this study for attendance management is that once employees are made aware that their absenteeism rates will be measured and communicated to them they will gain a feeling of being studied or observed. This alone will likely have a positive effect on behaviour and with little other intervention the organization can expect improvements in attendance. However, these improvements will be temporary at best. The simple reason for this is that without changes in the stimulus the feeling of being observed will subside over time. Also there is a tendency in most organizations for initiatives to begin with a flurry of communications and related activities and then to abate.

So we know that initiating an attendance management program will have some degree of success in the beginning we also need to be aware that in order to sustain improvements the program has to be designed in a way that will make it a feature of the sustained culture of the organization.

3.3 — The Pygmalion Effect

The Pygmalion effect, also known as the Rosenthal effect or teacher-expectancy effect, describes how an individual or group of individuals will outperform a comparator group simply because he or they are expected to.

In their study *Pygmalion in the Classroom* (1968), Robert Rosenthal and Lenore Jacobson found that if teachers were led to expect enhanced performance from some children, then the children did indeed show that enhancement. In some cases such improvement was about twice that shown by other children in the same class. Teachers were told that certain students had higher IQs than others and those students tended to outperform the others even though they had no real advantage in IQ scores.

The purpose of the experiment was to support the hypothesis that reality can be influenced by the expectations of others. This influence can be beneficial as well as detrimental depending on which label an individual is assigned. Rosenthal posited that biased expectancies can essentially affect reality and create self-fulfilling prophecies as a result.

The implications for attendance management are that the expectations of acceptable attendance levels have to be established in the minds of the managers and supervisors. If they believe that the current level of absenteeism is an acceptable norm then they will manage in ways that ultimately maintain that norm. If they, on the other hand, believe that substantial improvements are possible they will act in ways that will support the achievement of those objectives.

Another implication is that positive support will yield positive improvements. Discipline tends not to be effective because it implies the employer anticipates that the person will continue to fail to live up to expectations. Using positive reinforcers is a far more effective way to encourage an employee to improve attendance than meting out penalties for failing to meet attendance objectives.

3.4 — Jastrow's Expectancy Effect

In another series of industrial experiments workers being trained on punch card machines at the U.S. census bureau were told that the inventor of the machine expected it to be capable of processing about 550 cards a day. The observed group was able to attain that level of productivity but was unable to improve upon it. However a second group of keypunchers who were isolated from the expectation were soon doing 2,100 per day. (In Rosenthal & Jacobson, *Pygmalion In The Classroom*, 1968.)

A fixed expectation may create a threshold expectation that becomes difficult to break through. Many casual observers in Canada believe that 8% absenteeism is an accepted norm. This translates into an average of 19 days away from work for every employee. Managers and supervisors who truly believe this to be the norm will communicate this expectation to employees. Breaking through this barrier will be difficult.

The important message here is that expectations should not be fixed but rather communicated as a moving target. The underlying theme in an effective attendance management program is to continuously improve performance towards an ideal of zero absenteeism.

3.5 — The Placebo Effect

Most of us are familiar with the term *placebo*. The placebo effect is the term applied by medical science to the therapeutic and healing effects of inert medicines based solely on the power of suggestion. Technically, this phenomenon is also known as subject-expectancy effects because the medicine works due to the individual believing it will work.

The placebo effect occurs when a patient takes an inert substance (sometimes called a sugar pill) in conjunction with the suggestion from an authority figure or from acquired information that the pill will aid in healing and the patient's condition improves. This effect has been known for years.

Developing expectations in the minds of employees and their supervisors works in the same way as a placebo. The trick is to convince the individual to make lifestyle changes that will improve their health. Put another way, the organization does not have to make any real changes to the environment to improve employee attendance, it only needs to convince employees that improvement is necessary and will happen.

3.6 — Expectancy Theory

Expectancy theory predicts that employees in an organization will be motivated when they believe that:

- putting in more effort will yield better job performance.
- better job performance will lead to organizational rewards, such as an increase in salary or benefits.
- these predicted organizational rewards are valued by the employee in question.

This theory was introduced by Victor H. Vroom. It assumes that behaviour results from conscious choices among alternatives whose purpose it is to maximize pleasure and minimize pain. Together with Edward Lawler and Lyman Porter, Vroom suggested that the relationship between people's behaviour at work and their goals was not as simple as was first imagined by other scientists. Vroom realized that an employee's performance is based on individual factors such as personality, skills, knowledge, experience, and abilities.

As a result he introduced three variables within the expectancy theory:

1. Valance: This refers to the strength of an individual's preference for a particular outcome. For the valance to be positive, the person must prefer attaining the outcome to not attaining it.

2. Instrumentality: This factor is the instrumentality of the first level outcome in obtaining the desired second level outcome. It is the degree to which a first level outcome will lead to the second level outcome.

3. Expectancy: It is the probability or strength of belief that a particular action will lead to a particular first level outcome.

Individuals consider the probability that their efforts will lead to a required performance level (E>P expectancy). If the probability is relatively high, then the person will behave in a way to yield the expected performance. At the same time the individual will assess the probability that successful performance will yield certain outcomes (P>O expectancy). If the probability that it will yield a given outcome and that outcome has a high preference for it then he will behave accordingly.

Expectancy theory tells us that individuals will be motivated to perform if they believe:

- There is a positive correlation between effort and the expected outcome.
- Favourable performance will result in a desirable reward.
- The reward will satisfy an important need.
- The desire to fulfill the need is strong enough to make the effort worthwhile.

The implications for attendance management are that the individual needs to believe that he can take actions that will lead to a positive improvement in attendance. If he believes that he can correct the problem than he needs to also believe that he will be rewarded in some way and that the reward fulfills a need. Finally fulfilling that need has to be important enough to make it worth the effort needed to realize an improvement.

This does not necessarily mean that the organization needs to offer a financial inducement to get people to attend work regularly. Recognition from a supervisor that the person has made an effort and improved may be a substantial reward for the individual. Acceptance and praise by a supervisor consistently ranks high amongst employees as a motivator. Implicit in attendance management efforts is the distant but real threat that a failure to improve could lead to the termination of the employment relationship. Therefore another salient and important reward is the removal of that threat.

3.7 — Learning Theory and Mixed Consequences

There are many variants of learning theory, but one of the most cited is the behavioural school that describes behavioural or operant conditioning, which occurs when a response to a stimulus is reinforced. Basically, operant conditioning is a simple feedback system: if a reward or reinforcement follows the response to a stimulus, then the response becomes more probable in the future. If a punishment or pain follows the response, then the response become less probable in the future.

Simply put if an individual's performance improves and she receives a positive reinforcement such as praise from the supervisor, it becomes highly likely that she will continue to strive to improve. If there is no reinforcement than the probability of continued improvement falls off, unless the individual receives some intrinsic reward from having improved (e.g. feels better about their self-perception).

Performance will also improve if an adverse consequence is taken away. For example, discussions about poor attendance performance may be seen as an adverse consequence (i.e. an unpleasant experience). The fact that such meetings will not be necessary if attendance improves may motivate some employees to improve.

Punishment is used to inhibit bad behaviour. Thus when the behaviour stops the punishment also stops.

The implications for attendance management are that the program design should consider different consequences depending on the behaviour being addressed and individual factors.

3.8 — Implementing an Attendance Management Program

The motivational theories cited above provide us with the foundations to build an effective attendance management system. Based on those theories our system should address the following elements:

- Employees should be made aware that their absenteeism rates will be measured and individual rates will be communicated to them on a regular basis.
- Employees with high absenteeism rates will be told that they will be required to meet with a supervisor to discuss their attendance.
- Expectations will be clearly defined for all employees.
- Those expectations will not be fixed but rather the organization will strive to continuously improve upon the overall attendance performance.
- Individuals will be counselled on how to improve.
- Individuals will be rewarded with praise and support for achieving improved attendance.
- The consequences for failing to improve for the organization and the individual will be made clear to everyone.

Thus a significant element in implementing an attendance management program is effective communications. More specifically the organization must clearly define its expectations and ensure every employee is aware of those expectations.

The second element is to ensure that supervisors are trained on how to consistently counsel and coach employees to make improvements in their attendance. In reality only the individual can actually do something to make improvements. He has to believe that improvements are possible and worthwhile. Otherwise it is unlikely that the individual will make the effort.

A third element is consistency. An ad hoc attendance blitz may yield results, but they will be short-lived. An effective attendance management program has to become part of the fabric of the organization's culture. In the beginning the program likely will yield significant positive results. After the initial "bang" future improvements will become more difficult to achieve and will require a concerted and sustained effort (this follows the economic theory of diminishing returns). Hence steps need to be taken to add preventative programming to address more persistent or problematic issues and to address underlying causal factors before they are manifest in a declining attendance rate.

These proactive or preventative programs include:

- employee wellness programs
- Employee assistance programs
- attendance recognition programs
- human resources management policies

A specific step-by-step implementation schedule can be found in the appendix to this chapter.

3.9 — Implementing a Wellness Program

Employee Wellness Programs include a diverse set of initiatives designed to engage employees in activities to improve their health and/or cope with the everyday stressors they encounter in striking a work-life balance. Wellness programs are strictly voluntary and may include such things as:

- subsidized membership in a fitness cub
- smoking cessation programs
- lunch-and-learn seminars
- on-site health clinics
- executive health monitoring
- on-site fitness programs or work-out facilities
- healthy snack programs

Since participation is voluntary the organization may want to survey employees to determine the level of interest before embarking on any of the more expensive initiatives.

When starting a program, the organization needs to designate an individual to coordinate thc activities. A basic wellness program may involve little more than setting a place aside in the cafeteria where employees can pick up pamphlets and brochures on health related topics. A full program may involve subsidized memberships in clubs and weekly guest speakers providing lunch and learn seminars to employees. Regardless someone needs to coordinate these activities and keep them fresh.

Specific goals for a wellness program will include impacting on absenteeism. While these programs are never introduced in isolation and therefore the direct correlation may be difficult to ascertain, one of the functions of the wellness coordinator should be to publicize the absenteeism rate and find ways to celebrate any notable reductions.

3.10 — Implementing an Employee Assistance Program

Employee assistance programs (EAPs) are employer-sponsored interventions designed to assist employees in dealing with personal issues that may affect their performance (including attendance at work). Some large corporations have internal staff to manage the EAP initiative while others use third-party experts to provide different levels of intervention.

The most common form of EAP deals specifically with substance-abuse problems such as alcoholism or drug dependency. The EAP process is seen as being independent of any other internal processes such as discipline. In a typical EAP dealing with substance-abuse employees are provided with a 1-800 number they can call at any time to seek help and guidance for their dependency issues. The help line serves as a referral service where the individual can find out where to go for help. An alternative to this is the establishment of internal referral agents who individuals can approach on a confidential basis in order to seek the same type of guidance. Often the referral agents are recovering addicts themselves, which lends credibility and confidence to the program.

This level of EAP is helpful but does not address two important issues. First, with respect to people with substance dependencies the first hurdle is often realizing or admitting that there is a problem. Thus, a more sophisticated approach is to have third-party agents available to simply discuss personal issues. These agents can assess the true nature of the underlying problem and direct the employee to seek the appropriate professional help.

The second set of issues the basic program does not address is the fact that there are many other potential personal issues that can affect an employee's performance and/or attendance including:

- family conflicts and marital breakdowns
- financial difficulties
- work-life balance
- legal difficulties

A full EAP may provide initial counselling to help determine the exact nature of the employee's problems and follow-up treatment with the appropriate professional support. The underlying problem may also not lie strictly with the employee but may involve a spouse or child. Full-service programs offer treatment options for all members of the immediate family and provide access for them around the clock.

The right choice of program is a matter of budget and perceived need. EAPs only work well if there is assurance of confidentiality. Unfortunately this may be seen as interfering with the assessment of the efficacy of the programs (and a reliable measure of the return on investment).

Nevertheless, most human resources practitioners who have had any experience with EAPs believe that the programs pay for themselves and provide an important element in creating a positive employee relations environment.

3.11 — Attendance Recognition Programs

Some managers oppose rewarding employees for simply doing their jobs (i.e. reporting to work as scheduled). Unfortunately this narrow view ignores the purpose of a recognition program. The intent is not only to reinforce good behaviour so that the individual is apt to repeat it but also to create role models for others to aspire to.

Public recognition of high performance is a substantial reward in itself in any group. A small investment in a recognition program can pay huge dividends in reducing costs by contributing to the reduction of absenteeism and the maintenance of low absenteeism rates. There are many varieties of attendance recognition programs (see sample policy appended to this chapter).

3.12 — Leadership Behaviour

It may be stating the obvious but in order to promote excellence in attendance the leaders themselves need to maintain excellent attendance. In some large organizations supervisors and second-line managers may tend to exhibit behaviour more akin to the people for which they are responsible then the management team to which they report. Hence these employees themselves may be high users of sick time and other absences.

When this occurs any initiative to address the behaviour of frontline employees alone will fail. In these cases a longer-term approach may be needed whereby absenteeism amongst supervisors and second-line managers is corrected first. In the absence of exemplary management behaviours any efforts to improve attendance will fail.

Appendix A — Attendance Management Program Implementation Steps

1. Measure the baseline rates of absenteeism by individual, department, and location. Identify the different types of absences and measure each separately.

2. Develop a business case for senior management. The business case should quantify the current levels of absenteeism, their identified causes, and the cost of absenteeism. The program elements being recommended can be associated with the various causes of absenteeism as follows:

- casual absenteeism: attendance monitoring program and employee counselling
- culpable absenteeism: progressive discipline
- workplace injuries: injury management program and claims management processes
- pattern absenteeism: employee assistance programming

3. Identify the goals of the attendance management program, such as reduce absenteeism by 50% each year, which would represent savings over the next five years of $5 million.

4. Establish a cross-functional task force to review the business case, plan objectives, and plan text for presentation to the senior management team.

5. Present the plan to senior management for approval and buy-in. Ensure attendance management objectives are made part of the measurable performance objectives for every manager.

6. Communicate the attendance management program to all managers and supervisors through a series of training sessions.

7. Communicate the attendance management program to all employees (and their representatives, if applicable). Make sure the program objectives are clearly communicated. Provide copies of the plan to everyone.

8. Begin monitoring all future attendance and red-flagging employees with absenteeism issues.

9. Meet with all employees who have records that exceed the local averages for their business units. This is the beginning of counselling for these employees.

10. Meet with all others and review their records and thank them for their positive contributions. Subsequently meet with this group once each year.

11. Implement the employee assistance program if it is not already in place. Make sure it is well promoted and someone is designated as its coordinator to ensure employees have consistent access to it.

12. Regularly communicate progress towards goals to everyone.

13. Implement an employee wellness program. Where possible establish employee wellness committees to coordinate these activities.

14. Establish a long-term disability review committee that will regularly review cases of long-term absences and ensure those employees are being monitored and that there is regular communication with them.

15. Establish a WSIB/WCB injury/claims management process.

16. Institute an attendance excellence recognition program and initiate by celebrating the accomplishments of those who maintain perfect attendance.

17. Review the efficacy of all attendance-related programming annually and ensure the relevance of the established objectives.

Appendix B — Sample Policy Employee Assistance Program

Policy Objective

The objective of the Employee assistance program is to foster and maintain the well-being and productivity of employees by providing confidential assistance or short-term counselling to those who are experiencing personal or work-related problems. In addition, the program aims to assist employees at the earliest possible moment in remedying personal problems and concerns that may adversely influence their job performance by providing professional assistance. Finally, the program seeks to promote the well-being of employees through activities, which are designed to prevent problems and enhance work performance.

Objectives

1. To establish and implement guidelines for dealing with any problem that may cause a decline in work performance

2. To inform employees about the program

3. To provide channels of correct and effective referral for assessment, treatment, and follow up so as to ensure maximum assistance

4. To monitor effective policies and procedures governing confidentiality

Policy statement

ZAR Productions recognizes that it is possible in the work environment to identify employees with problems, including those related to substance abuse, and to motivate them to seek assistance or treatment at an early stage. Although there are numerous organizations in the community to help people with various problems, assistance is often required to determine the most appropriate resource. To this end, ZAR Productions makes available to employees a confidential and voluntary employee assistance program (EAP) without prejudice to job security or career progression.

Application

This policy and the associated programming are available to all ZAR Production Employees and members of their immediate family (including spouses, children, and stepchildren).

Responsibilities

The human resources department will ensure that:

- An EAP coordinator is appointed.
- Employees are provided with EAP services that conform to this policy.
- The confidentiality and privacy of EAP information is respected and maintained.
- EAP practitioners abide by ZAR Productions Code of Ethics.
- EAP services are accessible to disabled employees.
- EAP services are available in both official languages.
- Employees are kept informed about the program and how to access its services.
- Managers and supervisors are provided with education on matters related to the program and informed of their responsibility to refer employees with work performance problems related to personal difficulties to their departmental EAP.
- Where employees are likely to be involved in critical incidents because of the nature of their work, a procedure is established to provide an initial stress debriefing session as soon as possible after such an incident and EAP follow-up if required.
- The quality and accountability of the EAP is periodically assessed.

Monitoring

To assess the effectiveness of this policy, the human resources department will prepare and submit a report once each calendar year to the senior management committee of ZAR Productions on program structure and a statistical summary of its EAP activities, including the use of any outside agencies or service providers. The statistical reports should not permit the identification of clients.

Referral Procedure

1. Emphasis will be placed on *voluntary self-referrals*. Every effort will be made to encourage employees, either through self realization, or from informal suggestions from others, to initiate entry into the program by making contact with the employee assistance coordinators. This initial contact usually occurs by telephone. To provide confidentiality, the coordinators have private, direct phone access with a private voice mail service. The coordinators will meet with the employee to make an initial assessment of the problem.

2. Another option is through the supervisor who will meet as early as possible with the employee to discuss privately any concerns with deteriorating job performance and to inform the employee of the availability of the employee assistance program. It is still up to the employee to become voluntarily involved in the program.

3. Employee assistance coordinator will take every reasonable precaution to protect the privacy of the individual and maintain the confidentiality in all voluntary self-referrals cases.

4. Mandatory referrals may occur if the employee raises the issue that a substance dependency or other personal problems as a mitigating circumstance during a disciplinary interview or as a defense in a termination grievance.

5. Where the referral is mandatory the employee and his representatives (if applicable) will be required to sign a last-chance agreement. A term of that agreement will allow the employee assistance coordinator to monitor the employee's participation and to report to the employee's supervisor if any term or condition of that agreement has been breached.

Appendix C — Sample Employee Attendance Recognition Program

Purpose

ZAR Productions places a high value on excellence in attendance. Our employees are missed when they are away from work. While occasional absences may be unavoidable for some employees others are able to maintain perfect or near perfect attendance. We believe these employees should be recognized for their efforts and accomplishments. Fortunately every year the ranks of these high achievers keep growing.

Definition of Excellent Attendance

Excellent attendance is defined as having zero or only one day of absence in a calendar year. Absences under this program do not include absences for bereavement, jury duty, duty as a subpoenaed witness, or any approved leave under our human resources policies.

Employee Role & Responsibility

Employees who achieve excellent attendance are expected to take off their excellent-attendance award day(s) and enjoy them!

Management Role & Responsibility

- Maintain accurate attendance records for employees.
- Develop and implement ways to recognize employees with excellent attendance. Recognition of employees with excellent attendance should be done throughout the year. Employees who achieve excellent attendance over incremental periods (monthly, quarterly, semi-annually) should be recognized for their efforts and encouraged to move toward greater attendance goals. Examples of recognition include but are not limited to draws for gifts/gift certificates, lunch with management, recognition at employee meetings, and letters from management.

Eligibility

All employees below the rank of director are eligible participants. Employees must have excellent attendance for the entire calendar year.

Awards

Every employee who has achieved attendance excellence in the previous calendar year will receive a pin marking the accomplishment and a congratulatory letter from our CEO. In addition recipients will receive days off with pay (excellent attendance award days) and a cash reward according to the following schedule:

Years of Excellence	Excellent Attendance Award Days	Cash Reward
1 - 2	1	$50.00
3 - 4	2	$75.00
5 - 7	3	$100.00
8 - 9	4	$150.00
10+	5	$200.00

Excellent attendance award days must be used by December 31 of the year in which they are awarded.

Employees who experience lapses in excellent attendance may be eligible for reinstatement of previous years of excellent attendance providing:

- An employee must have previously had at least three consecutive years of excellent attendance under this program.
- An employee subsequently completes one year of excellent attendance.
- No more than two years of ineligibility for this award have lapsed.
- Example: an employee with five years of excellent attendance experiences two consecutive years in which he is ineligible for excellent attendance. The following year the employee has excellent attendance. The employee's five years are reinstated and now he has six years of excellent attendance.

Employees who think they may be eligible for past year's credits must contact their supervisors who will contact the human resources department about the issue.

Chapter 4 — Resolving Absenteeism Issues

4.1 — Tracking Absenteeism

In Chapter 2 we discussed how "That which gets measured gets managed." Conceptually measuring absenteeism is relatively simple. In large organizations it can become more difficult because of the numerous different types of schedules employees may be working. For this reason the best measure is a relative measure of absences to scheduled shifts expressed as a percentage.

Let's review how we calculate the measure of absences. The calculation for casual absenteeism typically only includes absences of one to three days (though some organizations may include all absences from one to five days in length). We usually use days absent and days scheduled as opposed to hours in order to keep matters relatively simple.

The total absenteeism rate is the total number of days worked divided by the total number of days scheduled for each employee. For example an employee who is scheduled to work a five-day week and has three weeks' vacation and ten statutory holidays is scheduled to work 235 days per year. If this employee is absent 12 days his absenteeism rate is (12/235) X 100 = 5.1%.

This can be compared to the simple average of all employees. If the individual exceeds the average then he is considered to be a high user.

To calculate the average take the total number casual absences divided by the total number of scheduled days for all employees. If we had 25 employees all working five days a week with three weeks' vacation and ten statutory holidays the denominator would be 5875. If these 25 employees together were absent for 527 days the absenteeism rate would be (527/5875) X 100 = 9%.

These measures provide a baseline for comparisons. We also need to track absences for each individual. This can be done through a time-and-attendance module that is part of the time-keeping and payroll system or can be done relatively simply using manual cards. These are available through most office supply companies. They simply show the days in each month on a single card. A check mark can be used when the employee reports to work and letter codes can be used to indicate types of absences. A line is usually drawn through days not scheduled.

A - Absence Without Leave

B - Bereavement

E - Excused Absence
H - Holiday
J - Jury Duty
L - Late
LE - Left Early
NC - No Call, No Show
OT - Overtime shift
S - Sick
V - Vacation

One of the most problematic aspects of attendance management is identifying triggering events. Tracking absenteeism, particularly with large complements of employees, can be time consuming and somewhat bureaucratic. Supervisors charged with this responsibility tend to record absences only weekly or monthly. Similarly in larger organizations the task may be given to an HR clerk who records the data only weekly or monthly.

The issue though is not one of recording. The records are used to analyze patterns and trends. Each instance of absenteeism or tardiness needs to be looked at as a potentially triggering event. If the employee is a high user of sick days and the process of counselling has begun then follow-up interviews will already have been scheduled and the facts can be reviewed then. If the person is on the cusp then her counselling will start once the problematic trend has been identified.

Culpable instances automatically trigger a disciplinary response. One event of not calling to report an absence gives rise to discipline regardless of the record. This is precisely why we make the distinction between innocent absenteeism and culpable attendance issues. It ultimately makes tracking and reacting to absenteeism simpler.

4.2 — Discipline and Tardiness

It is a relatively common belief that being late is at times unavoidable. Hence a single incident of tardiness does not give cause to discipline an employee. Traffic conditions, weather, and other unforeseen obstacles may conspire to keep one from making it to work on time. Habitual tardiness, however, is culpable or blameworthy. The individual can choose to take into account the time it takes to travel to work and adjust according to the conditions.

In determining if being tardy is worthy of discipline the supervisor needs to look at how the triggering event fits into a pattern of behaviours. In this way he can determine if the act is attributable to the individual or to external circumstances.

Culpable tardiness refers to lateness caused by conditions under the control of the individual (such as the motivation to get to work on time). Innocent tardiness would then be lateness caused by external factors such as the weather, traffic, or a faulty automobile. While these definitions are intuitively correct they may not be of much assistance to the supervisor at first glance.

No rational person who is late would offer up "I just didn't feel motivated to get going this morning" as a reason for his tardiness. Instead there is usually an excuse attached to the lateness such as, "I overslept," "my car wouldn't start," "my alarm clock didn't go off," etc. Any one of these is a plausible explanation and thus one might presume that there is little one can do to hold the individual accountable for having bad luck.

We can look to attribution theory to help us sort out when we can consider the behaviour, regardless of the reported reasons, to be within or beyond the control of the individual. We determine if behaviour is internally or externally driven by examining the following questions about the behaviour:

- Is it similar to the person's past behaviour in similar circumstances? (consistency)
- Is it similar to the behaviour of others under the same circumstances? (consensus)
- Is it similar to the person's behaviour in different situations? (distinctiveness)

If a person is rarely late (or never) than an incident of tardiness has low consistency and is likely caused by external factors (or is innocent). Alternatively if the person is often late than an incident of tardiness has high consistency and is caused by internal factors (or is culpable behaviour).

Consider when a snow storm occurs. Many employees are late arriving (high consensus). So the individual, regardless of his record, is more than likely innocent. Alternatively, if after a mild sprinkling of snow the individual with a record of habitual tardiness is the only one reporting late (low consensus) than the behaviour can be considered blameworthy.

If when previous storms have occurred an individual has still managed to make it to work and this time he was late the behaviour is high in distinctiveness. Thus we can logically attribute the behaviour to the storm. If however the individual is always late when there is a snowfall (low distinctiveness) then we can attribute the tardiness to the individual's failure to adjust for the prevailing conditions.

Thus we must make judgments based on the available information to determine how we are going to treat incidents of tardiness. We must be careful though and ensure we have tracked the information accurately and are categorizing the behaviour as culpable or innocent based on the facts.

Some supervisors are concerned with making judgments because they equate this with playing favourites. There is nothing wrong with treating people differently based on their behaviour. We do need, however, to be cautious not to make errors of judgment based on perceptual biases. For example, a supervisor might tend to believe that an employee's tardiness was externally caused if the supervisor also arrived late. Conversely if the supervisor was on time then she might be prone to ignore the possibility of an external cause. This is why the perceptions should be based on the behaviours of others and not on the observer.

Supervisors tend to look for some black and white measure to determine if disciplinary action should be taken. We stress that by looking at the circumstances and using the above concepts to judge the behaviour the supervisor is going to be more successful in curbing the unwanted behaviours. Arbitrators tend to look for the same types of facts (consistency, consensus, and distinctiveness) to make their determinations as to whether or not discipline was justified.

Rather than triggering discipline on the third or fourth time the person is late the supervisor should gather some information about recent past behaviours. By analyzing the records for the business unit she might find that over the past quarter the average number of lates per employee was 1.5. Therefore, in the absence of an external determinants that are judged to be external causes then discipline should be meted out on the second incident of lateness in the quarter.

Discipline should follow progressive steps. Therefore the first triggering event, following the second incident of lateness, is merely a reminder of the requirement to be on time (sometimes referred to as a written-verbal warning). The third event of lateness results in a written warning that future discipline will follow a repeated offense, and so on.

Some programs offer a reprieve if there has been signs of a significant turnaround in behaviour with respect to tardiness. So if the employee is on time for every scheduled shift during the last quarter then subsequent disciplinary action will involve repeating the last step rather than progressing to the next. This is referred to as negative reinforcement where a desired behaviour (reporting to work on time) is rewarded by removing a negative consequence (a progressive step in the disciplinary process).

By using averages the supervisor will have a factual basis for differentiating between excusable levels of tardiness and habitual tardiness. Once the person has triggered some level of disciplinary response then each incidence of lateness can be looked at as a potential trigger unless it can be excused because of known external factors.

Another point of confusion: what happens when the employee offers documented proof that his lateness was caused by an external factor like a car breakdown? The same rules of perception apply. If the excuse offered is low in consistency then it can be accepted. However, if this is the fifth time the individual's car has broken down over the past six months (high consistency) then the behaviour can still be attributed to internal factors. The person obviously does not have the motivation to ensure his car is in good running shape to get him to work on time, or to make alternate arrangements because his car is unreliable. Therefore the documented proof does not provide a reason to excuse the behaviour.

4.3 — Discipline and Culpable Absenteeism

We have defined culpable absenteeism as absences for reasons that are not legitimate and are therefore blameworthy. Some acts of culpable absenteeism may constitute just and sufficient cause for termination even if there is only one occurrence.

The employee has an obligation to report any absence to the employer on a timely basis and to provide a reason for the absence. The employer is also entitled to require supporting evidence from the employee to justify the absence. An employer is entitled to end the employment relationship if the employee has not reported the absence in a timely manner or if the employee fails to provide a legitimate reason for the absence. However, the employer must provide the employee with an opportunity to provide an explanation for the absence and/or his failure to report it in a timely manner.

Some company policies and collective agreements specify that a failure to report any absence for three days will lead to automatic termination unless the individual can provide an explanation satisfactory to the company as to why the absence was not reported. Similarly if an individual cannot provide evidence that an absence of three days or more was justified because of sickness, injury, or family emergency he may be summarily dismissed.

Employees are not entitled to take scheduled time off work unless they have a legitimate reason for not being able to attend or they have been authorized to take leave of their schedule. Employees who absent themselves for reasons that are not considered legitimate may be subject to disciplinary action and in some cases even a single incident may be considered a breach of the employment contract and just cause for dismissal without notice. Typically one instance of "playing hooky" for a day will lead to a lesser penalty such as a suspension without pay or a final written warning.

Culpable absenteeism is blameworthy absenteeism. Taking a sick day when not sick is culpable behaviour worthy of some discipline. Other forms of culpable absenteeism may include absences due to self-inflicted illness such as a hangover brought on by overindulgence or injuries caused by extreme recreational activities. The common element being that the individual has direct control over the absence and therefore the employer is not obliged to excuse the absence.

These are usually not treated as culpable because of a lack of precision in our understanding of culpable behaviour versus innocent behaviour, hence, the need for some precision in writing out an attendance policy.

Progressive discipline is a widely accepted hierarchy of disciplinary measures wherein the penalty for misconduct becomes progressively more severe and culminates in the termination of employment. The idea is that the penalties will serve as a warning that if immediate corrections in behaviour do not occur then the employee will move closer to the point of discharge.

A typical progression looks like this:

First Offense	—	Verbal Warning
Second Offense	—	Written Warning
Third Offense	—	One-Day Suspension
Fourth Offense	—	Three-Day Suspension
Fifth Offense	—	Termination of Employment

Typically culpable absenteeism involves acts of volition that call for starting the disciplinary steps at the level of a suspension. An absence due to overindulgence the night before might only justify a verbal or written warning. However, taking time off without a legitimate reason is far more serious. If the employee is claiming a sick day when he is not sick then it is a form of fraud. Not to overstate the case but it is a serious breach of trust and is worthy of much more than a warning.

Again we sometimes become confused because excessive use of sick time is not usually culpable as the person has a reason for not reporting to work. Typically, abuse or misuse of sick time is not obvious, though it is often suspected. Hence it should be relatively rare to see discipline for playing hooky. If there is direct, clear and cogent evidence that the person called in sick when she was not in fact sick then stern discipline is warranted.

We sometimes hear of humorous examples where the evidence has been uncovered by coincidence. The employee calls in sick to attend a baseball game only to find that his seats are next to his boss, or an employee attends a hockey game while off sick and discovers that his face was shown on national TV when the cameras panned the audience. Unfortunately the HR director was watching the game that night and recognized the culprit.

Another example of culpable absenteeism worthy of a harsh penalty is the unauthorized extension of a leave of absence. An employee is planning a trip overseas and asks for four weeks' vacation. He is denied the leave because of production requirements and company policy and is only granted two weeks' vacation. However, mysteriously he becomes ill on the last day while travelling and misses his flight out. He is unable to book another flight for, you guessed it, two additional weeks.

The simple way to treat this is to not excuse the absence unless the company is satisfied that the story is true. The author has encountered dozens of these situations and in not one case was the employee able to substantiate the illness or the airline ticket bookings or both. This represents an act of insubordination and may be grounds for termination. In these cases the employee should be advised as soon as he reports that he will be unable to return at the appointed time that he will have to provide documented evidence of his illness and of his original airline booking and the changes thereto.

4.4 — Conducting a Disciplinary Interview

Disciplining an employee, for whatever reason, is not a pleasant experience for either the supervisor or the employee. One tip for supervisors is to get to know your employees. Make sure you are communicating with them regularly and that you show an interest in them as people. This does not mean you need to become fast friends, but you should be able to connect with them on a personal level. It is far easier to deal with difficult issues with someone you know and can have a discussion with.

The early steps of the progressive discipline process are intended to be relatively mild reminders of the organization's rules and policies. It is very important to address relatively minor issues right away. It is easy to overlook a minor transgression and delay taking action. For instance, an employee is late for the third time in a month. The supervisor is busy and decides to speak to the employee at a later time. The later time turns out to be after the employee has been late several more times and now a minor issue has become bigger.

Had the supervisor addressed the first incident of lateness the situation would have been different. The reminder he would have delivered to the employee would have been nothing more than a reminder that there is a company policy on lateness and the employee's tardiness is being monitored. In most instances this would be enough to get the employee's attention and a repeat of the behaviour would be less likely.

By delaying taking action the supervisor has to deal with several instances of tardiness beyond the threshold. Though the appropriate form of action is still a gentle reminder of the company policy on lateness, the supervisor may now be frustrated by the employee's excessive lateness. This is likely to come across in the supervisor's approach to the problem and the effectiveness of the interview will be diminished.

In any disciplinary interview the secret is to get to the point quickly and not to dwell on the matter. The supervisor should stick with the facts and remind the employee of the company policies. In the case of any attendance-related misconduct the supervisor should have the employee's record available and the overall attendance statistics. Vague statements like "You are always late" will result in the employee being confrontational, whereas if the supervisor provides the employee's attendance records the employee cannot dispute the documented facts before her.

Importantly, except of course in the case of a termination, the supervisor should end the interview with words of encouragement that would restore the employee's self-esteem. Let the employee know that you value her work and that you believe that she can correct the problem.

The other important elements of discipline are to be consistent in its application. Consistency is easier to maintain when actions are taken immediately to address issues and when the policies are clearly communicated and enforced at the time the misconduct takes place.

Even when terminating an employee the interview will be much easier when policies are well-known, reasonable and the proper steps have been taken. The same guidelines apply. Do not make the issue personal. The action is being taken because of behaviour — not because the person is "good or bad."

4.5 — Counselling and Innocent Absenteeism

As we have stressed throughout this work taking disciplinary action or punishing an employee for being sick or injured is not appropriate. Punishment is used to extinguish an unwanted behaviour. However, an employee cannot directly or immediately control the fact that he is prone to illness and injury.

An employee can be encouraged to reflect on his lifestyle and make changes that may help him become healthier and attend work more regularly. The employee can also be coached to understand the impact his absence has on the organization. It cannot be stressed enough that the supervisor must be sincere and demonstrate that she genuinely cares about the employee's welfare. When an employee knows he is cared for he is more likely to reflect on his actions and take steps to improve.

There may even be an underlying element of guilt associated with counselling employees on attendance. If the employee believes that the supervisor cares for him then he will feel some guilt when booking off sick in the future. In some cases casual absenteeism is the result of an employee feeling disengaged or alienated in the workplace. Hence an employee who experiences a slight sniffle and a few minor aches and pains in the morning may be prone to book the day off whereas an engaged employee will still report for work (though no one wants an employee who has a significant illness to come to work and risk his health or the health of others).

Like discipline, counselling should be consistent and follow the behaviour closely. In cases where the organization is just beginning to actively manage attendance supervisors will be talking to employees who may have several years of problematic attendance for the first time. It is important that the supervisor make it clear that the program is not a temporary fix and that there will be scheduled follow-ups with the employee.

In truth the supervisor cannot do much to correct the employee's attendance problem. Counselling is about making the individual aware that there is a problem (based on factual data) and about encouraging the individual to take action to correct the problem. The supervisor can ask if there is anything he can do to help and make suggestions that the employee seek help from a physician or from the employee assistance provider. In the end though the supervisor must make it clear that the employee is responsible for taking whatever steps necessary to improve his attendance.

Of course one of the important elements throughout the counselling is to help the employee maintain his self-esteem. The supervisor should use words of encouragement and show that she cares for the employee as a person. Notwithstanding, the employee needs to be aware of the consequences if the excessive absenteeism persists. This is why counselling is structured in a progressive manner whereby the third and fourth counselling are handled by more senior managers. In the fourth or fifth session the employee will need to be told that a failure to correct the problem could result in termination (because the contract is frustrated by the employee's inability to attend to work regularly).

Probably the most important aspect of attendance counselling is scheduled follow up. The supervisor should schedule a specific day and time in the future to discuss the employee's attendance again. A single interview will not result in any lasting behavioural changes. Nor does it truly demonstrate that the supervisor cares. Once an employee becomes involved in attendance counselling he can expect that there will be several interviews.

The timing and script of each interview will depend on the employee's subsequent behaviours. If there is improvement the interview will focus on that and further discussions will be spaced farther apart. In an effective attendance-management program every employee will have at least one attendance interview each year. Those with perfect or near perfect attendance will be thanked for their efforts and may receive some other form of recognition. Employees with problematic records may have several interviews.

In some cases an employee may reveal important information to the supervisor that was previously unknown to the organization. For example, the employee may be suffering from a chronic condition that interferes with regular attendance. In these cases the supervisor should defer the matter to a trained human resources specialist who can consider what accommodations might be necessary and provide specialized assistance through the company's EAP program or through other available resources.

4.6 — Absenteeism and Terminations For Cause

We have dealt with the issue of discipline and culpable absenteeism above. Employees who have excessive records of innocent absenteeism may also be subject to termination for cause even though their behaviour is not blameworthy.

Technically these administrative terminations, as they are sometimes called, are based on the fact that the employee is unable to fulfill her side of the contract by attending work regularly. While this is akin to frustration of contract the termination actually takes place when the employee has returned to work and is at the time healthy. The notion is that the employee's past behaviour (excessive absenteeism) is a predictor of her future behaviour. If the company has documented its attempts to assist the employee and those attempts have failed it will have cause to terminate the employee.

At the point of discharge employees may become more forthcoming and admit to underlying issues that might mitigate in their favour. The company should consider any such admissions carefully and take them under advisement. A termination might be reconsidered under such circumstances; therefore, a trained human resources practitioner should be involved in the termination interview.

4.7 — Identifying Mitigating Circumstances

A note of caution: employers cannot ignore any signs that there may be an underlying problem that has caused the employee's attendance issues. Supervisors may believe that they are not trained or qualified to identify signs of, for example, substance abuse amongst employees. That simply is not true.

There are often obvious indicators that the employee with problematic attendance has a chemical dependency. People who are hungover from a night of overindulgence look hungover. Employees who report to work with the smell of alcohol on their breath have probably been drinking. Bloodshot eyes, looking constantly tired, and poor personal hygiene may all be signs that there is a problem.

Moreover, other employees are apt to talk about the person's problems and word often gets back to the supervisor. None of these things can be overlooked. The supervisor is perfectly entitled to present his observations or the observations of others to the employee. He cannot diagnose the actual dependency, but he can point out the presence of the indicators. The employee may deny the problem, but the supervisor has an obligation to disclose his suspicions.

If the employee does deny that there is a substance abuse issue the supervisor should move on. The only thing he can do is offer any assistance available under an EAP program. If there is a problem it will only be addressed when the individual is ready to admit it and take responsibility to correct it.

4.8 — Managing Pattern Absenteeism

One form of problematic casual absenteeism is so-called pattern absenteeism. Some employees will be absent on particular days of the week or at given times of the year. These patterns may be a clue to the underlying problem or may indicate that the behaviour is not innocent but rather is culpable.

The most commonly referred to pattern is the Friday-Monday pattern. This is where the employee's absences are always on either a Monday or Friday. A variation of this is any pattern where the days taken off come at the beginning or end of the employee's work cycle, or immediately follow pay day. This is usually considered as a potential indicator of substance abuse. Employees tend to behave themselves during the week but binge on weekends or after being paid. The supervisor should point out the existence of the pattern and have the employee explain what might be causing it.

Another pattern that can only be detected over several years is the taking of days off at particular times of the year. One such pattern is the taking of excessive time in the first quarter or first half of the year. This is common in organizations with strong cultures of entitlement and a fixed number of sick-day benefits. The employee may be taking the time early to ensure he gets his full entitlement in during the year and does not lose the benefit. While this is misuse it is difficult to manage because it takes several years to detect and prove. It is best handled as innocent.

Annual patterns may also appear during odd times. Some employers, for example, see a spike in absenteeism in the fall. The same set of employees all seem to be prone to a mysterious illness in the early part of October. Apparently this illness is known as "Hunting Season." When there is a suspicion of this kind of abuse the supervisor should insist that employees present doctors notes to substantiate why they are off and ask that the employee call in regularly.

Some employers who have experienced this pattern have accommodated it by scheduling production so that the company can allow the maximum number of employees to take time off and use their vacation credits or lieu time.

Finally there is a pattern related to statutory holidays whereby some employees are prone to taking the day immediately before or the day immediately following a holiday to maximize the time off. Some collective agreements and company policies set out to combat this by disqualifying the person from receiving holiday pay if they are absent on either of the scheduled days immediately prior to or following the holiday. In any case the employee who has the misfortune of being sick around the time of a statutory holiday should be asked to provide a doctor's note.

4.9 — Managing Short-Term Disability Claims

Short-term disability claims tend to be of a lesser concern to employers. These involve absences of greater than three consecutive days. They are not considered controllable as they likely involve a relatively serious illness or injury that prevents the person from being at work. As well it is relatively rare for an employee to have a large number of short-term disability claims.

Nevertheless the supervisor should make regular contact with the employee to demonstrate that the company cares and wishes the individual a speedy recovery. In some cases the supervisor may be suspicious that the claim is not legitimate and is willing to call the employee to check up on them. When this happens the employee will sense that the supervisor does not trust him and will likely be confrontational.

We offer two points of advice to the supervisor. First, all short-term absences should be considered to be innocent unless there is compelling evidence to the contrary. Secondly, all employees who are off should be called to show them that the company and the supervisor genuinely care.

In rare instances the individual may have a problem or series of problems that causes multiple short-term disability claims over a relatively short period of time. This could be an indication of a chronic illness, or may be an indicator of a problematic pattern that needs to be addressed.

The approach to this type of occurrence is similar to any pattern of absenteeism. The supervisor needs to document the concern and present the facts to the employee.

An example of this is the employee who experiences a number of injuries due to recreational activities. The company cannot insist on the employee stopping such outside activities, but it can treat the absences as culpable since there is an act of volition. In other words the employee can be given a choice. Either you stop engaging in activities that interfere with your ability to perform your duties (including the duty to report to work) or you cannot work here any longer.

If the issue is one of chronic illness then the company needs to understand what the underlying cause might be. In some cases the absences might be related to a single chronic condition. In others the absences may be related to the general poor health of the individual that causes a susceptibility to illness. In the former case, the company will have an obligation to consider what steps need to be taken to accommodate the employee's disability (whether it is transitory or permanent). In the latter case the absences should be treated the same way as any other pattern of excessive absenteeism.

In any case problematic patterns of absenteeism should be managed with the assistance of a trained human resources practitioner.

4.10 — Managing Chronic Sickness

Chronic ailments may be permanent or transitory. In either case the employer needs to deal with these as it would any other form of disability.

Some chronic conditions will require the employee to be frequently absent over a fixed period of time while they seek treatment. These absences may be for part of a day, a full day, or for a number of days. The employer needs to know what to expect and should schedule the person's work around these treatments. To some extent, the employee has a duty to accommodate the employer by ensuring the appointments for treatment are scheduled when possible to cause the least inconvenience to the company. However, this is usually not possible and should not be pressed as an issue.

In some cases the proper accommodation may be to have the employee absent herself for the duration of the treatment regimen and return after it is complete or at a time when the schedule is minimally disruptive to her work routine.

If the employee has a permanent condition that causes him to be frequently absent the employer needs to consider if the level of absenteeism can be tolerated without undue hardship to the company. Obviously in senior positions or specialized functions accommodation may be difficult or impossible. In other situations the frequent absences may have little impact on overall productivity.

If the expected level of absenteeism does cause undue hardship the employer will need to consider placing the person in an alternate position in order to accommodate the disability. If this is not possible then the contract of employment may be deemed frustrated and the employer will be entitled to terminate the employee.

4.11 — Managing Workplace Injury Claims through Transitional Work Plans

Early and safe return to work (ESRTW) policy has been designed to meet the company's obligations under the *Workers' Compensation Act* and to provide employees with meaningful and productive work during their recuperation from occupational illnesses and injuries. While most organizations treat lost time due to workplace injuries separately from other absences they nevertheless contribute to overall absenteeism.

Some losses due to workplace injuries, particularly those short-term absences of one or a few days, are very similar to casual absenteeism. Employees may be prone to take advantage of company policies or the lack thereof, in order to take a few days off. In addition an employee may be apt to malinger after a recuperative period and delay returning to work unless there are proactive efforts to get them back as quickly as possible.

The primary goal of an ESRTW policy is to speed up the rehabilitative process and minimize the negative impact to both the employee and the company of prolonged absences due to occupational illnesses or injuries. ESRTW policy and programs should not be used under any circumstances where the assignment of duties poses a potential risk of further injury to the individual or poses any risk to others.

These programs are not designed to avoid lost-time injuries per se and must only be applied to situations where the individual can be returned to his regular duties with modifications or other meaningful work.

The assignments under such a policy should not be "make work" programs. Otherwise the program devolves into a means to avoid recording incidents as lost-time accidents and will provide little if any real motivation for the employee to participate. Employees will view any program that seems solely established to manage statistical results as insincere.

Thus the work provided should be meaningful and productive. If there is no value-added from the work performed by employees on modified work assignments or involved in transitional return-to-work programs the program may be costly and lead to poor morale and reduced overall productivity. On the other hand, if the work is productive and meaningful employees are more likely to want to participate. In addition there are significant cost advantages to the company, but only if the programs are implemented correctly and with the right motivation.

Companies are legally obliged under both human rights legislation and workers' compensation statutes to make reasonable accommodations for injured workers and to make productive, meaningful work available to employees injured on the job, on either a transitory or permanent basis.

It is also the duty and obligation of employees to fully cooperate in these efforts to accommodate their injuries. This cooperation includes:

- cooperating with any efforts to investigate the root causes of the incident that caused the injury or illness
- consenting to the release of all relevant medical information needed to determine how the injury needs to be accommodated
- providing any medical forms or other documentation needed by the company in a timely manner
- being readily accessible at all times during working hours
- participating in any meetings (with their representative present where appropriate) to discuss accommodation
- participating in any training needed in order to assume new or modified duties
- scheduling medical visits, physiotherapy sessions, and any other outside appointments outside of their scheduled working hours to every extent possible

ESRTW programs may include the following program alternatives:

- return to full Duties without restrictions

- temporary modified duties
- gradual return to full duties
- permanent accommodations
- labour market re-entry.

4.12 — Return to Full Duties without Restrictions

Obviously if the workplace injury does not restrict the individual from performing his regular duties he should return to work immediately.

4.13 — Temporary Modified Duties

In the majority of cases the injury will prevent the employee from performing the full range of the primary duties of the job. The company needs to consider what duties can be performed to determine if some duties can be reassigned to others, performed by the employee with assistance from others, or performed by the employee with mechanical assistance.

If the person's restrictions prevent them from performing the essential duties of the job to any degree then the employer needs to consider what other positions can be made available that fit the person's restrictions. In some cases the alternative work may involve the assignment of duties that are not necessarily attached to another position. However, employers are cautioned not to create "make work" programs in order to accommodate employees. These tend to be nothing more than excuses to reduce lost days and do not involve any activities that are actually useful or meaningful. As such they will not be motivating to the employee.

The company should establish a written modified-duties policy. Many companies experience the problem of modified duties lasting much longer than expected. This is an indication that the assignment is interfering with the employee's recuperation or that the employee is not motivated to return to full duties in his former position.

This can be overcome by establishing a fixed number of weeks for the modified work assignment. For example the policy might state that temporary modified duties will be made available whenever the prognosis is for the employee to fully recover from his injuries within a six-week period. If the recovery is expected to last longer than six weeks the employee should be allowed to rest at home until he has recovered to the point that full recovery will fall within the six-week window.

In the event that an employee is assigned to temporary modified duties and has not fully recovered within six weeks the modified duties could be extended for an additional period of up to six weeks. It is, however, recommended that no temporary modified duty assignments continue past twelve weeks.

4.14 — Gradual Return to Full Duties

In cases where the nature of the injury prevents the individual from working a full shift, or in cases where the employee is expected to return to work after an extended absence a work-hardening schedule or gradual return to work may be indicated.

This might involve one or two weeks where the individual works four hours per day, followed by one or two weeks at six hours per day, followed by one or two weeks at eight hours maximum, and then a lifting of all time restrictions (whereby the employee can then work any available overtime hours). Like any modified-duty assignment such gradual returns should be completed in a fixed period not to exceed twelve weeks. Otherwise the individual's recovery is better facilitated by bed rest at home.

Some work-hardening programs include prescribed exercises or physical therapy. When there is an occupational health nurse on staff these other activities should be monitored to ensure the employee is getting the full benefit of the rehabilitation efforts.

4.15 — Permanent Accommodations

Permanent accommodations must be considered for any employee whose injuries prevent them from performing the full range of the essential duties of their pre-injury position. In some cases the permanent accommodation will involve amending the job requirements to take out aspects of the position that the individual is restricted from performing. In other cases these functions might be assigned to others or others may be assigned to assist the individual in performing those specific duties.

In other cases the employer may need to provide a mechanical device to assist the individual (such as a lifting device or a device to facilitate access for the individual).

Where the position cannot be reasonably modified to accommodate the person's injuries, or it is cost prohibitive to do so then the employer is obliged to see what other positions might be available to assign the employee to. In some cases this may involve retraining the person but the employer is not obliged to retrain the person to a position that is higher than the pre-injury job. However, there are many examples of injured workers who have successfully transitioned into supervisory roles after being injured on the job.

If accommodation is not possible then the person may be eligible for retraining assistance in another field.

4.16 — Labour Market Re-entry

Labour market re-entry programs are available to injured workers through the Worker's Compensation Boards. Employers should consider carefully if this is the best alternative from a cost and morale point of view. Training an employee for a position within the company may be less costly and have a greater positive impact on employee morale.

However, when there simply are no viable alternatives the employee can receive vocational rehabilitation assistance that will include retraining and job search assistance. These programs can be very costly to the former employer so she should be monitored and managed closely by a workers' compensation claims specialist.

4.17 — Last-Chance Agreements

When an employee's performance has fallen to the point where the company has just and sufficient cause to terminate the employment relationship there may be mitigating circumstances to lead the employer to give him one last chance. This involves establishing a formal written agreement with the employee, or contract, wherein the employee undertakes to take specific steps to resolve any issues that affect his ability to attend work regularly.

Last-chance agreements should not be used simply as a means of settling a termination grievance. There must be the presence of mitigating circumstances that were previously unknown to the employer. These circumstances also need to be of a nature that the employee, with assistance, may be able to control. Typically last-chance agreements are used as a form of accommodation for employees who have substance-abuse problems that have affected their attendance (or other aspects of employee performance).

Last-chance agreements are used in post-termination situations or at the point of discharge. The employer must have just and sufficient cause to terminate the employee. They are not appropriate in situations where an employee has voluntarily come forward to admit that he has a problem that he would like assistance to resolve. Otherwise the last-chance agreement becomes a deterrent to those who are able to admit to a dependency before it manifests into a cause for termination. However, some organizations may use a similar "social contract" with employees who come forth to seek help.

A last-chance agreement is not appropriate when there is a dispute about whether or not the company had cause for termination. These agreements should not be imposed on an employee. An employee who feels compelled or coerced into signing such an agreement will not likely buy into the need for reform or rehabilitation and those efforts are likely to fail. Given that the last-chance agreement is intended as a contract there must be a meeting of the minds.

In addition if the employer does not have just cause for termination or if just cause is in dispute, then it is likely that the employee will not fully embrace the need to make the vital changes in his lifestyle necessary to truly make a turnaround in behaviour. The employer's arbitrary actions will sit on his mind and will interfere with his soul-searching. If the employee has an opportunity to blame others for his situation he will not fully commit to the course of action needed. In these defective agreements we typically see a lack of clarity with respect to exactly what actions the employee must take during the period covered by the last-chance agreement.

In order for a last-chance agreement to be effective the following elements must be indicated:

- The company has just and sufficient cause to terminate the employee.
- The employee (and his representatives) recognize that the employer has just and sufficient cause for termination.
- The employee freely admits to having a problem which represents a mitigating factor under the circumstances.
- The employee truly has a problem that must be addressed.
- The terms and conditions of the Last Chance Agreement are specific and time bound.
- The onus is placed on the employee to take the necessary actions to correct the problem.
- The consequences are unequivocal.

Sample Last Chance Agreement

Terms of Settlement

Between

Bob Smith

(Herein referred to as "the Employee")

And

Amalgamated Manufacturing Employees Union Local 230

(Herein referred to as the "Union")

And

ZAR Productions

(Herein referred to as the "Company")

Whereas the parties acknowledge that the Employee has a record excessive absenteeism that exceeds the business unit's average rate of absenteeism; and

Whereas the Company has terminated the Employee for excessive absenteeism and the Union has grieved that the termination was unjust; and

Whereas the Employee acknowledges that his absenteeism is excessive and that he must correct his behaviour in order to attend to work regularly; and

Whereas the Employee has admitted to alcohol dependency, which has been a contributing factor to his excessive absenteeism; and

Whereas the parties are desirous of making the necessary accommodations to assist the Employee in seeking the appropriate treatment of his alcohol dependency and resolving any other lifestyle issues that contribute to his excessive absenteeism;

Therefore the parties have resolved to enter into this agreement to establish the future terms and conditions the Employee must abide by in order to be reinstated and to retain his employment with the Company.

The following terms and conditions have been agreed to be:

1. The Employee will be suspended from active duty without pay for the period from the date of his termination until he has successfully completed the rehabilitation steps prescribed below.

2. Notwithstanding item 1 above, the Employee may apply for short-term disability benefits under the Company's health and welfare plan, and nothing in this agreement shall be construed as rendering him ineligible for such benefits.

3. The Employee shall seek a referral to an appropriate treatment program for alcohol dependency and upon successful completion of that program submit a certificate to the company as evidence of his successful completion.

4. Upon the submission of the certificate described in 3 above the Employee will be returned to active duty in the position he occupied at the time of his discharge with his full seniority intact.

5. The Employee agrees to attend a prescribed after-care program (like Alcoholics Anonymous) at least monthly for a period of at least eighteen months from the date of his reinstatement.

6. The employee agrees to refrain from the use of alcohol at all times, and will provide a doctor's note to attest that any future absence is not related to the use of alcohol if and when required to do so by the Company

7. The terms and conditions of this agreement will remain in place for a period of eighteen months from the date the Employee returns to active duty.

8. Upon his return to active duty the Employee will maintain regular attendance, not to exceed an absenteeism rate equal to the business unit average. He also acknowledges that he will not be granted time off for personal business. Appointments will be made on his time away from work. Approved time off will only be granted for documented family emergencies and instances of personal illness, which will each be documented for every instance during the eighteen month period.

9. Any breach of the terms and conditions of this agreement will be deemed a culminating incident and will be further considered just and sufficient cause to terminate the Employee's employment.

10. In addition any breach of company rules or misconduct that would give rise to a disciplinary response will be deemed to be a culminating incident and just and sufficient cause for termination for the life of this agreement.

11. The Employee and the Union agree that any grievance related to a termination under this agreement will be restricted to whether or not there is sufficient evidence to prove that a culminating incident occurred and that the Employee and the Union will not grieve the quantum of the penalty in the case where the culminating incident is proved.

12. The parties hereto acknowledge that the terms and conditions of this settlement represent reasonable accommodation under the *Human Rights Code* of Ontario and any other applicable statutes.

13. The Union and the Employee acknowledge that this settlement represents a full and final resolution to all prior grievances related to the Employee and his employment with ZAR Productions.

Last-chance agreements cannot include any terms that provide for differential treatment of the individual with respect to conditions not directly related to the cause being addressed. Using the substance-abuse problem as a typical example, the parties can agree to conditions such as monitoring the employee's attendance at after-care treatment programs and the requirement that the employee certify that future absences are not related to his addiction. These conditions are directly related to the problem being addressed and are therefore *bona fide* even though the person is being treated differently. However, with respect to absences the company can only expect the person to attend regularly and match the average expected of any other employee.

The employee should not be expected to maintain attendance at a level that exceeds the average. The fact that he had a prior problem with substance abuse does not mean that he will not catch a cold or have a legitimate family emergency just as any other employee might have.

4.18 — When is a Last Chance Not a Last Chance?

Arbitrators and other third-party adjudicators have at times ruled that in spite of a breached last-chance agreement the employee should be given another opportunity to rehabilitate himself. This can frustrate managers and supervisors alike who may believe that "a contract is a contract."

Certainly one reason an arbitrator may give an employee another chance is that the Agreement was defective. It is important to first ensure the employee is entering into the agreement with a full understanding of the terms and conditions and has had the opportunity to consider his alternatives. An agreement that has been compelled or forced upon the employee will not stand. In theory if the employee has a full understanding and has accepted the terms voluntarily he will be likely to accept the consequences of a breach.

Another defect may be that the agreement is not deemed to truly represent an accommodation of the employee's disability. This is only partly covered by inserting a clause indicating that the parties turned their collective minds to the issue of accommodation and accepted that the agreed upon terms dealt with it adequately. However, given the nature of alcohol and drug dependencies relapses are not uncommon. The employer should consider the possibility of a relapse in enforcing the terms of the agreement.

Rather than writing in a provision dealing with relapses the employer can establish a practice that will enforce the terms and conditions. Writing in a provision may be seen as giving the employee a "get out of jail free" card that allows for a relapse. Instead, any instance where the employee has taken a step back should be documented in the form of a written reminder and final warning.

In some cases, supervisors fail to enforce the terms and conditions when there is a relapse. In fact the employee may have several absences and several instances where he has fallen back to drinking before the supervisor takes action. This can be seen as tacit acceptance by the employer and render the agreement null and void. It is essential that every transgression be dealt with while allowing some leeway for the earnest employee who is making an effort to reform may make the difference in helping him make a full recovery.

Arbitrators may also consider the circumstances that existed prior to the parties entering into the last-chance agreement. If the agreement itself represented the first opportunity the employee had to admit to the problem and seek help then a single transgression may not be sufficient to give cause to the employer to terminate the individual. However, if the company had a well-promoted and active employee assistance program in place and had made efforts to uncover the root cause of the employee's past absenteeism then the terms are more likely to be upheld.

This is particularly true if the agreement is being monitored by a trained professional who is documenting relapses and serving proper warnings to the employee. The employer will not have to excuse other breaches such as the person's failure to keep appointments for assessment or treatment. Nor would an employer have to tolerate the employee's lack of honesty in disclosing relapses. So the monitoring of the last-chance agreement is essential. Large organizations typically have an occupational health nurse or an employee assistance program director monitor employees on these and other programs. The monitors can exercise some judgment as to whether or not a relapse constitutes a significant breach of the terms and conditions of the agreement. However, these professionals should be given written guidelines to follow in order to maintain consistency in the application of "forgiveness."

Last-chance agreements will also be voided if they contain any terms or conditions that impose differential treatment on the individual. The exceptions, as noted above, are those terms and conditions that are necessary to address the employee's dependency. Even though the cause that led to the initial termination was excessive absenteeism, the company cannot impose an expectation that the employee will have a better attendance record than others in the future. It can, however, insist that his record of absenteeism not be worse than the average.

Another element to consider is the full range of mitigating circumstances. An employee with short tenure will not be given the same latitude or consideration as an employee with long service. Often an employee with short service remains terminated until he has completed a course of treatment and can certify that the problem has been addressed before being reinstated. A long-service employee may be conditionally reinstated so that he has access to benefit plans and other assistance.

4.19 — Monitored Referral Programs

Wc differentiate terms and conditions of employment imposed on people who have not been terminated from last-chance agreements. Instead we might refer to these agreements as monitored referral programs (MRPs). These are actually an important part of a comprehensive EAP. These MRPs need to be crafted with the same care as a last-chance agreement. The only differences being that for some breaches the penalty will fall short of termination and will be in line with the employer's progressive discipline policies.

MRPs typically are used in organizations that do not have full-time EAPs or in instances where the employee has admitted to a problem to her supervisor well in advance of a threat of termination or discharge.

Chapter 5 — Legal Issues Surrounding Attendance

5.1 — Frustration of Contract

What is Frustration of Contract Under Employment Law?

The doctrine of frustration of contract occurs when one party is unable to discharge her obligations under the contract and the other party is entitled to sever the relationship without notice. In employment contracts this doctrine has been commonly applied to cases involving employee absences. When an employee becomes injured or ill and the condition interferes with her regular attendance at work the employment contract may be said to be frustrated. Certainly this is not the case when the absence is transitory or short-term. However, if an individual's injury or illness is of a chronic or permanent nature and is likely to continue to interfere with the regular discharge of his duties to the employer, including the duty to attend at work regularly, then the employer may be entitled to deem the contract to be frustrated and to dismiss the employee without notice or severance.

This doctrine has become very controversial in recent years and may be less relevant in the employment context. Before an employer could claim that an employment contract had been frustrated due to illness or injury to the employee the employer would have to demonstrate the following:

- The employee's pattern of past absences demonstrated his inability to attend work regularly.
- The nature of the individual's injury or illness was permanent and, therefore, it had become impossible for the individual to perform his duties to the employer including the duty to attend at work regularly.
- The employer had attempted to discharge its duties to accommodate the individual to the point of undue hardship and found it impossible to do so.

A contract is said to be frustrated when one of the parties is unable to fulfill her obligations due to some unforeseen circumstances. In the employment context we usually use the term *frustrated contract* to refer to terminations resulting from long-term illnesses or injuries. An employer does not have just cause to summarily dismiss an employee simply because he/she has been absent from work. However in situations where the employee suffers from a permanent condition or injury that prevents her from fulfilling her obligations to the employer the employment contract may become frustrated.

In some situations the concept of frustration may be obvious. An employee who has a serious and permanent condition that makes it impossible to perform the essential duties of her job or any other job the employer might have available the contract is frustrated. However, in many situations employees suffer from chronic conditions or from a series of seemingly unrelated conditions that contribute to a lengthy pattern of excessive absenteeism. Based on such a history, the employer may believe he has the right to declare that the employment contract has been frustrated.

Whether or not the incapacity of an employee due to illness or injury will can be considered as frustrating the employment contract depends on several factors including the length of the current absence, the nature of the incapacity (e.g. is it permanent or transitory), the terms of the employment contract itself and the employee's length of service with the employer.

If, for example, the employment contract provides for short-term sick leave benefits the contract cannot be said to be frustrated during the period in which benefits are payable. This differs from provisions for long-term disability benefits in part because there is an expectation that employees will occasionally be away from work for short-term periods due to illness or injury, but in such cases are expected to return to work. Long-term disability benefits do not necessarily contemplate that the person will actually return to work.

The nature of the individual's work also may be a significant determining factor. When an employee is one of many employees in the same job classification the relationship will be more resilient, precisely because the absence will not significantly disruptive to the employer's enterprise. However, if the employee occupies a key post and it is necessary for the employer to find a permanent replacement because of a prolonged absence then the contract may be more vulnerable to frustration due to unforeseen circumstances. This argument may cut the other way. In *White v. F.W. Woolworth Co.*,[1] the Newfoundland Supreme Court, Appeal Division, noted the argument by the employer that the employee occupied an important position would heighten the employer's interest in continuing the individual's employment in order to retain the value of the expertise of a long-term employee.

This indicates that service or seniority as another important factor in determining whether or not the contract can be deemed to be frustrated. The absence of a senior employee in a key position may be tolerated for a longer period of time than a junior employee in the same position. In the case of a

[1] *White v. F.W. Woolworth Co.* (1996), 1996 CarswellNfld 205, 22 C.C.E.L. (2d) 110 (Nfld. C.A.); leave to appeal refused (1997), 161 Nfld. & P.E.I.R. 90 (note) (S.C.C.).

senior employee the employer is more likely to choose other options to fill the void left by her absence in order to retain the individual and her acquired expertise. These options might include hiring an interim executive, seconding someone from another division, or appointing another employee into an "acting" role. These options are less likely to be used to protect the tenure of a junior employee. In these instances the employer's interest may be better served by hiring a permanent replacement.

One of the more controversial aspects of frustration in the employment context is the nature of the illness or injury itself. This involves a consideration of how long the illness or injury has already lasted and the employee's prospects for recovery. The greater the degree of incapacity and the longer the period over which it has persisted and is likely to persist, the more likely it is that the employment relationship has been frustrated. However before deeming the contract to be frustrated the employer must discharge its responsibilities to accommodate the individual under the applicable employment legislation, which may include re-employment obligations under a workers' compensation statute or the duty to accommodate under human rights legislation.

Employers may find it increasingly difficult to determine if the nature of the employee's condition is permanent, chronic, or transitory. Privacy legislation has given rise to the belief that employers are not entitled to personal medical information and hence employees and their physicians are reluctant to provide the information necessary to determine if the employment relationship should be preserved. This is further complicated when the employer maintains disability payments through a third-party insurer or administrator. These third parties invariably will not disclose any "confidential" medical information provided to them to support a claim for benefits.

5.2 — The "Two Year" Rule

Short- and long-term disability plans are generally structured to protect an employee's income for a period of time when he is unable to perform the essential duties of his own job. Thereafter long-term disability payments will continue if the person is unable to perform the essential duties of any occupation. Commonly the period during which the person is entitled to receive benefits because he cannot work at his own job is defined as two years (though this may differ depending on the particular terms of the employer's benefit plans). Similarly some workers' compensation statutes extend the employer's obligation to return the employee to his pre-injury position for a period of two years.

The rationale is based on evidence that disabilities that prevent people from working at their own jobs for periods of up to two years are not uncommon. Alternatively, it is highly unlikely for an individual to return from a disability that kept her away from work for a period of two years or more. It is safe to assume, as many employers do, that an employee who has been absent for a period of two years or more is not going to be returning. It is at this point that many employers deem the employment contract to be frustrated. Again the rationale is based on the relatively safe assumption that the length of the absence itself determines that the individual's condition is more than likely permanent.

At one time it was standard practice for employers and unions to negotiate a provision in the collective agreement that provided for the loss of seniority rights and the termination of employment when an employee had been absent due to illness or injury for a given period (often one or two years). These clauses ran into problems and arbitrators now will void any such clause as violating the individual's rights under human rights legislation.

Essentially, while the two-year rule may serve as a guideline for employers to review the likelihood of an employee's return to work and to assess whether or not the duty to accommodate had been fully discharged it cannot be relied on as an absolute indicator that the employment contract had been frustrated.

5.3 — Frustration and Long Term Disability Benefits

In *Sylvester v. British Columbia*[2] the British Columbia Court of Appeal saw the existence of the long term disability plan as, in effect, a term in the employment contract that implied the parties contemplated the employee may, at some point during his employment, be disabled from working for a long time. The Supreme Court of Canada, however, said that while the underlying assumption of a long term disability plan is that an employee may be disabled for a long period of time, the assumption that underlies the contract of employment is the employee is able to do the work. It is arguable that there is, in effect, two contracts arising out of the same employment relationship.

This suggests that while an employment contract could not be said to be frustrated while an employee was in receipt of short-term disability pay-

---

[2]*Sylvester v. British Columbia*, 1997 CarswellBC 1024, 1997 CarswellBC 1025, [1997] 2 S.C.R. 315 (S.C.C.).Case summary by Timothy J. Delaney at http://www.lklaw.ca/Publications/Employment%20TERMINATING%20THE%20EMPLOYMENT%20OF%20A%20DISABLED%20OR%20ILL%20EMPLOYEE.pdf.

ments, because there was an expectation that the individual would likely return to work, the same rationale does not necessarily apply to long-term disability cases.

However, the fact that an individual has been found to be entitled to long-term disability benefits does not automatically indicate in any way that the employment contract has been frustrated.

While the doctrine of frustration of contract remains relevant in the employment context there have been a number of court decisions and recent legislative changes (e.g. under the *Employment Standards Act of Ontario, 2000*) that bring its application under question. In another British Columbia Court of Appeal decision, *Bohun v. Similco Mines Ltd.*,[3] the court raised just this question of relevance.

Mr. Bohun had worked for approximately 20 years as an accountant for Similco Mines Ltd. He left work suffering from chronic refractory depression. He was notified approximately eight months later that he was dismissed, which was to take effect 14.7 months later. The defendant, however, regarded the disability benefits as the only payments to which the plaintiff was entitled on termination. The evidence established that at the time Mr. Bohun was dismissed he was expected to be able to return to work in approximately one and a half months. However the termination of his employment had an adverse effect on his condition and made his return to work impossible.

The British Columbia Court of Appeal found that Mr. Bohun was terminated by his employer before frustration could have been claimed. As such, he was entitled to be paid notice and severance.

In the *Bohun* decision the British Columbia Court of Appeal suggested that the law of frustration should not apply to an employment relationship, particularly one which contains a long term disability plan. The suggestion would seem to be that because the parties contemplate that an employee can be on disability coverage for a long time (indeed permanently to age 65); the law of frustration may not apply.

However, in *Bohun* because there was evidence that the employee was going to return to work when his employment was terminated. The termination set back his condition and, it was argued, rendered him permanently disabled. Thus, the frustrating event had been, in effect, induced or aggra-

---

[3] *Bohun v. Similco Mines Ltd.*, 1995 CarswellBC 244, 6 B.C.L.R. (3d) 22 (B.C. C.A.).Case summary by Timothy J. Delaney at http://www.lklaw.ca/Publications/Employment%20TERMINATING%20THE%20EMPLOYMENT%20OF%20A%20DISABLED%20OR%20ILL%20EMPLOYEE.pdf.

vated by the employer. The case illustrates the importance of being absolutely certain that the contract has been frustrated, otherwise the employer may be liable for damages such as the provision of proper notice and severance payments upon termination.

In *Antonacci v. Great Atlantic and Pacific Co. of Canada*[4], the decision of Justice Swinton suggested that if an employer has a long-term disability plan, it could never argue that employment has been frustrated since a long-term disability is contemplated. However, long-term disability benefits continue to age 65 under disability insurance policies in most cases, regardless of termination of employment. The employee is, therefore, not prejudiced by the termination. Consequently, if medical evidence determines that returning to work will never occur, the employer may be successful in asserting that the contract of employment has been frustrated.

The state of the law regarding frustration remains confusing for employers. It seems evident that the doctrine can only be relied on in limited situations where an employee is clearly permanently disabled, or otherwise unable to attend at work regularly. It is also evident that the employer must make every reasonable effort short of undue hardship to accommodate the individual before the employee could be terminated. Finally there are questions regarding how the employer should consider the effect of his long-term disability coverage with respect to the employment contract.

The more compelling issues with respect to the continued relevance of the doctrine of frustration in the employment context concern the individual's eligibility for notice and severance payments upon termination. The intent of the doctrine was for one party to claim that he had cause to sever a contract that had become impossible of performance due to unforeseen or fortuitous circumstances. Recent decisions in Ontario have all but erased this by requiring employers to pay notice and severance under circumstances where an employment contract has been frustrated because of illness or injury.

5.4 — Frustration of the Employment Contract under the *Employment Standards Act of Ontario, 2000*

Under the *Employment Standards Act of Ontario*, R.S.O. 1990 employees whose "contract of employment" had "become impossible of performance or been frustrated by ... illness or injury" were exempted from receiving

[4]*Antonacci v. Great Atlantic & Pacific Co. of Canada* (2000), 2000 CarswellOnt 61, 181 D.L.R. (4th) 577 (Ont. C.A); additional reasons at (2000), 2000 CarswellOnt 356, 181 D.L.R. (4th) 577 at 589 (Ont. C.A.).

notice or severance upon termination. The Act was subsequently amended following an Ontario Court of Appeal decision (*Ontario Nurses' Association v. Mount Sinai*[5]) such that the provision that exempted employers from paying severance due to frustration of employment did not apply in cases where the *Human Rights Code* prohibited severing the employee. However, in 2005 the *Employment Standards Act* was further amended to clarify the exemption as follows:

1.

(1) Paragraph 4 of subsection 2(1) of Ontario Regulation 288/01 is amended by striking out "Subject to the *Human Rights Code*" at the beginning.

(2) Section 2 of the Regulation is amended by adding the following subsection:

(3) Paragraph 4 of subsection (1) does not apply if the impossibility or frustration is the result of an illness or injury suffered by the employee.

2. Clause 9(2)(b) of the Regulation is revoked and the following substituted:

(b) the impossibility or frustration is the result of an illness or injury suffered by the employee.

[6]Ergo if an employer was to terminate an employee because the employment was frustrated as a result of an illness or injury then the employer would have to pay severance. However, there are a number of related issues which are not clearly contemplated by this change in the regulations. For example, if an employee is receiving disability payments from an insurance carrier one line of thought followed in several cases has been that notice and severance ought not be payable until those payments are exhausted.

The controversy around the issue of severance and the frustration of an employment contract due to a disability arises from the Mount Sinai case. In it a nurse with 13 years' service was terminated for innocent absenteeism. The hospital denied her statutory severance pay in accordance with an exemption in the *Employment Standards Act, 1990* [ESA 1990]. The case ultimately found its way to the Court of Appeal which held that para. 58(5)(c) of the ESA 1990, which provided an exemption from the payment of severance pay if the employee's contract of employment had become impossible

[5]*O.N.A. v. Mount Sinai Hospital* (2005), 2005 CarswellOnt 1714, 75 O.R. (3d) 245 (Ont. C.A.).

[6]O. Reg. 549/05.

of performance or frustrated by illness or injury, violated subs. 15(1) of the *Charter of Rights and Freedoms* [Charter] and was therefore void.

Initially an Arbitration Board had ruled that the Act did not discriminate against the employee because the provision was not based on the existence of a disability but merely dealt with a situation where the employment contract was no longer viable. On appeal however the Divisional Court found that the exemption under the Act denied disabled employees a benefit to which they would have been entitled but for their disability thus violating "the very core of the values contemplated in s. 15(1) of the *Charter*" (para. 47).

The counter-argument made at the appellate level by both the employer and the Ontario Attorney General was that the dominant purpose of statutory severance payments is to compensate terminated employees who remain in the workforce for the loss of seniority, accumulated benefits and job-specific skills which a long-serving employee suffers when terminated. The financial needs of employees whose contracts have been frustrated due to a disability are typically met through other avenues such as disability benefits. In the view of many employers removing the exemption essentially created an opportunity for "double dipping."

The Court of Appeal rejected this argument. It found that the exemption was based on "an impermissible stereotype that disabled persons cannot fully participate in the workplace" (para. 26). Essentially the court found that despite the individual's inability to fulfill their employment obligations to the present employer it remains feasible that with retraining or some form of accommodation the individual may possibly remain in the workforce. The Court found that the general assumption that disabled employees will not work again is false because disabled employees may be able to find suitable alternative employment, and may undergo training to acquire new skills to accommodate their special needs.

The denial of equitable treatment under the statute in effect represented an affront to the dignity of the disabled employee. contract of employment had become impossible of performance or frustrated by illness or injury, violated subs. 15(1) of the *Charter of Rights and Freedoms* [Charter] and was therefore void.

Furthermore, in the Court of Appeal's opinion, a "crucially important" aspect of the dignity of disabled people was affected by the denial of equality of treatment and compensation. In this regard, the Court accepted that one of the main purposes of severance pay is to compensate long-serving employees for contributions they have made to their employer. In the Court's view, to deny severely disabled employees severance pay was to devalue their contributions relative to that of other terminated employees. Essentially, the differential treatment permitted under the ESA was held to be discriminatory because it was based on a stereotypical assumption that perpetuated the view that disabled employees are less capable or worthy of recognition as members of society.

Finally, the Court of Appeal found no rational connection between denying payments to employees whose contracts have been frustrated due to illness or injury and the legislative objective of facilitating re-entry of terminated employees to the workforce. As such, the impugned provision was not saved by s. 1 of the *Charter.*

At the time of Tilley's termination, the statutory provision at issue was contained in the *ESA 1990*. Since then, that version of the *ESA* was repealed and replaced by the *Employment Standards Act, 2000* [ESA 2000]. The equivalent provision to the one at issue in the Mount Sinai case was then addressed at s. 9 of *Termination and Severance of Employment, O. Reg. 288/01*, which provided that an employee is not entitled to statutory severance pay if the contract of employment has become impossible to perform or frustrated, unless the impossibility or frustration is the result of an illness or injury suffered by the employee and the *Human Rights Code* prohibits severing the employment.

The statutory severance pay exemption in the *ESA 2000* was similar but not identical to the exemption that was at issue in the *Mount Sinai* case. Unlike the predecessor provision, it clearly established that an employer could rely on the statutory severance pay exemption only in cases where it has met its obligations to maintain the employment of a disabled employee under the *Human Rights Code.* As noted above the Act has again been amended to bring greater clarity to the regulations and remove the aspect with respect to fulfilling obligations under the *Human Rights Code.*

5.5 — Application Under Workers' Compensation Statutes

Under the Workplace Safety Insurance Board (WSIB) policies it is recognized that the WSIB is obligated to accommodate injured workers under the *Human Rights Code.* They have determined that programs such as the labour market re-entry (LMR) process are governed by the Code. Under LMR, WSIB works with the employee and all other interested parties to establish a plan to retrain the individual in order that they may find suitable alternative employment. These programs are entered into when accommodation with the pre-injury employer is impossible.

If the employer (and WSIB) was not obligated to accommodate the injured employee and the employee's employment contract is severed at that point due to frustration based on the injury, then the employer might be absolved of any associated costs under the LMR. This would undoubtedly be a better alternative cost-wise, but it would be detrimental to the injured employee.

Obviously this is not the intent. Rather the employer is obligated to fund the LMR for the individual and this is recognized as a form of accommodation. It also is obvious that under an LMR the employee will be severed at the point when they seek alternative employment. Hence there seems to be no logical connection with the reasoning provided under the Tilley case.

The statutes seem to be black and white, and therefore at some point of time injured employees who have entered the LMR program *and* who are unlikely to return to work for the company will be eligible for severance pay. The problem is identifying when it could (or should) be determined that the injured employee is unable to return to work to the pre-injury employer.

Typically an injured worker would have to reach his maximum medical recovery (MMR) point before LMR would be considered. This often occurs after three years have elapsed from the original date of injury and all other issues (initial future economic loss awards, non-economic loss awards, etc.) have been resolved. This is important from a company's point of view as it determines whether or not the cost of LMR will be included under the WSIB's new experimental experience rating (NEER) program.

While LMR is initiated only when it has been determined that the company cannot accommodate the employee's injuries, this is partly based on the individual's skill set at the time. If the individual can be retrained for another occupation that the pre-injury company employs it is possible, at least in theory that the employee could return to her pre-injury employer. Thus it could be premature to terminate employment.

Another aspect that needs to be considered is the level of WSIB benefits the individual is receiving. Typically injured employees are entitled to full loss of earnings (LOE) benefits while they are being retrained. These benefits are reduced once the person actually re-enters the workforce. This can in certain circumstances provide an incentive for the pre-injury employer to "hire" the person into another occupation; an incentive the payment of severance would erase. In other respects it could be argued that the payment of full LOE benefits represents accommodation while the individual's employment has been retained (and thus leaving the door open for her possible return to work).

The jurisprudence as it exists today provides few if any guidelines with respect to WSIB cases. Hence employers may want to establish policies to determine when they would pay notice and severance to employees disabled due to workplace injuries as follows:

- An employee who is injured and unable to perform his pre-injury occupation cannot be terminated (except where just cause exists) during the period when the employers obligation to reemploy continues to be in effect (i.e. two years from the original date of injury).
- Subsequent to the expiry of the employer's obligation to re-employ in order for an individual to be eligible for severance pay the following conditions must be met:
  - The injured employee must have reached maximum medical recovery.
  - The injured employee must have entered into or been declared ineligible to participate in the LMR program.
  - If the injured employee has entered into the LMR she must have exhausted the retraining effort.
  - The injured employee must no longer be eligible to receive full LOE benefits.
  - The company must terminate the individual's employment by written notice.
- It is understood that as a condition of receiving any severance pay under the terms of this agreement the employee will sign a release acknowledging that the company had exhausted its obligations to accommodate the individual and the employee will waive any claims whatsoever against the company arising out of her employment with the company or the termination thereof.
- The parties agree that the terms of this settlement comply with their respective obligations under the *Employment Standards Act*, the *Human Rights Code*, the *Workplace Safety Insurance Act*, and any other applicable statutes.

5.6 — Assessing Damages for the Wrongful Dismissal of Disabled Employees

Accepting that the doctrine of frustration cannot be used as cause then employers will under certain circumstances owe disabled employees damages for terminating their employment. Clearly Ontario *Employment Standards Regulations* require the employer to pay the individual notice and severance upon termination.

An employee who is wrongfully dismissed while absent from work due to illness is entitled to damages for the salary the employee would have earned had the employee been working during the noticc period, just as an employee who is wrongfully dismissed while working enjoys such an entitlement. The fact that the employee could not have worked during the notice period is irrelevant to the assessment of damages.

The Supreme Court of Canada in *Sylvester v. British Columbia* made it clear that benefits received by the employee pursuant to a disability plan will be deducted from the award for damages for reasonable notice. Thus, for example, if an employee was receiving disability benefits at 70% of his usual salary, the employer would only be required to "top up" the salary to 100% during the notice period.

An employee who arranges his own private disability insurance will not have those funds deducted from the notice period damages. It is important to note that in Sylvester the employer was the Government of British Columbia. The Government of British Columbia had set up and funded its own disability plan for employees. Most employers, however, usually arrange disability coverage through private insurance plans for their employees, where the employees may or may not contribute directly to funding the plans. The question then is, are these benefits deductible?

The answer to this question is affected, in part, by the question as to when the notice period begins to run following the dismissal. This question also affects the issue of mitigation. In *Sylvester* (and also reflected in *Bohun*), the British Columbia Court of Appeal held that the notice period should run from the date of the employee's wrongful dismissal. In other words, if an employee was absent from work due to an illness for two years and was dismissed six months following her absence from work, the notice period would run from the dismissal, six months after the date the employee last worked, prior to the illness. Therefore, the notice period would run during the period of disability.

Conversely, the Ontario Court of Appeal in *McKay v Camco*[7] held that the notice period should be suspended and run following the period of disability. This contrasts with the court's decision in 2001 in *Sills v. Children's Aid Society of Belleville (City), Hastings (County) & Trenton (City)*[8] wherein the court stated that the approach in *Sylvester* makes some practical sense. At the time that the court is asked to assess damages the employee

[7] *McKay v. Camco Inc.* (1986), 53 O.R. (2d) 257 (Ont. C.A.).

[8] *Sills v. Children's Aid Society of Belleville (City), Hastings (County) & Trenton (City)* (2001), 53 O.R. (3d) 577 (Ont. C.A.).

could still be on disability leave and may remain so for years to come. Assessing damages to run after the period of disability ends may not be practical. The Ontario Court of Appeal, in another post-*Sylvester* decision called *Whyte v. Viceroy Fluid Power International Inc.*, ruled that workers compensation benefits received during the notice period were deductible from the damages awarded.

The deductibility issue was considered again by the Ontario Court of Appeal in the case of *McNamara v. Alexander Centre Industries Ltd*[9]. In that case Mr. McNamara had worked for the defendant for 24 years. He was terminated after advising his employer that he would be off work indefinitely due to medical reasons. He was summarily dismissed without notice or severance.

At trial the court found Mr. McNamara had been wrongfully dismissed. Damages were assessed at 24 months notice. The employer argued that the disability payments paid by London Life under an employer sponsored plan during those 24 months should be deducted from the award. The Court of Appeal refused to deduct the disability benefits. It said:

> If the disability benefits are deducted, McNamara will receive his full salary for the entire notice period. However, that salary will be less than it might have been if he had not bargained a trade-off between salary and benefits, and he will forfeit all of the disability payments. ACI, on the other hand, will derive a huge benefit from the deductibility scenario, solely because it chose an employee's new disability, after 24 years of loyal service, as the moment and reason to fire him. ACI's windfall for acting abominably will be $163,000.

It is not clear whether or not an employer is entitled to deduct benefit payments (whether accrued through an employer sponsored plan or under a workers' compensation scheme). It would seem that the answer depends on the governing jurisdiction and the circumstances of the case. However, given the reduced relevance of the doctrine of frustration this question is bound to be tested in the future.

In limited circumstances, an employer may have cause to dismiss an employee if the employment contract has been frustrated in performance by an illness or injury. However, as decisions in British Columbia and Ontario have demonstrated the doctrine of frustration is becoming less relevant in the employment context (and may disappear altogether in the near future).

In the absence of cause an employer cannot dismiss an employee without providing sufficient notice and severance. There are some questions that remain to be answered with respect to the deductibility of any disability

---

[9] *McNamara v. Alexander Centre Industries Ltd.* (2001), 53 O.R. (3d) 481 (Ont. C.A.); leave to appeal refused (2001), 2001 CarswellOnt 3807, 2001 CarswellOnt 3808 (S.C.C.).

benefits the employee may be entitled to. As such employers are less likely to dismiss an employee who is receiving disability or workers' compensation benefits for frustration and more likely simply to keep the individual on the books as an employee. This may have other unforeseen consequences down the road (like employees who have been absent for many years suddenly reappearing ready to return to work).

5.7 — Duty to Accommodate

Under the Ontario *Human Rights Code*, section 17 creates an obligation to accommodate, specifically under the ground of disability. It states that a right is not infringed if the person with a disability is incapable of performing or fulfilling the essential duties or requirements attending the exercise of the right. However, this defence is not available unless it can be shown that the needs of the person cannot be accommodated without undue hardship.

The Ontario Human Rights Commission in its policies emphasizes the need for individualized accommodation, because the ground of disability "means vastly different things depending upon the individual and the context." Further, the duty to accommodate requires that the most appropriate accommodation be determined and then be undertaken, short of undue hardship. The most appropriate accommodation is one that most respects the dignity of the individual with a disability, meets individual needs, best promotes integration and full participation, and ensures confidentiality.

Accommodation will be considered appropriate if it will result in equal opportunity to attain the same level of performance, or to enjoy the same level of benefits and privileges experienced by others or if it is proposed or adopted for the purpose of achieving equal opportunity, and meets the individual's disability-related needs. If the accommodation meets the individual's needs and does so in a way that most respects dignity, then a determination can be made as to whether or not this "most appropriate" accommodation would result in undue hardship.

Nothing in the Code or in section 17 specifically restricts the requirement to accommodate a worker with disability to the pre-disability position. Thus, accommodation could entail retraining an individual to be able to perform work in another position. The Code and the Commission's polices do not speak specifically to retraining for positions that are external to the organization.

5.8 — The OC Transpo Case

In a case before the Ontario Human Rights Commission a tribunal found that the Ottawa-Carleton Regional Transit Commission (OC Transpo) did not demonstrate that it had attempted to accommodate the employee up to the point of reasonable hardship:

> The Complainant, Mr. Parisien, was a bus driver with the Ottawa-Carleton Regional Transit Commission (otherwise known as "OC Transpo"). He was employed there for over 18 years. During the 18 years he was absent for approximately 1,664 full days and 33 part days, mostly because of illness, due to post-traumatic stress disorder, which was brought about as a result of two violent incidents that occurred while at work. The symptoms included anxiety and gastro-intestinal problems. According to Mr. Parisien's doctor, he was "preoccupied with being assaulted" while driving his bus route, "to the point of almost paranoid feelings."
>
> Mr. Parisien received treatment in the form of cognitive behavioural therapy and medication. His driver's licence was downgraded due to his disability, meaning that he was no longer able to drive a bus. His psychiatrist later filled out a Ministry of Transportation form stating that Mr. Parisien was ready to regain his Class "C" driver's licence. Mr. Parisien's psychologist and psychiatrist also wrote a letter to OC Transpo, explaining that he was ready to return to work, but that it would be best for him to initially return on a part-time basis.
>
> OC Transpo's Health Unit wrote a letter to the Superintendent of Operational Personnel, which concluded:
>
> > Taking into consideration the medical information on file at present, the fact that Mr. Parisien does not hold a class "C" licence at present, as well as his past record of attendance, the Health Unit is not fully convinced at this time that Mr. Parisien will be able to perform his duties as a bus operator on a regular basis.
> >
> > If the Transportation Division is able and prepared to offer Mr. Parisien alternate employment, we will contact his medical advisors to quantify his restrictions and to obtain a more complete prognosis. Please advise us as to your decision.
>
> Mr. Parisien was subsequently dismissed for chronic innocent absenteeism. He filed a grievance against OC Transpo.
>
> OC Transpo argued that they were not discriminating against Mr. Parisien based on his disability. They pointed out that Mr. Parisien was terminated "because of the poor prognosis of his regular and reliable attendance". They further argued that their treatment of Mr. Parisien, under their policy on innocent absenteeism and their Attendance Management Program, was no different from any other employee who had a poor attendance record.
>
> According to the Tribunal, OC Transpo developed an Attendance Management Program "in honest and good faith belief that it was necessary to maintain reasonable levels of attendance," however an intention to discriminate is not a requirement in order to amount to discrimination under the law. It was also found that accommodating Mr. Parisien's return to work on a part-time basis would not amount to undue hardship on the part of OC Transpo.

> The Tribunal ordered reinstatement of Mr. Parisien, as well as damages for lost income and the sum of $3,500 for hurt feelings.[10]

According to Eric Roher and Michelle Henry in a *Canadian Employment Law Today* article:[11]

> Based on the test established by the Supreme Court of Canada in *British Columbia v. B.C.G.S.E.U.* (also known as the *Meiorin* case) the arbitrators ruled the employer had failed to establish a *bona fide* occupational requirement for the discrimination since it did not demonstrate any effort was made to accommodate the disability to the point of undue hardship. In the tribunal's view "tolerating" absenteeism could constitute an acceptable type of accommodation. Even where innocent absenteeism justified dismissal in accordance with labour arbitration law, the tribunal's view was this did not mean the dismissal was in accordance with human rights law.

5.9 — Coast Mountain Bus Company

In another case under British Columbia Human Right Coast Mountain Bus Company[12] also recently discovered, attendance management programs can quite easily fall afoul of human rights legislation when dealing with employees who are disabled, even where such absences are treated as innocent absenteeism not giving rise to disciplinary sanctions.

> Coast Mountain Bus Company (CMBC) operates transit services in the Greater Vancouver area. CMBC had an Attendance Management Program which inducted operators into the program if they had absenteeism rates at or above the company average. At the initial stage, letters would be sent to the operators notifying them that their attendance was considered to be unacceptable. These employees would have quarterly attendance reviews, which could simply result in monitoring of their attendance, informal discussions with their supervisors, or progression through a series of more formal stages of the Attendance Management Program.
>
> If there was insufficient improvement, employees would be sent a formal letter and moved to Level 1 of the Program. The next phase was Level 2, when the employee could be asked to provide a medical assessment from his/her doctor. Once the information in the medical assessment was considered by CMBC, employees could be moved to Level 3, which included a formal letter outlining prescribed attendance targets, or "parameters," which the employee was required to meet. Termination could result from an employee's failure to meet these parameters. The Program was administered by the Attendance Management Department, the Occupational Health Group and supervisors in the line.

---

[10] *Parisien v. Ottawa-Carleton Regional Transit Commission*, 2003 CarswellNat 3230, [2003] C.H.R.D. No. 6 (Can. Human Rights Trib.)

[11] Eric Rohler and Michelle Henry, "Duty extends to a broad range of areas," *Canadian Employment Law Today* 411 (April 14, 2004).

[12] *CAW-Canada, Local 111 v. Coast Mountain Bus Co.*, 2008 BCHRT 52 (B.C. Human Rights Trib.).

According to the union, the Attendance Management Program failed to consider the underlying causes of absenteeism in individual cases and dealt with sick and injured workers "mechanistically and punitively" by initiating employees into the program without regard to the circumstances, and by only considering accommodation during the later stages of the Program. The union also argued that there was no actual policy on accommodation within the Attendance Management Program (there was a separate policy on accommodation which was not part of the Attendance Management Program).

The union and several employees with disabilities objected to the Attendance Management Program on the grounds that it amounted to systemic discrimination against them based on their disabilities, especially those with chronic or recurring disabilities. They brought a complaint before the British Columbia Human Rights Tribunal, arguing that this was an infringement of section 13 of the B.C. *Human Rights Code*, which protects employees from discrimination based on physical or mental disabilities.

CMBC argued that the Attendance Management Program was required in light of the fact that transit operators had high rates of absenteeism. However, fewer than 20% of its operators had absenteeism rates that were at or above the company average. The company therefore argued that average attendance could not be construed as being "normal". The union did not object to the existence of the Attendance Management Program per se, but did object to the way it was applied.

According to the Tribunal, the Attendance Management Program amounted to prima facie discrimination. Induction into the Attendance Management Program was stressful for many employees and had "negative employment-related consequences" including termination in some instances. Applying the Supreme Court of Canada's Meiorin[13] test, the Tribunal held that, having proved prima facie discrimination, it was then up to CMBC to prove that its conduct was justified by satisfying three requirements: (1) that a standard was being adopted for a purpose or goal rationally connected to the function being performed; (2) that the standard was adopted in good faith for the purpose of attaining the goal or purpose; and (3) that the standard is reasonably necessary to accomplish the goal or purpose because the employer cannot accommodate such individuals without undue hardship. CMBC satisfied the first two requirements but failed the third one:

> [W]hile CMBC led evidence of the substantial cost of employee absenteeism to its operation, that evidence related to the global cost of absenteeism to its operations. There was no evidence on which I could assess the cost related specifically to those employees with chronic or recurring disabilities. Thus, there is no evidence before me on which I could find that considering accommodating those with such disabilities at an earlier stage in the Program, or expanding the possible accommodation options available in the manner outlined above, would so escalate costs to CMBC as to create an undue hardship.

---

[13] *British Columbia (Public Service Employee Relations Commission) v. B.C.G.E.U.*, 1999 CarswellBC 1907, 1999 CarswellBC 1907, 1999 CarswellBC 1908 (S.C.C.).

The Tribunal further commented:

> The evidence before me established that, in applying the Attendance Management Program, CMBC treats individuals with chronic or recurring disabilities as "attendance problems" and forces them into the AMP process. Although they may eventually be accommodated in the later stages of the process, this approach ignores the stress and anxiety experienced by employees who are placed on the Attendance Management Program and the frustration and anger which may result when the fact that they have a disability is seemingly ignored. It imposes on an employee a standard, average attendance, which the employee may be unable to meet. As outlined above, it is not sufficient to say that, at some point in the process, there may be an accommodation reached, after the employee has exceeded the standard. In fact, such an approach is contrary to the directions of the Supreme Court of Canada in Meiorin and Grismer[14], which indicate that there must be accommodation within the standard, not just a standard set with the possibility of accommodation at the end stages.

According to the Supreme Court of Canada in the *British Columbia (Superintendent of Motor Vehicles) v. British Columbia (Council of Human Rights* case, the Meiorin test for accommodation "ensures that each person is assessed according to his or her own personal abilities rather than presumed group characteristics. Failure to accommodate may be shown by evidence that the standard was set arbitrarily, or that individual assessment was unreasonably refused, or in some other way."

At times supervisors at CMBC had refused to hear information from disabled employees related to their accommodation for reasons of privacy. Because supervisors had a key role to play in the process, including monitoring attendance and providing coaching to employees with attendance management problems, the Tribunal felt this was unacceptable:

> Thus, the evidence before me indicates that the structure in place to protect confidentiality and information issues, in practice, leads to situations where decisions under the AMP are made with incomplete information. CMBC is not taking into account all of the information it has available to it, and its failure to do so means that any accommodation process which may be required cannot be commenced at an early stage.

The Tribunal did not strike down the Attendance Management Program in its entirety, but ordered "CMBC to cease and desist in its application of the Attendance Management Program to operators with chronic or recurring disabilities, where those disabilities are the cause of some or all of the absenteeism considered excessive under the Attendance Management Program." Also, Tribunal-assisted mediation was ordered for disabled employees with chronic or recurring conditions currently going through the Attendance Management Program process. Employees with chronic disabilities who had progressed to Level 3 of the Attendance Management Program were each awarded $5,000 or $6,000 for injury to their dignity, feelings and self-respect. However, the Tribunal refused to interfere with arbitration deci-

---

[14] *British Columbia (Superintendent of Motor Vehicles) v. British Columbia (Council of Human Rights)* (1999), 1999 CarswellBC 2730, 1999 CarswellBC 2731 (S.C.C.).

sions which dealt with employees who had already been terminated under the Attendance Management Program.

Lessons for employers:

- Sufficient communication is vital between different departments, including line managers, human resources, and occupational health. While privacy concerns are legitimate, sufficient information needs to be provided to supervisors in relation to an individual's condition and the specific accommodations he requires, especially where the employee's immediate supervisor is involved in monitoring absenteeism and providing coaching to individual employees with attendance management issues.
- Employees with disabilities should not be moved through the progressive steps of an attendance management program in a "mechanistic and punitive" manner prior to attempting to accommodate them. To do so is discriminatory.
- Once an employee who has a disability which is shown to result in elevated rates of absenteeism returns to work, it is inappropriate to hold that person to the same standards of attendance required of all employees.
- Employers should consider what would be a normal attendance target for employees with specific disabilities. Such employees should not be held to the same targets as the general employee population.

5.10 — Family Status: What should Be Accommodated?

A British Columbia health-care worker was discriminated against because of her duty of care to her disabled child, the British Columbia Court of Appeal ruled in *Campbell River & North Island Transition Society v. H.S.A.B.*, a 2004 decision[15].

Shelley Howard worked as a youth support worker for the Campbell River & North Island Transition Society, a Campbell River, B.C.-based non-profit society that deals with family violence. She had four children, one of whom had a behavioural disability that required special parental attention.

[15] 2004 CarswellBC 1012, [2004] B.C.J. No. 922, 2004 BCCA 260, 127 L.A.C. (4th) 1, 28 B.C.L.R. (4th) 292, 240 D.L.R. (4th) 479, 50 C.H.R.R. D/140, 2004 C.L.L.C. 230-019, 196 B.C.A.C. 236, 322 W.A.C. 236 (B.C. C.A.).

Howard was considered a "very good employee" from the date when she started in 1993 until 2001, when the society changed her shift from day to evening. She was concerned the new shift would interfere with her ability to care for her son's special needs, which included caring for him after school. The society refused to reinstate her to her old shift and she went on medical leave due to stress.

The arbitrator and British Columbia Court of Appeal found the society interfered with Howard's ability to carry out her "substantial parental obligation" when it changed her hours of work and therefore discriminated against her based on her family status as a parent of a special needs child.

Thomas Gorsky and Stephen Shore[16] made the following observations regarding the *Campbell River* case:

> There are a multitude of considerations under the framework of family status accommodation. As with so many human rights issues, there are often no simple answers and each case must be considered on its own merits.
>
> What is clear is an employer must be aware of these issues so if a family status question does arise it is identified promptly and addressed thoroughly. The British Columbia Court of Appeal in *Campbell River & North Island Transition Society v. H.S.A.B.* developed a three-step test to determine whether an employer is at risk of discriminating against employees.
>
> Human rights legislation across Canada prohibits certain types of workplace discrimination, but day-to-day compliance in ever-changing workplaces can present difficulties for employers. Family status is one type of protected ground for which there has been little judicial guidance.

5.11 — What Is Family Status?

Under the Ontario *Human Rights Code*, family status is defined as "the status of being in a parent and child relationship." Because human rights legislation is broadly construed, adopted children, stepchildren and foster children qualify, as will an individual who has assumed the role and obligations of a parent. Whether this definition will automatically be applied to grandparents and grandchildren and other extended relationships is doubtful.

---

[16]Thomas Gorsky and Stephen Shore, *Canadian Employment Law Today* 501 (January 16, 2008; online January 31, 2008).

5.12 — What Constitutes Unlawful Discrimination?

An employer might have a workplace rule that work begins for everyone at 8:30 a.m. sharp. On the surface, this does not appear to discriminate because the rule applies to everyone.

However, even though not intended, such a rule can adversely affect individual employees with family commitments. For example, a parent may be unable to organize a daycare schedule with her work schedule. The question is whether the employer is required to relax the schedule as part of its duty to accommodate.

The duty to accommodate has been expressly stipulated under the Code with regard to accommodation of disabled employees, but there is no explicit reference to a duty to accommodate an employee on account of family status. While this might suggest there is no duty, the Supreme Court of Canada has made it clear that whether mentioned in human rights legislation or not, a duty to accommodate can arise in the context of most prohibited grounds of discrimination.

5.13 — The Three-Step Test

In *Campbell River & North Island Transition Society v. H.S.A.B.*, the British Columbia Court of Appeal came up with a three-step test to determine whether a workplace rule might run afoul of human rights legislation. Employers should consider whether:

- The rule is rationally connected to the performance of the job.
- The employer adopted the particular standard in a good-faith belief it was necessary to the fulfillment of a legitimate work-related purpose.
- It is impossible to accommodate an individual employee adversely affected by the rule, without imposing undue hardship upon the employer.

The first two steps are often not the main point of contention, but the third is frequently controversial.

5.14 — When Is The Need for Accommodation Triggered?

In *Campbell River*, the court found the duty to accommodate is triggered if a workplace rule "results in serious interference with a substantial parental or other family duty or obligation of the employee." The court recognized family demands create many potential requests for accommodation, but only the more pressing demands will trigger a legal right to accommodation.

From this analysis, a parent's desire to leave work early to attend a child's soccer practice is not sufficient. However, a parent's need to accompany a severely handicapped child to school will likely meet the test.

Generally, when an obligation is one which only the parent can fulfill, and one which can only be satisfied by revision of a workplace rule, a duty to accommodate will likely be triggered.

If an employer is asked to accommodate an employee on the basis of family status, it would be advisable to show an open mind as failure to do so has been the ignition switch for many human rights complaints. It should collect all available information, including allowing the employee an opportunity to state her case as to why her particular circumstances constitute a substantial obligation and in what manner the workplace rule seriously interferes with the fulfillment of that obligation.

5.15 — Accommodation and undue hardship

The search for accommodation is one in which the employee has a duty to participate. An employee must be open to all options which would alleviate the disadvantage. As well, an employer is justified in limiting accommodation to the minimum of what is required to meet the employee's need.

The duty to accommodate is not a duty to provide "perks" to an employee. In *Campbell River*, the court considered medical evidence that the child had a "major psychiatric disorder and the parent's attendance to his needs during after-school hours was an extraordinarily important medical adjunct to the son's well-being." On the basis of this evidence, the court was prepared to find the ability of the parent to be at home during after-school hours was a "substantial parental obligation" for which the employer should offer accommodation.

As a rule, employers are held to a very stringent level of hardship before undue hardship will be found. If it becomes the issue over which the employee's request is ultimately decided, the employer will have a high onus to meet in order to demonstrate accommodation will result in undue hardship.

There are several circumstances where family status may have to be accommodated. If an employer has strict rules for scheduling or changing shifts, these may have to be revisited in the search for accommodation. An attendance management program must be administered in a way that does not punish an employee for an absence that is a result of family obligations.

If family status or another protected ground for discrimination comes into play, an employer may be required to accommodate an employee beyond the minimum standards provided under the relevant *Employment Standards Act*, such as if an employer fails to consider an employee with caregiving responsibilities for promotion.

5.16 — McGill University Health Centre

In another case the Supreme Court of Canada took a different view of the duty to accommodate and upheld a provision in a collective agreement that allowed for termination of disabled workers after three years:[17]

> The McGill University Health Centre terminated an employee who had been off work for three years because of a disability. The collective agreement allowed for terminations of disabled workers after three years. The union claimed this was a failure to accommodate the disability and a violation of Quebec's Charter of Human Rights and Freedoms.

However, the Supreme Court of Canada found the collective agreement provision limiting disability leave was justified, noting further accommodation would have a negative impact on the hospital and reach the point of undue hardship. The three-year limit stipulated in the collective agreement was not a violation of the charter as it surpassed the minimum requirements. The court found the three-year limit was recognition of the hospital's duty to accommodate and an identification of the point it would face undue hardship. Once the employee's leave reached that point, the hospital had the right to terminate her.

"Undue hardship resulting from the employee's absence must be assessed globally starting from the beginning of the absence, not from the expiry of the three-year period," the court said.

In a *Canadian Employment Law Today* article,[18] Brian Johnston made these observations following the *McGill* case:

> ... if a non-unionized employee misses too much time, the employer may be able to say the employment relationship is frustrated and allow it to end without economic consequences to the employer. The common law principle of frustration is consistent

[17]*Syndicat des employés de l'Hôpital général de Montréal c. Sexton*, 2007 CarswellQue 110, 2007 CarswellQue 111 (S.C.C.).

[18]Brian Johnston, "Sick day limits are legal," *Canadian Employment Law Today* 482 (March 28, 2008; online May 8, 2007).

with the concept of innocent absenteeism, which has been enshrined for many years in unionized situations. ....

However, a more recent and favourable decision for employers dealing with the limits of work absences was released by the Supreme Court of Canada on January 26, 2007. In *McGill University Health Centre v. Syndicat des employés de l'Hôpital général de Montréal*, the court supported a labour arbitrator's award upholding the termination of an employee after three years' absence due to disability, pursuant to a collective agreement provision. The provision stipulated after 36 months of absence an employee would lose seniority rights and employment if absent due to illness or accident, other than an industrial accident or occupational disease. The union had grieved the termination, relying upon the Quebec *Charter of Human Rights and Freedoms* provision. ...

Parties to a contract (whether a collective agreement or an employment contract) cannot contract out of a person's fundamental rights. In *McGill*, the fact the three year period was negotiated was only a consideration when assessing the duty of "reasonable accommodation." A worker's sick day allotment can't be negotiated to be shorter than what human rights legislation allows. A collective agreement can't establish a level of protection lower than the basic level provided by legislation.

The court in *McGill* also noted accommodation is not standard but needs to be flexible according to the situation.

An employer can establish a "hard line" with associated consequences with respect to sick-day usage and not presumptively violate human rights principles. However, that limit has to respect statutory entitlements and be consistent with the individualized nature of accommodation. A hard-line limit itself can be evidence of reasonable accommodation as an employer establishes *bona fide* measures to ensure employees' regular attendance.

5.17 — Hydro-Québec v. Local 2000 of the Canadian Union of Public Employees

In a 2008 case the Supreme Court of Canada ruled that an employer's duty to accommodate a worker has to be balanced with an employee's duty to work. This may lead to changes in the way in which we interpret what is meant by undue hardship. The case involved the provincial utility *Hydro-Québec v. Local 2000 of the Canadian Union of Public Employees (or Syndicat des employéees de techniques professionelles et de bureau d'Hydro-Québec),*[19] and centred around an employee with a history of mental and physical health problems.

The Supreme Court found that the test should not be whether or not it is impossible for the employer to accommodate but if accommodation creates undue hardship for the employer. The purpose of the duty to accommodate

[19] 2008 CarswellQue 6436.

"is not to completely alter the essence of the contract of employment, that is, the employee's duty to perform work in exchange for remuneration." In a case of chronic absenteeism, if the employer can show it has taken steps to accommodate the employee but she's still unable to go back to work in the foreseeable future, the employer will have established undue hardship.

In the Hydro-Quebec case the employee suffered from several different medical problems that resulted in her having missed 960 days of work over a seven year period. During an extended leave between February and July 2001 she was terminated. The employer had made several accommodations for the individual over the years, including lighter duties and gradual return to work after lengthy absences. Immediately prior to her termination, her doctor recommended she stop working for an indefinite period. An assessment ordered by the company concluded she was not able to "work on a regular and continuous basis without continuing to have an absenteeism problem as in the past." She was then terminated.

The union grieved her termination. The arbitrator sided with the employer. Based on assessments conducted by experts for the company and those conducted by experts for the union, the arbitrator noted, "the employer would have to periodically, on a recurring basis, provide the complainant with a new work environment, a new immediate supervisor and new co-workers to keep pace with the evolution of the 'love-hate' cycle of her relationships with supervisors and co-workers."

The ruling was further upheld by the Superior Court. However, the Court of Appeal the court noted that the employer had not proven that accommodation was impossible. Up to then the yardstick for what would be considered "impossible" came from a 1999 Supreme Court decision regarding a discrimination lawsuit by female firefighter Tawney *Meiorin*. In the Meiorin ruling the court noted: "A rule or standard must accommodate individual differences to the point of undue hardship if it is to be found reasonably necessary. Unless no further accommodation is possible without imposing undue hardship, the standard is not a (bona fide occupational requirement) in its existing form and the prima facie case of discrimination stands."

When the Hydro-Quebec case went before the Supreme Court the standard for accommodation was given some additional clarity. In over-ruling the Court of Appeal decision, the Supreme Court noted that "what is really required is not proof that it is impossible to integrate an employee who does not meet a standard, but proof of undue hardship, which can take as many forms as there are circumstances." This seemingly paves the way for employers to make decisions based on the particular circumstances of each case.

Employers don't have "a duty to change working conditions in a fundamental way," wrote the high court in the unanimous ruling. What's more, the test of undue hardship is not whether it's impossible for an employer to accommodate an individual employee's needs — it's just whether the accommodation would cause the employer undue hardship. In the Hydro-Quebec case the employee's horrific attendance record in the past and the prognosis that it was likely to continue to be excessive in the future created an undue hardship for the employer. It had tolerated the excessive absences for long enough.

Essentially the court recognized that there are obligations on both parties to be able to fulfill the duties under the employment contract. It is not reasonable to insist that an employer change the fundamental nature of that relationship in order to accommodate the individual. Hence there are limitations as to what the employer has to accept. With respect to absenteeism the employer does not have to indefinitely tolerate a high level of absences even if those absences are caused by legitimate medical issues.

Specifically the Court noted:

> "The test for undue hardship stated by the Court of Appeal is erroneous. The test is not whether it was impossible for the employer to accommodate the employee's characteristics. Although the employer does not have a duty to change working conditions in a fundamental way, it does have a duty, if it can do so without undue hardship, to arrange the employee's workplace or duties to enable the employee to do his or her work. The test for undue hardship is not total unfitness for work in the foreseeable future. If the characteristics of an illness are such that the proper operation of the business is hampered excessively or if an employee with such an illness remains unable to work for the reasonably foreseeable future even though the employer has tried to accommodate him or her, the employer will have satisfied the test. The employer's duty to accommodate ends where the employee is no longer able to fulfill the basic obligations associated with the employment relationship for the foreseeable future. In the instant case, the arbitrator had not erred in law, and there was no justification for interfering with his assessment of the facts.
>
> The Court of Appeal also erred in holding that the duty to accommodate had to be assessed as of the time the decision to dismiss the complainant was made. It is instead necessary to assess the duty to accommodate globally in a way that takes into account the entire time the employee was absent."

5.18 — Absenteeism and Grievance Arbitration

Attendance management is at the best of times a complex subject given that we are dealing with a variety of different behaviours. Each type of absence from the workplace can trigger a different response by the supervisor depending on whether or not the behaviour is culpable or non-culpable and depending on the nature of the absences. Complicating this further is the fact that an individual may have absences related to several different causes. An individual with a poor record of casual absenteeism (non-culpable) may also have a record of tardiness (culpable). He may also have experienced both short-term absences (casual) and long-term illnesses.

Sorting out all of this can be problematic for any supervisor. In a unionized environment the supervisor is also confronted with the complexities associated with interpreting the collective agreement and understanding how the company's actions will be treated at arbitration. In this chapter we will examine examples of how arbitrators treat discipline related to attendance management.

Typically the reported cases deal with employees who have been terminated for attendance-related behaviour or misconduct so it is worth beginning with a look at the considerations an arbitrator will take into account when assessing whether or not a company has cause to end the employment relationship due to attendance related issues.

Certainly one of the first considerations is whether or not there is evidence, either direct evidence or an inference drawn from the employee's past attendance record, that the employee simply is not capable of maintaining regular attendance at work in the future. In cases where an employee is not in a position to fulfill her fundamental duty to attend at work regularly in the future, regardless of whether or not the employee is deemed to be at fault, a discharge may be justified on "administrative grounds." This is analogous to termination due to frustration of contract.

Arbitrator Shime noted in a case involving the U.A.W. and Massey-Ferguson:

> In so far as the general issue of absenteeism which was raised by the company is concerned, we are satisfied that the employer may justifiably terminate an employee if the employee is not capable of regular attendance and the company may consider the employee's past attendance record and his medical history for the purpose of drawing inferences or arriving at a conclusion about the employee's future prospects with respect to attendance.[20]

With respect to excessive absenteeism the company must prove that an employee's record is not only excessive but is excessive to the extreme that it calls into question the employee's capacity or willingness to provide regular attendance at work. The pattern of absence might be used as evidence that the employee is prone to illnesses or injury that prevents him from attending regularly or it might be relied on to demonstrate a general attitude on the employee's part with regard to regular attendance at work.

---

[20] *U.A.W., Local 458 v. Massey-Ferguson Industries Ltd.* (1972), 24 L.A.C. 344 (Ont. Arb. Bd.).

Alternatively a termination might be justified on disciplinary grounds where the absences carry a culpable connotation calling for progressive discipline that culminates in termination. In this case the company would have to show that the instances relied on for discipline were examples of culpable behaviour, that it followed a stepped progression of sanctions to provide the employee with ample opportunity to correct his behaviour, that it clearly made the employee aware of the potential consequences of his absenteeism, and that the incident relied on to terminate him truly was a culminating incident.

Culpability is a necessary element in defending a termination for absenteeism based on disciplinary grounds (as opposed to an administrative termination). Therefore the company relying on an excessive record of absenteeism would have to show evidence that the pattern reflected specific abuses on the part of the employee or demonstrated a wanton disregard for his responsibilities and obligations to the company to report to work regularly. Hence in managing attendance the company must be aware of the reasons for a given absence. It cannot simply assume that a given absence is not justified but must make an effort to enquire as to why an employee is absent. It can insist where warranted that the employee provide proof that a given absence was indeed justified. If such documentation is not provided then it is reasonable for the company to conclude that an absence was not justified and to treat it as a culpable absence.

Noting the distinction between an administrative termination for excessive non-culpable absenteeism and attendance abuse Arbitrator Palmer noted:

> Quite simply, it is my view that the purpose of discipline (as opposed to discharge) is to attempt to alter corrigible behaviour. Put another way, it is hoped that by imposition of discipline the recipient of such will be made more aware of the impropriety of his conduct and will attempt to change in the future. Obviously, where the conduct complained of cannot be altered, discipline is inappropriate. In the instant case, for example, the two week period when the grievor was not allowed to work cannot improve his health in the future...
>
> In my view, the appropriate response to excessive absence due to illness is dismissal where the facts justify a conclusion by the company that the pattern absences is both inconsistent with continued employment and is indicative of likelihood that such absences will continue in the future.[21]

In that case Palmer pointed out the irony that the company's imposition of a two-week suspension could not be justified because the employees absences were explainable, however under the circumstances in his view the com-

[21] *Canadian Ohio Brass Co. v. Teamsters, Chemical, Energy & Allied Workers, Local 1345* (1981), 1 L.A.C. (3d) 256 (Ont. Arb. Bd.).

pany would have been justified if it had terminated the employee for "administrative" reasons.

Specifically a company will want to be sure that the culminating incident it relies on to justify a discharge for culpable absenteeism is itself an example of culpable misconduct worthy of a disciplinary sanction. An employer must establish first that the final incident which gives rise to the decision to terminate the employee is culpable. Only then can it rely on prior incidents included in the employee's record of discipline to support the decision to end the employment relationship. If the final incident is not worthy of discipline the employer cannot then rely on the past record to justify its actions.[22]

5.19 — Innocent Absenteeism

Arbitrator Brandt noted:

> It has now become accepted and recognized that an employer may terminate its contractual relationship with an employee where, through absenteeism which well may be innocent and excusable, but is nevertheless continuous, recurring and intermittent, the employer has simply lost the benefit of its bargain. In contractual terms the employer contracts that it will pay wages for work performed and there comes a point where, through what may be a blameless set of circumstances, the employee can no longer deliver what he promised, viz., his skills and labour. The interest that the company has in ensuring as far as possible consistency in attendance justifies termination in these situations.[23]

We distinguish between innocent absenteeism (illness and injury) and culpable absenteeism. In the former the employer accepts that the employee through no fault of his own is unable to attend at work and perform his normal duties. Innocent implies that the employee was not directly responsible for the absence or the underlying cause of the absence. Therefore some arbitrators have found that being hungover from the night before or suffering from an injury due to recreational activities does not represent innocent behaviour.

For the most part an employer must accept an employee's explanation that he is absent for a short period (one or two days) due to an illness or injury without corroborating evidence such as a doctor's notes. The reasoning behind this is that it simply does not make sense to burden our medical care

---

[22] *Emery Worldwide (C.F. Co.) v. S.T.E.C., Local 156* (1992), 31 L.A.C. (4th) 341 (Can. Arb. Bd.).

[23] *Allied Chemical Canada Ltd. v. U.A.W., Local 89* (1975), 9 L.A.C. (2d) 300 (Ont. Arb. Bd.).

system with requests for doctor's certificates to justify every absence. One arbitrator put it this way:

> Many short-term illnesses, as any mortal human being knows well, are not amenable to medical treatment. Were the requirements of many collective agreements enforced to the letter, employees with common colds who ought to be home in bed with a hot drink would be forced to attend at their doctors' offices, and physicians who ought to be meeting the treatable medical needs of their patients would, to satisfy some employer, be certifying the existence of cold symptoms which can be best cured by the body's own defences.[24]

Thus while it is an inherent right for the company to demand an acceptable reason for an employee's absence it must have good and sufficient cause to require that employee to certify an absence of a short duration (a day or two). The rationale may be based on probable grounds to suspect that the absence was not legitimate or based on the employee's overall pattern of absenteeism.

5.20 — Pattern Absenteeism

There are different types of patterned absenteeism that may give rise to disciplinary actions. A common pattern is for the employee to take days off in conjunction with unscheduled days such as weekends and statutory holidays. The inference being that the employee's actions are an indication that the days off are for reasons other than being sick and demonstrate a clear abuse of leave from work. However, perhaps obviously, in order to demonstrate that the record of absences represented a pattern that indicates abuse the company will have to present evidence of the pattern.

In most matters where an employee is going to be held to account for a given behaviour he must be given notice at the time of incident so he can provide a timely explanation. However, in the case of a pattern of absenteeism the employer may not be aware of a potential abuse until several incidents have occurred and the pattern emerges. In this case the employee is not necessarily being asked to account for each and every incident of absence but rather will be required to answer for the pattern of absenteeism as a whole. The company may draw an inference from a persistent pattern that the record itself is evidence of abuse in cases where the incidence rate of absences coinciding with other days off reasonably leads one to conclude that it is unlikely for the pattern to have occurred by mere chance.[25] Thus

---

[24] *St. Jean de Brebeuf Hospital v. C.U.P.E., Local 1101* (1977), 16 L.A.C. (2d) 199 (Ont. Arb. Bd.).

[25] *Canada Post Corp. v. C.U.P.W.* (1992), 26 L.A.C. (4th) 180 (Can. Arb. Bd.).

the pattern has to have persisted for some time. In other cases where there is evidence of a pattern that raises suspicions of abuse but falls short of conclusively demonstrating abuse the company may need to present "further and better evidence" of an abuse.[26]

5.21 — Culpable Absenteeism

In some instances a single absence may provide just and sufficient cause to warrant the discharge of an employee, particularly if it undermines the employment relationship or breaches the employer's trust in the employee. In most cases where immediate discharge is justified the employee has deliberately misled the employer as to the reason for an absence in order to attend to some other activity such as personal business, working on behalf of the union or working for another employer.

Examples include:

- A local union president was terminated for absences when she attended a week long union conference despite the fact that the company had withdrawn its specific authorization for the leave to attend the conference. Her explanation for her absence was less than candid.[27]
- Falsification of medical records for the purposes of claiming sick pay has been considered by arbitrators to be an attempt to defraud.[28] This includes an instance where an alleged a medical emergency in order to be granted special leave[29] and another wherein the employee was collecting weekly indemnity benefits while working for another employer.[30]
- Fraudulent claim for workers' compensation benefits when the employee alleged a lost-time injury but was actively engaged in construction work and supervision.[31]

---

[26] Ibid p. 188 (*Re Alexander Knox* (unreported)).

[27] *Guelph General Hospital v. C.U.P.E., Local 57* (1982), 5 L.A.C. (3d) 289 (Ont. Arb. Bd.).

[28] *Forrester v. Canada (Treasury Board)* (1981), 2 L.A.C. (3d) 182 (Can. Arb. Bd.).

[29] *Canada Post Corp. v. C.U.P.W.* (1990), 10 L.A.C. (4th) 393 (Can. Arb. Bd.).

[30] *Midas Canada Inc. v. U.S.W.A.* (1993), 37 L.A.C. (4th) 1 (Ont. Arb. Bd.).

[31] *Steels Industrial Products v. Teamsters, Local 213* (1991), 24 L.A.C. (4th) 259 (B.C. Arb. Bd.).

- Falsification of timecards in order to be paid for time not actually worked is typically considered a firing offence in the absence of mitigating factors.[32]

Certainly lesser penalties may be meted out in cases where the incident was not serious enough to warrant the termination of employment. Examples of disciplinary actions that have been upheld at arbitration include:

- An employee was suspended for two days for taking a day off from work to participate in a Day of Protest[33] (in a similar case 18 employees were suspended for 1 day for taking time off to protest actions by the Anti-Inflation Board[34]).
- An employee was suspended for five weeks after he went on a hunting trip during his medical leave.[35]

Arbitrators have used their discretion in numerous cases to substitute a lesser penalty based on mitigating factors such as an employee's clean disciplinary record, length of service, financial hardship, and demonstrated remorse[36]. In cases of "time theft" where employees booked time worked when they were engaged in other activities or simply were not attending to their work arbitrators have considered such factors as the level of supervision, the employer's consistency in the keeping of records and possible condonation as factors in considering the right level of disciplinary response.[37]

However, most examples of culpable absenteeism involve short-term absences of one or two days. Here the distinction between what constitutes innocent absenteeism due to illness or injury and what constitutes culpable behaviour becomes somewhat murky for frontline supervisors. Clearly an absence for a *bona fide* illness or injury constitutes innocent behaviour and thus does not justify a disciplinary response. However, the employee has a duty and obligation to notify the employer in a timely manner of any absence and has an additional duty to provide an explanation to the employer as to why the absence from work is necessary. Failure in either regard constitutes culpable behaviour even in instances where the underlying reason for the absence is in itself legitimate and innocent. Obviously then any ab-

---

[32] *Phillips Cables Ltd. v. I.B.E.W., Local 625* (1993), 32 L.A.C. (4th) 153 (N.S. Arb. Bd.).

[33] *Photo Engraving & Electric Typing v. G.A.U., Local 28B* (1977), 1977 CarswellOnt 697, 15 L.A.C. (2d) 148 (Ont. Arb. Bd.).

[34] *Saskatchewan Wheat Pool v. G.S.U.* (1976), 12 L.A.C. (2d) 371 (Sask. Arb. Bd.).

[35] *Kenroc Tools Corp. v. U.S.W.A.* (1990), 17 L.A.C. (4th) 416 (Ont. Arb. Bd.).

[36] *Stelco Inc. (Hilton Works) v. U.S.W.A.* (1994), 40 L.A.C. (4th) 229 (Ont. Arb. Bd.).

[37] *Toronto (City) Board of Education v. U.A., Local 46* (1993), 38 L.A.C. (4th) 288 (Ont. Arb. Bd.); affirmed (1994), 1994 CarswellOnt 1827 (Ont. Div. Ct.).

sence which is not justified due to a reasonable or satisfactory reason would also be considered as culpable and worthy of progressive discipline. Furthermore a termination for culpable absenteeism would have to rely on a culminating incident, which in itself would have to warrant a disciplinary response (though the incident itself may not be related to absenteeism).

In *Allied Chemical*[38] Arbitrator Brandt noted that disciplinary action could not be taken against an employee for absenteeism related offences based solely on a review of his past record. Rather a culminating incident had to occur in order to trigger the disciplinary response. The same would not hold true in cases where the company is dealing with innocent absenteeism which might result in administrative actions being taken.

5.22 — Notification of Absence

Employees must inform their employers of any expected absence. Only in rare exceptions where circumstances prevent an employee from reporting an expected absence would such behaviour be accepted.

One arbitrator noted:

> An employee's obligation is to keep himself available and able to work for his employer, and while recognizing that emergencies or illness may prevent an employee from working, there remains a responsibility on the employee, regardless of shop rules, to keep his employer informed. If the employer does not accept the explanation, then that may be another matter, but certainly an employee must advise the company if he is to be absent from work. The need for this is obvious for the efficient operation of a plant. An employee who relies on others to carry out his responsibilities does so at his peril, as the prime obligation is on him alone and he must answer for any failure by his agent for that purpose.[39]

Jurisprudence has been very clear and consistent on this point. Only in extraordinary circumstances where there was a physical impairment that prevented the employee form reporting an absence has he been relieved of this obligation. The fact that reporting may be inconvenient, costly, or difficult does not excuse a failure to report. Nor is the employer under any obligation to accept a report from another employee or another individual on behalf of the employee. Rather the employer has the right to expect the employee to report an absence directly.

---

[38] *Allied Chemical Canada Ltd. v. U.A.W., Local 89* (1975), 9 L.A.C. (2d) 300 at p. 302-303 (Ont. Arb. Bd.).

[39] *International Union, District 50, Local 13286 v. Stauffer Chemical Co. of Canada* (1970), 22 L.A.C. 42 at p. 44 (Ont. Arb. Bd.).

5.23 — Explanation For Absence

In addition to being required to provide adequate notice employees are required to provide a reasonable explanation to justify their absences. Even if the absence itself is justifiable a failure to provide a timely explanation may give rise to a disciplinary sanction.

5.24 — Loss of Seniority Clauses

Many collective agreements contain clauses that describe when an employee might lose his seniority and be deemed to be terminated from employment. Typically these clauses dictate that an employee will lose seniority if he quits voluntarily, is terminated for cause or is absent for a period of time without notification to the company or without an explanation that is acceptable to the employer. A typical such clause reads like this:

Seniority rights shall cease and employment will be terminated for any employee who:

(a) voluntarily quits the employ of the Company

(b) is discharged and such discharge is not reversed through the grievance procedure

(c) is absent for three (3) working days or more, unless he has a justifiable reason satisfactory to the company

(d) fails to return to work within seven (7) days after notification to his address on record with the Company. The employee must notify the Company within two (2) working days of his intention to return to work, unless the employee has a justifiable reason satisfactory to the company for not giving such notice.

(e) fails, unless the employee has a justifiable reason, acceptable to the Company, to report for work to their immediate supervisor on the first day following the expiration of an approved leave of absence

(f) is laid off for a continuous period of more than twelve (12) consecutive months, for employees with less than two (2) years seniority. Employees with more than two (2) years seniority, shall loose recall rights after twenty-four (24) consecutive months of lay off.

A key issue is the interpretation of what constitutes "justifiable reason satisfactory to the company." The plain meaning of the words allows the employer to determine whether or not it finds the explanation to be "satisfactory." Thus it would appear that an arbitrator must allow the company's decision as to whether or not it found the reason to be satisfactory to stand unless there was evidence that the employer's actions had been arbitrary, discriminatory or in bad faith.

This standard for arbitral review was established by the Ontario Divisional Court in a 1981 case[40] in which the company had refused to participate in a temporary absence program and to accept the employee's incarceration as the reason for his absence. The issue is not whether or not an arbitrator would have accepted the reason given for the absence but rather whether or not the company had the unfettered right to determine if the reason was satisfactory to it.

In that case the applicant union had argued that the exercise of a management right was reviewable to ascertain if it was fair and reasonable. The Court cited the Toronto Police Board decision[41] and found that an arbitrator could not substitute his view as to what might be deemed reasonable;

> If such a term were to be implied, it would mean that every decision of management made under the exclusive authority of the management rights clause would be liable to challenge on the grounds that it was exercised unfairly and discriminatively. In our opinion, this would be contrary to the spirit and intent of the collective agreement.

It should also be noted that the clause specifically refers to a length of absence of three (3) days or more without notice or without a "justifiable reason satisfactory to the company." Essentially this is an alternative ground for the employer to rely on to that of just cause by imposing a loss of seniority and termination of employment. Since the cause specifically talks to a given period of time an unreported absence without notice or reasonable excuse could not be relied on to justify a termination on its own. Instead the company would have to employ progressive discipline and such an absence could only be relied on as cause to terminate if it formed the culminating incident in a progression of successive disciplinary actions.

A distinction is drawn between an employee who is discharged for cause and one whose employment is terminated due to a deemed terminated clause. In the case of discharge for cause many collective agreements require the company to provide notice to the employee and to ensure he has a

---

[40] *U.G.C.W. v. Libbey-St. Clair Inc.* (1981), 1981 CarswellOnt 1146, 33 O.R. (2d) 760, 125 D.L.R. (3d) 702 (Ont. Div. Ct.).

[41] *Toronto (Metropolitan) Commissioners of Police v. Police Assn. (Metropolitan Toronto)* (1981), 124 D.L.R. (3d) 684, 42 N.R. 272 (Ont. C.A.); leave to appeal refused (1981), 39 N.R. 449 (S.C.C.)

steward present when being notified that he is being discharged. This issue was described in length by Arbitrator O'Shea in a 1976 case:[42]

> The provisions of art. 7.03 and art. 8.13 may appear, at first reading, to be somewhat contradictory. Indeed, apart from the provisions of art. 7.03, we would likely find that a "termination" for unauthorized absence was tantamount to a "discharge". However, it is clear that the parties have distinguished between the word "termination" and the word "discharge". Article 7.03 provides that employment shall be terminated for such matters as the case where an employee "resigns", or "is discharged", or is "laid off for lack of work" or "is absent for more than three (3) working days without notifying his foreman or the Industrial Relations Department," etc. The intention of the parties thus expressed clearly contemplates a distinction between "termination of employment" and "discharge." Although discharge results in and may be said to mean termination of employment, termination of employment does not necessarily mean discharge. To use an analogy, while a sore finger is a sore thing, a sore thing is not necessarily a sore finger.
>
> Accordingly, we find that since an employee's employment may, among other reasons, be terminated by reason of his discharge or by reason of his absence for a period exceeding three working days, it therefore follows that the parties intended to distinguish the latter cause for termination of employment from the act of discharge. We therefore find that termination of employment because of absence for a period exceeding three working days is something separate and distinct from "discharge" as used in the collective agreement.

The implications for an employer are two-fold. First care must be exercised in constructing the wording of the deemed terminated clause and any other clauses related to termination or discharge to ensure a consistency in intent and in wording is maintained. Secondly, an absence of less than the period stipulated under the "deemed terminated" clause is not a "freebee" for the employee but rather is only distinguished by the level of response. An absence of three days or more without notification and suitable explanation will result in loss of seniority and termination of employment. Absences of less than three days without notification or suitable explanation or unexcused and unauthorized absences and may be dealt with under the company's progressive disciplinary policy and practices.

Another controversy companies should be aware of is the distinction between a loss of seniority and the termination of employment. While many arbitrators see a loss of seniority as being tantamount to a loss of employment some have ruled that in the absence of specific wording stipulating that the loss of seniority will be considered the same as a termination of employment then the loss of seniority merely changes the employee's status to that of a probationary employee. To overcome this ambiguity negotiators

---

[42] *Steel Co. Canada (Swansea Works) v. U.S.W.A., Local 3767* (1976), 12 L.A.C. (2d) 245 (Ont. Arb. Bd.).

have moved to include the words "and will result in the termination of employment."

5.25 — *Keays v. Honda Canada*[43]

Keays has been one of the most controversial and closely watched employment law case in years. The initial ruling was considered a landmark because of its application of punitive damages against an employer who had dismissed an employee under its Attendance management program. It was an extreme case wherein the employer was found to have made numerous errors in judgment in handling the management of an employee with a chronic medical condition. The potential implications for all employers were considerable. Effectively the lower Courts' decisions in Keays placed quite a chill on Attendance management programs for all employers.

The following is a brief summary of the history of the case:

During his 14 years of employment with Honda Canada Inc Mr. Keays suffered from chronic fatigue syndrome (CFS). His medical problems caused him to be frequently absent from work. When his medical condition was diagnosed as chronic fatigue syndrome, Mr. Keays was placed on short-term disability leave and, later, on long term disability leave. At one point, he was absent from work for 2 years before his LTD benefits were terminated by the insurer. After returning to work, Keays continued to experience health problems requiring frquent absences.

Around the time of his return from LTD the company had implemented an Attendance management program. One of the requirements imposed on Mr. Keays because his absences exceeded the norms of the program was to supply medical evidence to substantiate his absences. Mr. Keays complied with the company's requirements by obtaining a medical certificate which confirmed that he would likely be absent from work approximately 4 times each month. In the month just prior to his dismissal, Mr. Keays had to be absent from work approximately 14 times. In response, the employer required Mr. Keays to meet with its company doctor who, in turn, concluded that the employee did not suffer from any medical condition which prevented regular work attendance. In fact, Honda's doctor recommended that Mr. Keays be returned to physically demanding functions on the plant assembly line.

Mr. Keays was concerned by the suggestion that he should be returned to more physically demanding work. He retained a lawyer who contacted the

---

[43] 2008 CarswellOnt 3743.

company and requested an opportunity to mediate the dispute concerning Mr. Keays' absenteeism. Honda refused that invitation and, instead, insisted that Mr. Keays consult with the company's occupational specialist. When Mr. Keays questioned why this second consultation would be necessary (given his previous consultation with the company physician), he was fired for insubordination.

Keays sued for wrongful dismissal. The decision of Mr. Justice McIsaac[44] represented a departure from employment law practices. Mr. Justice McIsaac determined that the company's decision to dismiss Mr. Keays for insubordination was totally disproportional to his alleged "wrongdoing" and, therefore, there was no "just cause" for dismissal. In arriving at that conclusion, the Court considered Mr. Keays' "long service to Honda Canada, the fact that his alleged wrongdoing did not demonstrate low moral character, that Mr. Keays had been respectful to Honda Canada in raising his concerns regarding the absenteeism issue, that his concerns were grounded in legitimate human rights concerns, that the company had alternate means of discipline available to it, and that Mr. Keays did not cause any disruption in the manufacturing processes; and Mr. Keays' specialized employment training was not easily "portable" to a different industry."

Having concluded that the Keays' dismissal was not for "just cause", the Court commenced its assessment of damages. On the subject of "reasonable notice", the Court considered Mr. Keays' lack of significant formal education, his age (35) and the fact that Mr. Keays' circumstances should not lead to a lesser reasonable notice award than would be afforded to a management employee. In consideration of all these factors, the Court awarded Mr. Keays 15 months of reasonable notice (or 1.07 months' salary per year of service).

Next, the Court considered the Wallace Factor in the context of the Keays' dismissal circumstances. In that regard, Mr. Justice McIsaac referred to the relatively recent Ontario decision in *Gismondi v. Toronto*. In *Gismondi* case, it was concluded that Wallace Factor damages were not limited to employer acts which occur at the time of dismissal but, additionally, contemplate ". . . pre and post-termination circumstances so long as they formed a component of the manner of dismissal." The Gismondi decision expands the application of the Wallace Factor in an important way, since it allows for consideration of employer "bad faith" conduct which has occurred either before a dismissal or after a dismissal, and not just bad faith behaviours "in the course of" dismissal (as was originally contemplated by Canadian Courts in the post-Wallace era).

---

[44] 2005 CarswellOnt 1131 (Ont. S.C.J.)

In *Keays*, the court concluded that Honda Canada had misrepresented medical evidence concerning Mr. Keays by suggesting that his condition did not justify absenteeism from work. "The Court characterized this misrepresentation as callous and insensitive". Furthermore, in the courts view the company had refused to fairly and reasonably mediate its dispute with Mr. Keays concerning absenteeism - in spite of the employee's request to do so. After analyzing all of the company's behaviour in respect of Mr. Keays' disability, the Court concluded that the company's "egregious bad faith" warranted a Wallace Factor increase from 15 months' of reasonable notice to 24 months.

Then, the Court turned its mind to the subject of "punitive damages". Punitive damages assessments are particularly disconcerting for Canadian employers, who have been largely shielded from such awards. In his decision, Mr. Justice McIsaac referenced the long-accepted principle that "punitive damages are exceptional and are only available if there is an independent actionable wrong." In other words, an award of punitive damages is arguably unavailable unless the employer's behaviour gives rise to a potential lawsuit beyond "breach of contract for reasonable notice"

In this case, the Court found as follows:

> I have no difficulty in finding that the plaintiff has proved that Honda committed a litany of acts of discrimination and harassment in relations to his attempts to resolve his accommodation difficulties. When he began to push them on his concerns by having his lawyer attempt to advocate for him, they imposed the most drastic form of harassment possible: they terminated him.

Having concluded that the circumstances of the case permitted consideration of punitive damages award, the Court then reviewed the "catalogue of considerations" for punitive damages. In the end, the Court awarded $500,000.00 in punitive damages to Mr. Keays.

This award was initially upheld on appeal but punitive damages were reduced to $100,000. Keays was awarded $610,000 for costs.[45]

At the heart of the controversy is the company's belief that Keays was malingering and that there was no objective findings of a medical cause for his lengthy and persistent absences. This is not an uncommon trap for employers to fall into. Given the rise of absenteeism and the numerous dubious claims made to substantiate absences it is not surprising that a company would be suspicious of a claim related to Chronic fatigue syndrome — a disease that is difficult to diagnose and treat.

---

[45] 2005 CarswellOnt 5885 (Ont. C.A.)

It also remains difficult for employers to understand precisely what their obligations are to disabled employees. On a different scale a small employer might not be in a position to accommodate an employee like Keays because to do so could constitute undue hardship for the employer. However, Honda is a large multinational capable of accommodating Keays without an adverse impact on its operations in terms of impact on the bottom line. Nevertheless, accommodation of disabled employees has an impact on operations and organizational culture.

If the company believed Keays was malingering then it could reasonably conclude that it was not required to accommodate him (since there would be no disability to accommodate) and to do so would adversely affect the efficacy of its Attendance management program. The problem here was that there were objective findings of the existence of a disability that the company chose to ignore in light of the findings of its own experts.

Its steadfast assertion that the disability did not warrant accommodation and its rather quick decision to terminate the employee were viewed by the court as reprehensible conduct perpetrated in bad faith. If the refusal to cooperate had persisted after the company provided an explanation for wanting to investigate the matter further then it may have been justified in claiming cause to end the relationship. After 14 years of service however the courts believed it was a bit too quick in pulling the trigger.

Of course much attention has been paid to the size of the award. In applying the one month formula to Keays' employment the court ignored the principles laid down in other cases that reasonable notice and severance for non-managerial staff ought to be capped at twelve months. Further in applying Wallace Damages for the employer's bad faith actions the court was also quite generous. However, the court's decision can partly be explained by emotional factors.

The individual was disabled and unable to enjoy a full range of activities including attending work on a regular basis. The employer, a large multinational, seemingly ignored his disability and acted in a callous unfeeling way. Hence the court exercised as much latitude as it could to ensure the employee was well compensated for the breach of contract under the circumstances.

What is more surprising is the imposition of punitive damages beyond the award of increased notice and severance following the principles of the "Wallace Bump". The court relied on the principle of a separate actionable wrong to look beyond compensation for the breach of the employment contract and reward punitive damages to dissuade Honda from similar conduct and to send out a general deterrence to all employers with respect to handling employees with disabilities with some degree of sensitivity and care.

The court's intent was obviously to send a message to employers who seem intent on "playing hardball" with employees who have disabilities. However, the decision is controversial precisely because opinions will differ as to whether or not Honda was merely playing "hardball" or whether it had legitimate concerns that the employee was malingering. In cases such as those involving Chronic Pain Syndrome diagnosis is difficult and cannot be proven on an objective basis. It seems reasonable that an Employer acting in good faith could conclude that the employee was not making reasonable efforts to fulfill his obligation to make every attempt to report to work regularly. The scare put into employers because of the early rulings in *Keays* demonstrates the need to exercise due diligence in managing these claims.

Cases like Keays are relatively rare. Companies who face an issue involving a long-term disability and difficult circumstances surrounding accommodation should consult with a legal expert before taking drastic action. If a dispute arises about medical findings ensure that the company's position is based on an experts medical opinion that trumps any medical evidence that the employee has. In the Keays' case the company relied on the opinion of its own doctor who had not actually examined Keays. A specialists opinion will be given far more weight than a General Practitioner but only if the specialist actually examines the patient.

Also, be fully aware of the company's obligations under human rights legislation to "accommodate" disabled workers to the point of undue hardship. Employers are not permitted to take hard lines against disadvantaged employees who suffer from mental or physical challenges, nor should they be allowed to do so. Rather, it is incumbent upon employers to at least consider available options for permitting continued employment. In the case of an employee with a proven disability it will not be likely possible to terminate the employment relationship on the supposed "strength" of an Attendance management program. This is precisely why the Programs contained herein focus on using non-punitive measures to deal with non-culpable absences and why long-term or chronic conditions are separated under different processes.

One significant reason for dealing with these cases separately is that the web of legal considerations makes them very difficult to manage even for a seasoned human resources practitioner well-versed in the legal ramifications. Supervisors and managers will have their hands full dealing with casual absenteeism and tardiness. Let the experts deal with the tough cases.

Update:[46] On Feb. 20, 2008, the Supreme Court of Canada heard the appeal in the landmark case of *Keays v. Honda Canada Inc.* The appeal raised issues with respect to the relationship between human rights protections and the common law, in particular whether courts can apply common law principles to provide the same protections available through human rights legislation.

Keays had sought to refine the manner in which courts approach human rights violations in an employment law context byasking the Courts recognize a tort of discrimination and harassment. This would be accomplished by incorporating human rights codes into employment contracts and recognizing a duty on employers to prevent the creation of a poisoned work environment. Courts would have concurrent jurisdiction to ensure employees have direct access to a remedy with no loss of procedural safeguards or expertise and the courts would have direct means to remedy discrimination by awarding damages separate from existing damages for wrongful dismissal, bad faith, mental distress and punitive damages.

Honda objected to a common law action for a breach of the code — a breach of statutory duty — arguing for the greater expertise of tribunals as well as the need to avoid a multiplicity of proceedings creating a two-tier system to enforce human rights violations where courts are utilized by the wealthy for greater damage awards.

The lower courts found Keays, who was disabled by chronic fatigue syndrome, was wrongfully terminated to evade Honda's duty to accommodate him under human rights law. They further found the decision to terminate Keays was "planned and deliberate" and "made in retaliation for his retainer of counsel to advocate for his human rights." Prior to termination, Honda asked Keays to attend a medical assessment after receiving medical notes from his physician that didn't satisfy it. Keays asked Honda to clarify the purpose of the assessment, which Honda refused to do and instead terminated him for his refusal to meet with the doctor who was to perform the medical assessment.

Honda dropped its allegations of cause for Keays'dismissal in its appeal. Instead it argued that the appropriate notice period was 8 to 10 months, rather than the 15 months assessed by the trial judge. The Supreme Court citing the principles of *Bardal v. Globe & Mail Ltd.* (1960), 24 DLR (2d) 140 (Ont.H.C.) stated:

> the reasonableness of the notice must be decided with reference to each particular case, having regard to the character of the employment, the length of service of the

---

[46] See Ronald Minken, Protect human rights through courts: Keays reproduced in *Consult-Carswell*, www.consultcarswellonline.com.

> servant, the age of the servant and the availability of similar employment, having regard to the experience, training and qualifications of the servant.

Therefore, the Court found that the trial judge had erred in finding that Honda'sflat management structure was a factor in determining his reasonable notice, rather than examining his actual functions. Nevertheless on the basis of the Bardal factors there there was no basis to interfere with the 15 month notice assessment.

As for damages for conduct in the manner of dismissal, The Court reconsidered the Wallace approach and made important clarifications to the law. It considered its recent decision in *Fidler v. Sun Life Assurance Co. of Canada*, [2006] 2 S.C.R. 3 and concluded that the "normal distress and hurt feelings resulting from dismissal are not compensable". Damages resulting from the way in which an individual is terminated from employment are only applicable if the employer acts in "bad faith". The court also noted that these damages when they do apply are separate damages. Unlike the decision in Wallace the Supreme Court holds the view that these special damages should not be awarded as an extension of the notice and severance period.

In Keays specifically the court did not agree that Honda had acted in bad faith and it set aside the nine (9) months of additional severance awarded by the lower courts. Following this there was no basis in the case, according to the Supreme court, to award punitive or aggravated damages.

Importantly the Supreme Court also held that the Court of Appeal erred in concluding that Honda's "discriminatory conduct" amounted to an independent actionable wrong for the purposes of allocating punitive damages.

In the 1981 Supreme Court of Canada decision of *Seneca College of Applied Arts and Technology v. Bhadauria*, [1981] 2 S.C.R. 181, the Court held that the legislature intended to exclude the courts in favour of an administrative regime to achieve its human rights objectives through legislation precluding the use of courts as the primary forum for human rights complaints. (Following amendments to the *Ontario Human Rights Code* which came into effect on June 28, 2008, courts may be able to entertain claims for breach of the code when they are connected to another claim that must be advanced through the courts, such as wrongful dismissal. If, however, there is no other claim, the only recourse is through the administrative regime of the human rights commission).

Finally Honda was awarded costs on the appeal and cross-appeal and the cost premium was set aside. In a partial dissent, Justices LeBel and Fish would have upheld the award of Wallace damages.

Hopefully this decision will allow employers to take comfort that they can develop policies to address chronic absenteeism issues free of the fear that their actions could lead to outrageous awards for damages. Mr. Justice Bastarache, who wrote the majority opinion, stated:

> . . .I accept that the need to monitor the absences of employees who are regularly absent from work is a *bona fide* work requirement in light of the very nature of the employment contract and responsibility of the employer for the management of its workforce.

Appendix

Campbell River & North Island Transition Society v. H.S.A.B.

2004 CarswellBC 1012, 2004 BCCA 260 (B.C. C.A.)

Low J.A.:

1 This is an appeal from a decision of an arbitrator appointed under a collective agreement to adjudicate a grievance brought by the appellant union on behalf of one of its members, an employee of the respondent transition society. The parties are agreed that this court has jurisdiction to hear the appeal under s. 100 of the *Labour Relations Code*, R.S.B.C. 1996, c. 244. There is a general issue of law involved that is not included in s. 99(1).

2 The legal issue turns on the meaning and scope of the term "family status" found in s. 13(1) of the *Human Rights Code*, R.S.B.C. 1996, c. 210 ("the *Code*"). That provision reads:

> 13(1)A person must not
>
> (a) refuse to employ or refuse to continue to employ a person,
>
> (b) discriminate against a person regarding employment or any term or condition of employment
>
> because of the race, colour, ancestry, place of origin, political belief, religion, marital status, family status, physical or mental disability, sex, sexual orientation or age of that person or because that person has been convicted of a criminal or summary conviction offence that is unrelated to the employment or to the intended employment of that person.

3 The appellant contends that the employer refused to continue to employ or otherwise discriminated against the employee, Shelley Howard, regarding her employment or a term or condition thereof because of her family status. The appellant says that the respondent, by changing Ms. Howard's hours of work, failed to accommodate her particular family situation.

4 The arbitrator stated the union's position as follows: the employer was "under a duty to accommodate [Ms. Howard's] hours of work so that she is better able to care for her son who has both medical and behavioural problems."

5 The respondent's position as stated by the arbitrator was that "it is not under any legal duty to accommodate [Ms. Howard], but nonetheless, it has made attempts to accommodate her."

6 (The second respondent represents the respondent society and others in collective bargaining and grievance matters. It was not a party before the arbitrator. It is not clear to me why it was added as a respondent in this court and it did not participate in the appeal. In these reasons, I will simply refer to the respondent by which I will always mean the respondent society, the employer.)

7 The facts are easily stated. Ms. Howard is married with four children, the third of whom, a boy now aged thirteen, has severe behavioural problems requiring specific parental and professional attention. She began working for the respondent in early 1993 as a casual transition house worker and later that year became a part-time child and youth support worker. She worked at Ann Elmore Transition House run by the respondent. It is a safe shelter for women suffering marital abuse, and for their children.

8 The respondent is a non-profit society incorporated in 1985 to provide to the community of Campbell River services and education directed at ending family violence. In addition to operating the shelter, it offers counselling, assistance to children affected by family violence and public education.

9 The arbitrator, Stan Lanyon, Q.C., made the following findings of fact with respect to the work schedule of Ms. Howard and the adjustment therein made by the respondent that gave rise to the grievance:

> The Grievor is described as a "very good employee." She is hard working and very helpful to other employees; a person who is always willing to perform duties outside of her job description. She is also described as very flexible and willing to work additional hours on short notice. Her normal part-time hours are 24 hours per week, however, she has agreed on many past occasions to work evenings, weekends and statutory holidays. A normal shift for "front line workers" is 12 hours a day, 4 days on, and 5 days off.
>
> On July 12, 2001, Valery Puetz, Coordinator of the Transition Society, notified the Grievor, that as of September 4, 2001, her hours would be changed from her current 8:30 a.m. to 3:00 p.m. shift to 11:30 a.m. to 6:00 p.m., Monday through Thursday. She was informed that she would continue to have "a flexible schedule" and that she could adjust her hours to include school presentations.
>
> The Grievor and Puetz had had previous discussions about her reduced workload; the number of children requiring counseling during her shift had gradually declined. The Grievor was doing child-minding in the mornings, which often [proved a] very busy period. These discussions concerning the Grievor's workload first arose in the year 2000.
>
> In the Spring of 2001 the Grievor and Puetz once again discussed her declining workload. They did so in preparation for a strategic planning meeting which was to take place in the Summer of 2001. Puetz asked the Grievor to come back with six or seven possible programs for her position. Neither the Grievor nor Puetz wanted to

> lose this part-time position. The Grievor came up with some options and they agreed to take these to the strategic planning committee. One such proposal was to expand the existing healthy relationships program taught in the local schools.
>
> When the issue of the Grievor's position was raised at the Board's strategic planning meeting it opened up a wider discussion of her position and her hours of work. In the end, the Board decided to change the hours of work for the Grievor's position so that counselling services could be offered to a greater number of school aged children; thus the change in hours to 11:30 a.m. to 6:00 p.m. (In fact, the position currently has been operating from 2:30 to 9:00 p.m., Tuesdays to Fridays. Puetz stated that with these new hours the workload has been "overwhelming" because there has been a substantial increase in non-resident clients seeking counselling).

10 Ms. Howard was concerned about her new work hours because she attended to the needs of her son after his school hours. However, she worked the new hours from 4 September to 17 September 2001. Later on the 17th, she attended a meeting of the board of the respondent to express her concern. She explained her son's situation and submitted a letter from Dr. Mark Lund, the boy's paediatrician. Six fellow employees provided written support for Ms. Howard resuming her former hours of work. They also attended the meeting but were not permitted to speak. The Board deliberated and decided that the new hours would be maintained. The next day Ms. Howard received a letter from Ms. Puetz so advising her. The letter contained a proviso that there would be a reassessment of the new schedule after six months and that Ms. Howard's input would be welcome.

11 The arbitrator found that on the day she received the letter Ms. Howard had "a severe anxiety or panic attack." She did not return to work. Her doctor diagnosed post traumatic stress disorder and provided a note stating that she needed to be off work for six weeks. On his advice, Ms. Howard did not return to work after that time and she never did return. The doctor testified before the arbitrator that Ms. Howard's condition was caused by her employment circumstances.

12 On 26 September 2001, Ms. Puetz sent a letter to Ms. Howard enclosing some forms needed for a claim for sick benefits. She stated in the letter that she hoped Ms. Howard "will be able to return to work soon."

13 On 1 October 2001, the appellant union informed the respondent by letter that the respondent had to accommodate Ms. Howard's family situation and reinstate her hours of work from 8:30 a.m. to 3:00 p.m. Ms. Howard remained on sick leave for a period of time after which she received employment insurance benefits. Her doctor testified before the arbitrator that she was fit to return to her employment as of April 2002 but that because of the stress she could never again work for the respondent. Before the arbitrator, the appellant sought compensation to Ms. Howard for lost salary as well as punitive damages. It did not seek reinstatement of Ms. Howard.

14 In his medical report dated 16 August 2001, Dr. Lund stated that Ms. Howard's son "is a very high needs child with a major psychiatric disorder". His need for consistent parenting is best served by his mother, particularly after school. The doctor reported that she should be available to her son after school, something he considered to be "an extraordinarily important medical adjunct to [the son's] ongoing management and progression in life."

15 Following the decision of the Canadian Human Rights Tribunal in *Lang v. Canada (Employment & Immigration Commission)* (1990), 12 C.H.R.R. D/265 (Can. Human Rights Trib.) and other arbitral authorities, including *Campbell v. Shahrestani*, [2001] B.C.H.R.T.D. No. 36 (B.C. Human Rights Trib.), the arbitrator concluded that the term "family status" in s. 13(1) of the *Code* includes the relationship of parent and child. The respondent does not dispute that conclusion.

16 The arbitrator then noted that the "principal characteristic of the parent-child relationship is the parent's obligation to care for [the] child." He recognized this as a fiduciary obligation, referring to *M. (K.) v. M. (H.)*, [1992] 3 S.C.R. 6 (S.C.C.). He also referred to sections 2 and 4 of the *Child Family and Community Service Act*, R.S.B.C. 1996, c. 46 in which the general nature of parental duties is spelled out.

17 Then the arbitrator defined what he saw as the central issue before him:

> However, what is clear from these fiduciary and statutory duties is that the fundamental obligation for the care of children rests with the parent, not the employer. If that is the case, can the Legislature have intended that the words "family status" in the *Human Rights Code*, be read to shift some significant part of that fundamental obligation, from parents to employers? Is, for example, an employer legally obligated to accommodate all employees who have children, simply because of their status as a parent?

18 The core of his analysis commences two paragraphs later:

> In the case before this board, the Grievor has experienced, and continues to experience, both demanding and difficult childcare obligations. Her son requires special care. This is supported by the medical evidence. These difficulties are shared by other parents, especially those who have special needs children. The circumstances of these parents, as well [as] parents of other children, will vary greatly. Some will have excellent childcare arrangements, others will not; some have extended family members, who can assist, others do not; some will be able to afford exceptional care, especially for special needs children, and others will not.
>
> Thus, the circumstances of child-care will vary from parent to parent, and indeed may vary for the same parents, over different periods of time. A parent may have what they consider to be exceptional childcare arrangements one year, and yet be searching desperately the following year to find even adequate care. Changes in employment may have an adverse [effect] on these childcare arrangements. In other circumstances, changes in employment may assist a person in their childcare arrangements.

> Were these different circumstances of employment, and varying degrees of difficulty in child-care arrangements, intended to be captured by the words "family status"?
>
> I conclude that these differing circumstances, many of which may result in individuals trying to balance work and child-care arrangements, are not the kind of circumstances that raise an issue of discrimination based on the prohibited ground of "family status." Rather, the Legislature by deliberately employing the words "family status", was concerned with discrimination based upon the very status of being a parent, or other family member. For example, had the Employer refused to employ the Grievor, because she was the parent of a special needs child, that would, in my view, violate section 13 of the Human Rights Code. It would not make sense, that one could not discriminate, based on the prohibited grounds set out in section 13, against an employee, but could do so against one of their family members. This would defeat the very purpose of the Human Rights Code.
>
> Thus family status in these circumstances deals with the status of parent and child, and not with the individual circumstances of a family's needs, such as those concerning childcare arrangements. I therefore conclude that all parents that experience difficult childcare arrangements, as a result of their employment, are not a class or category that section 13 of the Human Right Code seeks to protect.
>
> I find that the Employer had the right to change the shift, and that its purpose in wanting to extend counselling services to school aged children was a reasonable one. It would be ironic indeed, if the Employer was not at liberty to change the hours of work of the Grievor's position, in order to make counselling service available to students, who may well have needs as serious as those of [the Grievor's son].

19 After considering the decision of the Canadian Human Rights Tribunal in *Brown v. Minister of National Revenue (Customs & Excise)* (1993), 19 C.H.R.R. D/39 (Can. Human Rights Trib.), the arbitrator said (p. 17): .I have found that the words "family status" refers to the status of being a parent per se, and not to the innumerable (and yet important) circumstances that arise for all families in regard to their daycare needs. I therefore decline to follow *Brown*, supra.

20 The reasons of the arbitrator continue:

> Does this mean that the Grievor is faced with either working the new shift or losing her job? Without a finding of discrimination, and no duty to accommodate, what is the Employer's obligation to the Grievor? There may well be situations where a Grievor is faced with the Hobson's choice of either working the new shift, or losing their employment. However, most employers, as a matter of good labour relations, permit employees to deal with a wide variety of family matters: medical emergencies, domestic problems, and childrens' school activities. Many collective agreements provide special leave to deal with such issues (Article 20 of this Collective Agreement).
>
> .....
>
> What were some of the options which the Grievor had in regard to this workplace under this Collective Agreement? First, five of the six employees who signed the petition testified that they were willing to participate in an "accommodation" of the Grievor. This was never explored. Second, the Collective Agreement provided some

> contractual options: for instance, two Memoranda of Agreement, attached to the Collective Agreement, provide for job sharing and flexible work hours. Third, if extra time was required to obtain a resolution to the dispute there are both paid and unpaid leaves. Fourth, the Grievor could have assumed casual status and worked relief. Fifth, there were lay-off and bumping rights. It must be remembered that the position held by the Grievor included not only that of Child Counsellor, but also of Transition House Counselor; other employees were capable of performing the Child Counselling position and the Grievor was capable of performing the Transition House Counselling position. Thus, the Collective Agreement offered both the potential of different hours of work, and different classifications.
>
> However, what is clear is that the Grievor was not entitled to keep either her same hours of work or her same position. The Employer had the right to change the hours of work of that position in order to extend a much needed service to the community.

21 The appellant union does not challenge the conclusions of the arbitrator that there was no tort and no breach of the collective agreement committed by the respondent society. Nor does it dispute the conclusion of the arbitrator that the changes in the working hours of Ms. Howard were a work-related requirement of the respondent society made in good faith. The arbitrator said that the respondent's "purpose was simply to offer counselling services to children who would otherwise not be able to access them."

22 The appellant union says that the arbitrator erred in not finding that the respondent breached s. 13(1) of the *Code* by discriminating against Ms. Howard on the basis of family status. It also says that the arbitrator erred in declining jurisdiction under s. 37(2)(d)(iii) of the *Code* to award damages.

23 The appellant asks this court to set aside the award of the arbitrator and to remit the matter back to him with the following directions:

(a) that "family status" under s. 13 of the *Code* includes the fiduciary obligation of parents to care for their children;

(b) that the respondent discriminated against Ms. Howard contrary to s. 13 by not reasonably accommodating her particular family status; and

(c) that the arbitrator must fashion an appropriate remedy in damages under s. 37 of the *Code*.

24 The appellant begins its argument by referring to the ruling of the Supreme Court of Canada that human rights legislation is "quasi-constitutional. and must be interpreted" in a liberal and purposive manner in order to advance the broad policy considerations underlying it ..: *A. v. B.*, [2002] 3 S.C.R. 403 (S.C.C.), at para. 44, and other cases cited therein.

25 The appellant contends that the arbitrator held that there had to be an intention on the part of the employer to discriminate against the employee when he gave an example in his reasons (quoted at para. 18 above) of a circumstance in which the employer would have discriminated "based upon

the very status of being a parent". The appellant says that this is contrary to s. 2 of the *Code* that states that no intention to contravene the *Code* is required.

26 I do not accept this argument. The arbitrator gave an example in which intention to discriminate might be inferred. But it was an example only and he did not discuss intention. It cannot be said that he required proof of intention. Read as a whole, his reasons do not identify the error alleged. The arbitrator did not dismiss the grievance on the basis of absence of intention to discriminate on the part of the respondent employer.

27 The appellant's argument continues with the assertion that the arbitrator failed to apply the law by rejecting as part of "family status" the parental obligations that flow from that status. In *Brown*, supra, the tribunal considered s. 3 of the *Canadian Human Rights Act*, R.S. 1985, c. H-6 that contains wording very similar to the wording of s. 13(1) of the *Code* in this province. One of the issues in the case arose out of denial by the employer of the employee's request for only day-shift work due to difficulties she had encountered in arranging daycare for her child after expiration of her maternity leave.

28 The tribunal in *Brown* said this:

> We can therefore understand the obvious dilemma facing the modern family wherein the present socio-economic trends find both parents in the work environment, often with different rules and requirements. More often than not, we find the natural nurturing demands upon the female parent place her invariably in the position where she is required to strike this fine balance between family needs and employment requirements.
>
> It is this Tribunal's conclusion that the purposive interpretation to be affixed to s. 2 of the C.H.R.A. is a clear recognition within the context of "family status" of a parent's right and duty to strike that balance coupled with a clear duty on the part of an employer to facilitate and accommodate that balance within the criteria set out in the Alberta Dairy Pool case [[1990] 2 S.C.R. 489]. To consider any lesser approach to the problems facing the modern family within the employment environment is to render meaningless the concept of "family status" as a ground of discrimination.

29 The arbitrator declined to follow *Brown*. He agreed that it is desirable to expand employer obligations .that better [enable] families to balance the care of their children with their work.. But he said that the Legislature has occupied this area by enactment of ss. 50 to 54 of the *Employment Standards Act*, R.S.B.C. 1996, c. 113. He held that it was not correct to do indirectly through the *Code* what the Legislature declined to do directly through specific legislation. Therefore he restricted "family status" under the *Code* "to the status of being a parent per se" without regard to the "innumerable (and yet important) circumstances that arise for all families in regard to their daycare needs."

30 Sections 50 to 54 of the *Employment Standards Act* deal with four specific matters — pregnancy leave, parental leave, family responsibility leave and bereavement leave. It cannot be said that the scope of family status in s. 13(1) of the *Code* is determined by the more specific statute. I cannot find any wording in either statute that would lead to that conclusion. Section 13(1) of the *Code* legislates against discrimination "regarding....any term or condition of employment." On the reasoning of the arbitrator those words would be superfluous. In my opinion, the arbitrator erred in considering the provisions of the *Employment Standards Act* when attempting to determine the scope of the term "family status" in s. 13(1) of the *Code*.

31 Although it was not so stated by the arbitrator, it seems to be clear from the authorities that the first issue is whether the appellant has made out a *prima facie* case of discrimination that requires consideration of the issue of accommodation: see *British Columbia (Public Service Employee Relations Commission) v. B.C.G.E.U.*, [1999] 3 S.C.R. 3 (S.C.C.) and *British Columbia (Superintendent of Motor Vehicles) v. British Columbia (Council of Human Rights)*, [1999] 3 S.C.R. 868 (S.C.C.), at para. 20.

32 The appellant argues that the circumstances of this case give rise to a *prima facie* case on the basis that family status should be given a very broad scope as the board did in the passage quoted above from the decision in *Brown*. The appellant also relies on *Woiden v. Lynn*, [2002] C.H.R.D. No. 18 (Can. Human Rights Trib.), also a decision of the Canadian Human Rights Tribunal.

33 In *Woiden*, the tribunal considered complaints by four female employees that the respondent, the senior manager at their place of employment, discriminated against them by sexual harassment and on the basis of sex. One of the four complainants also alleged that the respondent discriminated against her "on the ground of family status by requiring that she change her work hours in a manner that was incompatible with her obligations as a single mother of three children." The respondent required that employee to work extended hours upon pain of dismissal. In the decision, there was no exploration of the evidence on this issue and no elaboration of the facts. There was a finding that "the extended hours limited [the complainant's] ability to work because of the basic needs related to her particular family situation." The respondent, who was a manager and not the corporate employer of the complainant, did not appear at the hearing or present evidence in any other manner. The tribunal apparently assumed discrimination and had before it no evidence or submission that imposition of the extended hours was a bona fide occupational requirement and that the respondent could not accommodate the complainant without incurring undue hardship to the employer. The tribunal found discrimination based on family status. It defined family status discrimination as .practices or attitudes that have the

effect of limiting the conditions of employment of, or the employment opportunities available to, employees on the basis of a characteristic relating to their family..

34 The appellant argues that, as the mother of a special needs child who required her attention as the person most effective in attending to his needs at a critical time of the day, Ms. Howard was discriminated against on the basis of family status to a greater extent than the employees in the *Brown* and *Woiden* cases.

35 In my opinion, the tribunals in both *Brown* and *Woiden* conflated the issues of *prima facie* discrimination and accommodation. They seem to hold that there is *prima facie* discrimination whenever there is a conflict between a job requirement and a family obligation. In each decision there is an overly broad definition of the scope of family status that I consider to be unworkable. I find both decisions unhelpful in defining family status under s. 13(1) of the *Code* for the purpose of determining whether *prima facie* discrimination is proven.

36 What then needs to be established in order to prove *prima facie* discrimination based on family status? The respondent relies on *Wight v. Ontario (Office of the Legislative Assembly)*, [1998] O.H.R.B.I.D. No. 13 (Ont. Bd. of Inquiry), a decision of the Ontario Board of Inquiry (Human Rights Code). In that case, the employee was on pregnancy leave during a high-risk pregnancy and delivery. The employer ordered her to return to work but she refused to do so until she had secured adequate daycare for her children. She was dismissed from her employment. One of her complaints under the applicable human rights code was that her dismissal amounted to discrimination on the basis of family status. In an extremely lengthy decision, the board found that the employer had breached other provisions of the code but had not discriminated on the basis of family status. That issue turned on the facts of the case and I am unable to find in it any useful definition of the scope of family status in human rights legislation.

37 The Supreme Court of Canada did deal with the concept of family status in human rights legislation in *B.*, supra, and in *Canada (Attorney General) v. Mossop*, [1993] 1 S.C.R. 554 (S.C.C.). In *B.* the majority of the court upheld the decision of the Ontario Court of Appeal that family status did encompass discrimination claims based on the particular identity of the complainant's child. *Mossop* was a bereavement leave claim and turned on whether family status included a homosexual relationship. The majority determined that it did not. Neither case addressed the question of whether family status includes parental or other family obligations.

38 The parties have cited no other cases that assist in providing a working definition of the parameters of the concept of family status as the term is

used in the *Code*. In my opinion, it cannot be an open-ended concept as urged by the appellant for that would have the potential to cause disruption and great mischief in the workplace; nor, in the context of the present case, can it be limited to "the status of being a parent per se" as found by the arbitrator (and as argued by the respondent on this appeal) for that would not address serious negative impacts that some decisions of employers might have on the parental and other family obligations of all, some or one of the employees affected by such decisions.

39 If the term "family status" is not elusive of definition, the definition lies somewhere between the two extremes urged by the parties. Whether particular conduct does or does not amount to *prima facie* discrimination on the basis of family status will depend on the circumstances of each case. In the usual case where there is no bad faith on the part of the employer and no governing provision in the applicable collective agreement or employment contract, it seems to me that a *prima facie* case of discrimination is made out when a change in a term or condition of employment imposed by an employer results in a serious interference with a substantial parental or other family duty or obligation of the employee. I think that in the vast majority of situations in which there is a conflict between a work requirement and a family obligation it would be difficult to make out a *prima facie* case.

40 In the present case, the arbitrator accepted the evidence of Dr. Lund that Ms. Howard's son has a major psychiatric disorder and that her attendance to his needs during after-school hours was .an extraordinarily important medical adjunct. to the son's wellbeing. In my opinion, this was a substantial parental obligation of Ms. Howard to her son. The decision by the respondent to change Ms. Howard's hours of work was a serious interference with her discharge of that obligation. Accordingly, the arbitrator erred in not finding a *prima facie* case of discrimination on the basis of family status.

41 The appellant contends that we should advise the arbitrator that the respondent breached s. 13 of the *Code* by not accommodating Ms. Howard's parental obligation. The arbitrator did not address that issue and, in my opinion, this court should not do so in the first instance.

42 The issue of accommodation arises out of s. 13(4) of the *Code* that reads:

> 13(4) Subsections (1) and (2) do not apply with respect to a refusal, limitation, specification or preference based on a bona fide occupational requirement. (emphasis added)

43 In the application of this sub-section and others like it in human rights legislation, McLachlin, J. (as she then was) in the *B.C.G.S.E.U.* case (cited in para. 31 above) enunciated the analysis to be employed:

> 54 Having considered the various alternatives, I propose the following three-step test for determining whether a prima facie discriminatory standard is a BFOR [bona fide occupational requirement]. An employer may justify the impugned standard by establishing on the balance of probabilities:
>
> (1) that the employer adopted the standard for a purpose rationally connected to the performance of the job;
>
> (2) that the employer adopted the particular standard in an honest and good faith belief that it was necessary to the fulfilment of that legitimate work-related purpose; and
>
> (3) that the standard is reasonably necessary to the accomplishment of that legitimate work-related purpose. To show that the standard is reasonably necessary, it must be demonstrated that it is impossible to accommodate individual employees sharing the characteristics of the claimant without imposing undue hardship upon the employer.

44 The appellant concedes the first two stages of the analysis.

45 The authorities make it clear that reasonable accommodation is the responsibility of both sides - the employee and the union on the one hand and the employer on the other. The present case has the added factor of the effect of Ms. Howard's illness on the issue of accommodation. It is for the arbitrator to resolve this issue.

46 It is not appropriate for us to discuss the issue of damages. That is a matter for the arbitrator to address if he finds against the respondent on the accommodation issue.

47 I would allow the appeal and remit the grievance back to the arbitrator.

Levine J.A.

I agree.

Smith J.A.

I agree.

Appeal allowed.

CAW-Canada, Local 111 v. Coast Mountain Bus Co.

2008 CarswellBC 1110, 2008 BCHRT 52 (B.C.H.R.T.)

T. Beharrell Member:

I. Introduction

1 The complainant, the National Automobile, Aerospace, Transportation and General Workers of Canada (CAW.Canada) Local 111 (the .Union.), filed a complaint on behalf of its members employed by the Coast Mountain Bus Company Ltd. (.CMBC., or the .Company.) as transit operators who have disabilities and, as a result, have been placed in CMBC's Attendance Management Program (the .AMP. or the .Program.) because of their higher than average non-culpable absenteeism rates. The Union alleges that the AMP discriminates against operators with respect to their employment on the basis of both actual and perceived mental and physical disabilities, contrary to s. 13 of the *Human Rights Code*. CMBC denies that the AMP is discriminatory.

2 This complaint has given rise to many preliminary and procedural decisions. I will not reiterate those decisions here, except where necessary to this decision.

3 A number of witnesses testified at the hearing. Bob Jones, a transit operator and the Chair of the Union's AMP Committee, and Don MacLeod, former president of the Union, testified for the Union, as did the following transit operators who have been subject to the AMP: Virginia Young, Shailendra Prasad, Susan Lieb, Gary Templeman, Cynthia Cable, Dwayne Mayes, Sergio Da Luz, Susan Welch, Carlos Fernandes, Gerry Essex, Christopher Watson and Kevin Minch.

4 Colin Kelly, Director of Corporate Attendance Management, and Ana Lopez, the Manager of Corporate Health, testified for CMBC. In addition, the parties entered an agreed statement of facts in support of a preliminary application: *CAW-Canada, Local 111 v. Coast Mountain Bus Co.*, 2005 BCHRT 242 (B.C. Human Rights Trib.). The agreed statement of facts was also entered as an exhibit for the purpose of the hearing on the merits.

5 There was a great deal of evidence presented in the course of the 25 days of hearing. Much of that evidence consisted of personal information. CMBC consistently took the position that such information was confidential, and could only be used with the consent of the affected employee, or by order of the Tribunal. This issue was first dealt with in *Freeman v. Coast Mountain Bus Co. (No. 3)*, 2005 BCHRT 57 (B.C. Human Rights Trib.).

There, in ordering CMBC to disclose a large amount of information, the Tribunal wrote:

> Given the systemic nature of the complaint, and the nature of the information which would be required to make out such a complaint, I find that the privacy concerns at issue are best resolved by ordering that the information be disclosed to Mr. Freeman's agent, for review with Mr. Freeman only, and that neither Mr. Freeman nor his agent disclose or rely on the information of any operator who does not provide written authorization for the use of their information in the complaint proceeding, except with leave of the Tribunal. (para. 41)

6 The Union was subsequently substituted for Mr. Freeman as the representative complainant, but the order continued to apply, with appropriate modifications.

7 At the hearing, written or oral authorizations for the use of personal information were provided by each of the employees who testified on the Union's behalf. CMBC raised an issue about the use of documents containing personal information where there was no authorization by the employee in question. After submissions by the parties, I ruled that the parties would be allowed to introduce and rely on the documents at issue, but that in any decision of the Tribunal (or any other public disclosure of the information) the names of the operators in question would be excised, and those individuals would be identified by employee number only. Thus, in this decision, where an individual did not testify personally, and I was not provided with a written authorization for the use of their personal information, I refer to them by their employee number.

II. Evidence

8 CMBC operates conventional buses, smaller community shuttles, and the SeaBus, all in the Greater Vancouver area. In order to provide these services, CMBC employs, among others, approximately 2,600 bus drivers, known as .transit operators. or .operators.. The transit operators work out of a number of depots in different geographic locations across Greater Vancouver.

9 The Union is the exclusive bargaining agent for the operators. The terms and conditions of their employment are governed by a collective agreement between CMBC and the Union.

10 Other groups of CMBC employees are represented by different unions. The maintenance employees (including SeaBus employees) are represented by CAW, Local 2200 (.Local 2200.); the office employees by Canadian Office and Professional Employees Union, Local 378 (.COPE.); and the front line Supervisors by Canadian Union of Public Employees, Local 4500 (.CUPE.).

11 It was generally agreed by the parties that absenteeism among urban transit operators is higher than in other occupations. Some of the reasons for this higher absenteeism relate to the requirements and stresses of the job.

12 Below, I will first give a brief description of the AMP as it was at the time the complaint was filed. The purpose for this is to put some of the evidence into context. I will then outline the circumstances that gave rise to the implementation of the AMP. I will then outline the various departments involved in implementing the AMP, and other collective agreement provisions, benefits, and corporate policies which interact with it.

13 I will then discuss, in some detail, the various stages of the AMP, followed by the evidence with respect to the experience of a number of employees who have been affected by the AMP.

14 Finally, I will discuss the evidence relating to the impact of the AMP on CMBC's operations.

A. Brief Description of the AMP

15 As noted above, this complaint centres on CMBC's attendance management program. Although the Program will be described in some detail below, in order to put some of the evidence into context, I will first outline the main stages of the Program, as it existed at the time the complaint was filed.

16 The AMP is, in essence, a program through which CMBC first identifies operators who have unacceptable levels of absenteeism, and then provides them with notice that it considers their attendance to be unacceptable. CMBC reviews the attendance of its employees every three months, at what are termed .quarterly meetings.. Employees identified pursuant to this process may simply be monitored, or may be progressed through a series of stages. First, employees may have informal discussions with their Supervisors about their attendance. If there is insufficient improvement, employees will be advanced to Level 1, and provided with a formal letter outlining CMBC's concerns. If there continues to be insufficient improvement, employees are advanced to Level 2, at which CMBC may ask them to provide a medical assessment from their physician with respect to their state of health. After considering the information provided in this medical assessment, CMBC may proceed to a Level 3 interview, at which time an employee is provided with a formal letter requiring them to meet prescribed attendance targets, also known as parameters. If an employee fails to meet those parameters, CMBC may proceed to consider whether or not the employee should be terminated at an Employment Status Review (.ESR.). Employees may be terminated for failure to meet Level 3 parameters.

B. Background to the AMP

1. First discussions about an attendance management program - 1996

17 In 1996, the Auditor General of British Columbia conducted an audit of the productivity of the transit operators of B.C. Transit (CMBC's predecessor). The purpose of the audit was to assess B.C. Transit's degree of success in maximizing the productivity of its transit operators.

18 Mr. MacLeod, a former president of the Union, testified that, prior to the audit, absenteeism had not been raised as a major issue at B.C. Transit. This changed during the audit process.

19 Mr. MacLeod stated that the concept of an attendance management program was first raised by B.C. Transit in mid-1996, when he was the vice-president of the union then representing the transit operators (ICTU, Local 11, which was succeeded by the Union in February 2000. For the purposes of this decision, both will be referred to as the .Union.). In mid-1996, Mr. MacLeod attended a meeting with two senior representatives of B.C. Transit, where the issue of attendance was raised. B.C. Transit reported that 20-25% of transit operators had extensive, chronic absenteeism, and that something needed to be done. Mr. MacLeod testified that his initial response was concern with the broad-brush approach. He was concerned about pervasive problems in the system: lack of equipment, passenger load, and increased ridership. He felt it was more important to establish the reasons for absenteeism and the contribution of system problems to absenteeism. B.C. Transit was not receptive to these comments. Mr. MacLeod testified that he and other Union representatives left the meeting feeling that the company was not concerned with addressing the underlying issues causing absenteeism, but rather was simply interested in reducing its benefits costs.

20 Later in 1996, there was a meeting between B.C. Transit and representatives from each of the unions representing its employees. This was a more extensive presentation of the proposed attendance management program. Mr. MacLeod testified that the focus of this meeting was on the reduction of the costs of absenteeism, not in dealing with the underlying causes. The Union disagreed with this approach.

2. Auditor General's Report - 1997

21 The Auditor General released his report, entitled *B.C. Transit: Managing Operator Productivity.Performance Audit*, in June 1997. The audit raised some issues about the absenteeism rate among Vancouver-based transit operators.

22 The Auditor General compared the attendance statistics of B.C. Transit operators with those at five other North American transit companies, and found that the average annual absenteeism at the other companies was 13 days per operator. At B.C. Transit, operators averaged 37 days absence per year: significantly more than double the average rate. Mr. Kelly testified that the Auditor General's statistics in this regard included absences on long-term disability for over one year. When B.C. Transit reviewed the attendance data with respect to absences up to one year, it determined that the average was 27.4 days absent, per transit operator, per year.still more than double the average rate at the other North American transit companies surveyed.

23 The Auditor General also found that the importance of regular attendance was never communicated to employees; that there were inconsistencies in monitoring; and that there was no clear corporate policy on attendance.

24 As a result of his findings, the Auditor General recommended that B.C. Transit implement a comprehensive strategy for attendance management. In response to this recommendation, B.C. Transit introduced an attendance management program in 1997 which has been continued by CMBC with respect to all its employees.

3. AMP: 1997-1999

25 B.C. Transit introduced the first version of the AMP in 1997. From its inception, the company's Supervisors have been central to its administration. In 1998, B.C. Transit issued a .Supervisor's Guide for Managing Employee Attendance.. This Guide was revised by CMBC in 1999, and on an almost annual basis thereafter.

26 Until recently, there was no employer policy document relating to the AMP. The Supervisor's Guide is the most comprehensive statement about it.

27 The content of the AMP will be discussed in some detail below. In general, Mr. Kelly testified that, from its inception, the purpose of the AMP has been to lower absenteeism and to make employees aware of the importance of good attendance. As a result, the focus of the AMP is on all types of absences, including: short-term disability ("STD"); long-term disability ("LTD"); and absences while on workers' compensation benefits (.WCB.). For the purposes of calculating the average absenteeism rate for CMBC employees, STD absences, as well as both LTD and WCB absences of up to one year are counted. However, for the purpose of calculating an individual's absenteeism rate, all absences are included, including LTD and WCB absences over one year.

4. Policy Grievance: 1999-2000

28 From the outset, the Union had significant concerns with the AMP, related both to its terms and its application. For example, the Union was concerned that CMBC was attacking sick people on the basis of absences beyond their control, and that CMBC was blinding itself to the underlying causes of absenteeism in favour of an approach that dealt with sick and injured workers mechanistically and punitively.

29 As a result, in 1999, the Union filed a policy grievance against the AMP which resulted in an arbitration award: *CAW-Canada, Local 111 v. Coast Mountain Bus Co.* [2000 CarswellBC 2850 (B.C. Arb. Bd.)], unreported award, December 13, 2000 (Dorsey) (the .Policy Decision.). In the Policy Decision, the arbitrator found that the AMP was, in some cases, being administered in an unfair and unreasonable manner, and to this extent allowed the grievance. For example, the arbitrator found that treating time at work doing something other than operator duties (*e.g.* graduated return to work (.GRTW.), and alternate duties) as an absence was contradictory, unfair and unreasonable (p. 95). The arbitrator also found that using absenteeism beyond an employee's control, such as an absence while receiving WCB benefits as a result of being assaulted while at work, or as a result of a motor vehicle accident, to induct or progress an employee in the AMP was unreasonable and unfair (p. 100 and 103).

30 However, the arbitrator also found that these issues were subject to individual grievances and did not render the AMP as a whole unfair and unreasonable.

31 The arbitrator ordered CMBC to amend the Program in some regards: for example, to expressly state, and to illustrate with examples, absenteeism circumstances that will not trigger induction of a transit operator into or progress an operator through the Program (p. 101).

32 The arbitrator also found that CMBC failed to give appropriate notice of the AMP to its employees, and ordered CMBC to do so (pp. 106-107). CMBC issued that notice (the .Notice.) in January 2001.

33 In *CAW-Canada, Local 111 v. Coast Mountain Bus Co.*, 2005 BCHRT 242 (B.C. Human Rights Trib.), the Tribunal held that the Policy Decision did not prevent the Union from bringing this complaint to the Tribunal.

34 The Policy Decision did not settle the issues between CMBC and the Union with respect to the AMP and, in some cases, gave rise to additional disagreements between the parties. Among those disagreements, the parties are at odds over whether the Policy Decision means that time spent awaiting a rehabilitation assignment, or on a GRTW, can be used to trigger an employee's induction or advancement into the AMP. The parties also disagree about whether absences related to motor vehicle accidents generally

should not be taken into account in AMP decisions, or only those that have been accepted as WCB claims.

C. Departments involved in administering the AMP

35 There are a number of CMBC departments involved in administering the AMP. The two primary departments are the Attendance Management Department and the Occupational Health Group. I will briefly describe those departments here, although I return to them in more detail later in this decision.

1. Attendance Management Department

36 The Attendance Management Department plays a key role in implementing and applying the AMP. The Department's responsibilities include: reviewing the attendance of all CMBC employees; providing training in attendance management processes for Supervisors; generating bi-weekly reports to senior management about attendance/absenteeism in different areas; and acting as a resource to Supervisors and managers who are looking for assistance in dealing with employees with attendance problems.

2. Occupational Health Group

37 The Occupational Health Group (.OHG.) also plays an important role in the implementation and application of the AMP. Ms. Lopez testified that there are four Occupational Health Nurses (.OHNs.), three part-time and one full-time, who report to her, as well as a coordinator and an occupational health clerk.

38 The OHG's broad responsibilities include: liaising with employees, Supervisors and insurers on STD and LTD claims issues; administering the health and wellness program; being the primary contact for the Employee Assistance Program (.EAP.); and dealing with accommodation issues, including temporary rehabilitation assignments, GRTW coordination, permanent accommodations, and medical severances.

39 Ms. Lopez testified that OHNs spend a great deal of their time on the phone with employees, benefits providers, and others. Approximately 50% of an OHN's day is spent on the phone with employees. The work is divided between the OHNs by depot, with each OHN being responsible for two or more depots. One OHN is also the WCB case manager. Ms. Lopez testified that each OHN has approximately 85-100 active case files at any one time.

40 If an employee is off work because of illness, they are required to submit an STD claim form. Where the absence is longer than three days, the form needs to be accompanied by supporting medical information. The OHG be-

comes aware of the employee's absence once they receive the STD claim form. If the employee is still off work once this form is received, the OHN initiates a call to the employee. If an employee is off for an extended period of time, there is generally regular contact between the OHN and the employee, which ranges from every seven to ten days. In circumstances where an employee is waiting for medical intervention or an appointment with a specialist, the OHN will contact the employee after these appointments.

41 In addition, and as discussed in more detail below, the OHG is the department charged with the collection and use of confidential medical information.

42 Specifically with respect to the AMP, Ms. Lopez testified that the OHG is involved at a few different stages. First, an OHN will provide information to the Attendance Management Department for the purposes of their review prior to a quarterly meeting. Second, the OHG will be involved in organizing any medical assessments required as part of the process. Third, the OHG can be involved in discussions involving an Employment Status Review. In addition, the OHG is also involved in any accommodation or GRTW arrangements. Each of these stages will be described in more detail below.

D. Collective Agreement Provisions, Benefits, and Corporate Policies which interact with the AMP

43 The AMP does not exist in a vacuum. There are other collective agreement provisions, benefits, and policies which exist along side, and interact with, it.

1. Benefit Plans

44 First, and as outlined above, the terms and conditions of employment of CMBC operators are governed by the collective agreement in place between the Union and CMBC (the .Collective Agreement.). Under the Collective Agreement, employees absent from work due to non-work related illness or injury have access to both STD and LTD benefits.

45 The STD plan is provided for in Article 12.02 of the Collective Agreement. Pursuant to Article 12.02, CMBC agrees to provide an STD plan which will provide a benefit payable for employee absences arising from non-occupational injury or illness. Employees can take up to three working days on STD without providing a doctor's note. From the fourth day onward, medical support is required. If such information is not provided, the employee will not receive benefits. The STD plan is funded by CMBC, and administered by Great West Life (.GWL.) on an administrative services only (.ASO.) basis. This means that CMBC pays the total cost of benefits to

GWL, which pays the benefits to the employee. In addition, CMBC pays GWL an administration fee.

46 Under the STD plan, employees are entitled to a benefit equivalent to 100% of their regular daily earnings for the first eight weeks of absence, and to 85% of their regular earnings from weeks nine to seventeen of the absence.

47 The LTD plan is also administered by GWL, on an ASO basis, and is funded completely by employee contributions. The LTD plan is overseen by a health and benefit trust, which is comprised of an equal number of representatives from CMBC and the Union. The trust determines the amount of the LTD premiums. The amount of the benefit provided has generally been determined by collective bargaining. At one time, the benefit provided was approximately 60% of regular daily earnings at the time of the commencement of the disability, but in the current collective agreement, the benefit provided is 50%. LTD benefits are provided from the 17th week of absence on, pursuant to the provisions of the LTD plan.

48 Mr. Kelly testified that LTD benefits are received on a tax-free basis to the employee. The plan was originally designed to provide a smooth transition from the STD benefit (85%, taxable) received during the last eight weeks on STD to a non-taxable 60% payment from the 18th week of absence onward. However, over time, with increases to taxation, the LTD benefit began to exceed the STD benefit, and so it was perceived as an incentive for employees to stay on LTD. Mr. Kelly testified that this was one reason for reducing the benefit to 50% of daily earnings.

2. Collective Agreement Provisions

49 In addition to the benefit plans, the Collective Agreement contains other provisions which interact with and affect the administration of the AMP. Two provisions relate to the confidentiality of medical information.

50 Article 12.04 of the Collective Agreement provides as follows:

> **12.04 Medical Certification**
>
> Confidentiality of Medical Information.all personal medical information required or provided pursuant to this Plan [*that is, the Wage Protection Plan, including STD and LTD*] shall be made available only to the carrier administering the Plan and to the Employer's Occupational Health Group. **Where it is in the best interests of the employee, and where it will assist the Company to make informed decisions, the Union will encourage the employee to disclose the medical information to particular members of the Company.** The information shall be treated in strict confidence and will be administered in compliance with the Freedom of Information and Protection of Privacy Act.
>
> The cost of any medical forms required under the above Plans shall be borne by the Employer.

> The Employer will notify the Union in writing of any changes in the members of the Occupational Health Group. (reproduced as written)

51 The bold face type indicates new language, which was agreed to in the last round of collective bargaining, in 2004.

52 In addition, Letter of Understanding #4, appended to the Collective Agreement, provides, in part:

> The Employer agrees that Medical information shall be treated in strict confidence and shall remain confidential and in the hands (files) of the Occupational Health Group. Further, that Management shall not have access to these same confidential medical files for any reason, nor shall management require, or be provided with, any information in those files. Members of the Occupational Health Group will sign a document acknowledging their obligations to comply with this Letter of Understanding.

53 Pursuant to these provisions, medical information received by CMBC with respect to an employee is to be held solely within the OHG and is strictly confidential.

54 Mr. Jones testified that one of the problems the Union has with the operation of the AMP is the way CMBC interprets its confidentiality obligations. Specifically, Mr. Jones testified that, although it seems that the OHG generally receives a great deal of medical information with respect to employees who have been placed on the AMP, the type of information communicated to Supervisors who are charged with making decisions about advancement on the AMP is very limited in nature.

55 Mr. Jones agreed in cross-examination that, pursuant to the language of the Collective Agreement, the Union can encourage the employee to discuss their medical information, but ultimately, medical information is the employee's confidential information and it is the employee's decision whether to release that information.

3. Corporate Policies

56 In addition to the benefit plans and Collective Agreement provisions, CMBC also has several policies in place which address disability and accommodation issues. Ms. Lopez testified about these policies, which include: the Disability Management Policy; the Accommodation of Employees with a Permanent Disability Policy; the Safety and Health Policy; and the Substance Use Disorder Policy.

57 In general, Ms. Lopez testified that the OHG is involved in accommodation issues both as part of, and outside, the AMP. In either case, accommodation issues come to the OHG on the basis of medical information that indicates that the employee requires accommodation and is unable, either permanently or temporarily, to continue in their own job.

58 I will discuss each of the policies in turn.

a. Disability Management Policy

59 The purpose of the Disability Management Policy is to provide rehabilitation work assignments for employees who are temporarily unable to perform their regular work duties due to limitations and restrictions arising from their disabilities. In such cases, the OHG will work with employees on an individual basis in order to determine whether they have any limitations or restrictions and, if so, what type of temporary alternate work would assist them in successfully returning to work in their own occupation.

60 There are four primary types of rehabilitation positions (also known as temporary alternate placements): Utility Operator (which is a position within the Union); and Building Service Worker, Service Person, and Interior Cleaner (which are Local 2200 positions). The Utility Operator position conducts all-door boarding on the high-volume University routes, assists operators at bus loops (changing signs, loading passengers), and answers customer enquiries. A Service Person sweeps buses and move them around the yard. Interior Cleaners clean the inside of the buses. Building Service Workers clean CMBC's facilities. In addition, there are also less frequently used types of rehab positions, including yard sweeper and cleaner, and parts truck driver. These are also Local 2200 positions.

61 Ms. Lopez testified that, in the year and a half before she gave her evidence (in October 2006), a Union employee had been placed in a temporary placement in lost property, within COPE jurisdiction, but that placements outside of Local 111 or 2200 are rare.

62 Temporary alternate placements are a maximum of six months in duration (although they can be extended to a year based on agreement with the relevant union). In some cases, there can be changes in a temporary alternate placement where, for example, an employee is unable to continue in a placement because of medical reasons, or where the six month placement ends and the employee is unable to return to their own occupation.

63 In addition to coordinating temporary work assignments, the OHG's responsibilities under the Disability Management Policy include monitoring GRTW arrangements where an operator is returning to their own position. Ms. Lopez testified that an OHN assists in such arrangements once they receive a recommendation for a GRTW from the employee's doctor or the insurance carrier. The OHG will communicate with the appropriate Supervisor about implementing the recommended schedule.

64 With respect to the interaction between the Disability Management Policy, as it relates to GRTWs, and the AMP, there was uncontested evidence from Mr. Jones that when an employee is on a GRTW, hours that the employee is not at work are taken into account for the purposes of the AMP. That is, if an employee is working four hours a day on a GRTW, and their

regular shift is eight hours, the four hours a day that they are not working are considered hours of absence for the purposes of the AMP.

65 Statistics provided by Ms. Lopez indicated that, in 2005, there were 128 temporary alternate placements in rehabilitation assignments; and, in 2004, 124 such placements (some employees may have been placed in more than one assignment). In addition, in 2005 there were 223 GRTW placements of transit operators, and in 2004 there were 259.

b. Accommodation of Employees with a Permanent Disability Policy

66 CMBC also has a policy relating to the accommodation of employees with permanent, as opposed to temporary, disabilities. The purpose of this policy is to comply with CMBC's obligation under the *Code* to accommodate employees with permanent disabilities to the point of undue hardship.

67 Where the OHG has medical information that an employee is unable to work in their own occupation and requires accommodation, the OHG will look at the limitations and restrictions of the employee as outlined by their doctor. Sometimes the employee will undergo a Functional Capacity Evaluation to determine if the employee can perform work in an accommodated position.

68 The first step in the process involves looking at whether it is possible to modify the employee's own job. Ms. Lopez did not give any examples of this among transit operators, but did provide an example from the Local 2200 jurisdiction where a work area had been modified to accommodate an employee's disability.

69 If the employee's own job cannot be modified, the next question is whether the employee can be accommodated in another position within their own bargaining unit; and, if not, whether they can be accommodated in a position within another bargaining unit. In the case of Local 111 employees, CMBC looks specifically at the Local 2200 bargaining unit, and then at externally posted vacant positions in other union jurisdictions. The provision of accommodated positions to operators in union jurisdictions other than Local 2200 is a relatively recent and emerging development. Ms. Lopez gave two examples of cases where such an accommodation had occurred.

70 Ms. Lopez testified that in 2005 there were nine or ten permanent accommodations of Local 111 operators arranged in the Local 2200 jurisdiction; and that, to the date of her testimony in 2006, there had been eight such placements.

71 Ms. Lopez also testified about the scope of the Accommodation of Employees with a Permanent Disability Policy. She was asked in cross-examination whether, if a doctor identifies that an individual has a chronic condi-

tion, they would be considered to have a permanent disability. She replied in the negative. A permanent disability means that an individual is permanently disabled from their own occupation. The policy is triggered when the OHG receives information that the employee requires permanent accommodation in another job.

72 In cross-examination, Ms. Lopez was asked about the OHG's approach in cases where an employee's doctor indicated that the employee was capable of performing the work of an operator; but where it was clear that the employee was not meeting attendance parameters under the AMP. Specifically, Ms. Lopez was asked whether, in such a case, the OHG would consider whether an accommodation was required or appropriate. Ms. Lopez stated that, if the medical information indicated the employee was capable of performing the work of an operator, then no. If the medical information indicated that the individual was capable of returning to their own (pre-disability) job, then no accommodation would be considered.

73 At Level 3 of the AMP, which will be outlined in more detail below, employees are required to meet certain attendance parameters that are based on average attendance rates of their employee group. Ms. Lopez was asked whether, if an individual for whom she was seeking an accommodation was on the AMP and was required to meet attendance parameters, the OHG would recommend removal from those parameters. Ms. Lopez testified that the OHG had to deal with each individual case on its own merits. Ms. Lopez was then asked whether she could recall recommending that an operator be removed from parameters, and she replied that she could not recall ever doing so.

74 Mr. Kelly gave evidence with respect to the expectations placed on employees who have been moved to an accommodated position. He testified that the expectation is that they will perform at an acceptable level, including regular attendance. He stated that this was the purpose of an accommodated position. If an employee still isn't capable of meeting attendance expectations, Mr. Kelly testified that CMBC may look at a different accommodated position, but the focus would be on whether a position was available in which the employee could meet an acceptable standard.

75 Ms. Lopez confirmed this testimony: when employees are placed in a permanent accommodation, they are advised that they must meet attendance requirements. If they are unable to do so, that is addressed under the AMP. Ms. Lopez was asked whether she was aware of attendance requirements being waived with respect to an employee in a permanently accommodated position, and she said she was not.

c. Substance Abuse Policy

76 Pursuant to the Substance Abuse Policy, CMBC provides interest free loans to employees undergoing treatment for addiction issues, based on the recommendation of a specialist.

77 The OHG may become aware of an employee's substance abuse issue in a number of ways. First, the employee may self-disclose, contacting the OHG and seeking assistance. Where the employee self-discloses, the OHG gives the employee the names of three specialists whom they can attend for the purpose of undergoing an Independent Medical Examination (.IME.). The OHG will arrange an appointment with the specialist chosen by the employee. Once the employee attends the IME, a report, including treatment and monitoring recommendations, is provided to the OHG. An OHN reviews the IME with the employee, discusses the treatment recommendations, and assists the employee in obtaining a spot at a facility if such treatment is recommended by the specialist and desired by the employee. In addition, the OHN advises the employee of the treatment loan available: a maximum of $2,500, interest free, one time loan paid directly to the treatment facility. The loan is forgivable, and is forgiven if the employee successfully completes the treatment and monitoring requirements.

78 In other circumstances, the OHG may receive medical information from the employee's doctor or specialist. Ms. Lopez did not specifically testify about the procedure followed in such circumstances, but it appears that, under the Substance Abuse Policy, if CMBC has reasonable grounds to believe that an employee has a substance abuse or addiction problem, and is impaired or using drugs or alcohol while at work, the employee may be required to attend an IME. While awaiting the IME and the results from it, the employee will be placed on .to be qualified. (.TBQ.) status. This is a designation CMBC uses where an employee cannot return to work until their physician specifies that they are fit to return to work in the safety sensitive position of transit operator. It appears that the other provisions of the Substance Abuse Policy would also be available to such employees.

79 In cross-examination, Mr. Jones was asked about a specific employee who had gone through this program. Mr. Jones agreed that the employee's disability was effectively accommodated by CMBC. Mr. Jones stated that CMBC and the Union both respond very quickly to substance abuse problems of which they become aware.

4. Employee Assistance Program

80 Ms. Lopez also testified about the EAP, which is available to all employees and their dependents. The EAP provides confidential assistance to employees through face-to-face counselling, telephone and internet counselling, other internet services, e-learning courses, and other resources. There

is no limit on the number of visits an employee may make to EAP counselling. The EAP is provided by an independent provider, unconnected to CMBC.

E. The Attendance Management Program

81 As outlined above, CMBC first published the Supervisor's Guide for Managing Employee Attendance (the .Guide.) in 1998. The Guide describes, for the Supervisor, the issues surrounding attendance, CMBC's expectations for good attendance, what a Supervisor should do to promote and recognize good attendance, and how to deal with employees who have problem attendance on a regular basis.

82 The Guide has been regularly revised from 1998 to the date of the hearing. Mr. Kelly was instrumental in drafting the Guide and the subsequent revisions. He testified that the revisions take into account concerns raised by Supervisors and employees, ensure that it is still current and viable, and incorporate changes to the AMP resulting from arbitration awards and human rights decisions.

83 In addition, in June 2005, CMBC issued a Corporate Policy Statement entitled .Attendance Management.. The Policy Statement is consistent with the material outlined in the Guide. Mr. Kelly testified that, previous to this, the Guide was the only reference to the AMP, and he felt that it was preferable to have the AMP outlined in a separate document.

84 At the commencement of the hearing, the applicable Guide was the 2004 revision. By the end of the hearing, the 2006 revision had been distributed. Mr. Kelly testified that there had been no substantive changes between the two revisions. He testified that one of the concerns addressed in the 2006 revision was the elimination of anything in the Guide that suggested that progression through the AMP was a lock-step process, and that the main change made to the 2006 revision was to clarify that the interventions undertaken under the AMP had to be appropriate to each individual situation.

85 Below, I will outline the components of the AMP, based on the oral and documentary evidence before me. In doing so, I will rely primarily on the 2004 revision of the Guide, but will include elements of the 2006 revision where appropriate. Unless otherwise indicated, references are from the 2004 revision of the Guide.

1. Summary of CMBC's attendance policy

86 The Guide articulates CMBC's attendance policy as follows:

> All Coast Mountain employees are expected to fulfill the requirements of their jobs on a regular basis. This means that, except for reasonable causes, employees are required to be at work when scheduled. It is recognized that most employees will, at

> some time in the course of their employment, be temporarily absent from work due to illness or injury. However, employees are expected to take reasonable steps to maintain their health and fitness at a level which allows them to attend work on a consistent basis.
>
> For those employees who are suffering from longer term illnesses or work related injuries, Coast Mountain Bus Company will make genuine efforts, through rehabilitation programs and/or alternate assignments, to assist affected employees to regain their health and return to work. Coast Mountain will also use its best efforts to accommodate employees who have permanent medical disabilities. (p. 2)

87 The Guide then discusses attendance management principles, and the responsibilities of various groups. Supervisors (known as .Operations Supervisors. for transit operators) play a key role in the administration of the AMP, and have primary responsibility to:

a) Communicate the Company's attendance expectations to their employees,

b) Promote a positive work environment,

c) Monitor employee attendance and positively reinforce good performance,

d) Maintain contact with employees who are absent from work for extended periods,

e) Meet individually with employees who exhibit excessive absenteeism, to review their attendance records, express the Company's concerns, counsel regarding available assistance and caution about the possible consequences of continued, unacceptable absenteeism. (pp. 2-3)

88 The Guide also outlines the following principles:

> Employees who, because of a legitimate disability, cannot return to their normal work assignment, either temporarily or permanently, may be accommodated through re-training, rehabilitation or alternate-work programs developed under Coast Mountain's disability management program.
>
> Termination of employment may result in cases where reasonable time and opportunity have been afforded to an employee to attain acceptable levels of attendance, but whose absenteeism continues to be excessive and there is no reasonable likelihood of the employee attending work, in the future, on a regular and consistent basis. (p. 3)

2. Identifying potentially problematic absenteeism

89 Mr. Kelly testified that the focus of the AMP is to identify employees who have a pattern of .problem absenteeism.. In this regard, the Guide outlines absenteeism benchmarks, and what constitutes problem absenteeism, in the following manner:

> CMBC's overall .average. is not a reliable indicator of the attendance performance of most employees. A more accurate reflection is the .median. average, where, on a

continuum representing all CMBC Operators, the operator at the halfway point would be absent approximately 6 days per year.

There are many employees who generally have good attendance records but who may experience a serious medical condition resulting in a lengthy absence. These employees are NOT considered as having attendance problems.

The Company's main focus for improving attendance performance will be on those employees who exhibit high rates and/or frequencies of absence, year after year, for a variety of reasons but without any indication of a chronic disability that may require some form of accommodation.

CMBC will also scrutinize the attendance performance of more junior employees for indications of emerging attendance problems as well as those employees whose absenteeism rates may not be higher than the average but whose frequency of absences are disruptive and costly.

Over the longer term, CMBC is targeting an average annual absence rate of 6% for its operator workforce or approximately 15 days per year (combined STD, WCB and LTD < 1 year). ***This should not be construed as acceptable attendance on an individual basis***. ... (Emphasis in original, pp. 5-6)

90 Similarly, the 2006 revision of the Guide states:

At CMBC, attendance data, evaluated over several years, shows that 50% of the employees in the employee-group with the highest rate of absenteeism, have less than 6 absence-days per year and 75% of all employees are absent less than 10 days. In fact, fewer than 20% of employees, in any given year, actually experience absenteeism that is at or above the overall average. That is why the ***average rate of absenteeism should not be construed as being normal, nor should it be regarded as acceptable.*** Employees who occasionally exceed the 10-day range may not be a concern, but those who consistently exceed 10 absence-days and 2 or more occasions per year may require attention. (Emphasis in original, p. 9)

91 Thus, while the standard used within the AMP is the .average. attendance rate, CMBC is quick to point out, both in the Guide, and in Mr. Kelly's oral evidence, that the average is not an accurate representation of the absenteeism rate of most employees. Fewer than 20% of employees each year have absenteeism in excess of the .average..

92 In addition, the 2006 Guide contains the following statement:

Some employees may have disabilities that impact on their work performance. Having a disability does not lessen the obligations on the employee to meet acceptable performance standards, including attendance, however, it may impose on CMBC, a duty, to the point of undue hardship, to search for an accommodation that will enable the employee to meet acceptable standards in the performance of meaningful work. When you encounter an employee whose excessive absenteeism may be at least partly associated with a temporary or permanent medical condition or disability, you must refer the employee to the Occupational Health Group (OHG). The OHG is responsible for coordinating all accommodation efforts, based on the circumstances of each individual case. (p. 9)

93 The Guide then outlines the levels and types of absenteeism which trigger active monitoring. Employees are credited with hours worked for all the

time they are on annual vacation, statutory holiday, banked overtime leave, jury duty and any other paid leaves of absence. The absences which are included in the absenteeism calculation are STD, LTD, and WCB. Mr. Kelly testified that LTD and WCB absences of up to one year only are taken into account in determining the overall attendance statistics. However, with respect to any individual employee, the entire length of any LTD and WCB absences is taken into account.

94 The Guide also provides a discussion of the types of absenteeism which may be viewed as .problem absenteeism.. The 2004 Guide states that problem absenteeism may be indicated where one or more of the following conditions are present:

a) The frequency of absences and/or the rate of absenteeism is consistently higher than the average for the employee's work group;
b) The reasons for the employee's absences are unknown or poorly understood by the supervisor;
c) The supervisor is uncertain as to whether the employee is taking reasonable steps to deal with the absences;
d) Absences exceed the normal period of recovery for the particular disability;
e) The absenteeism is chronic in nature; the absences are repetitive and there is no indication that the employee's level of absenteeism will improve in the future. (p. 10)

95 Employees are identified for active attendance monitoring under the AMP through a progressive screening process. Mr. Kelly gave evidence about his department's role in this process. He stated that, on a quarterly basis, he reviews the attendance of all employees. He calculates what the average absence rate has been for the previous 12 month period, and reviews all employees who are at or above the average for that period. Then, he looks to see if their current absence rate (for the previous 12 months) is indicative of their attendance history over the past several years. If it seems that their absenteeism rate is persistently at the average or higher, the employee is identified for discussion at the quarterly review meeting. Mr. Kelly testified that the average rate of absenteeism is a benchmark used to initiate the process.

96 Mr. Kelly stated that, at this stage in the process, he is reviewing employees who could possibly represent ongoing attendance problems. The decision he makes at this stage is whether or not to include an employee for discussion at a quarterly review meeting.

97 Mr. Kelly testified that he exercises his discretion in deciding whether to move employees forward to discussion at a quarterly review. He gave ex-

amples of employees who may not be moved forward for discussion at a quarterly meeting. For example, where he was aware of particular circumstances from previous reviews; in cases where it has been determined that there is no cause for concern; employees who are approaching retirement in the next few years; and employees with a long history of good attendance, followed by a few more recent years of high absenteeism.

98 Mr. Kelly testified that the list of employees that is generated out of this process is sent to the OHG, which identifies any employee on the list with special medical issues that should be taken into account.

99 Ms. Lopez's evidence in respect of this procedure was slightly different. She stated that, in practice, the OHG is generally provided with a list of employees for whom return to work information is sought. That is, the information requested is generally about employees who are off work, and information is required about their ability to return to work (.RTW.), and when that return might occur. With respect to these employees, Ms. Lopez testified that the OHG would not provide any confidential medical information, but only a prognosis for their return to work. Examples of the information provided were given, as follows:

- RTW anticipated in two months;
- Employee commencing GRTW in two weeks;
- No RTW date known at this time; or
- Likely unable to RTW as operator; currently exploring accommodation options.

100 Given that Ms. Lopez is the head of the department giving the information in question, to the extent that there is inconsistency between her evidence and that of Mr. Kelly, I prefer her evidence about the type of evidence that is sought and provided.

3. Quarterly Review Meeting

101 As noted above, and subject to the discretion described by Mr. Kelly, employees who indicate a trend toward higher than average absence rates, or who have absence rates that are consistently higher than the average, are placed on a list for discussion at quarterly review meetings. The Guide notes that employees whose absence frequency is a concern are also identified for discussion. Absence frequency refers to the number of periods of absence during the year. For example, an employee who was absent on one occasion for 50 days, and an employee who was absent on one occasion for one day would both have an absence frequency of one.

102 As their name suggests, quarterly review meetings are held quarterly (*i.e.*, every three months). With respect to transit operators, one such meet-

ing is held for each depot. They are normally attended by the respective Supervisor and/or Manager responsible for the depot, and representatives from the Labour Relations and Attendance Management Departments.

103 Ms. Lopez testified that OHNs do not attend the quarterly review meetings in person (although they did at one time), but they are available by phone should the participants wish to contact them for more information. Ms. Lopez states that this has never actually occurred.

104 Mr. Kelly testified that the meeting is run by the Supervisor, who reviews the list of employees with the other individuals participating in the meeting. Mr. Kelly stated that the role of the Supervisor is extremely important, as s/he is the one individual who has had direct contact with the employee. Often, Supervisors will be privy to the employee's particular circumstances and situations which may prevent intervention by CMBC.

105 The participants review the list that has been generated by Mr. Kelly's department, and annotated by the OHG, in order to determine whether there is a legitimate concern for each listed employee's ability to attend work regularly in the future. The participants will also consider information relating to the employee's attendance record, interview history, recent discussions, and any follow-ups.

106 Mr. Kelly testified that the participants may also consider the proximity of the employee to mandatory retirement, the employee's past attendance history, whether the group has been advised that the employee has a disability which interferes with their ability to attend regularly, and whether any accommodation is required.

107 After this discussion, the group determines whether employees should remain on the list, whether intervention is warranted, whether intervention should be delayed pending medical testing, and, if intervention is warranted, at what level.

108 If the participants determine that there is no legitimate concern about ongoing attendance, usually no action is taken. Mr. Kelly testified that an employee would not be introduced or advanced into the AMP on the basis of their absenteeism alone, but rather on the basis of their pattern of absenteeism, and whether it indicates the possibility of continued high absenteeism in the future.

109 If the participants decide that there is a legitimate concern about attendance, the action taken will depend on whether the employee has previously been talked to about attendance issues. The intervention in question could range from an informal meeting to a decision about whether to continue the employee's employment. The quarterly review is not just the first step in the AMP process, but an ongoing procedure by which employees are identified and discussed. An employee could be raised for discussion on one oc-

casion, or could be discussed at each quarterly review meeting for a number of years, depending on whether they are experiencing ongoing attendance issues.

110 Each of the levels of the AMP (except the ESR) involves an attendance interview with the appropriate Supervisor. In the 2004 Guide, the levels are identified as: informal interview, formal interview (Level 1 interview, Level 2 interview, Level 3 interview), and ESR. In the 2006 Guide, they are identified as: informal interview, formal interview (review of attendance record and formal indication of concern; and advanced concern interview) and ESR. Mr. Kelly testified that the reason for this change was that CMBC never intended to have the various levels of the AMP seen as a necessary progression, where you could only move in order from Level 1 to Level 2 to Level 3 (or conversely from Level 3 to Level 2 to Level 1). He testified that the changes were made to clarify that the interventions undertaken under the AMP had to be appropriate to each individual situation.

111 Although the various stages have slightly different names in the two Guides, the content of the interviews is roughly the same. I will outline the process as it is described in the 2004 Guide, and will note changes in the 2006 Guide where necessary.

4. Informal Interview

112 The informal interview is generally the first interview held with an employee whose attendance has been identified as a concern. According to the Guide, the purpose of an informal interview is:

> ... to let employees know that their rate or frequency of absences, or both, is being noticed, and to give them an opportunity to resolve their absence issues without going through a formal process. It is also an opportunity for an employee to give the supervisor some insight regarding the reason for the absences, and how the employee has been dealing with the absences, and perhaps a commitment to a timeline for seeing an improvement. (p. 13)

113 In the 2006 Guide, an additional purpose of the informal interview is identified: to convey CMBC's expectation that the employee will take all reasonable steps to minimize their absences in the future and to make the employee aware of the resources available to assist them (p. 11).

114 The informal interview is conducted by the employee's Supervisor. As with any AMP interview, the employee is entitled to Union representation, and there is a specific process through which the fact of the meeting is communicated to both the employee and the Union.

115 At the meeting, the Supervisor will inform the employee that their attendance has come to CMBC's attention, that the Supervisor has some concerns with the attendance, and hopes that any issues with absenteeism are short term in nature. The Supervisor asks if there is anything he or she can

do to assist, advises of the existence of the EAP, and states that the employee can contact an OHN for any assistance.

116 Informal interviews are not confirmed by letter, but are documented in the attendance management system.

117 In an informal interview, as with any other interview conducted in the AMP, the employee is advised that their attendance record is taken into account with respect to vacancies and promotions. Mr. Kelly was asked about the purpose of this in cross-examination, and he replied that, if the employee has demonstrated difficulties in regular attendance at their current job, and then applies for another job within the company, it is equivalent to moving the problem around. Vacancies are posted for a purpose: to get the job done. Lack of regular attendance is a big problem, so CMBC wants to address the attendance issue first.

5. Formal Interviews

118 The Guide notes that formal attendance interviews should be conducted only with employees who exhibit signs of problem absenteeism, and should be carried out in a timely manner (the 2004 Guide indicates within a month of a return to work from absences, the 2006 Guide indicates within three weeks). Mr. Kelly stated that a formal interview is conducted with an employee who has likely already received an informal interview, but whose attendance has not shown satisfactory improvement.

119 Consistent with the Policy Decision, the Guide states that the formal introduction of an employee into the AMP or advancement to the next level of the AMP should not be triggered by: an absence resulting from an isolated illness or injury which causes an anomalous spike in an otherwise acceptable attendance record; a WCB-absence arising from an assault on the job; or a WCB-absence caused by a motor vehicle accident on the job.

a. Level 1 Interview/Formal Indication of Concern

120 The first formal interview is the Level 1 interview, referred to in the 2006 Guide as a .Formal Indication of Concern.. At a meeting at this stage, the Supervisor will inform the employee that the purpose of the interview is to make them aware of CMBC's concern regarding their attendance record, and to offer any assistance that would lead to more acceptable attendance. The Supervisor is instructed to tell the employee that the only person in the Company to whom the employee may be required to provide personal medical information is an OHN. The Supervisor informs the employee that the Supervisor will not ask the employee for, and the employee is not obliged to divulge, any such information. Following these opening remarks, the employee is provided with a copy of their absence record, and the Supervisor

explains how it has prompted the interview. The employee is advised that if the absenteeism levels demonstrated in the record were to continue, it would indicate an inability to attend work in a regular and consistent fashion, and could not be tolerated by CMBC.

121 The employee is then given statistical information about the attendance levels of the majority of employees doing the same job. Other information is given to the employee, including information relating to available resources that could assist them in achieving and maintaining acceptable attendance. The 2006 Guide states:

> Advise employees of the resources that are available to them and where their work performance or attendance is being affected by an ongoing medical condition ask them to discuss the matter with the OHN as soon as possible.
>
> - Employees who cannot return to their own occupation either temporarily or permanently can contact the professional staff in our OHG for assistance (may include temporary alternate work or graduated-returns to work).
> - The confidential services of the EAP are available to assist employees and members of their immediate family. (p. 14)

122 At the conclusion of the interview, the employee is advised that the Supervisor will continue to monitor their attendance and, depending on the level and sustainability of the employee's attendance, may schedule another interview in the coming months.

123 The interview is confirmed with a letter, the outline of which is provided in the Guide. This letter, and all AMP letters, are copied to Labour Relations, the OHG, the employee file, the Corporate Attendance Management Department, and the employee's union.

124 In the 2004 Guide, the sample letter for the Level 1 interview states:

> This letter will confirm my meeting with you on (*date*), during which we discussed your attendance record, which is a concern to the Company. Our records show that you have been absent from work for __________ days on __________ separate occasions over the past 12 months. The attached document gives a breakdown of your absences, in hours and by type, on a monthly basis, for the entire period your attendance is being reviewed.
>
> The importance of regular attendance at work cannot be overstated. Your attendance record shows a level of absenteeism that is well above the average for employees with similar positions at Coast Mountain Bus Co. If your absenteeism were to continue at current unacceptable levels it would indicate an inability to attend to your job in a regular and consistent fashion, and could not be tolerated. You should also be advised that attendance records are one of many factors taken into account when considering employee applications to fill vacancies or promotions.
>
> If there are circumstances that exist, relevant to your absences, we urge you to advise us so that we may provide you with the appropriate support. As discussed, Coast Mountain Bus Co. will ensure that every assistance is available to you and that all benefits to which you are entitled, whether for sickness or injury are placed at your disposal. The Employee Assistance Plan [telephone number provided] and

> the services of the Occupational Health Nurse [telephone number provided] are available to you. If you wish to utilize these support services, please feel free to contact them directly.
>
> I will continue to monitor your attendance and look forward to seeing a significant improvement. If circumstances warrant, I will schedule a meeting with you to review your progress. (p. 20)

125 The sample letter provided in the 2006 Guide is worded slightly differently, but is similar in nature. In particular, it includes the following paragraphs:

> The Company understands that most employees will be absent occasionally due to sickness or injury and we accept that your absences have been for legitimate medical reasons. Our concern, however, is that your absenteeism consistently exceeds the norm for your peer group and, if it were to persist, would have negative implications for our costs and service reliability.
>
> We discussed the need for you to show meaningful and sustained improvement, going forward, and you were encouraged to contact the confidential resources listed below if you think they could be helpful. You were also advised that attendance records are taken into account when considering employee applications to fill vacancies and promotions. (p. 17)

126 Mr. Kelly testified that, in his experience, Supervisors generally follow the wording of the sample letters provided.

127 Mr. Jones testified about his experience in Level 1 meetings. He agreed that the Supervisor would give the information outlined above to the employee. However, he stated that, if an employee chooses to discuss the reasons for absenteeism, or that their absenteeism is related to a chronic disability, the conversation is shut down and the Supervisor will inform the employee that she or he should speak to an OHN, as it is not the responsibility of the Supervisor.

128 Pursuant to the 2004 Guide, if there was no significant improvement in an employee's attendance, they could be advanced to the next stage of the AMP. As the 2006 Guide introduced some structural changes in this respect, I will first outline the 2004 process (Level 2 and Level 3 interviews), and then discuss the changes to the process in the 2006 Guide.

b. 2004 Guide: Level 2 Interview

129 If an employee's attendance does not show significant improvement over the months following a Level 1 interview, the Guide indicates that a further interview should be scheduled. The Guide states that, prior to the interview being conducted, the Supervisor is to contact an OHN to determine the appropriateness of requesting a medical assessment. The Level 2 interview is conducted by the Supervisor, with his or her manager in attendance.

130 In the 2004 Guide, the purpose of the Level 2 interview is stated to be, among other things, to request a medical assessment from the employee. In the Notice issued by CMBC in January 2001, and discussed at paragraph 32, the purpose for requesting the medical assessment is stated to be two-fold:

> First, to determine an employee's ability to perform their duties and attend work on a regular basis;
>
> Second, to determine if the employee has a medical disability that is causing him/her difficulty in performing his/her job or attending work on a regular basis and which may require some form of accommodation.

131 At the interview, after discussing the employee's attendance record since the last interview, the Supervisor is to provide the employee with an opportunity to discuss any reasons for his or her absences, and to ask if they are availing themselves of any medical or other assistance to address their issues. In addition, the Guide states that the Supervisor should:

> Advise the employee that CMBC is unwilling to tolerate his/her ongoing, excessive absenteeism and unless an accommodation for a chronic medical condition is required and available, a continuation of unacceptable absenteeism could result in termination of his/her employment. (p. 16)

132 Where appropriate, the Supervisor is to request that the employee contact an OHN within five working days to discuss arrangements for a confidential medical assessment. The purpose of this assessment is to help determine if any underlying health reasons are contributing to their attendance problems and also to assess their fitness for regular work. Written confirmation of the interview is provided to the employee. The sample letter included in the Guide states:

> This letter confirms the matters discussed with you at our meeting of (*date*). In attendance were (*names of Manager/Union Reps*). The purpose of this meeting was to discuss your attendance record.
>
> You have been counselled in the past about this matter. As recently as (*date*), you attended an interview with myself and (*names of other persons*). At that time, you were informed that we were concerned about your absenteeism and the importance of regular attendance at work was strongly emphasized.
>
> Since that interview you have been absent from work on (X) occasions for a total of (Y) days. Your apparent inability to attend to your duties on a regular basis is putting your continued employment with Coast Mountain Bus Company in serious jeopardy.
>
> A professional opinion as to the state of your health would assist all concerned in determining your future with Coast Mountain Bus Company. Therefore, we request that you contact our Occupational Health Nurse within five (5) working days from the date of this letter, [phone number provided] for the purpose of arranging a medical assessment, setting out your fitness to perform your work and your ability to maintain regular attendance in the future.

> The Company expects to receive your doctor's report within 30 days of today's date, following which another meeting with you will be scheduled to discuss the Company's expectations for your attendance. If you choose not to provide a medical assessment, the Company may not have full information regarding your medical status and will be forced to rely solely on your attendance history to determine your future employability.
>
> If you have any questions or concerns about this matter, I can be reached at __________. If you wish to utilize the confidential support services of the Employee Assistance Plan [phone number provided], please feel free to contact them directly. (p. 21)

133 Where the employee chooses to comply with the request for a medical assessment, the OHG provides a questionnaire to them to provide to their doctor, which is to be returned to the OHG after it is completed.

134 The purpose of the assessment is to provide information with respect to whether there is a medical condition which would prevent the employee from performing their job duties as a transit operator, or from attending work on a regular and consistent basis. Ms. Lopez summarized the types of questions asked in the questionnaires as follows: what the employee's capabilities are (can the employee perform the full duties of the job); does the employee require accommodation; what are the employee's limitations and restrictions; and whether there is anything restricting the employee from attending work on a regular and consistent basis.

135 After the OHG receives the completed assessment, an OHN will e-mail information distilled from that assessment to the employee's Supervisor. In general, the information provided to the Supervisor includes whether the employee is able to attend work or not, and, if so, whether the employee is able to continue in their own occupation.

136 If the report from the doctor indicates that there is no chronic medical disability issue, or that there is a disability that should not affect future attendance, CMBC advises the employee that no relevant disability has been identified and therefore no accommodation is required. At that point, CMBC outlines the attendance parameters applicable to the employee. Mr. Kelly testified that, where an employee has been cleared to work as a transit operator, he assumes that the clearance includes the medical opinion that the individual is capable of regular attendance: *i.e.*, meeting or beating the average attendance rate.

137 Conversely, if the report indicates that there is some chronic medical issue, the OHG will have a discussion with the employee about what the doctor's report says about accommodation, and will explore those options with the employee.

138 In circumstances where limitations and restrictions have been identified by the employee's physician, the OHG will approach the employee's Super-

visor to see if they could accommodate them. The employee may be assigned to temporary alternate work while other options are explored. Mr. Kelly testified that sometimes employees decline accommodation, but that does not diminish the employee's requirement to provide regular attendance in their particular job.

139 In cross-examination, Ms. Lopez was asked whether the fact that an employee has had persistently high absenteeism would, in and of itself, raise the issue of whether some accommodation was required. She replied that it would not. For example, the OHG may not have any medical documentation that accommodation is required, or the employee may have refused accommodation. Ms. Lopez was then asked if OHNs write to an employee's doctor with information about attendance rates and ask whether, given the employee's medical condition, accommodation would be required with respect to these rates. Ms. Lopez stated that this was not the process. Rather, where it is appropriate, an OHN will enquire from the doctor if accommodation is required where an employee is unable to return to work. Ms. Lopez further stated that, if the medical information indicates that the employee is able to return to work, there is no need for an accommodation.

c. 2004 Guide: Level 3.Medical Assessment Follow-Up

140 The 2004 Guide states the following with respect to processing the information contained in the medical assessment:

> A discussion among the employee's supervisor, Manager, the OHN, Labour Relations and the Attendance Management Committee should occur as soon as possible after receipt of the requested medical assessment. If an ongoing medical disability is identified, this same group will attempt to resolve any accommodation issues arising. If an accommodation is made, involving alternate work, the arrangements for same will be handled by the appropriate person in the Human Resources Health group.
>
> If a chronic medical disability is not indicated, the group will assess other comments, treatments or health-regimen recommendations made by the medical practitioner and determine the appropriate corporate attendance expectations to be conveyed to the employee. (p. 17)

141 Similarly, in the Notice, CMBC made the following statements about the Level 3 process:

> ... Generally, where the medical information indicates that the employee has no chronic or ongoing medical conditions, the employee will be expected to meet the rate of attendance of his/her employee group. ...
>
> On the other hand, if the medical information indicates that the employee has a medical disability, CMBC will explore opportunities for accommodation of that employee. CMBC has a corporate policy dealing with accommodation of employees with medical disabilities. ...

142 After the information is assessed, the Supervisor arranges a meeting with the employee for the Level 3 interview. At this interview, CMBC communicates its attendance expectations and the possible consequences to the employee of being unable to meet those expectations. The interview is confirmed in writing to the employee.

143 As outlined in the sample letter in the Guide, the Level 3 letter sets out the history of the employee's attendance interviews, and indicates what the OHN has advised about the results of the medical assessment (*i.e.*, whether or not the employee's doctor reported a chronic medical condition, and whether it affects the employee's ability to work). If the results of the medical assessment indicate that there is no medical condition, or that the medical condition should not prevent regular attendance, the employee's attendance record is reviewed and compared with the annual average rate. Attendance parameters are then provided to the employee, in the following terms:

> Without intending to suggest that any particular rate of absenteeism is acceptable, and after reviewing the particular circumstances of your case, Coast Mountain Bus Co. expects you to maintain an attendance performance that is at least equal to the average for employees in your group. Specifically, Coast Mountain expects that you will not be absent more than __________ days per year, for a period of two years.
>
> If, at any time between (*date of #3 interview and date one year hence*), or between (*date one year hence and date 2 years hence*), your absenteeism exceeds __________ days, Coast Mountain Bus Co. will conduct a review of your employment status. Under consideration at such a review will be whether or not to terminate your employment for excessive, non-culpable absenteeism. (p. 22)

144 In addition, the letter notes that CMBC will continue to monitor the employee's attendance in order to assess their overall ability to attend work on a regular and consistent basis. Staying within the prescribed number of days during the assessment period is stated not to be acceptable if it is achieved without due regard to the frequency of the absences. The employee is advised that absence frequency in the transit operator group averages less than two per employee, per year.

145 The letter ends:

> You have now been clearly advised that continued, excessive absenteeism could result in the termination of your employment. We sincerely hope that you are able to use this opportunity to demonstrate your ability to attend at work, in the future, on a consistent and regular basis, by meeting the expectations outlined above. (p. 22)

146 Mr. Jones testified that, despite the fact that CMBC would ask for a medical assessment at Level 2 stage, in his experience, moving to Level 2 invariably led to also moving to Level 3 with parameters being imposed. In other words, Mr. Jones testified that, despite the request for a medical assessment, CMBC would not exercise any discretion in imposing parameters

on an employee at this level. Further, those parameters were always the same: the average attendance rate for transit operators.

147 Mr. Kelly also testified that, despite the statement that such parameters are imposed .after reviewing the particular circumstances. of each case, the attendance parameters imposed at Level 3 are always based on the average absenteeism rate for transit operators. In the time period covered by the evidence, the parameters have ranged from 17 to 24 days in a 12-month period, depending on what the average employee absenteeism rate was at the time.

148 The Union took issue with the manner in which information from the medical assessment was interpreted and communicated to Supervisors by the OHNs. Examples of this will be discussed below with reference to the experiences of specific employees. When Ms. Lopez was questioned about the role of OHNs in this regard, she stated that the information in question comes from the employee's physician, and is simply passed on by the OHN in a manner that maintains the employee's confidentiality to the greatest degree possible. She stated that, if there was something in the information that was unclear, an OHN would seek clarification from the doctor.

d. 2006 Guide: Advanced Concern Stage

149 As noted above, the 2006 Guide provides for a somewhat revised process. There was, however, no evidence before me with respect to the practice under the 2006 Guide. Pursuant to the 2006 Guide, the specific process followed varies depending on whether there is any indication that the employee has an ongoing medical condition or disability. In cases where there is no indication that an employee has an ongoing medical condition or disability, the Level 2/3 process is, in essence, collapsed. No medical assessment is sought, and the employee is simply placed on parameters.

150 The two-stage process is, however, retained in cases where CMBC has some knowledge that the employee may have a disability or chronic medical condition.

151 In either case, pursuant to the 2006 Guide, an .Advanced Concern. interview should be held where an employee's attendance remains unacceptable following two or more attendance interviews.

152 Where there is no indication that the employee has an ongoing medical condition or disability, the Supervisor will conduct another formal interview where parameters will be set in accordance with the peer group average. At this stage, the employee is also strongly cautioned that their ongoing employment could be in jeopardy if they are unable to meet those targets.

153 Mr. Kelly testified that two management employees will attend this interview on behalf of CMBC. One will have the discussion with the em-

ployee, while the other will take notes. The employee is told that they are at a very serious stage. They have had a lengthy period of unacceptable attendance, and at least two previous discussions of their attendance without any improvement. The employee is advised that it may be in their interest to talk to their doctor about CMBC's concern regarding their attendance. Specific attendance parameters are set for the employee, and the employee is advised that the purpose of these parameters is to assess whether they are capable of providing regular attendance in the future.

154 Mr. Kelly was asked about the options open to an employee in such an interview to raise issues and concerns they may have. Mr. Kelly responded that an employee was free to tell CMBC anything they want. The purpose of the meeting is to advise the employee of CMBC's concern. The employee has the opportunity to say anything that will assist the Company in understanding the situation and in getting the employee to acceptable attendance.

155 Mr. Kelly stated that, in such an interview, where an employee raised disability related issues, they would be referred to an OHN, and the fact that this discussion took place, and the referral to an OHN, would be noted in the letter.

156 Following the interview, the employee is provided with a letter similar to the sample letter outlined in the 2006 Guide, which provides, in part:

> ***(Supervisors Note * The information in the following 2 paragraphs must accurately describe the circumstances relevant to the employee being discussed and must be approved by the OHN before this letter is issued.)*** The most recent information on your medical file, according to our Occupational Health Nurse (OHN), indicates that you are fit to perform your regular duties and that you do not have a medical condition requiring the Company to investigate accommodation options for you. On that basis, we have established specific attendance guidelines, as set out below, that are intended to measure your ability to maintain acceptable attendance in the future.
>
> If our information regarding your medical condition is incorrect or out of date, we urge you to contact our OHN immediately for the purpose of arranging to have your doctor respond to a questionnaire that would confirm your medical situation.
>
> .
>
> If forthcoming information changes our understanding of your medical condition, and/or our duty to accommodate you, the circumstances of your case will be reviewed.
>
> In the interim, however, it is our understanding that your medical fitness is sufficient to meet the attendance expectations outlined below, without an accommodation.
>
> Our records show that (from the date of the last interview or in the latest 12-month period, or you recently returned from a lengthy absence, etc. whichever is appropriate) you were absent on __________ occasions for a total of __________ compressed-work days and __________ regular days. In addition, our records show that your pattern of excessive absenteeism has persisted for several years. Since

> __________ your absenteeism has averaged __________ days per year. (Combined WCB, STD and LTD).
>
> In comparison, absenteeism among all other employees in your group, in the preceding 12-month period, averaged __________ regular days or __________ compressed-work days (based on combined WCB, STD and LTD up to one year).
>
> On that basis, and taking into account the particular circumstances of your case, CMBC expects that you will not be absent more than __________ days per year, for the next 2 years.
>
> If, at any time between *(date of #3 interview and date one year hence)*, or between *(date one year hence and date two years hence)*, you are absent more than __________ regular days or __________ compressed-work days, Coast Mountain Bus Company may conduct a review of your employment status, at which time termination of your employment for excessive, non-culpable absenteeism, will be considered.
>
> .
>
> If I can offer you any assistance towards this goal, please let me know. ... If you wish to utilize the confidential support services of the Employee Assistance Plan [telephone number provided], please feel free to contact them. (pp. 18-19)

157 Mr. Kelly testified that, with respect to the part of the letter in which the employee's attendance record is recounted, the description of the date range chosen to outline the attendance record is determined by the facts of the case. For example, if the date of the last interview was eight months ago, it would not be appropriate to use the last 12-month period as a benchmark. It would be more appropriate to use the period of time since the last interview. Alternatively, if an employee had experienced a lengthy absence of 9-10 months, it would not be useful to talk about days absent, but rather the length of the absence in months.

158 The letter sets out two one-year assessment periods. If an employee is not able to meet attendance parameters set out in either of the two one-year periods, the Company may conduct an ESR, and may terminate the employee's employment.

159 In contrast to this process, in cases where it is strongly indicated that an employee may have an ongoing medical condition or disability, the Guide states that .it may be more appropriate to request that the employee have his/her doctor fill out the questionnaire before establishing any attendance targets.. (p. 14)

160 In such cases, the 2006 Guide provides the following form of letter to be used:

> This letter confirms the matters discussed with you at our meeting on (date). In attendance were (names of Manager/Union Reps). The purpose of the meeting was to discuss your attendance since our pervious discussion on (date).
>
> Since that interview (or in the last 12 months, or whatever description is appropriate to the circumstances) you have been absent from work on (x) occasions for the total

of (y) days. Our concern is that your ability to attend regularly at work in the future, could be compromised if positive steps are not taken to identify and address any underlying contributing factors.

We accept that your absences have been caused by legitimate medical problems; however, we would like to determine the following:

If you have any previously undiagnosed conditions contributing to your absenteeism;

If reasonable health regimens or medical treatments are available that could help prevent or delay the onset of predictable health problems and improve your attendance in the future; and/or

If the overall condition of your health is sufficient to meet the demands of your job.

Therefore, we urge you to contact our Occupational Health department at [number], before noon on (date), to arrange for you to take a medical questionnaire to your treating physician for completion. Your compliance with our request is voluntary but without it, any decisions regarding your ongoing employment will be made on the basis of the information we have on file and your attendance history.

If you agree to our request, we will expect the completed questionnaire to be returned within 30 days of today's date. Your personal medical information is kept strictly confidential in our Occupational Health department. It will not be shared with Management staff unless you provide written consent to do so.

Following receipt of the requested information, I will schedule another meeting to discuss you circumstances and the Company's expectations. (pp. 20-21)

161 If the employee contacts an OHN, and obtains a medical assessment, the procedure followed is the same as that outlined in the 2004 Guide.

e. Employment Status Review

162 Under both the 2004 and 2006 revisions of the Guide, an ESR may be conducted when an employee who has been prescribed attendance parameters has exceeded those parameters.

163 Mr. Kelly testified that exceeding Level 3 parameters does not inexorably lead to the ESR process. For example, where the absence that causes the employee to exceed the parameters relates to a WCB assault or motor vehicle accident, the ESR process will not be triggered. Mr. Kelly also testified about other cases where exceeding Level 3 parameters did not lead to an ESR, some of which will be outlined later in this decision.

164 Mr. Kelly testified that the purpose of such a review is to enable CMBC to determine what the next step should be in the management of the employee, and to assess whether accommodation issues need to be dealt with. CMBC is trying to determine whether or not the absences that caused the employee to exceed the parameters are a reliable indicator of what the employee's attendance might look like in future, and to assess whether the employee has been given an appropriate opportunity to demonstrate regular attendance.

165 Where it is decided that an ESR is appropriate, the meeting is attended by a number of very senior management employees, including the responsible Director (for operations, the Director of Service Delivery), Manager and/or Supervisor, as well as representatives from Labour Relations, Occupational Health, and Corporate Attendance Management, who together comprise the Employment Status Review Committee (.ESRC.). In addition, Ms. Lopez testified that the OHN involved would attend the meeting, and sometimes so would she. At the meeting, information relating to the employee's attendance is reviewed, including the following:

- The attendance record (most recent five years);
- Reasons given for absences;
- Supervisor notes of attendance related interviews;
- Copies of related correspondence with the employee; and
- Relevant information forwarded through the OHN.

166 The OHN will provide information relating to the employee's prognosis, advise whether the employee has any disabilities, and advise whether accommodation issues have been explored or rejected. This information will again be given on a general basis only, so as to respect confidentiality concerns. The OHN will then leave the meeting before any decisions are made.

167 Mr. Kelly testified that the ESRC considers whether there are disability and accommodation issues arising from the employee's situation. On the basis of the review, the ESRC may take a number of steps. For example, the ESRC may ask for more medical information and delay any decisions until such information is received; it might decide that termination at the current time is not appropriate; or it might decide that termination is appropriate. According to the Guide, the ESRC may also make recommendations regarding alternate employment and/or amended attendance expectations for a specified period of time. Where the employee remains employed, their attendance will continue to be monitored for adherence to any specified attendance expectations. Any further indications, within the specified period, of an inability to maintain acceptable attendance, may cause a re-initiation of the ESR process.

F. Employee Experience with the AMP

168 Both CMBC and the Union provided evidence with respect to the experience of employees within the AMP. As noted above, the Union called 12 transit operators to testify about their experiences. Mr. Jones also gave evidence for the Union with respect to his experience dealing with operators

involved in the AMP. CMBC's evidence in this regard was given by Mr. Kelly.

169 In general, the Union sought to show that the AMP was applied mechanistically, and inexorably processed disabled operators towards termination. CMBC's evidence, in contrast, sought to highlight the discretion and flexibility provided for in the AMP.

170 Below, I will first outline the overall statistics provided by Mr. Kelly. I will then consider the Union's evidence relating to the experience of individual transit operators, followed by CMBC's evidence.

1. Statistics

171 Mr. Kelly testified about the number of transit operators who can be considered to be .on. the AMP.

172 First, Mr. Kelly testified that the number of transit operators discussed at quarterly meetings has ranged from 370 to 576. For the period of April to June 2006, the most recent period for which statistics were available, there were 530 Local 111 operators discussed.

173 Of the 530 operators discussed at quarterly meetings in June 2006, only 293 could be considered as being .on. the AMP. Of these, 123 were at the informal stage: 115 were at Level 1; 1 was at Level 2; and 30 were at Level 3. In addition, 24 were at some other point in the process. From 2000 to 2006, the number of transit operators on the AMP at any given time has ranged from 235 to 366.

174 Mr. Kelly testified that 11 transit operators have been terminated as the end result of the AMP process. All 11 terminations were grieved, and six operators were subsequently reinstated (either as the result of an arbitration award, or as a resolution to the grievance prior to arbitration). At least one employee who was reinstated is no longer employed by CMBC.

2. Union evidence relating to the experience of individual transit operators

175 As previously discussed, where individuals testified directly at the hearing, I will identify them by their full names in this decision. Where evidence was given about specific employees, but those employees did not testify, I will refer to the employees by their employee number.

176 Mr. Jones testified in general terms about his experience representing transit operators with respect to the AMP. He stated that those transit operators frequently feel intimidated, and under pressure to perform. Some have expressed suicidal thoughts to him. Many have told him that they have

come to work sick, injured, or under the influence of medication, to avoid being recorded as absent.

177 Mr. Jones testified that the Union viewed the AMP as a discriminatory and flawed policy. He stated that there is no accommodation process incorporated within the AMP in practice. While the Guide may pay lip service to accommodation, that is not reflected in the practice.

178 Mr. Jones conceded that some operators have been accommodated within the AMP, but said that in the vast majority of cases there is no individual assessment or accommodation, and no meaningful accommodation alternatives. In addition, CMBC has failed to consider the issues underlying high absenteeism.

a. Cynthia Cable

179 Ms. Cable was employed by CMBC from June 1993 until April 2005. Her level of absenteeism was a concern to the Company from at least 1996. During the period from 1996 to the termination of her employment in 2005, her rate of absenteeism ranged from a low of 11.41% to a high of 93.68% of her scheduled work hours in a year.

180 Ms. Cable has suffered from at least three disabilities during her employment: two physical (a chronic heart condition known as patent ductus arteriosus, and cervical spondylosis). In addition she suffers from a mental disability which has been variously diagnosed as depression, cyclothemia, dysthemia and borderline personality disorder.

181 Ms. Cable was absent from July 6, 1998 to June 25, 1999 for investigation into two dizzy spells. The cause was not definitively diagnosed. Ms. Cable was off work again from December 27, 1999 until November 15, 2001 for pneumonia, followed by the investigation and treatment of her heart condition. It took some time to diagnose this condition, but Ms. Cable had surgery in 2001. She testified that she continues to have problems with arrhythmia. Following the surgery, Ms. Cable entered an acute depression.

182 When Ms. Cable returned to work in November 2001, it was on a GRTW. On January 11, 2002, shortly following her return to work on a full-time basis, Ms. Cable had an informal discussion with her Supervisor regarding the AMP. In April 2002, she was denied admission into line supervisor training as a result of her attendance history. In August 2002, Ms. Cable was placed on Level 1 of the AMP. At that time, CMBC noted that she had been absent from work for 25 days on three occasions over the past 12 months.

183 After the Level 1 meeting, Ms. Cable contacted an OHN, asking for her support to be removed from the AMP, given her disabilities. The OHN told her that she would provide such support when Ms. Cable was at Level 2 of

the AMP, and her doctor returned a medical questionnaire stating that she had chronic medical conditions.

184 On January 19, 2003, Ms. Cable attempted suicide. She was absent from work until May 16, 2003, suffering from depression.

185 Before allowing Ms. Cable to return to work, CMBC required her to undergo an IME, which was conducted in April 2003. The report indicated that Ms. Cable was fit to return to work, and she did so the following month.

186 Shortly thereafter, on July 7, 2003, Ms. Cable had a Level 2 meeting. At that meeting, her Supervisor noted that, since August 2002, she had been absent from work on two occasions for a total of 90 regular days and 25 part-time days. She was asked to provide a medical assessment, which she did shortly thereafter.

187 Neither party provided me with a copy of the medical assessment, but it appears to have identified two medical conditions: a chronic heart condition with arrhythmias, and borderline personality disorder; and it stated that Ms. Cable had permanent physical impairments/disabilities but was capable of unrestricted work as a transit operator. The medical questionnaire did not ask whether Ms. Cable's chronic medical conditions would affect her ability to attend work on a regular basis.

188 On August 29, 2003, Ms. Cable had a Level 3 meeting. In the letter given to Ms. Cable after that meeting, her Supervisor noted the following:

> The doctor you attended forwarded the results of your medical assessment to our Occupational Health Nurse who, in turn, advised us that you have a chronic medical condition. However, we are further advised that the condition does not require an accommodation and should not prevent you from performing your job duties as a Transit Operator or from attending work on a regular and consistent basis.

189 The letter went on to state that, in the last 12-month period, Ms. Cable's absence rate had been 47.26%, based on three absences for a total of 118 days. It is not clear on the evidence before me whether the .25 part-time days. referred to in the Level 2 letter were subsequently considered as full-time absences.

190 As a result, Ms. Cable was placed on parameters for two years, with a target of 18 days of absence per year (the annual average rate of absenteeism at the time).

191 On September 16, 2003, the Union grieved Ms. Cable's placement in Level 3 of the AMP. CMBC denied the grievance, stating that the OHN had informed CMBC that, although Ms. Cable had chronic medical conditions, her physician did not believe they prevented her from performing the unrestricted duties of a transit operator and attending work on a regular and consistent basis.

192 Also in September 2003, Ms. Cable asked for accommodation for a pinched nerve and possible cervical spondylosis in her neck. From December 2003 to April 2004, Ms. Cable elected to drive a route serviced by a diesel bus, rather than the trolley routes which she otherwise preferred. She found the steering, and other aspects of the diesel bus, easier to cope with.

193 In April 2004, CMBC accommodated Ms. Cable by allowing her to drive a diesel bus on a route normally serviced by trolley buses. However, CMBC understood that, in the future, Ms. Cable would sign up for a designated diesel route to assist in accommodating her condition. On June 1, 2004, Ms. Cable's Supervisor provided her with a letter which stated:

> Eventually, although the Company was able to accommodate you for the April sheet by putting a diesel on your trolley work, the Company will be unable to continue this arrangement. Therefore, at the May sign-up and all subsequent sign-ups, as long as you are subject to your doctor's instructions that you are restricted to diesel buses, you will be required to sign diesel work. In light of your seniority, you should have no difficulty signing diesel work at the Oakridge Transit Centre. Alternatively, such work is also available to you at all of the Company's other depots, and you may exercise your seniority to transfer to another depot, where all of the work is diesel.

194 Thus, Ms. Cable's Supervisor advised her that she would have to sign for diesel work, and that she would not be accommodated on a trolley run. The Supervisor noted that any duty to accommodate owed by CMBC carried a corresponding duty on her part to facilitate the accommodation, and, in this case, CMBC felt that included signing for diesel work.

195 Ms. Cable objected to this as undermining her seniority rights. She testified that CMBC wanted her to sign for work outside of her seniority rights, that is, sign for a diesel route instead of the route of her choice. In addition, she stated that her .medical community. was located in the downtown core, and this made the trolley routes the most convenient for her.

196 Also in June 2004, CMBC agreed that an investigator would conduct an independent investigation into a number of complaints brought by Ms. Cable, including a complaint of harassment and discrimination relating to the AMP, the outstanding AMP grievance, and a human rights complaint filed by Ms. Cable which related to her removal from the line supervisor training.

197 The first year at Level 3, from 2003 to 2004, Ms. Cable was absent for 26 days. Her employment was not terminated at that time. The second year at Level 3, from 2004 to 2005, she was absent for 24 days.

198 Ms. Cable testified that the absences she had while on Level 3 related to her cervical spondylosis, as well as a root canal that aggravated her arthritis, followed by a bout of the flu. She also testified that she took several steps to avoid exceeding the parameters set for her. For example, she booked off without pay for medical procedures.

199 During the course of one of Ms. Cable's absences, an OHN suggested to the management group that CMBC offer Ms. Cable a permanent accommodation in an alternate position. Ms. Cable was provided with a letter to that effect on June 24, 2004. In that letter, Ms. Cable was asked to contact the OHN by July 5. If she did not, CMBC would assume that she was not interested in participating in a search for an accommodation in an alternate position. Ms. Cable returned to work two days after the letter was sent. She did not contact the OHN with respect to any potential accommodations.

200 On March 4, 2005, CMBC provided Ms. Cable with a letter which noted that she had exceeded her parameters. The letter stated:

> On the basis of medical information supplied by your doctor(s), our Occupational Health department has suggested that alternate work may be an option for you to explore to enable you to attend work on a regular and consistent basis. However, you have not participated in previous efforts to discuss alternate accommodation options and you did not respond to a letter dated June 24, 2004 from S. Hentzen, Director Employment Services, in which you were asked to participate in the accommodation process.

201 CMBC indicated that it was not prepared to continue to tolerate Ms. Cable's level of absenteeism, and that it would be conducting a review of the circumstances of her case for the purpose of identifying any further accommodation options that would enable her to attend work on a regular and consistent basis.

202 In her testimony, Ms. Cable stated that she believes that CMBC wanted to offer her another position (*i.e.*, not as a transit operator). However, the Union advised her not to discuss this option, as she was not disabled from her own occupation, and she loved her job.

203 Meanwhile, on November 17, 2004, the investigation report into Ms. Cable's various complaints was released. The findings in that report included the following:

- CMBC did not discriminate against Ms. Cable by placing her in the AMP;
- CMBC has an ongoing duty to accommodate Ms. Cable's cardiac and mental disabilities within the AMP when it receives specific information from her specialists about her needs in that regard. The Company must make it clear to Ms. Cable exactly what information they require from her specialists. Ms. Cable has an obligation to provide that information to the OHN;
- CMBC has an ongoing duty to accommodate Ms. Cable's cervical arthritis by allowing her to perform work within her physical capabilities;
- In the past, CMBC has not met its duty to accommodate Ms. Cable's cardiac and mental disabilities within the AMP; and

- CMBC was meeting its duty to accommodate Ms. Cable's cervical arthritis. Ms. Cable had not met her duty to cooperate in the search for a suitable accommodation of her condition.

204 Ms. Cable testified that she did not receive any information about the investigation report until March 18, 2005, when she and her Union representatives met with the Company to discuss the findings.

205 As a result of that meeting, Ms. Cable was asked to provide additional medical information to Ms. Hentzen, so that the Company could assess her current limitations and restrictions, and consider appropriate accommodations.

206 On April 1, 2005, Ms. Cable e-mailed Ms. Hentzen with a number of concerns, including concerns about some of the information requested. Ms. Hentzen replied to Ms. Cable in a letter dated April 13, 2005, reiterating the need for Ms. Cable to provide all of the information sought by CMBC. In addition, CMBC sought an IME with respect to Ms. Cable's psychiatric condition. Ms. Hentzen indicated that the information should be provided by May 2, 2005, and that Ms. Cable should contact an OHN to schedule the IME appointment by April 22. The letter concluded:

> If we don't hear from you by these dates, we will not be in a position to accommodate your continuing request to sign a trolley route and be assigned a diesel bus. With respect to the current sign-up, the Company has provided you with a diesel bus on your trolley route even though the OHN does not currently possess medical information which indicates that such an accommodation is necessary. The Company has allowed this as part of our good faith efforts to canvass all necessary accommodation options. However, we require you to provide medical information at this time to support that the accommodation you have requested is necessary. If such information is not provided, you will no longer be assigned a diesel bus on a trolley route.

207 Ms. Cable objected to the request for a psychiatric IME. She stated in her testimony that she didn't see any reason for it, as two years had passed since her major psychiatric problems. No one explained to her why it was necessary. As a result, she asked for a further meeting to discuss the issue, but that request was never responded to.

208 On April 28, 2005, Ms. Cable's Supervisor wrote to her terminating her employment as a result of her excessive, non-culpable absenteeism. The Supervisor referenced Ms. Cable's .persistent absenteeism., and stated that CMBC had determined that all reasonable efforts to accommodate her disabilities had been exhausted, and she was unlikely to be able to fulfill her employment obligations in the future.

209 Ms. Cable testified that, while she had not met the parameters imposed by CMBC, her attendance had improved during her two-year monitoring period, and that she had only exceeded the parameters by a relatively small margin.

210 The Union grieved the termination. In the letter denying this grievance, CMBC stated:

> The medical information provided to the Company was that Ms. Cable's disabilities could be accommodated if she were to drive only diesel coaches. Through several sign-up periods, the Company accommodated Ms. Cable by providing a diesel coach on the trolley work she insisted on signing. Ms. Cable repeatedly ignored the Company's request that she co-operate in the accommodation process by signing diesel work. This resulted in cost and disruption to the Company. Notwithstanding that Ms. Cable was provided with diesel coaches, she was unable to meet the attendance parameters set out for her during a 2-year assessment period.
>
> .
>
> Before Ms. Cable's employment question was decided, a final review was undertaken. The findings in regard to her medical condition were that she had many different ailments contributing to her absenteeism. The Company had exhausted all reasonable efforts to accommodate her disabilities with little cooperation from Ms. Cable. The Company considered that it was unlikely that Ms. Cable would be able to fulfil her employment obligations in the future, by attending at work on a regular and consistent basis.

211 Ms. Cable testified that, prior to the termination of her employment, she was never told that if she failed to sign for diesel work she would be terminated. If she had been, she would have signed for such work and then grieved it. Further, CMBC had never raised the issue of cost and disruption to it as a result of the diesel issue. Finally, she testified that, while the letter refers to .different ailments., the bulk of her absences were caused by three diagnosed chronic conditions.

212 The Union's grievance was dismissed at arbitration: *National Automobile, Aerospace, Transportation and General Workers of Canada (CAW.Canada), Local 111 v. Coast Mountain Bus Company*, unreported decision, May 26, 2006 (Dorsey). The arbitrator found that, while the decision to dismiss Ms. Cable was *prima facie* discriminatory, CMBC had met its duty to accommodate her to the point of undue hardship. The arbitrator stated:

> The watchword for the disabled employee from the Supreme Court of Canada in the process of finding an accommodation is facilitating, not combating.
>
> .
>
> Ms. Cable's conduct was not to make suggestions. It was to dictate the one and only accommodation acceptable to her ...
>
> Ms. Cable firmly and successfully resisted all suggestions and efforts to explore or consider accommodation in suitable alternate employment from September 2003. She was adamant she was staying in her own job and, except for one sign-up, she was unwilling to make any concession to the full exercise of her personal choice by signing-up for a trolley route. She forced the entire obligation was on the employer to make the necessary operational changes to provide her with a diesel bus for a trolley route regardless of the reason the route was a trolley route or the inconvenience to the employer or public.

.

The employer was not able to successfully fulfil its duty to accommodate Ms. Cable after September 2003 because she .went to war. with the employer. The employer made concessions to allow her to drive a diesel bus on a trolley route in anticipation she would later sign-up for a diesel route. She did not.

.

The employer was actively, honestly and in good faith seeking to discharge its duty to accommodate Ms. Cable, who was failing to facilitate a search for an appropriate and reasonable accommodation. She was frustrating the process. (pp. 41-3, reproduced as written)

b. Virginia Young

213 Ms. Young started her employment at CMBC in 1990. During her employment with CMBC, she worked out of both the North Vancouver and Burnaby depots.

214 In early 1998, Ms. Young had a Level 1 interview. Her attendance improved thereafter, but in May 2000, Ms. Young experienced a recurrence of a previous back injury, resulting in a prolonged absence from work.

215 On August 3, 2000, Ms. Young's Supervisor sent an e-mail to Mr. Kelly, asking for direction. He stated that he was planning on doing another Level 1 interview with Ms. Young, but wanted to know if he could do a .Level 1 with conditions., due to her previous Level 1. Mr. Kelly responded by reviewing her history, and stating:

> I agree that she should be interviewed again at Level #1, but not before you talk to the OHN to determine her RTW status and whether or not her current absence is related to a chronic disability, or is a one-off situation. And although I don't think there are any conditions we can impose in order to escalate the gravity of the Level #1, it might be useful, at the Level #1 interview, to state the concerns you've raised and that CMBC is paying close attention to the uniqueness of her case.

216 Ms. Young returned to work in mid-January 2001 on a GRTW basis. She started off working two hours a day, and increased to full-time by the end of the month. At that time, her Supervisor met with her and provided her with a Level 1 letter. The Union filed a grievance with respect to this letter, which was denied by CMBC in the following terms:

> The Company has acknowledged that an absence from an isolated illness or injury will be counted in an employee's absence rate but will not cause an employee to be introduced into the Program or into the next level of the Program. However, the Company's interpretation of this is that the illness or injury must be truly .isolated.. In other words, the Employee's Attendance Record was always good in the past so that the one illness or injury alone would not cause the employee to be introduced into the Program or into the next level. It is the Company's position that the absence at issue in Operator Young's case is not a truly .isolated. absence as Operator Young's overall absenteeism problems did not result from that one isolated absence alone.

217 Ms. Young's attendance did not improve to the satisfaction of CMBC. From February to December 2001, Ms. Young was absent on four separate occasions for a total of 19.5 days. Ms. Young attributed the bulk of these absences to ongoing back problems. She testified that she often reported to work in pain, as she felt she had no option, given her placement on the AMP.

218 On December 20, 2001, Ms. Young attended a Level 2 interview, at which she was asked about any continuing problems, in response to which she stated that she did not have a medical problem at that time. In her testimony, she stated that she was unable to give a clear answer about the nature of any continuing problem, because she didn't have any answers. She testified that her Supervisor was well aware of her situation and her back problems.

219 The Supervisor's notes of that meeting indicate that Ms. Young stated that she was not seeking professional assistance. Ms. Young testified, however, that she was asked if she was under a doctor's care, and had responded yes. She also testified that she did not recall being asked if she was seeking professional assistance, and was not sure what that term meant.

220 Ms. Young testified that, at the Level 2 meeting, she was advised that, unless she was able to provide evidence of a diagnosed chronic medical condition, and a prognosis for regular attendance in the future, continuation of excessive absenteeism would likely result in non-culpable termination. The Supervisor's notes also indicate that Ms. Young was advised that employees who cannot return to their normal work assignment, either temporarily or permanently, because of a legitimate disability may be accommodated through retraining, rehabilitation or alternate work programs. Ms. Young testified that she could not recall whether that was raised with her or not. Ms. Young agreed that she was advised to contact an OHN within five working days to set up an appointment to obtain a confidential medical assessment. She did so.

221 The Company reviewed the medical assessment, and held a Level 3 meeting with Ms. Young. In the Level 3 letter, dated January 31, 2002, CMBC stated:

> The doctor you attended forwarded the results of your medical assessment to our Occupational Health Nurse who, in turn, advised us that you do not have a medical condition which would prevent you from performing your job duties as a Transit Operator or from attending work on a regular and consistent basis.

222 Ms. Young was placed on parameters, in the following terms:

> ... the annual average rate of absenteeism among all other employees in your group, for the last 12 months, is 9.6%, which equates to 25 regular 7.5-hour days or 20 compressed 9.4-hour days (based on combined WCB, STD and LTD up to one year).

> Without intending to suggest that any particular rate of absenteeism is acceptable, and after reviewing the particular circumstances of your case, Coast Mountain Bus Company expects you to maintain an attendance performance that is at least equal to the average for employees in your group. ...
>
> If at any time between January 29, 2002 and January 29, 2003, or between January 29, 2003 and January 29, 2004, your absenteeism exceeds the equivalent of 25 regular 7.5-hour days or 20 compressed 9.4-hour days, Coast Mountain Bus Company will conduct a review of your employment status. Under consideration at such a review will be whether or not to terminate your employment for excessive, non-culpable absenteeism.

223 In September 2002, Ms. Young experienced a recurrence of her back problems, and booked off work. By October 16, 2002, she had exceeded the attendance parameters. On the same date, Mike McComber, the manager of the North Vancouver depot, wrote a memo to the ESRC which included the following statement:

> The Union has been in several times to suggest that Operator Young is looking for an accommodation. Each time we have referred them to the OHN. To date neither the Union nor the Operator has followed up with the OHN.

224 The Union provided CMBC with a letter from Ms. Young's family doctor which stated:

> This patient is diagnosed with mild degenerative disc disease of the lumbar spine, sciatica and possible new disc herniation. This condition is aggravated by her job as a bus driver. I have enclosed a copy of Ms. Young's MRI report to further substantiate her condition. New disc herniation will be ruled out by a CT scan, which is pending.

225 The Union requested that CMBC delay any decision on Ms. Young's future until after this CT scan, in order to determine an appropriate accommodation for Ms. Young. However, on October 28, 2002, Ms. Young was terminated for non-culpable absenteeism.

226 The Union grieved the termination and the matter was set for arbitration in November 2003. In addition, Ms. Young filed a human rights complaint relating to her termination, but this complaint was deferred pending the outcome of the arbitration.

227 Shortly before the arbitration hearing, the parties agreed that Ms. Young would be reinstated and made whole. In addition, she would undergo an IME. If she was capable, she would be reinstated as a bus driver. If she was not physically capable of that job, the parties would search for an accommodated position. The arbitrator was to retain jurisdiction over the aspect of the settlement relating to accommodating her return to work.

228 Following her reinstatement, Ms. Young attempted to return to work as a transit operator, but this was not successful. By June 2004, Ms. Young realized that she could not return to bus driving, and sought an accommodation from CMBC.

229 In July 2004, Ms. Young underwent testing for a Customer Information Clerk position. Customer Information Clerks answer CMBC's information line and provide bus and route information, and take complaints. Ms. Young was informed that she had not successfully completed the testing.

230 On August 12, 2004, an OHN wrote to Ms. Young's family doctor, stating that CMBC was making efforts to place her in a suitable accommodation. He was provided with information about the Service Person, Building Service Worker and Utility Operator positions, and asked for information about whether Ms. Young could perform any of them. He replied that Ms. Young could perform the Utility Operator position.

231 Ms. Young was placed in the Utility Operator position. The position was scheduled to start on September 7, 2004. However, the placement was preceded by a three-day project which involved placing information into .info tubes. located at bus stops. Ms. Young participated in this project, but it aggravated her back injury. When she reported for work as a Utility Operator she experienced excruciating pain within three hours, and had to leave the job.

232 After the experience with the Utility Operator position, Ms. Young also discovered that she had received 81% on her Customer Information Clerk testing, where a passing mark was 82%. She was not offered the opportunity to retake the test, and was informed that she could not do so for six months.

233 Also, after the outcome of the Utility Operator posting, Ms. Young was asked to come in for clerical office testing. However, her doctor felt that her back was in too acute of a state to sit for any length of time.

234 On December 16, 2004, Ms. Young's employment was again terminated by CMBC. That termination was upheld at arbitration: *Coast Mountain Bus Co. v. National Automobile, Aerospace, Transportation and General Workers of Canada, Local 111 (Young Grievance)*, unreported decision, April 1, 2005 (Dorsey). The arbitrator held that he only had jurisdiction to determine whether CMBC fulfilled its duty to accommodate Ms. Young after her reinstatement, and that it had done so to the point of undue hardship.

235 In March 2006, Ms. Young's individual human rights complaint was dismissed on the basis that the substance of that complaint had been appropriately dealt with in the arbitration proceedings: *Young v. Coast Mountain Bus Co.*, 2006 BCHRT 149 (B.C. Human Rights Trib.).

c. Kevin Minch

236 Kevin Minch was employed by CMBC for just over 16 years, and normally worked out of the Burnaby Transit Centre. His employment was also terminated through the AMP.

237 Mr. Minch had ongoing high levels of absenteeism throughout his employment. From 1996 to 1999, he was absent between 39% and 98% of the time. Mr. Minch testified that his absences were due to a variety of problems including a number of surgeries for different reasons.

238 As a result of his absenteeism, Mr. Minch was given an informal interview in February 1999, and was placed on Level 1 on March 16, 2000. At that time, Mr. Minch had been absent from work for 60 days on two separate occasions over the preceding 12 months.

239 In 2000, Mr. Minch's absenteeism rate fell to 15.5%. In 2001, he had an absenteeism rate of almost 75% and, as a result, on November 26, 2001, he was advanced to Level 2 of the Program. In the letter confirming the Level 2 meeting, Mr. Minch's Operations Supervisor noted that, between the Level 1 and Level 2 interviews, Mr. Minch had been absent from work on two occasions for a total of 108 days. He was asked to provide a medical assessment, but did not do so.

240 Mr. Minch was advanced to Level 3 of the AMP on December 13, 2001. He was placed on parameters of 24 days for a two-year period. Because Mr. Minch worked a compressed work week (.CWW.), the applicable parameters were amended to 19 CWW days per year in a letter dated March 5, 2003. In that letter, CMBC noted that Mr. Minch had been absent 23 CWW days in the first year of the Level 3 parameters. However, since Mr. Minch had not been properly advised of the number of CWW days allowed, CMBC did not conduct an ESR. The letter also stated, with respect to the status of Mr. Minch's second year on parameters:

> Company attendance records show that since December 13, 2002, you have been absent from work for 4 complete CWW days, plus the absence-hours associated with a gradual return to work beginning on December 23, 2002. Those GRTW absence hours represent the difference between your hours worked and the 9.23 hours of a CWW day and total 142.78 absence hours, which equates to 15.2 CWW days. You resumed fulltime work on February 17, 2003, leaving you with 37.22 hours or 3.96 CWW days remaining before you would exceed the parameters set out in the December 13, 2001 letter.

241 Despite this, Mr. Minch successfully completed the second year of his monitoring period, and was removed from Level 3 on December 14, 2003. The letter acknowledging this was dated January 2, 2004, and noted that Mr. Minch would be monitored as if he were at Level 1 of the AMP for the next year.

242 From May to July 2004, Mr. Minch was absent as a result of a gall bladder operation. Mr. Minch was moved to Level 2 of the AMP on Octo-

ber 4, 2004. He was asked to provide a medical assessment, but it does not appear that he did so.

243 Shortly after being placed on Level 2, Mr. Minch was involved in an on-the-job motor vehicle accident, and suffered an injury to his collarbone which resulted in an absence from October to December of 2004. Mr. Minch testified that his doctor told him that the ligament holding his collar bone in place was stretched, and looser than it should be. The condition might eventually require surgery.

244 Mr. Minch was moved to Level 3 on March 3, 2005, and placed on parameters of 20 days of absence for two years. The Union grieved that action, but the grievance was denied.

245 In the second year of monitoring, Mr. Minch exceeded the parameters. Mr. Minch testified his absences during this period were largely the result of two concussions he suffered within six months in late 2005 and early 2006. Neither was work-related. Mr. Minch agreed that these were not his only absences, but they represented the majority of his absences.

246 The first concussion resulted in an absence of approximately three weeks. Mr. Minch was cleared to return to work in early November 2005. Partially as a result of this absence, Mr. Minch exceeded his Level 3 parameters. On November 16, 2005, CMBC provided him with a letter which advised him of that fact, and informed him that his employment status was under review. In addition, Mr. Minch was requested to provide CMBC with a medical assessment for this purpose. He did so. The medical assessment indicated that he did not have a chronic medical condition, or any temporary or permanent limitations or restrictions. However, his doctor did note the following:

> **4. Are you aware of any other medical reason(s) that would prevent Mr. Minch from attending work as a Transit Operator on a regular and consistent basis in the future?**
>
> Possible unpredictable events or trauma which aggravates his chronic left collar bone.breast bone joints laxity (i.e. popping out of joints). Unlikely under normal job duties and circumstances.

247 On January 17, 2006, CMBC wrote to Mr. Minch, advising that his employment would not be terminated:

> Although most of your absenteeism is unrelated to an ongoing disability, we are aware that you have one, ongoing medical condition. Notwithstanding the Company's willingness to conduct a search, the nature of your ongoing medical condition makes it unlikely that any accommodation would lead to an improvement in your attendance. Each time your ongoing condition resolves, you are cleared to return to work as a transit operator and you have not requested an accommodation. The latest information from your doctor is that you are able to work as a transit operator and that is your preference.

> Nevertheless, since alternate work opportunities do not seem to be a viable option, we are prepared to provide you with one final opportunity to demonstrate your ability to attend regularly at work.
>
> Your attendance will continue to be monitored and if you are unable to attain an acceptable level of attendance, going forward, we will again consider terminating your employment for persistent and excessive, non-culpable absenteeism.

248 Mr. Minch suffered the second concussion in April 2006, and was off work as a result from April 19 to May 7. He then attempted to return to work prior to being cleared by his doctor, because he was concerned about his status on the AMP. He drove for one shift, but he experienced dizziness, headaches, and a loud ringing in his ears. He testified that he may have phoned the OHN and explained his situation: that is, that he had a head injury but was concerned about his number of absences. She told him that he was not safe to drive and, as a result, placed him on TBQ status. Mr. Minch was then off work until May 24, 2006.

249 Mr. Minch started a three-week GRTW on May 25, 2006. On Monday, June 5, when he was starting his third week on that schedule, he received a phone call from his Supervisor. He was told not to report for work, as his employment status was being reviewed. He was later informed by his Union representative that CMBC planned to terminate his employment. That was approximately three days after the initial phone call from his Supervisor.

250 On June 8, 2006, Mr. Minch was formally advised that his employment with CMBC was terminated as a result of his persistent and unacceptable absenteeism. The Union grieved this termination, but it was upheld at arbitration, after Mr. Minch's testimony before me: *Coast Mountain Bus Company -and- Canadian Auto Workers, Local 111 (Kevin Minch Termination Grievance)*, unreported award, January 30, 2007 (Chertkow). The arbitrator found that Mr. Minch's absences which led to his termination were not caused by a .disability. for the purposes of the *Code*.

d. Christopher Watson

251 Mr. Watson has been employed by CMBC as a transit operator since July 1996. From 1998 to 2003, Mr. Watson had rates of absenteeism that were significantly in excess of the average. During this time, Mr. Watson was absent from work on many occasions due to a variety of illnesses, injuries and disabilities.

252 At the time he gave his evidence, Mr. Watson had recently suffered from a stroke, and was clearly not fully recovered. He was shown a copy of an arbitration award relating to his employment with CMBC: *Coast Mountain Bus Co. v. CAW-Canada, Local 111* [2004 CarswellBC 3608 (B.C. C.A.A.)], unreported decision, December 29, 2004 (Gordon). He tes-

tified that he agreed with the arbitrator's recounting of his employment history, and was not significantly challenged on those issues in cross-examination. Therefore, for the purposes of this decision, I will rely on the arbitrator's recounting of Mr. Watson's employment history.

253 In January 1998, Mr. Watson was placed on Level 1 of the AMP. The letter confirming his placement on Level 1 noted that he had been absent for a total of 16 days on four separate occasions over the past 12 months. It is not clear on the evidence why this triggered his initiation into the AMP, but it may be due to the fact that his frequency of absence was higher than the average. In any event, his placement into the AMP was not grieved.

254 Following his placement at Level 1, Mr. Watson had a high level of absenteeism in 1998, due largely to a work-related injury that resulted in pulled muscles in his neck and shoulder, and recurrences of this problem. He was off work for approximately a year, and returned on a GRTW.

255 In April 1999, Mr. Watson was driving his bus when he was cut off by another vehicle. He was forced to brake in order to avoid a collision. He felt a sharp pain in his chest and severe heart pounding. He was subsequently assessed by his physician, who reported his symptoms as: depression, anxiety, insomnia, lack of concentration and volatile temper. CMBC placed him on TBQ status. Mr. Watson returned to work in May 1999, after being off work for 23.5 days.

256 Shortly after his return to work, Mr. Watson experienced a recurrence of chest pain due to a similar traffic incident. He was again placed on TBQ status, and was absent for a further 27 days.

257 In August 1999, Mr. Watson was involved in a motor vehicle accident at work when a truck cut him off and struck his bus. Mr. Watson was off work for 21 days between August and November 1999 as a result of injuries resulting from this accident. In addition, he was absent for a further 40 days in 2000 as a result of ongoing neck/shoulder/back and other medical problems related to the 1999 accident. His WCB claim relating to these absences was denied, as the WCB found Mr. Watson's injuries to be related to a pre-existing condition.

258 In late June 2000, Mr. Watson sustained another work-related injury to his shoulder and back. He was absent 29.5 days and spent 23 days on a GRTW on modified duties.

259 On September 12, 2000, Mr. Watson was driving his bus when one of his passengers told him that another passenger was carrying a bomb on the bus. Mr. Watson contacted Transit Communications (.T-Comm.) who advised him to .carry on. driving, and that a Supervisor would meet with him on his route. This never occurred. Eventually, the passenger who was reportedly carrying the bomb disembarked.

260 Mr. Watson was extremely disturbed by this incident, and by T-Comm's response to it. He subsequently booked off work for three days.

261 On September 18, 2000, Mr. Watson was again advised that he was being placed at Level 1 of the AMP. At that time, Mr. Watson had been absent from work for 80 1/4 days on eight separate occasions over the preceding 12 months.

262 In early 2001, Mr. Watson was absent for nine days due to digestive problems; and for 10 days due to headache, fever, nasal congestion, cough and other problems. All transit operators were off work from April 1 to August 6, 2001, due to a labour dispute.

263 In August 2001, Mr. Watson was placed on Level 2 of the AMP. The letter notes that, in the 11 months since the Level 1 interview, Mr. Watson had been absent from work on three occasions for a total of 28 days. He was asked to obtain a medical assessment, which he did.

264 This medical assessment was not put in evidence before me. However, it was in evidence before the arbitrator, and she records the findings of that assessment as follows:

> As requested, Dr. Wong completed the medical assessment. He described the cause of the grievor's limitations/disability as .extensive degenerative osteoarthritis of his cervical spine.3 levels.. ... Dr. Wong then diagnosed .a permanent physical impairment and/or disability.. His medical opinion was that the grievor was not capable of unrestricted work as a Transit Operator. Dr. Wong further opined that the grievor no longer met the physical demands of a Transit Operator and was .NOT. fit to be .driving a bus full of passengers.. Dr. Wong's recommendation was that the grievor should be .placed in a position other than actually driving a bus if such is available to him.. Finally, Dr. Wong's opinion was that placement in a position other than actually driving a bus would help the grievor attend his job on a regular basis in the future. (pp. 11-12)

265 According to Mr. Watson's evidence at the arbitration, neither Dr. Wong, nor any OHN, nor any other representative of CMBC, ever discussed this medical opinion with him.

266 On August 30, 2001, starting shortly after his placement at Level 2, and before Dr. Wong's initial medical assessment was received, Mr. Watson began an absence which ultimately lasted for 21 months, until June 2003. He initially reported his absence as being due to a pulled groin muscle. However, the absence was due to depression, anxiety disorder and lower back pain. For most of the 21 month period, Mr. Watson was on TBQ status. GRTW programs were unsuccessfully attempted in July 2002 and March 2003.

267 In early June 2003, Mr. Watson returned to work as a transit operator on a GRTW basis, after being cleared to do so by his psychiatrist. On July 7, 2003, he returned to work on a full-time basis, and was placed at Level 3

of the AMP. The letter confirming that placement stated that the medical assessment provided by Mr. Watson's doctor indicated that his current medical condition did not prevent him from performing his job duties as a transit operator, or from attending work on a regular and consistent basis. It appears that this refers only to the assessment provided by Mr. Watson's psychiatrist and not that provided by Dr. Wong. In any event, Mr. Watson was placed on parameters of 18 days of absence for two years.

268 For the remainder of 2003, Mr. Watson was off work on various occasions due to gastroenteritis, cystitis, and a gall bladder condition. These absences caused him to exceed his Level 3 parameters and, following an ESR, his employment was terminated on November 13, 2003.

269 The Union grieved his termination, arguing that Mr. Watson had two disabilities, which CMBC failed to accommodate.

270 CMBC denied the grievance, but it was upheld at arbitration. The arbitrator found as follows:

> I further accept the Union's submission that the AMP was administered in an unreasonable and discriminatory manner, that the grievor's advancement to Level 3 and the ESR Level, as well as the decision to terminate, were based, in part, on his disabilities, and that no process to search for a permanent accommodation was ever initiated by the Employer as required under both the AMP and human rights legislation. These deficiencies did not arise due to intentional conduct by those involved. I am satisfied that they arose instead due to departmental isolation and poor inter-departmental communication. (p. 54)

271 The arbitrator found that Mr. Watson had been subjected to systemic discrimination and that he had arrived at the ESR level on a discriminatory path. Further the arbitrator found that, absent the discriminatory application of the AMP, Mr. Watson may never have found himself at the ESR level facing termination. The arbitrator found that the Union had established *prima facie* discrimination, and that CMBC had not justified its treatment of Mr. Watson by establishing a *bona fide* occupational requirement. The decision to terminate was set aside, and Mr. Watson was reinstated to employment status.

272 As a result, on January 10, 2005, Mr. Watson was reinstated to employment with full back pay from the date of his termination. Prior to resuming his duties as a transit operator, Mr. Watson was required to undergo a functional abilities test, and was cleared to return to work in late February 2005. On March 2, 2005, Mr. Watson was placed on Level 3 of the AMP, and given parameters of 20 days absence for each of the next two years.

273 Between March 2, 2005 and February 20, 2006, Mr. Watson had seven sick leave absences for a total of 17.2 days. Thus, Mr. Watson was under the parameters set. However, given the number of absences and other con-

cerns that CMBC had, he was provided with a letter indicating CMBC's continuing concern with his level of absence.

274 The Union grieved this letter, contending that several of his absences were related to ongoing medical conditions. In a letter dated May 19, 2006, CMBC denied that grievance, stating that, based on the medical information it had available to it, only one of his absences was related to a chronic condition. CMBC informed Mr. Watson that his ongoing pattern of excessive absenteeism placed his employment in serious jeopardy.

275 At the time of his testimony before me, Mr. Watson was at Level 3 of the AMP, and had just suffered an additional health related problem (a stroke) which had caused him to exceed the parameters. No one from CMBC had contacted him with respect to his employment status. He testified that, based on his previous experience, he expected to be terminated when he returned to work.

e. Gerald Essex

276 Mr. Essex commenced employment with CMBC's predecessor in 1974, and has most recently worked out of the Richmond depot. He testified that he is four to five years from retirement and would, in fact, qualify for early retirement immediately.

277 Mr. Essex had higher than average absence rates in 1996, 1997, 1998 and 1999. He testified that these absences were caused by a number of different factors. In 1996, he broke his arm in a motorcycle accident. He was off work from July 1996 to the following May. His arm did not heal properly and it was still not resolved when he returned to work.

278 Shortly after his return to work from the arm injury, Mr. Essex was involved in a motor vehicle accident while in his personal vehicle. As a result of injuries sustained in that accident, he was off work for almost two months.

279 In addition, in 1998, Mr. Essex was off nine days with cold and flu, and eight days with sinusitis.

280 In October 1998, Mr. Essex broke his wrist in a hiking accident. He was off work for two to three months (into January 1999). He states that, during all of these absences, he was not offered alternate work. He also testified that he did not request alternate work, but that his doctor filled in all the forms that were required.

281 On February 15, 1999, Mr. Essex attended a Level 1 interview. The letter confirming this interview was not placed in evidence before me.

282 Later in 1999, Mr. Essex suffered a back injury as the result of a passenger assault. He was off work for one month. In addition, he was off two weeks for tendonitis in his shoulder.

283 On December 3, 1999, Mr. Essex attended a Level 2 interview, and was asked to provide a medical assessment, which he did. That assessment indicated that he did not have any medical disabilities which would prevent him from attending work on a regular and consistent basis in the future.

284 On February 14, 2000, Mr. Essex was placed on Level 3 of the AMP. The letter confirming this placement noted that Mr. Essex's average absence rate since 1994 was approximately 23.72%. In the past year, his absence rate was 22.56%, comprised of four absences totalling 61.5 days. Mr. Essex was placed on 20 day parameters for a one year period.

285 In 2000 and 2001, Mr. Essex had a significantly reduced level of absenteeism. He successfully completed his year of monitoring, and on February 14, 2001, Mr. Essex was returned to Level 1 of the AMP.

286 In January 2002, Mr. Essex had an operation on his left hand to correct a growth on the tendon. This condition, Dupuytren's contracture, resulted in him being unable to straighten one of the fingers of his left hand. Mr. Essex testified that the surgery was a fairly simple procedure, but required six weeks of recovery time.

287 On April 23, 2002, Mr. Essex was escalated to Level 2 of the AMP, and on June 9, he was placed on Level 3. The Union grieved Mr. Essex's placement at Level 3, but CMBC denied the grievance.

288 In July or August 2002, Mr. Essex was absent for four weeks as a result of shingles. Some of that time was counted as annual vacation, which Mr. Essex had previously booked and did not defer.

289 In January 2003, Mr. Essex was absent for one week as the result of a bad cold. As a result of these absences, Mr. Essex exceeded his parameters. On January 30, 2003, there was an ESR to discuss Mr. Essex's continued employment with the Company.

290 On February 3, 2003, when he returned to work from his most recent absence, Mr. Essex was advised that his employment was terminated for excessive non-culpable absenteeism. The Union grieved Mr. Essex's termination, and, through negotiations between the Union and CMBC, Mr. Essex was reinstated to employment on November 24, 2003.

291 Since his return to work, Mr. Essex has had rates of absenteeism well below the average.

f. Sergio Da Luz

292 Mr. Da Luz has been employed by CMBC as a transit operator since April 1997, most recently out of the Richmond depot.

293 Mr. Da Luz suffers from Crohn's disease and depression. Crohn's disease is a chronic incurable inflammatory bowel disease. The main symptoms are bowel urgency (recurrent diarrhea) and fatigue. In addition, Mr. Da Luz testified that the disease gives rise to a number of other problems, including a form of arthritis (as it is an inflammatory disease). In addition, it increases his susceptibility to viruses, as it lowers his immune system.

294 Mr. Da Luz was first diagnosed with Crohn's disease in March or April of 1998. In 1998 and 1999, Mr. Da Luz experienced periods of high absenteeism, but his attendance in 2000 was unremarkable.

295 In 2001, Mr. Da Luz experienced a 15% absence rate, based on five occasions of absence amounting to 25 days over the preceding 11 months. In November 2001, Mr. Da Luz attended an attendance interview, and was placed on Level 1 of the AMP. Mr. Da Luz testified that his Supervisor was aware that his absences were related to Crohn's disease.

296 The Level 1 letter to Mr. Da Luz states:

> The importance of regular attendance at work cannot be overstated and your current attendance record is unacceptable. You informed me that you have been diagnosed with a chronic medical condition. You need to contact the Occupational Health Nurse so that she may in turn contact your Doctor. This will enable the Company to ascertain how best to accommodate you with your condition and ensure you are managing it to mitigate your absences at CMBC.

297 The letter stated that Mr. Da Luz's Supervisor would monitor his attendance over the next six months, and might schedule a meeting with him to review his progress. There was no evidence before me with respect to whether there was any contact with an OHN at this time.

298 In 2002, Mr. Da Luz's attendance improved to a 9.77% absence rate, although the frequency of his absences increased. He was placed at Level 2 of the AMP. His Supervisor noted that, since the Level 1 interview he had been absent from work on seven occasions for a total of 21 days. CMBC requested a medical assessment. Mr. Da Luz provided the requested medical information.

299 On January 20, 2003, Mr. Da Luz was placed on Level 3 of the AMP, and was given a target of 20 days absence. In the letter recording the meeting, Mr. Da Luz's Supervisor noted that the medical assessment indicated that, while Mr. Da Luz did have an ongoing medical condition which could have attendance implications in the longer term, he was currently fit to per-

form his job duties as a transit operator and was capable of attending work on a regular and consistent basis. Mr. Da Luz was advised as follows:

> Without intending to suggest that any particular rate of absenteeism is acceptable, and after reviewing the particular circumstances of your case, Coast Mountain Bus Co. expects you to maintain an attendance performance that is at least equal to the average for employees in your group. Specifically, Coast Mountain expects that you will not be absent more than 20 regular days (7.5 hours), which equates to 7.9% absenteeism per year, for a period of 2 years.

300 In response to being placed on Level 3, Mr. Da Luz asked his physician, Dr. Linda Curtis, to clarify some of the answers she had given on the medial assessment. On February 12, 2003, Dr. Curtis wrote to CMBC, describing Mr. Da Luz's condition and main symptoms, and stating:

> In response to your questions, Mr. Daluz does have a permanent physical disability. Mr. Daluz is not capable of unrestricted work as a transit operator. Mr. Daluz is not fit to work in a safety-sensitive position when his Crohn's symptoms flare. Mr. Daluz' chronic illness will cause him more work absences than the average employee. I have seen no evidence that Mr. Daluz misses work inappropriately.

301 In reply, CMBC requested further information from Dr. Curtis about Mr. Da Luz's abilities and/or restrictions in relation to his medical condition and his employment needs for the purpose of possible accommodation. Dr. Curtis was also provided with job descriptions for accommodated positions. She replied on March 14, 2003. Some of the questions and answers provided in that letter are as follows:

> **2. Is any disability suffered by Mr. Da Luz, permanent or temporary? Are any restrictions permanent?**
>
> Disability may be total or partial. It depends on job duties and the current symptom severity. Each episode of disability is temporary, but the illness and the possibility of disability is permanent. ...
>
> **10. In your report dated February 12, 2003, you have stated .Mr. Da Luz is not fit to work in a safety-sensitive position when his Crohn's symptoms flare.. How will CMBC be made aware when he is experiencing a .flare-up. and is unsafe for him to drive?**
>
> He is responsible for notifying CMBC, as he has always done.
>
> **11. Is he currently experiencing a .flare-up.?**
>
> Level of symptoms can vary from day to day. In the past three months, he has been off for at most 2 consecutive days, this is a fairly typical pattern for him.

302 In that letter, Dr. Curtis also indicated that employment as a transit operator was not suitable on a long-term basis. She stated that Mr. Da Luz was permanently restricted from the position of transit operator, because of ongoing issues with his chronic illness which would not resolve. Dr. Curtis indicated that the Building Service Worker position was not an appropriate permanent accommodation, but that the Service Person position might be.

Dr. Curtis noted, however, that a graveyard shift was not ideal for individuals with Mr. Da Luz's medical condition and, in any event:

> He will still have absences due to fatigue, joint pains and bowels. This should be less frequent than in his current position, this is currently unknown.
>
> .
>
> I have never considered his level of absenteeism to be inappropriately high, considering his condition. He has not abused this process.

303 In 2003, his first year on the AMP, Mr. Da Luz exceeded his 20 day parameters. He testified that, in late 2003, his back started acting up (he testified that this is a symptom related to the Crohn's disease). At that time, he was interested in finding out if there was any alternate work he could do. He performed work as a vehicle maintenance man for a 5-6 week period on a GRTW basis. He was not able to work a full week at full shifts due to his medical condition. He testified that he later found out that these periods (days that he would normally work that he did not on the GRTW) were counted as absences for the purposes of the AMP.

304 In early 2004, Mr. Da Luz had discussions with CMBC with respect to alternate work. He testified that they discussed the Service Person position, but that he had concerns about his ability to do the work: with his arthritic condition, he couldn't do the sweeping and the hours were graveyard shift, which was not good for his health. He agreed in cross-examination that the graveyard shift was also problematic in terms of his childcare arrangements. He states that, at this meeting, he provided CMBC with a copy of his résumé, and they discussed his education, but he was told that CMBC was unable to accommodate him in a non-CAW bargaining unit across union jurisdiction.

305 On February 2, 2004, Ms. Hentzen wrote Mr. Da Luz, informing him that there was a vacancy for a full-time regular Service Person, and requesting a meeting with him and his Union representative to discuss a placement in that position. On February 24, 2004, CMBC received a letter from Dr. Curtis, stating that a Service Person shift ending at 2:00 a.m. would be appropriate. Mr. Da Luz testified that he did not recall being advised of a Service Person shift that ended at 2:00 a.m.

306 In March 2004, Mr. Da Luz, Ms. Hentzen, an OHN, Mr. Kelly and Mr. Jones had a meeting with respect to finding an accommodation for Mr. Da Luz. The Union took the position that Mr. Da Luz should be left in the transit operator job, with increased parameters. Mr. Da Luz testified that he understood that CMBC would be concerned if he refused an accommodation that could reduce his absences. Mr. Da Luz did not accept a placement into the Service Person position at that time. Mr. Da Luz stated there were a number of reasons for this, including the graveyard shift, and the fact that

he had tried the Service Person job previously, and had been unable to sustain a full week at full hours due to the physically taxing nature of the job.

307 Mr. Da Luz testified that he again exceeded the 20 day parameter in 2004. He stated that he was at the 20 day mark in December, late in the year. He didn't feel well one day, but went to work anyway. After working half a shift, he booked off. He then had a car accident, and was off for a number of months. He did not return to work until late October 2005. Mr. Da Luz testified that he experienced a great deal of stress while he was off work because he knew his employment was in jeopardy. He stated that in approximately April 2005, when he knew his job was on the line, his Crohn's disease acted up. He couldn't eat, lost about 20 pounds in three to four weeks, and was quite sick.

308 When Mr. Da Luz returned to work, he was advised that he had exceeded the parameters. However, CMBC did not terminate his employment. In a letter dated November 15, 2005, Mr. Da Luz's Supervisor advised him that CMBC was aware of his medical conditions and had offered him alternate positions for the purpose of facilitating better attendance at work. CMBC noted that Mr. Da Luz had declined these offers and insisted on remaining a transit operator. The letter stated:

> ... since you have declined alternate work opportunities and insist on returning to work as a transit operator, we can only provide you with a final opportunity to demonstrate your ability to attend regularly at work.
>
> We will consider your attendance to be within an acceptable range if your combined absences for STD, LTD and WCB total 19 days or less, in each of 2 consecutive 12-month periods, beginning from the date of this letter. Exceeding 19 days of absenteeism, in either period, may cause the Company to consider terminating your employment.

309 Mr. Da Luz had another lengthy absence, commencing in January 2006. He testified that this absence was due to surgery he required as a result of his Crohn's disease. Notes from a quarterly meeting held in early 2006 indicate: .abs Jan. 8 hospitalized due to disability. ESR may be required..

310 At the time of his testimony, in July 2006, Mr. Da Luz had been off work for approximately seven months. He had therefore greatly exceeded the 19 day parameters. He testified that no one has contacted him about his employment with CMBC, but he felt that, once he returned to work, his employment would likely be terminated. He agreed in cross-examination that the November 15, 2005 letter states that, if he exceeds the parameters CMBC .may. consider terminating his employment, and that he had exceeded the number of days in the past and had not been fired. However, he also noted that the November 15 letter referenced a .final. opportunity.

311 Mr. Da Luz testified that he found being placed on the AMP extremely stressful, and that he feels a high level of pressure. He knows there is always the possibility that he will lose his employment and his livelihood because of the time he takes off work, when he has no control over his illness.

312 He testified that he felt it was .ridiculous. that he was placed on the AMP when he was. He stated that if was missing 250 days a year, that would be one thing, but on many occasions his attendance was only a few days more than the .average. employee. Given his condition, he felt it was unfair that this level of absenteeism triggered him into the AMP.

313 Mr. Kelly testified that it was CMBC's view that Mr. Da Luz had, on at least two occasions, declined accommodation. Mr. Kelly stated that Mr. Da Luz insists on working as a transit operator, despite his doctor's advice to the contrary, and he is not capable of attending regularly.

g. Shailendra Prasad

314 Mr. Prasad started work as a transit operator in February 1990. He testified that he suffers from a number of medical conditions. First, he has a liver dysfunction relating to a bile duct disorder, which has required surgery on a number of occasions. Second, he has osteoarthritis, which is worst in his right knee joint as a result of a surgery he had on that knee. Third, he has Type 2 diabetes. He testified that he was being monitored as a borderline diabetic from 1999 until approximately 2002, when the diagnosis of full Type 2 diabetes was confirmed.

315 On February 3, 1998, Mr. Prasad attended an interview with CMBC where he was informed of its concern about his absenteeism. At that time, he had been absent from work for a total of 19 ¾ days on four separate occasions over the preceding 12 months. He was interviewed again in November 1998, and was advised that his absenteeism rate showed an encouraging improvement, but that it would continue to be monitored on an ongoing basis.

316 Between November 1998 and January 2000, Mr. Prasad was absent on two occasions for a total of 131 days. He testified that the majority of these absences were the result of surgery he required due to liver dysfunction. He was absent for approximately five months after that surgery.

317 In January 2000, Mr. Prasad attended a Level 2 interview, and was asked to provide a professional opinion with respect to the state of his health, which he did.

318 After reviewing the assessment, an OHN informed CMBC that Mr. Prasad was fit to perform his duties as a transit operator, that no significant health problems were anticipated, and that he could be expected to attend

work on a regular basis in the future. In his testimony before me, Mr. Prasad noted that this medical opinion would have been provided to the OHN following his surgery. At that time, there was no guarantee about his attendance levels. Mr. Prasad also agreed, in cross-examination, that he had not contested the OHN's report.

319 In the end result, Mr. Prasad was placed on parameters. He was required to be absent 20 days or less during the one year period from the date of the Level 3 letter (March 10, 2000). In addition, he was advised that the frequency of his absences should be in line with the average (two per year).

320 Mr. Prasad completed this one year Level 3 with one nine-day absence. However, in the six months following completing of the Level 3 monitoring period, Mr. Prasad had two absences for a total of 55 days and 38.54 part-time hours. Mr. Prasad testified that these absences were largely due to complications from his initial liver surgery, requiring further surgery. At the end of his period of absence, he returned on a GRTW. In addition, Mr. Prasad was away from work on a WCB claim in January 2002 resulting from a slip on ice.

321 As a result of these absences, on January 15, 2002, Mr. Prasad was again placed on Level 3 parameters. On this occasion, the average for employees in his group was 22 days per year, and Mr. Prasad was required to maintain this level of attendance for two years.

322 Mr. Prasad successfully achieved this level of attendance for two years, and was thus placed on Level 1 of the AMP. However, shortly thereafter he again had elevated absenteeism.

323 On June 11, 2004, Mr. Prasad attended a Level 2 interview, at which CMBC noted that, in the past 12 months, he had been absent from work on three occasions, for a total of 38 days. Mr. Prasad testified that these absences were largely due to arthritis, which was now affecting his shoulder, and complications from diabetes. However, in cross-examination, Mr. Prasad stated that he was not sure what the reason for the absences was. He agreed that some of the absences were unrelated to osteoarthritis.

324 As a result of the June 11 meeting, Mr. Prasad was required to obtain a doctor's report and provide it to an OHN. His physician, Dr. Bueno, completed the assessment and provided it to the OHN on July 27, 2004. That report included the following questions and answers:

1. Does Mr. Prasad suffer from a chronic medical condition? If yes, please describe.

1. Type II Diabetes Meillitus
2. Common bile duct disease requiring several surgeries ...
3. Osteo arthritis.post-traumatic ...

7. Does Mr. Prasad have a permanent physical impairment and/or disability?

CHRONIC illness as stated ...

8. Is Mr. Prasad capable of unrestricted work as a Transit Operator?

As long as there is no flare-up of his chronic condition or complication.

9. Does Mr. Prasad meet the physical demands of a Transit Operator?

Yes. As of lately.

10. Is Mr. Prasad fit to work in a safety-sensitive position?

YES. As long as he is not taking medications that are known to cause impairment for control of flare-up of his chronic condition.

.

12. Are there any other conclusions that apply in this case?

He has a chronic medical condition that can fluctuate in severity. When he is well, there is no restriction in participating as a transit operator. Fluctuations in these conditions may lead into periods of temporary disability which preclude maintaining regular attendance.

325 On October 1, 2004, Mr. Prasad attended a Level 3 interview. At that interview, and in a follow-up letter, CMBC reviewed the information it had received from the OHN:

> Our OHN has advised us that the medical questionnaire received from your Doctor indicates that you have three (3) medical conditions. We are further advised that all of these conditions are being regularly followed up and there is no requirement for an accommodation at this time. Given this information, you are expected, aside from an occasional flare-up of one of these conditions, to be able to attend work on a regular and consistent basis.

326 The letter continues:

> Our records show that since completion of the most recent 2-year monitoring period, on January 14th, 2004, you have been absent 33 ½ days on two (2) occasions, which equates to an annual absence rate of approximately 13%. In addition, our records show that, in the previous 5-year period, notwithstanding that you had specific attendance targets for 3 of those years, your average absence rate exceeded 13% or 34 days per year...

327 Despite the reference to absences resulting from .an occasional flare-up., Mr. Prasad was placed on a two-year monitoring period, on parameters that reflected the average absence rate:

> Without intending to suggest that any particular rate of absenteeism is acceptable, Coast Mountain Bus Company intends to closely monitor your attendance for the next 2 years. The Company will take into account the particular circumstances of your case and will use the current averages of 19 days on 2 occurrences per year as a guide in assessing whether or not your attendance is acceptable.
>
> If, at any time within 2 years of the date of this letter, your absenteeism exceeds 19 days per year, or 3 or more occasions, your ongoing employment status may be subject to review, at which time all aspects of your attendance history and prognosis

> for future attendance will be weighed against the appropriateness of terminating your employment for excessive, non-culpable absenteeism.

328 Mr. Prasad testified in November 2005, at which time he stated that, during his first year on monitoring, he met the parameters with 15 days of absence. Mr. Prasad testified that, during this period, some of his absences have been caused by infections in his neck and nose that did not heal properly as a result of his diabetes. He also stated that he had arranged to use all of his holiday time to have required knee surgery. He had delayed the surgery until he had enough holiday time available so that it would not count towards his attendance record. Once he arranged the time off, the surgery date was cancelled, and he had to try to arrange it again for the following year.

329 Mr. Prasad testified that, throughout his tenure with CMBC, and his interaction with the AMP, no accommodation was ever offered or made available to him. He agreed that he did not make enquiries about alternate work, either directly to CMBC or through the Union. He stated that he has returned to work on a GRTW basis on at least one occasion. It was put to Mr. Prasad in cross-examination that, during a grievance meeting resulting from a grievance of his most recent placement on Level 3, there was a discussion of accommodation into other positions. Mr. Prasad did not agree that such a discussion had occurred. No other evidence was called indicating that such a discussion had occurred. He agreed, however, that at the time of the meeting he was not particularly interested in accommodation in a job other than his own.

330 Mr. Prasad testified that, during his time in the AMP, he has worked hard to maintain regular attendance. He testified that he has followed his medical practitioner's advice about medication, diet and exercise. Mr. Prasad was cross-examined on this point, but stated that the only concern his doctor has ever raised with him with respect to his treatment was that he needed to take his medication on a consistent basis.meaning, at the same time each day. He agreed that, when he was first officially diagnosed with diabetes, he was angry and upset. His doctor spoke to him about the need to accept the condition and to learn how to effectively manage and live with it. He states that he has done so.

331 Mr. Prasad has taken vacation time and unpaid leaves of absence to tend to his medical needs in order to stay within the attendance parameters set by CMBC.

332 Mr. Prasad testified that he doesn't feel good about being in the AMP, and that if he didn't have medical conditions, he would not be in it. He is trying his best to get out of the Program any way he can, but he finds it

extremely difficult to do so, given the three disabilities he has to live with and manage.

333 He states that he has a family that he is responsible for supporting, and that his status on the AMP jeopardizes his employment. He finds it threatening and intimidating. He testified that he is doing his best to provide his services, but he feels like a gun is being held to his head. He finds it frustrating and stressful on top of a job that has more than its fair share of stressors.

h. Susan Lieb

334 Ms. Lieb commenced employment with CMBC in October 1998. In 1999, she had a level of absenteeism that was above the average.

335 Starting in May 2000, Ms. Lieb had a lengthy absence from work that lasted until July 2002. Ms. Lieb testified that this absence was caused by a WCB incident that occurred while she was driving a trolley bus. She turned the heater on in the bus, which caused a blast of smoke and fumes in her face. She thought that the bus was on fire, and therefore emptied out the passengers. She contacted T-Comm, and then lost consciousness.

336 As it turned out, the fumes which Ms. Lieb inhaled were toxic, and what followed was a two-year absence. Ms. Lieb testified that, during this period, her throat kept closing up, and her doctors were unable to determine the precise cause or treatment. She was eventually diagnosed with irritable larynx syndrome, and underwent surgery to improve the condition.

337 Ms. Lieb testified that, during her time away from work, she approached CMBC for assistance. She asked for access to a program about improving one's health, but the OHN advised her that the program was full. She stated that she requested accommodation into a light duty position. She was offered a position cleaning the buses or toilets, which Ms. Lieb was unable to perform because the dust and chemicals would aggravate her condition. She was told that CMBC was unable to offer her any other position, as they were not able to accommodate her across union boundaries.

338 Ms. Lieb eventually had surgery and, at the end of her recuperation period, she returned to work on a GRTW, working part-time for two weeks. Within a month of her return to work, in August 2002, Ms. Lieb was given a Level 1 interview.

339 At the time of the interview, CMBC noted that Ms. Lieb had been absent from work for 62% of her working hours from the start of her employment with CMBC. She was advised that her Supervisor would monitor her attendance over the next six months. Ms. Lieb testified that she was angry and confused by her placement on the AMP. She was devastated and in tears as a result of the interview. In her view, poor equipment had hurt

her.badly. She had been unable to work for two years, and had gone through much pain and fear, given that her disability related to her ability to breathe. She felt that she had gone through so much. Returning to work seemed to her like it was the end of her difficulties, and then she had to deal with the AMP issue.

340 Ms. Lieb had regular attendance until December 2002, when she was off work for 11 weeks. She testified that she experienced numbness down her left side, and was diagnosed with a possible stroke. Her doctor arranged for her to see a neurologist, and then to obtain a CT scan, and advised her not to work. She was placed on TBQ status by CMBC. She stated that she was panicked about potentially losing her job. When she eventually got the CT scan, it was not conclusive, and she had to wait for an MRI. The MRI didn't show anything, and she was able to return to work.

341 Ms. Lieb testified that, immediately upon her return to work, she was advanced to Level 2 of the AMP. The Level 2 interview was held on March 7, 2003. In the letter which followed that interview, Ms. Lieb's Supervisor stated that, since her Level 1 interview, she had been absent from work on one occasion for a total of 54 days. She was asked to obtain a medical assessment.

342 Ms. Lieb contacted an OHN with respect to the medical assessment, and provided the form to her doctor. Ms. Lieb testified that the form had been completed and she had assumed it was sent in. However, the OHN had not received a reply from Ms. Lieb's physician as of June 27, 2003. Ms. Lieb stated that she picked up another copy of the medical and provided it to CMBC. However, this did not happen until after the Level 3 interview, and so was not taken into account. As a result, CMBC proceeded with the Level 3 interview on the presumption that she did not have a medical condition which would prevent her from performing her job as a transit operator or attending work on a regular and consistent basis. Ms. Lieb was placed on parameters for two years, and required to be absent no more than 18 days a year during that period.

343 The Union grieved Ms. Lieb's placement at Level 3 of the AMP. The Union argued, among other things, that CMBC had failed to accommodate Ms. Lieb to the point of undue hardship. In its response to the grievance, CMBC stated as follows:

> The Company's Duty to Accommodate is a responsibility that we take very seriously. The Company is unaware of any occasion where it has failed to meet its duty to accommodate Ms. Lieb's medical condition. In fact, this grievance meeting was the first time that this issue had been raised. In every instance of a return-to-work following a medical leave, including her latest surgery, Ms. Lieb's healthcare providers cleared her as being fit and capable of returning to her safety-sensitive position

> as a transit operator. Accordingly, the Company was not under any obligation to provide an accommodation.
>
> However, if at any time Ms. Lieb is able to provide supporting documentation from a qualified medical practitioner, that an ongoing medical condition prevents her from attending at work or performing her work, and she wants to be accommodated, she should contact our OHN immediately.

344 While she was on Level 3, Ms. Lieb suffered a gall bladder attack, and had to be removed from her bus and taken to hospital by ambulance. She was advised to have her gall bladder removed, and that it would take four weeks to recuperate. She felt that she could not afford to be off for four weeks, because she would be fired if she was.

345 Ms. Lieb testified that she went to the Company and asked what the options were for having the operation. They said that they would look into it, but no accommodation was offered. Ms. Lieb was advised by the Union that they had asked CMBC to provide her with leave to have the operation, but CMBC refused. The OHN had stated that gall bladder issues could be controlled by diet. As no accommodation was forthcoming, Ms. Lieb had initially planned to wait to have the operation until after the conclusion of her two-year monitoring period. She was, however, unable to do so.

346 In August, Ms. Lieb had another gall bladder attack and needed to have an operation immediately. She stated that her doctor originally advised her to be off work for one month, but she returned after three weeks.

347 Despite this absence, on July 27, 2005, Ms. Lieb was advised that she had successfully completed her two year monitoring period. She was told that CMBC's policy was to continue to monitor employees who had successfully completed a Level 3 monitoring period as if they were at Level 1 of the AMP. Twelve months or more of good attendance would result in her complete removal from the AMP, but if Ms. Lieb's absenteeism rose to an unacceptable level, she would again be subject to a Level 3 monitoring period.

i. Gary Templeman

348 Mr. Templeman started work with CMBC on November 4, 1996. His attendance was unremarkable for the first three years of his employment. However, he had high absenteeism rates from 2000 to 2003.

349 Mr. Templeman testified that, from February 1999 to the end of December 2001, he was involved in four motor vehicle accidents in his personal vehicle. The first accident, in February 1999, did not result in any time off work. The three subsequent accidents caused him injuries which required time off work.

350 The second accident appears to have occurred in February 2000. Mr. Templeman sustained a number of injuries, including pain up and down his left side, and a blown rotator cuff which required surgery. From May 2000 to March 2001, while he was awaiting the surgery, Mr. Templeman worked on a part-time basis, 2 ½ to 3 hours a day. He testified that he thought he was helping out by doing what he could, but that these partial days of absence were then counted against him in the AMP.

351 In March 2001, Mr. Templeman had rotator cuff surgery on his left shoulder. He then had a third accident in April 2001. He was still experiencing a lot of problems with his shoulder, but did not know if they were the result of the initial injury or the more recent accident. Mr. Templeman commenced a GRTW in early October 2001, and returned to full-time hours in November 2001.

352 Mr. Templeman then had a fourth accident in December 2001, resulting in injuries to his neck, back and right shoulder. He was off work until March 2002, when he returned to work as a transit operator.

353 On April 2, 2002, Mr. Templeman had a Level 1 interview. During that interview, Mr. Templeman's Supervisor noted that he had been absent from work for 200 days, on two separate occasions, in the past year. In addition, the Level 1 letter stated:

> The importance of regular attendance at work cannot be overstated and your current attendance record is unacceptable. If there are circumstances that exist, relevant to your absences, we urge you to advise us so that we may provide you with the appropriate support. As discussed, Coast Mountain Bus Co. will ensure that every assistance is available to you and that all benefits to which you are entitled, whether for sickness or injury, are placed at your disposal. The Employee Assistance Plan [telephone number provided] and the services of an Occupational Health Nurse [telephone number provided] are available to you. If you wish to utilize these support services, please feel free to contact them directly.

354 Mr. Templeman testified that he contacted the EAP after his Level 1 interview. After speaking to a counsellor, he was diagnosed with PTSD as a result of the multiple traffic accidents. He was advised not to drive a bus, and went off work in May 2002.

355 In the fall of 2002, CMBC and Mr. Templeman began to search for alternate duties that he could perform. Mr. Templeman testified that the process involved was of concern to him. First, there were discussions about him pressure washing trolley buses, but this never came to pass. Then he was assigned to the Port Coquitlam garage, but the maintenance manager there refused to have him work due to his condition. Finally, he was assigned to a Building Services position. He performed this position from December 2002 to February 2003. He testified that the mostly janitorial duties which he was assigned involved sweeping, bending and lifting, which ag-

gravated his left shoulder and caused pain in his right elbow, lower back and feet. He feels that he was assigned duties which were not in accordance with the restrictions outlined by his physician, or the job descriptions that his doctor was provided with. The result was that he was in constant pain. He reported his concerns to his maintenance manager, but nothing was done as a result. Mr. Templeman testified that he just kept doing the duties, because he felt he had a gun to his head. He didn't want to refuse any work that CMBC asked him to do, because he was concerned that his job would be in jeopardy if he took any more time off.

356 Mr. Templeman testified that, eventually, he could not take the pain any more, and in early February 2003 went to his doctor, telling him that he could no longer do the work. The doctor asked him to explain the duties he was performing, and agreed that he could not do them. His doctor contacted his case manager at GWL, and Mr. Templeman was assigned to a fitness class, and also provided with counselling for his PTSD, both of which he attended from April 2003 to mid-August 2003. During this time, Mr. Templeman received LTD benefits.

357 Mr. Templeman returned to work on a GRTW in August or September of 2003.

358 On October 3, 2003, Mr. Templeman had a Level 2 interview. Between the Level 1 and Level 2 interviews, Mr. Templeman had been absent from work on four occasions, for a total of 183 days, and .24 GRTW days.. Mr. Templeman testified that these days included days he was working as a Building Services Worker, and days attending the fitness program approved by GWL.

359 In the Level 2 letter, Mr. Templeman was asked to obtain a medical assessment, which he did. Mr. Templeman testified that, when the assessment was conducted, he was back at work driving a bus. He testified that he was not .fit and able., but that a person could only take .so much..

360 On October 27, 2003, Mr. Templeman had a Level 3 interview. In the letter which confirmed that interview, Mr. Templeman's Supervisor stated the following with respect to Mr. Templeman's medical assessment:

> The doctor you attended forwarded the results of your medical assessment to our Occupational Health Nurse, who, in turn, advised us that you do not have a medical condition which would prevent you from performing your job duties as a transit operator or from attending at work on a regular and consistent basis. If you have information that does not accord with this opinion of your medical condition, or your condition changes significantly, we urge you to advise the OHN immediately.

361 In the letter, Mr. Templeman's Supervisor noted that the annual average rate of absenteeism among all other employees in Mr. Templeman's group, for the last twelve months, was 6.51% (17 days), and that Mr. Templeman was required to meet this standard for the following two years.

362 The Union grieved Mr. Templeman's placement on Level 3, in part because the GRTW days were taken into account in the calculation of his absences. In response, CMBC noted that the partial days used in the calculation did not play a significant role in progressing Mr. Templeman to Level 3, and therefore the grievance was denied.

363 Mr. Templeman testified about the frustration he experienced as a result of these events. He had suffered a series of injuries which required time off work, as a result of which he had been placed on the AMP. When he followed the directions of CMBC in the Level 1 letter and contacted EAP, he had been advised not to work. The rehabilitation placement arranged by the OHN had exacerbated his physical injuries. The fitness program he had been assigned by GWL had helped his condition, but was counted against him in the AMP. He was in pain, and depressed as a result of the PTSD, and he couldn't deal with the situation. Mr. Templeman felt that his only option was to go back, and drive his bus in pain. His condition didn't go away, it continued. Further, he was not receiving the treatment he needs because he was at work.

364 Mr. Templeman had surgery scheduled on his right shoulder, which he cancelled because he was on the AMP. Mr. Templeman agreed in cross-examination that he had informed an OHN in June 2004 that he was scheduled for shoulder surgery, but that he was concerned about undergoing the surgery because he was at Level 3 of the AMP. It was put to Mr. Templeman in cross-examination that the OHN had informed him that she could not give detailed medical information to his Supervisor because of the confidentiality provisions of the Collective Agreement, but Mr. Templeman denied this.

365 Mr. Templeman also testified that he brought a letter from his surgeon to his Supervisor. Mr. Templeman told his Supervisor that he needed shoulder surgery, but he was still on 17 day parameters. He was concerned that his job would be jeopardy if he underwent the surgery.

366 Mr. Templeman agreed that, although he brought his Supervisor a copy of the letter and asked him to put it on his file, he did not specifically ask him for an accommodation within the AMP. Mr. Templeman testified that, from his standpoint, his Supervisor should have understood what the issue was. It was his job to say whether or not Mr. Templeman could have time off. Mr. Templeman testified that he expected his Supervisor to inform him whether CMBC would grant him time off for the surgery. He testified that he never received this information, and therefore did not undergo the surgery.

367 Mr. Templeman successfully completed the first of his two years of monitoring. On August 23, 2005, just short of the conclusion of his second

year, he was advised that CMBC had agreed to conclude the monitoring period early. The letter informing Mr. Templeman of this stated:

> Our decision was based largely on the significant improvement you have shown and to alleviate your concern regarding a future absence that may be necessitated by a medical intervention. We appreciate the effort you have made to improve your attendance and sincerely hope that you will enjoy good health in the future.

368 Mr. Templeman testified that he understood this to relate to his need for shoulder surgery, but by that time (more than one year after he had raised the surgery issue with the OHN) he had lost trust in the Company. There were no assurances that his shoulder surgery absences would not trigger him back into the AMP. He testified that he still has not scheduled the surgery, because he doesn't know what will happen as a result.

j. Dwayne Mayes

369 At the time of his testimony, Mr. Mayes had been employed by CMBC as a transit operator for 11 years. For the first year, he worked out of the Oakridge depot, and then transferred to North Vancouver.

370 Mr. Mayes was unable to work from March 1997 to February 1999 as the result of a sprain and dislocation to his right ankle which he suffered while at work. He testified that he was unable to get the appropriate treatment for a significant period of time due to a dispute between the WCB and his physicians. He returned to work in February 1999. However, his ankle injury left him with reduced ankle strength which caused him some problems operating the brake pedal.

371 In January 2000, Mr. Mayes was absent from work as a result of gall bladder attacks which eventually required surgery.

372 In 2001, Mr. Mayes had a very low absenteeism rate. In 2002, that rate increased, and Mr. Mayes was absent for approximately 33% of his scheduled hours. Mr. Mayes testified that, at the time, he was experiencing severe digestive problems. He had four colonoscopies during that year, and was eventually diagnosed with irritable bowel syndrome (.IBS.). Mr. Mayes testified that CMBC was made aware of this diagnosis through the OHG. The following year, Mr. Mayes did not have any absences.

373 In 2004, Mr. Mayes re-injured his ankle. His injury occurred while at home and his WCB claim for a recurrence of his prior injury was not accepted. As a result of this injury, Mr. Mayes was absent from work from June 2004 to March 2005.

374 In September 2004, Mr. Mayes was fitted with an ankle brace. He discussed with his Supervisor whether he would be able to wear this brace while driving the bus, but was told that he could not, as it would be contrary

to the relevant regulations. He did not raise the issue of the brace again until October 2005.

375 In December 2004, in an attempt to return to work, Mr. Mayes was given a medical tryout at Oakridge. Mr. Mayes did not wear his ankle brace during this tryout, which was ultimately not successful.

376 On March 9, 2005, Mr. Mayes was given a rehabilitation assignment. His doctor had rejected the Utility Operator and Service Person positions, as he felt it would be more beneficial for Mr. Mayes to be off his feet. However, he approved a janitorial placement at the SeaBus terminal. Mr. Mayes testified that he was told that he would have the opportunity to sit down while working. He worked in this placement for two months, while continuing with physiotherapy treatments at night. He testified that the placement was not successful, as he found that walking on the hard surfaces at the SeaBus terminal made his ankle swell. When his ankle became swollen, the physiotherapist could not treat his initial injury and instead worked on reducing the swelling. Mr. Mayes testified that, while the rehabilitation assignment had got him back into the workplace in the short term, it had caused him more pain in the result. Mr. Mayes determined that he would prefer to be driving a bus.

377 In May 2005, Mr. Mayes returned to work as a transit operator. At that time, he was still not wearing the ankle brace, as he understood that he was not permitted to. Within a month, he had been involved in two motor vehicle accidents at work, the second of which reinjured his ankle joint.

378 As a result, Mr. Mayes was absent from June to September 2005. Although the latest injury to his ankle occurred as the result of a motor vehicle accident while driving a bus, because it was the re-aggravation of an existing injury, he was placed on LTD rather than WCB.

379 Mr. Mayes returned to work in October 2005. At that time, he was permitted to wear the ankle brace while driving, as it had been approved by the OHN. Shortly after his return to work, on October 25, 2005, Mr. Mayes was placed at Level 1 of the AMP. The letter indicated that, in the past twelve months, he had been absent from work for 168 days on two separate occasions.

380 Mr. Mayes asked for a follow-up meeting with his Supervisor to discuss his placement on Level 1, at which that placement was confirmed. In a letter confirming the meeting, the Supervisor wrote:

> You requested that I revisit your file and consider various medical issues that you divulged to me during that meeting. You explained that when you attended the Level 1 interview, you did not have an opportunity to ask questions or get clarification on certain points.
>
> .

> Your last absence was lengthy, due in part to the wait-times in the medical system, but this was not your only lengthy absence. During our discussion we examined your attendance from 2000 to 2006, and show that you had a lengthy absence in 2002, and again in 2000. (reproduced as written)

381 Mr. Mayes testified that he has maintained good attendance since returning to work in October 2005. However, he stated that he is still undergoing physiotherapy on his ankle and is waiting for a CT scan (ordered in June 2005). In addition, his IBS can cause absences when it acts up. He also testified that there is no way to predict what his attendance will be in the future. He stated that the things that happened to cause his absences .came out of the blue., so there is no way to predict if they might recur. This causes him a great deal of stress.

k. Susan Welch

382 Ms. Welch has been employed as a transit operator since July 1989, most recently in the Richmond depot. It does not appear that her attendance came to the attention of CMBC's predecessor, B.C. Transit, until 1998.

383 Ms. Welch was placed on Level 1 of the AMP in February 1998. As of that date, Ms. Welch had had two consecutive years of absence in excess of the average. Ms. Welch testified that, in 1996 her doctor found a lump on her thyroid, which led to an absence of approximately 3 months. In 1997, the majority of her absences related to a back condition.

384 Ms. Welch was placed on Level 2 of the AMP in January 1999. Between February 1998 and January 1999, she had been absent from work on six occasions for a total of 56 days. Ms. Welch testified that the majority of these absences related to a recurring neck problem, and a slipped disc in her back.

385 She was asked to provide a medical assessment, which she did. It appears that the medical assessment indicated that the causes of Ms. Welch's absences were widely varied. Her doctor indicated that she did not have a permanent physical impairment or disability, and could meet the physical demands of a transit operator.

386 After receipt of the medical assessment, Ms. Welch was placed on Level 3 of the AMP in May 1999. For a two-year period, Ms. Welch was required to meet the average absenteeism rate for transit operators, which at the time was 8.6% (the number of days this equated to was not outlined in the letter).

387 Ms. Welch's absenteeism rate for 1999, 2000 and 2001 was less than the average rate outlined by CMBC. As a result, Ms. Welch successfully completed her two-year monitoring period.

388 However, her absences increased in 2002, and in November of that year, Ms. Welch had a Level 1 interview. In that interview, her Supervisor noted that she had been absent from work for 61.5 days on three separate occasions over the preceding 12 months.

389 Ms. Welch testified that she was diagnosed with depression over 23 years ago, and has struggled with recurrences throughout her time as a transit operator. She testified that she believed that this was the cause of her absences in 2002.

390 Ms. Welch testified that, in December 2003, a regular passenger told her that he was going to rape her and there was nothing she could do about it. Ms. Welch was very concerned, and sent an incident report to CMBC and the Union. She also requested that her Supervisor put her on the spare board (a standby complement of operators available for dispatch to do previously unassigned work and to cover for operators absent for a variety of reasons) for a few days, so that she would not have to have contact with this individual. Her Supervisor refused. At a further meeting with management and her Union representatives, a different Supervisor accused her of flirting with the passenger. Ms. Welch was not challenged on this evidence in cross-examination.

391 In addition, Ms. Welch contacted transit security to ask for assistance, but she says she was told that such security is only for passengers, not for drivers.

392 Ms. Welch testified that, as she did not receive any assistance from CMBC, she went to the Richmond RCMP and filed a complaint. She stated that the officer she talked to there knew who she was talking about right away and said he was dangerous.

393 Shortly after this incident, there was a regular sheet change (there are .sheet changes., prior to which transit operators can sign up for routes on the basis of seniority, every four months). Ms. Welch had signed up for a different route. However, she found the new route very stressful: it was difficult to meet the timing points, and was very crowded. By February 2004, Ms. Welch had booked off for a longer period of time, and her psychiatrist subsequently diagnosed her with PTSD arising, not just from the incident with the passenger, but also from her subsequent treatment by CMBC in relation to it.

394 As a result, Ms. Welch was off work from February to April 2004. On July 2, 2004, Ms. Welch had a Level 2 meeting. The letter confirming that interview notes that, since November 2002, Ms. Welch had been absent on four occasions for a total of 61 days. The majority of this period related to her most recent absence.

395 Ms. Welch stated that, at the Level 2 meeting, she asked her Supervisor what type of help CMBC could provide. He responded that, if she had breast cancer, they would book her off in the afternoon for chemotherapy. Ms. Welch testified that she could not believe what he had said. She felt that, if that was the attitude, there was no assistance to be had from CMBC.

396 She was again asked to provide a medical assessment, which she did. After receipt of this assessment, Ms. Welch was placed on Level 3 of the AMP on September 24, 2004. The Union grieved this placement. The grievance was successful, and, as a result, Ms. Welch was returned to Level 1 in December 22, 2005. No evidence was given about the circumstances under which this grievance was resolved.

397 In January 2006, Ms. Welch had a lengthy absence from work due to shingles. She testified that she anticipated being returned to Level 2 as a result. She agreed in cross-examination that she returned to work in February 2006 and, as of the date of her testimony in July 2006, she had not been advised that she was being escalated in the AMP.

I. Carlos Fernandes

398 Mr. Fernandes has been employed by CMBC since October 1996, most recently in the North Vancouver depot. During his employment with CMBC, he has experienced two periods of higher than average absenteeism: the first in 1997 and 1998; the second in 2001 and 2002. Mr. Fernandes attributed both of these periods to diabetes.

399 Mr. Fernandes was first diagnosed with diabetes in late 1997. Prior to that time, he had been feeling very ill, but didn't know why. He went to his doctor, who referred him to a specialist. When the specialist ran some tests, including testing Mr. Fernandes' blood sugar, he was immediately told to book off work, which he did. Mr. Fernandes was away from work for two months, from late November 1997 until late January 1998.

400 At this time, Mr. Fernandes was diagnosed with Type 2 diabetes, which meant that he was not required to take insulin, but did need to take daily medication. After his blood sugar level came down, his doctor cleared him to return to work, which he did.

401 Between his return to work in February and September 1998, Mr. Fernandes was absent on three separate occasions, for a total of 11 days. In September 1998, Mr. Fernandes was placed on Level 1 of the AMP, but was thereafter dealt with on an informal basis (including meetings in April 1999 and December 1999).

402 On August 16, 2000, Mr. Fernandes was again placed on Level 1 of the AMP. In that letter, Mr. Fernandes' Supervisor indicated that, over the past

12 months, he had been absent from work for 25 days on eight separate occasions.

403 Mr. Fernandes testified that from early 2000 to August 2001 he had been slowly losing weight. At that time, he was not required by his specialist to report his blood sugar readings. He stated that he was not well informed about diabetes, so after his blood sugars came down to normal, he stopped testing. In late 2000, he started suffering from pains in his legs. He did not know what was causing them, and they slowly got worse. In addition, he was losing energy. He was concerned about his condition, but it did not occur to him that it was diabetes. As he was not well informed about the condition, he believed he was cured.

404 Mr. Fernandes stated that, by August 2001, his weight had dropped dramatically, and he eventually returned to his doctor. The specialist then determined that he had been misdiagnosed with Type 2 diabetes, and that he actually had Type 1 diabetes. Although he had continued to take his medication throughout this period, it was not doing any good. The specialist advised him not to work as of August 31, 2001, and he did not return until March 2002.

405 Mr. Fernandes was treated by the specialist with insulin injections, which significantly improved his condition. He initially returned to work in a rehabilitation position in the maintenance department. In November 2002, once his specialist was satisfied that his blood sugar levels were under control, Mr. Fernandes returned to work as a transit operator.

406 As a result, Mr. Fernandes' absence rate was 50.3% in 2001, and 35.67% in 2002, both significantly over the average.

407 On December 17, 2002, Mr. Fernandes was placed on Level 2 of the AMP and asked to seek a medical assessment, which he did. Mr. Fernandes testified that, during this meeting, he advised his Supervisor that most of his absences related to his diabetic condition.

408 With respect to the requirement to seek a medical assessment, Mr. Fernandes agreed in cross-examination that CMBC had a need to understand his new diagnosis and the impact it may have on his ability to drive buses. I note, however, that the medical assessment was sought in December 2002, after Mr. Fernandes returned to driving buses.

409 In any event, following the medical assessment, Mr. Fernandes was placed on Level 3 on February 11, 2003, on parameters of 20 days absent per year for a period of two years. The Level 3 letter states:

> The doctor you attended forwarded the results of your medical assessment to our Occupational Health Nurse who, in turn, advised us that you have a chronic medical condition. However, we are further advised that if you maintain the prescribed treatment regimen, your condition should not prevent you from performing the un-

> restricted duties of your job as a transit operator or from attending at work on a regular or consistent basis.

410 Mr. Fernandes testified that he agreed with this statement as far as it went, that is, that if he maintained appropriate treatment, his condition .should. not prevent him from attending at work. However, he noted that taking care of a diabetic condition was not an exact science, and there could well be periods of absence. Further, his doctor has advised him that there are many factors that could cause fluctuations in his blood sugar levels, including stress. His doctor has taught him how to recognize signs of problems, so that he can address them as soon as possible.

411 Mr. Fernandes testified that, in early 2003, he had a discussion with his Supervisor about corrective surgery that he needed as a result of a condition arising from his diabetes. He had been advised that he would require three weeks for the operation and recovery time. His Supervisor informed him that, if he took the three weeks, and then was subsequently absent for any other reason, he may be in danger of termination. He was told that the only way to safeguard his position would be to get the operation done during his vacation time. Mr. Fernandes was not challenged on this evidence in cross-examination. He testified that, as a result of this discussion, he had the surgery performed during his three weeks of vacation time.

412 After Mr. Fernandes successfully completed his monitoring period, he was returned to Level 1 on February 12, 2005. He was informed of this in a letter dated May 20, 2005. In early 2006, he was formally removed from the AMP. Mr. Fernandes testified that he was verbally advised of this.

413 Mr. Fernandes testified that the AMP had a negative effect on him, as he thought that he should not have been on it. As a result, he was stressed, angry and felt as if it was an injustice.

3. CMBC's evidence about accommodations under the AMP

414 CMBC's evidence about the various accommodations it has made under the AMP was given primarily by Mr. Kelly. In addition, Mr. Jones was cross-examined about his knowledge of the circumstances of some employees.

a. Mr. Jones: Cross-examination

415 With respect to employees who exceeded average attendance, but were not placed on the AMP, Mr. Jones agreed that employee E05435 had been off work for a significant amount of time, as his wife was ill with cancer. In addition, Mr. Jones agreed that employee E04939 has been off work for a long period of time as a result of a kidney transplant and resulting complications. With respect to both of these individuals, Mr. Jones agreed that,

although these individuals may have appeared on the quarterly reports on one or more occasions, they were never called in for any type of interview under the AMP.

416 Mr. Jones also agreed that there was at least one individual who had been permanently accommodated into an alternate position without ever having been placed on the AMP. This employee was diagnosed with a benign brain tumour which required two or three operations, and affected the employee's peripheral vision. The employee was placed in a permanent accommodation in Local 2200 driving a parts truck.

417 Similarly, there was evidence about another employee who had lost a leg as the result of an accident and was permanently accommodated as a Community Shuttle Bus driver.

b. Mr. Kelly: Level 3 expectations relaxed

418 Mr. Kelly testified about various circumstances in which expectations imposed at the Level 3 stage would be relaxed or suspended. For example, he testified that in some circumstances, expectations have been suspended while employees are awaiting medical treatment. Whether or not this is done will depend on the circumstances of each particular case. When the Company has information that the employee's medical issues will be resolved once they receive the necessary treatment, it may decide to suspend expectations.

419 Mr. Kelly gave the example of employee E05732. This employee was at Level 3 of the AMP, and indicated that they were afraid to get certain medical treatment because of their situation in the AMP. Mr. Kelly testified that the employee was advised that, if the medical procedure was designed to improve attendance (correct a medical condition), the employee should have it done. CMBC agreed, on a without prejudice basis, to extend the two-year Level 3 assessment period until the employee's return to work, and not consider absences relating to corrective surgery and recovery time. Thus, while the time the employee needed for the surgery and recovery was not considered for the purposes of the parameters; the assessment period was extended for an equivalent amount of time.

420 Mr. Kelly did not have a clear recollection of who originated the proposal, but he was sure that it was somebody from the Union, and that the Union raised the proposal because a similar approach had been taken earlier with another employee.

c. Mr. Kelly: Exceeding Level 3 parameters not leading to an ESR

421 Mr. Kelly also testified that exceeding parameters at Level 3 did not inexorably lead to an ESR. He gave a number of examples.

422 First, Mr. Kelly testified about employee E03590. Mr. Kelly was not absolutely certain of the circumstances of this employee's case, but stated he believed the employee had an on-the-job motor vehicle accident that led to an absence, and that the employee had been diagnosed with a disability that led to a period of treatment. Mr. Kelly testified that in neither case would the Company have proceeded to the ESR.

423 Mr. Kelly also testified about employee E07385. While at Level 3 of the AMP, this employee was sent to hospital with an aneurysm. This was about two years prior to Mr. Kelly's testimony. The employee continues to be employed in rehabilitation employment, although not able to return as a transit operator. The absence caused the employee to exceed the Level 3 parameters, but there was no follow-up with an ESR because the Company was advised of the circumstances of the employee's absence by the employee's daughter, and the information was followed up by the OHN.

424 Employee E08126 was hired when he was over the age of 60, and immediately ran into attendance problems. The employee was ultimately advanced to Level 3 of the AMP, and then had several absences related to a single WCB case. One involved corrective surgery. Given the nature of the surgery, the operator was not advanced to an ESR.

425 Employee E02494 was at Level 3 of the AMP and had exceeded the parameters when they required corrective surgery for a medical issue that had contributed to the previous absenteeism. Mr. Kelly testified that CMBC suspended the assessment period in order for the employee to have the surgery and allow for recovery time.

426 Employee E01700 was at Level 3 of the AMP when diagnosed with a disability. The employee went for several months of treatment and then resumed work. These absences caused the employee to exceed the Level 3 parameters. There were also personal issues at play. Mr. Kelly testified that the employee had recently resigned, but not because of any steps taken by CMBC.

d. Mr. Kelly: ESR not leading to termination

427 Mr. Kelly also gave examples of employees who were advanced to an ESR, but whose employment was not terminated, for a variety of reasons.

428 Employee E04998 has been advanced to Level 3 of the AMP on three occasions, and has exceeded the parameters imposed at that Level at least twice, both times resulting in an ESR. On both occasions, CMBC determined that termination was not appropriate. Among the reasons causing the employee's absences was a disability relating to migraine headaches. As an accommodation, CMBC was willing to have a higher tolerance for ab-

sences, and allowed the employee to use banked overtime for absences related to migraines (which would then not be recorded as an .absence.).

429 Notably, this was the only example in the evidence before me where a higher tolerance for absences was the accommodation arrived at. Mr. MacLeod, the former president of the Union, stated in his testimony that this was the only grievance he had been involved in where such an agreement had been reached.

430 The accommodation with respect to the migraines took place in 2003. The employee's overall absenteeism still exceeded the average, even after discounting the absenteeism relating to this condition. Nevertheless, CMBC provided the employee with a final opportunity to demonstrate regular attendance at work, and extended the assessment period for six months. Mr. Kelly testified that the reason for this extension was that CMBC was aware of some of the employee's medical conditions. Mr. Kelly testified that he did not think that this decision was reached as the result of Union intervention.

431 Mr. Kelly was asked whether any thought was given to accommodating this employee in another position. He testified that, initially, the accommodation for the migraine headaches seemed to be working well. In 2004-05, the employee had two WCB accidents. One arose out of an on-the-job motor vehicle accident, while the second was not. The fact that one was related to an on-the-job motor vehicle accident was the main reason why the CMBC did not consider termination. With respect to accommodation, Mr. Kelly testified that his understanding was that there was nothing to accommodate: there was no disability arising out of the incident, merely a period of recovery.

432 Mr. Kelly also testified that this employee is currently working in a Local 2200 job. He was not sure of the capacity in which the employee was working, but testified that the assignment to Local 2200 was the employee's decision.

433 In reference to the experience of this employee, Mr. Kelly agreed that it was possible, even where there was an accommodation with respect to a disability, that the absence record (related to that disability) could continue to play a role in future AMP decisions.

434 Mr. Kelly also testified, in general terms, about the circumstances of employee E06513. He stated that, while at Level 3, the employee experienced a four-month absence that caused them to exceed the parameters they had been placed on. However, the ESRC determined that the absence was not a reliable indicator of future attendance. As a result, the ESRC decided to extend the attendance monitoring period for four months to offset the length of the absence.

435 The letter provided to employee E06513 noted that, although asked to contact the OHN with respect to a medical assessment, they declined to do so. Mr. Kelly was asked in cross-examination why, in a case where it appeared the transit operator was not providing appropriate medical information and was exceeding the attendance parameters, a decision was made to give the operator another opportunity to demonstrate compliance. Mr. Kelly testified that his recollection was that the OHN advised the ESRC that the employee did not have an ongoing medical condition, and that the four-month absence was not a reliable indication of future attendance. Further, the employee had achieved acceptable attendance in at least three years, which was an indication that the employee was capable of providing acceptable attendance in the future. Mr. Kelly testified that, in all cases, decisions are based primarily on the individual circumstances and whether, given those circumstances, termination is appropriate. With respect to employee E06513, the consensus was that termination was not appropriate, but that an extension of the monitoring period was.

436 Mr. Kelly also testified that employee E04090 was at Level 3 and exceeded the applicable parameters, leading to an ESR. The absence which caused the employee to exceed the parameters lasted 38 days. The ESRC determined that the circumstances were not appropriate for termination, and extended the two-year period for a period of 38 working days.

437 In general, Mr. Kelly testified that he viewed the Union's approach of arguing that the Company should .not count. disability-related absences as simplistic. From the Company's perspective, he testified, it was not a question of .counting.. Rather, the Company is determining what is appropriate in all the circumstances. He asked what the alternative was: that the Company continue to tolerate absenteeism of 30-40%?

e. Mr. Kelly: Cross-examination

438 Mr. Kelly was asked, in cross-examination, about the utility of placing an operator on the AMP where the OHN is aware that the individual has a chronic disability. He was asked why, in such cases, CMBC advances people through the Program, rather than investigating possible accommodations earlier in the process. Mr. Kelly answered that people with disabilities have different tolerances or reactions to those disabilities. For example, diabetes can be restrictive for some individuals, while others manage it well and can perform their job without accommodation. Other individuals may have some absenteeism at the earlier stages, but, when they are properly diagnosed and their medication is balanced, they are capable of regular attendance.

439 Mr. Kelly testified that, for example, with respect to Mr. Da Luz, many people with his ailment are capable of managing it, and can come to work on a regular basis. The issue with Mr. Da Luz is that he sought the perfect accommodation: that absences related to his disability should never be counted. The Company was not prepared to give him a carte blanche. Further, CMBC offered Mr. Da Luz an accommodation, which he did not like and therefore did not accept. For CMBC the question is, what does the future look like? Mr. Da Luz has a poor prognosis for regular attendance, but his attendance may be improved with an accommodation outside a transit operator's job where he is not on the road regularly. However, Mr. Da Luz refused accommodation into another position. Mr. Kelly stated that, if Mr. Da Luz insists on driving a bus, CMBC has no option but to compare him to other operators.

440 Mr. Kelly was again asked why the Company puts some operators through the AMP process for years when it is apparent that they (1) have a chronic disability and (2) are demonstrably not meeting the attendance expectations. He again stated that disabilities do not affect everyone the same way, so it would not be appropriate to treat the entire group in the same manner. CMBC has to give employees the opportunity to demonstrate whether they can attend regularly. As long as the employee is capable of attending, there is no need for accommodation.

441 With respect to decisions to advance employees in the AMP in general, Mr. Kelly testified that CMBC takes a long hard look at the situation wherever an employee is being introduced into or advanced through the AMP. Where an employee is advanced to Level 3, it is because CMBC believes it is the appropriate thing to do, including in cases where someone has a disability. The employer is entitled, as part of the employment bargain with the employee, to regular attendance by employees. Mr. Kelly stated, however, that the Company takes the question of whether someone has a disability into account in every case. In this regard, Mr. Kelly testified that the Company .has to consider the duty to accommodate to the point of undue hardship. Can we accommodate this person somewhere else?..

442 In cross-examination, Mr. Kelly also testified about the way in which medical information is taken into account in making decisions with respect to the AMP. Using an example, he stated that, if the doctor said .an employee may experience slightly higher rates of absence., the Company would not do anything except wait and see if the employee could meet its attendance expectations, because there is no way of knowing what .a higher rate of absence. means.

443 In addition to questions about specific operators, Mr. Kelly was asked a number of hypothetical questions in cross-examination. For example, he

was asked about a Supervisor conducting an information interview with an employee. What would the Supervisor do if the employee indicated that they had recurring back problems? Mr. Kelly stated that the Supervisor would want to know if the employee was seeing their doctor regularly. Mr. Kelly was asked if the Supervisor would refer the employee to the OHN, and he replied .I don't think at that point it would be the focus of the suggestions.. While the Supervisor should suggest the availability of EAP and the OHN, beyond that there is not much more that the Supervisor could do. Mr. Kelly stated that Supervisors aren't medically trained.

G. Effect of the AMP on CMBC's operations

444 Mr. Kelly testified about the effect of the AMP in two areas: first, in reducing absenteeism, and second (but clearly related), in reducing costs to CMBC.

1. Reduction in absenteeism rates

445 As noted above, based on CMBC's review of the Auditor General's 1996 statistics, average absenteeism in 1996 was 27.4 days per transit operator per year or, in percentage terms, slightly over 10%.

446 Mr. Kelly testified that, at the time of the hearing, the absenteeism rate for transit operators represented by the Union was approximately 7.33%, or just slightly over 18 days per transit operator per year. He also stated that, at the same time, the *median* absence rate, that is, the number at which there are as many transit operators with higher absence rates as there are with lower, is five days (*i.e.*, 50% of transit operators have five days or less, while 50% of transit operators have five days or more). This is an absenteeism rate of approximately 2%.

2. Reduction in costs

447 When asked in cross-examination, Mr. Kelly estimated the cost savings brought about through the AMP at approximately $50-60 million over the first 10 years it has been in place. He testified that this was a rough calculation that he made in his head. He stated that the number of transit operators has increased by approximately 900 drivers since 1997. Taking into account this increase in staff, and the increase in wage rates; all things being equal (*i.e.*, if the absence rate was the same now as in 1996), that would have resulted in savings of $20 million in 2006 alone.

448 Mr. Kelly's evidence in this regard was explored in some detail. In essence, CMBC's costs from absenteeism arise in two, interrelated ways. The first relates the cost of replacing transit operators who are absent in

order to ensure that service delivery levels are not affected. The second relates to the cost of benefits paid to transit operators.

a. Replacement Costs

449 Replacement costs can be calculated in a number of ways. Two were dealt with in the evidence before me.

450 The first relates to the requirement to have sufficient stand-by transit operators to ensure that service delivery levels are not affected. A transit operator who is not able to work will generally be covered by a spare board operator. The spare board was described in the following manner in the Policy Decision, in a part of that award that was adopted by Mr. Kelly in his evidence:

> A spare board is a standby complement of operators available for dispatch to do previously unassigned work, to increase service for special events, such as professional sports games, and to cover for operators absent on temporary promotion, training, discipline, or illness or injury. An operator on a spare board is paid a straight time, standby rate until the start of work, then the applicable rate for the time worked. (pp. 7-8)

451 In fact, there are two types of spare board assignments. The first relates to transit operators who are on spare board stand-by. A stand-by assignment is considered a day's work, so an assignment on stand-by is the same as a complete day's work (7.5 hours). In the first two hours of a stand-by shift, if work becomes available, the stand-by transit operator is required to complete the full shift. Because of this, the transit operator could be assigned a full 7.5 hour shift after one or two hours of stand-by. That transit operator would therefore be paid overtime for the additional hour(s) worked.

452 The second type of assignment arises from routes that are posted as work assignments. Where an operator is absent, the first day of the absence would be filled as a stand-by assignment. If the absence continued, the operator's route would become a formal work assignment filled from the spare board.

453 The spare board is addressed in the Collective Agreement, under which there are a minimum number of operators required to sign spare board slots. It is currently equal to 8% of the routes available (called .indexes.), including holiday time and regular days off.

454 With respect to the minimum spare board allocation, Mr. Kelly testified that, in 1996, the requirement was 12%. Further, the reality in some locations was that the spare board operated at closer to 20% in order to provide required coverage for sick leave. Currently, spare boards operate at between 10-12%, which has led to a reduction in costs to CMBC. The amount of this cost reduction was not explored in the evidence before me, although Mr.

Kelly noted that this number could be calculated through knowing the absence rate in each year, and the cost for a full-time operator.

455 An alternate method of calculating the cost savings to CMBC from the operation of the AMP relates to the cost of providing replacement workers.

456 Mr. Kelly provided an estimate of the cost of replacement workers for 2005. He stated that his estimate was based on a calculation that the average cost of a full-time operator was $62,000 (wages and benefits), and that the productive time of each operator is approximately 1400 hours/year. In this regard, Mr. Kelly noted that the paid time for operators is approximately 1950 hours per year, but this includes unproductive time such as vacations, leaves of absence, statutory holiday time and sick time. 1400 hours is the net working time. Mr. Kelly testified that this was the number provided to him from the accounting department. No one from the accounting department gave testimony with respect to how this number was arrived at.

457 Taking the total absence hours of all operators for a one-year period, and dividing that by 1400, Mr. Kelly estimated that approximately 238 operators are required to cover absence hours. If the cost of each of these operators is $62,000, that means that the approximate operations cost of replacing absent transit operators is $14,756,000.

458 Mr. Kelly was asked how this compared with the replacement costs for transit operators in 1996. He stated that, applying the same absence rate in 2005 that existed in 1996, the cost would have been approximately $62 million. The actual cost in 2005 worked out to $41 million, approximately a $21 million savings to CMBC as a result of reduced absenteeism. It is not clear to me how these numbers are derived from the figures put in evidence before me.

459 In cross-examination, Mr. Kelly was challenged on a number of the assumptions underlying his calculations. For example, the Union asserted that a more realistic figure for the annual cost of an operator is $57,581.25. In addition, it was put to Mr. Kelly in cross-examination that the actual productive time of operators was 1557 hours per year, rather than 1400. On this basis, the cost of operator absences would be approximately $12,322,388 per year. Mr. Kelly testified that he did not know how the Company's figures were arrived at, so could not really respond to the Union's figures.

460 I need not reconcile the differences in calculations as, regardless of which is more accurate, it is sufficient to say that the cost of absenteeism is substantial, and there is a significant cost saving to CMBC in reducing absenteeism.

461 Mr. Kelly testified that, in order to maintain this reduction in costs, it is absolutely necessary to maintain acceptable levels of absenteeism. If absen-

teeism goes up, and exceeds the spare board allotments, that would lead to service cancellations.

462 In addition, Mr. Kelly noted that reducing absenteeism improves CMBC's ability to provide more and better service using the same number of staff.

b. Cost of benefits

463 With respect to the cost of benefits, Mr. Kelly testified that CMBC pays the costs of STD benefits. The cost of these benefits for all CAW employees (Local 111 and Local 2200) was approximately $8.5 million in 1996. In addition, the premiums paid by CMBC to WCB for all of its employees were approximately $3 million. Mr. Kelly also noted that the cost of LTD benefits was approximately $3.5 million, although these costs are borne by the employees, not CMBC.

464 In comparison, Mr. Kelly stated that, in 2005, the cost of STD benefits was $7.5 million, and the cost of WCB premiums was slightly less than $4 million. Thus, the overall costs of these benefits are approximately the same, although CMBC currently employs approximately 900 more operators than it did in 1996.

III. Analysis and Decision

465 The Union argues that the AMP systemically discriminates against employees who are disabled, or are perceived to be disabled, with respect to their employment, contrary to s. 13 of the *Code*. That section provides:

> (1) A person must not
>
> (a) refuse to employ or refuse to continue to employ a person, or
>
> (b) discriminate against a person regarding employment or any term or condition of employment
>
> because of the ... physical or mental disability ... of that person ...
>
> .
>
> (4) Subsections (1) and (2) do not apply with respect to a refusal, limitation, specification or preference based on a bona fide occupational requirement.

466 This complaint is not one of a single complainant, nor even of a series of individual complainants; it is a representative complaint of systemic discrimination practised against an identifiable class (see *CAW-Canada, Local 111 v. Coast Mountain Bus Co.*, 2005 BCHRT 478 (B.C. Human Rights Trib.). (*CAW No. 7.*).

467 Mr. Jones testified that the Union understood that the Company was entitled to have an attendance management program. He stated that the Union does not object to the existence of such a program in and of itself, but does object to the manner in which the AMP is applied. Specifically, in

the Union's view, the AMP is applied to operators based on statistical information without properly taking into account their individual circumstances. Further, the Union argues that there is no clear cut policy on accommodation *within* the AMP.

468 The ongoing human rights dispute over the AMP cannot be separated from the labour relations issues surrounding it. In the Union's eyes, the human rights and labour relations issues are one and the same. For example, the Union consistently took the position during the testimony of its witnesses, and in argument, that CMBC needs to take a broader approach to the issues causing absenteeism; that consideration should be given to the difficult and stressful work conditions dealt with by transit operators on a daily basis; and that WCB absences, in particular, should not be calculated in an employee's attendance record.

469 However, it is not for the Tribunal to determine whether the AMP, in its conception and implementation, constitutes .good labour relations.. Rather, the role of the Tribunal is to determine whether the AMP, as formally outlined in the Guide or other policy statements, or in its application in practice, is discriminatory for the purposes of the *Code*. It is this issue that I will consider in the remainder of this decision.

470 Given the Union's argument that the application of the AMP systemically discriminates against disabled employees, I will first consider what is meant by the term .systemic discrimination., especially in the context of a claim of discrimination on the basis of disability. I will then consider the appropriate test to be used, and apply that test to determine whether the AMP, as applied by CMBC, does, in fact, constitute a form of systemic discrimination. If I determine that the Union has established that the application of the AMP has an adverse impact on some or all members of the represented class, I will then consider whether it can be justified as a *bona fide* occupational requirement. If I find that it cannot, and it is therefore discriminatory, I will then turn to consider remedy.

A. What is systemic discrimination?

471 The leading case on systemic discrimination remains the decision of the Supreme Court of Canada in *Canadian National Railway v. Canada (Human Rights Commission)*, [1987] 1 S.C.R. 1114 (S.C.C.) (also known as .*Action Travail des Femmes*.). Although the case dealt specifically with discrimination on the basis of sex, it has been broadly applied. The Court referred to the 1984 *Report of the Commission on Equality in Employment* by Judge Rosalie Abella (as she then was), in the following manner:

> A thorough study of .systemic discrimination. in Canada is to be found in the Abella Report on equality in employment. ... Although Judge Abella chose not to offer a

precise definition of systemic discrimination, the essentials may be gleaned from the following comments, found at p. 2 of the Abella Report:

> Discrimination ... means practices or attitudes that have, whether by design or impact, the effect of limiting an individual's or a group's right to the opportunities generally available because of attributed rather than actual characteristics ... It is not a question of whether this discrimination is motivated by an intentional desire to obstruct someone's potential, or whether it is the accidental by-product of innocently motivated practices or systems. If the barrier is affecting certain groups in a disproportionately negative way, it is a signal that the practices that lead to this adverse impact may be discriminatory.
>
> This is why it is important to look at the results of a system ...

In other words, systemic discrimination in an employment context is discrimination that results from the simple operation of established procedures ... none of which is necessarily designed to promote discrimination. (para. 34)

472 While the definition noted above refers to an adverse impact because of .attributed rather than actual characteristics., that is because *Action Travail des Femmes* involved allegations of discrimination on the basis of sex. In contrast, the present case involves allegations of discrimination on the basis of disability. In this context, it is important to note that human rights law, including jurisprudence from the Supreme Court of Canada, has identified disability as a unique form of disadvantage, on the basis that the discrimination experienced by the disabled in society has been based not only on stereotypes about disability, but also sometimes on real features of disability itself. These different forms of discrimination experienced by the disabled were explained in *Eaton v. Brant (County) Board of Education* (1996), [1997] 1 S.C.R. 241 (S.C.C.), where Justice Sopinka made a distinction between two forms of discrimination: unfair treatment based on presumed characteristics of an individual, and unfair treatment based on the failure to take into account real characteristics. A unanimous Court held that both these forms of discrimination are relevant in the context of disability:

> The principal object of certain of the prohibited grounds is the elimination of discrimination by the attribution of untrue characteristics based on stereotypical attitudes relating to immutable characteristics such as race or sex. In the case of disability, this is one of the objectives. The other equally important objective seeks to take into account the true characteristics of this group which act as headwinds to the enjoyment of society's benefits and to accommodate them. (p. 272)

473 Thus, in the context of a claim of discrimination based on disability, systemic discrimination can be established both where a .system. operates on the basis of presumed, rather than actual, characteristics; and also where the .system. fails to take into account the actual characteristics or circumstances of those with disabilities.

B. Evidence relevant to a claim of systemic discrimination

474 A question which arises in this case is the nature of the evidence which is required to prove systemic discrimination. It is clear from the Tribunal's case law that statistical evidence, while it may be useful, is not necessarily required to prove such a claim: see *Radek v. Henderson Development (Canada) & Securiguard Services (No. 3)*, 2005 BCHRT 302 (B.C. Human Rights Trib.), para. 504.

475 Quite often, cases of systemic discrimination can be established through evidence from a number of individuals relating to their experience with the policies or procedures at issue. That was the case in *Radek*. In this case, the majority of the evidence led by the Union related to such experiences.

476 I find that in this case, as in *Radek*, statistical information is not central to the issues before me. Rather, the case before me is a case in which patterns of conduct or experiences of a number of individual operators may serve to highlight the facts upon which a discrimination analysis can be applied. In this case, the focus is on patterns of conduct that are part of the administrative structures of the CMBC workplace which may create or perpetuate a position of relative disadvantage for the disabled.

477 In the particular circumstances of this case, however, such evidence raises some complex issues about the use to which it can be put. That is because several of the operators who testified before me (Cynthia Cable, Virginia Young, Kevin Minch, and Christopher Watson) have also had some of their issues adjudicated before labour arbitrators. In addition, Ms. Cable and Ms. Young also brought individual claims before the Tribunal. Ms. Young's complaint was dismissed as a result of the arbitration award involving the same matters. Following the arbitration award in her case, Ms. Cable withdrew those parts of her complaint that related to the issues raised in the arbitration.

478 I find that, with respect to instances where arbitration awards have been rendered, it is not my role to reconsider those decisions with respect to the specific outcome for the individuals in question. To do so would run contrary to the principle of finality, which underlies the doctrine of *res judicata*. Specifically, judicial or quasi-judicial decisions should generally be conclusive of the issues decided. The Tribunal has addressed this issue in a number of decisions, including *Barter v. Insurance Corp. of British Columbia*, 2003 BCHRT 9 (B.C. Human Rights Trib.) and *C.S.W.U., Local 1611 v. SELI Canada*, 2007 BCHRT 404 (B.C. Human Rights Trib.). It has also been addressed by the Supreme Court of Canada in decisions such as *Danyluk v. Ainsworth Technologies Inc.* (2001), 201 D.L.R. (4th) 193 (S.C.C.).

479 At the same time, I find that I can consider the evidence before me as a whole, including that related to those individuals, to determine whether discriminatory patterns, such as those alleged by the Union, adversely impact employees with disabilities as a group.

C. Has systemic discrimination been proven in this case?

480 The fact that this case involves allegations of systemic discrimination does not change the basic framework by which the Tribunal analyzes issues of discrimination. In this case, as in all other cases under the *Code*, the burden of proof lies on the complainant to establish on a balance of probabilities that the respondent contravened s. 13 of the *Code*.

481 Specifically, the initial evidentiary burden lies on the Union to establish that the AMP is *prima facie* discriminatory on the basis of physical and mental disability. Therefore, I will first consider whether the Union has established that the AMP, as applied by CMBC, is *prima facie* discriminatory. If the Union does establish a *prima facie* case of discrimination, the onus shifts to CMBC to establish, on the balance of probabilities, that its conduct was justified.

1. Has the Union established a prima facie case of discrimination?

482 The test with respect to what constitutes a *prima facie* case of discrimination was established by the Supreme Court of Canada in *O'Malley v. Simpsons-Sears Ltd.* (1985), 7 C.H.R.R. D/3102 (S.C.C.):

> A *prima facie* case of discrimination ... is one which covers the allegations made and which, if they are believed, is complete and sufficient to justify a verdict in the complainant's favour in the absence of an answer from the respondent. (at D/3108)

483 To establish discrimination, a complainant need not prove that the protected ground was the sole or even the primary cause of the alleged behaviour; it is sufficient that the protected ground was one of the factors that influenced the conduct complained of: *Nixon v. Vancouver Rape Relief Society*, 2002 BCHRT 1 (B.C. Human Rights Trib.), para. 131.

484 The British Columbia Court of Appeal outlined the test for finding *prima facie* discrimination on the basis of disability in *Health Employers Assn. of British Columbia v. B.C.N.U.*, 2006 BCCA 57 (B.C. C.A.), in the following manner:

> [U]nder s. 13(1)(a), to establish a *prima facie* case of discrimination, an employee must establish that he or she had (or was perceived to have) a disability, that he or she received adverse treatment, and that his or her disability was a factor in the adverse treatment (para. 38).

485 CMBC concedes that some of its employees have disabilities, and that, in some cases, these disabilities are a contributing factor in the excessive absenteeism of some employees. I find, and it is not in dispute, that some

transit operators have disability-related excessive absenteeism that has led to their being subject to the AMP.

486 The Supreme Court of Canada has consistently emphasized the crucial importance of work as a fundamental aspect of a person's life. In addition, the Supreme Court and other tribunals have noted the close connection between work and human dignity, especially for those with disabilities: see *Martin v. Nova Scotia (Workers' Compensation Board)*, 2003 SCC 54 (S.C.C.), para. 104.

487 It is clear, on the evidence before me, that induction into the AMP is perceived by many employees to be extremely stressful. In addition, it can have negative employment-related consequences, including being considered with respect to promotions and transfers. Finally, induction into, and progress through, the AMP can, in some cases, lead to termination of employment.

488 As noted by the Tribunal in *MacRae v. International Forest Products Ltd.*, 2005 BCHRT 462 (B.C. Human Rights Trib.), termination of an employee because that employee is unable to attend work regularly due to a disability constitutes a *prima face* case of discrimination. However, such a termination can be justified by an employer who can establish that it could not have accommodated the employee's absenteeism without undue hardship:

> The present-day arbitral approach reflects what, in my view, is the inescapable conclusion that anytime an employer terminates an employee's employment due to absenteeism related to a disability, a *prima facie* case of discrimination on the basis of disability will have been established. Depending on the facts and circumstances, that discharge may ultimately be justifiable as having been based on a *bona fide* occupational requirement (.BFOR.) under the analysis prescribed by the Supreme Court of Canada in *British Columbia (Public Service Employee Relations Commission) v. B.C.G.S.E.U.*, [1999] 3 S.C.R. 3 ("*Meiorin*"). That includes showing that the employer could not have accommodated the employee's disability without undue hardship. But in all cases, the employer will be called upon to justify the discharge of a disabled employee's employment on the basis of excessive absenteeism as a BFOR. (para. 104)

489 Thus, it is clear that some CMBC employees have received adverse treatment, and that their disabilities were factors in that adverse treatment. With respect to some individual employees, then, a *prima facie* case has been established.

490 However, CMBC argues that, where the complaint relates to a policy as a whole, to find that policy itself to be *prima facie* discriminatory, it is not sufficient to establish that individual instances of discrimination are possible.

491 I have some concerns with this argument. It is difficult to conceive of how one would establish that a policy itself was discriminatory without looking at the outcomes (both individual and aggregate) of that policy. The Court in *Action Travail des Femmes* made this point when it endorsed the statement that it is important to look at the outcomes of a system. In my view, this includes the outcomes in individual cases.

492 I do, however, agree with the CMBC's argument to this extent: the question before the Tribunal is not whether a *prima facie* case of discrimination has been established with respect to any specific individual, but whether the AMP itself (in its conception or application) is *prima facie* discriminatory.

493 In this regard, I note that the Union does not dispute that CMBC is entitled to have an attendance management program, and to manage the attendance of its employees. Insofar as the AMP is applied to individuals who have recurring absences that are not disability-related, the existence of such a policy (in the absence of other concerns) is not problematic from a human rights perspective. The broader question before the Tribunal is whether the AMP has a discriminatory impact on those with disabilities who are less likely, because of their disabilities, to be able to meet the attendance requirements of the AMP. This question requires me to examine not just the terms of the Program as it is outlined in the Guide, but also the way in which the Program is applied in practice.

494 For the reasons outlined below, I find that there are a number of areas in which the AMP, in its application, has an adverse impact on those with disabilities, and in particular, those with chronic disabilities and those who suffer from a series of recurring disabilities that negatively affect their ability to attend work. By .chronic disability. I mean a disability which is ongoing for an extended period of time. By .recurring disabilities. I mean a series of disabilities over an extended period of time, which may or may not be related. I find, further, that the presence of a chronic disability or recurring disabilities is a factor in the adverse treatment. Below, I identify a number of issues which, taken together, lead to the conclusion that the AMP, as applied by CMBC, is *prima facie* discriminatory.

a. Information/Confidentiality Issues

495 The confidentiality of personal information is a major concern for both CMBC and the Union. This concern is enshrined in the Collective Agreement between the parties, including in Article 12.04, and Letter of Understanding 4, as noted above. Pursuant to the Collective Agreement, such information is held solely within the OHG, and is treated as strictly confidential.

496 The Union asserts that one of the problems with the operation of the AMP is the way that these confidentiality provisions affect the information that is available to those responsible for making decisions with respect to whether an employee is placed in or advanced through the AMP. I agree. While the OHG often receives a great deal of medical information about employees both before and during their placement on the AMP, the type of information communicated to Mr. Kelly, Supervisors and others who are charged with making decisions about placement and advancement in the AMP is extremely limited in nature.

497 It was evident, in the evidence before me, that this creates difficulties in the application of the AMP to employees with disabilities, and in particular to those with chronic or recurring disabilities, at at least two different stages: first, at the quarterly meeting stage; and second, with respect to AMP meetings between operators and their Supervisors. I will consider each of these in turn.

Quarterly Meetings

498 Mr. Kelly testified that he reviews the attendance of all employees on a quarterly basis. In doing so, he identifies all employees who are at, or above, the average absence rate for the previous 12 month period, and then reviews each identified employee's attendance history for the past several years. If it appears that their absenteeism rate is persistently at the average or higher, and where he is not aware of any circumstances which would cause him to exercise his discretion *not* to move these employees forward for discussion, they are identified for discussion at a quarterly review.

499 The list of employees generated by Mr. Kelly is sent to the OHG. Mr. Kelly testified that the OHG identifies any employees on the list with special medical issues that should be taken into account. However, on all of the evidence before me, it is clear that the medical information requested of and provided by the OHG is limited. Specifically, Ms. Lopez testified that the OHG is provided only with a list of employees about whom RTW information is sought (rather than a complete list of all employees to be discussed) prior to the quarterly meeting. She further testified that the focus of the information provided by the OHG relates to the employee's RTW prognosis, and not more general information about the causes of their absenteeism. She emphasized that the OHG does not reveal any confidential medical information at this stage.

500 Thus, the OHG, which is the holder of much of the medical information CMBC has with respect to an employee, does not provide *any* information at this stage unless that information is specifically requested. Further, the

only type of information which is requested of the OHG is RTW information.

501 At the quarterly meeting, CMBC management personnel from each depot review the list generated by Mr. Kelly, and annotated by the OHG, in order to determine whether an employee is appropriately placed on, or progressed in, the AMP.

502 Mr. Kelly testified that, in doing so, the attendees at these meetings will consider a number of factors, including whether the group has been advised that the employee has a disability which interferes with their ability to attend regularly, and whether accommodation is required. However, given the limited information provided by the OHG, the participants at a quarterly meeting do not have the full medical information necessary to determine whether an employee's absenteeism issue is disability-related.

503 The list of employees to be discussed at a quarterly meeting will include operators at many different levels of the AMP. The extent of information known to the group about the circumstances of each individual operator will vary widely depending on a number of factors, including past discussions about that operator. I note, however, that given CMBC's view on the confidentiality of medical information, it will always be the OHG that has the most specific medical information about the operator in question, and the OHG is not asked to provide such information. Nor is the OHG contacted in order to discuss questions which may arise during quarterly meetings. In this regard, Ms. Lopez testified that, even though OHNs make themselves available by phone during quarterly meetings, no OHN has ever been called upon to provide further information in the quarterly review process.

504 On the basis of all of the evidence before me, it is apparent that the decisions made at quarterly meetings are often made without taking into account the impact or role of disability on the absenteeism of the employee in question. As a corollary, the focus of the discussion is not to consider whether accommodation is appropriate. No consideration can be given to accommodation where no one is aware of the nature of the condition giving rise to the attendance issue.

505 A similar policy raised concerns in a case of individual discrimination in *Morris v. British Columbia Railway*, 2003 BCHRT 14 (B.C. Human Rights Trib.), where the Tribunal found as follows:

> Ms. Deveaux's ignorance of the effects of Mr. Morris' condition was furthered by BCRail's corporate policy under which Mr. Morris' superiors were not informed by Human Resources about the details of his illness or the effects which it could be expected to have on his performance. While confidentiality is laudable, BCRail's policy was so rigid that it ensured that Ms. Deveaux did not have available to her the

> information which might have enabled her to see how Mr. Morris' disability affected his performance. (para. 234)

506 Just as in *Morris*, CMBC's (and possibly the Union's) interpretation of its confidentiality obligations is so rigid that it ensures that decision makers do not have information before them which might enable them to make more appropriate decisions with respect to the treatment of individuals with disabilities within the AMP. The further result of this structure is that the issue of accommodation, if it arises, does so only at later stages of the AMP, and not as part of the initial consideration of any individual's circumstances.

507 There are at least two examples of the difficulties presented by this policy in the evidence before the Tribunal. There was evidence, for example, that the OHG was aware that Mr. Da Luz suffered from Crohn's disease while he was being placed on the AMP. Similarly, the OHG was aware of Mr. Fernandes' diagnosis of diabetes at the time as he was being placed on and advanced through the AMP. However, the OHG apparently was not asked whether there were any disability-related reasons for the absenteeism of either individual, and the OHG therefore did not provide any information to the AMP decision makers. Similar concerns, relating to poor inter-departmental communication with respect to pertinent medical information, were also noted by the arbitrator in Mr. Watson's case.

508 The result of this lack of information is especially notable with respect to Mr. Da Luz. In 2001, the year that he was first placed in the AMP, Mr. Da Luz experienced a 15% absence rate, based on five occasions of absences amounting to 25 days over the preceding 11 months. Mr. Da Luz testified that much, if not all, of this absenteeism was caused by his Crohn's disease.

509 Initially, .average. absenteeism was calculated on a depot-by-depot basis. Subsequently, the .average. used was the .average. absenteeism of all CMBC operators represented by the Union. There was no evidence before me with respect to the average absenteeism rate in 2001 at Mr. Da Luz's depot (Oakridge), but there is evidence that, in at least one depot (Burnaby), the average absenteeism rate in 2001 was 24 days (this is reflected in the evidence relating to Mr. Minch). Thus, Mr. Da Luz, whose absenteeism was likely only slightly over the average, and which was caused in large part by a chronic disability, was placed at Level 1 of the AMP. There appear to have been no enquiries made with respect to whether those absences were caused by a disability, and the OHG did not volunteer any information.

510 As in *Morris*, the importance that CMBC places on the confidentiality of an employee's medical information is commendable. However, it may be possible to take potential issues into consideration with relatively minimal

intrusions on that confidentiality. For example, prior to the quarterly meeting, Mr. Kelly could provide the OHG with a list and request information about whether there are disability-related reasons for the absences at issue. This would serve to identify those employees who may be in need of accommodation, and with whom CMBC might want to engage in discussion with, prior to, instead of, or in conjunction with, implementing the AMP process.

511 In this regard, I note that Article 12.04 of the Collective Agreement provides that an employee may disclose medical information to particular members of CMBC. Employees will frequently not know whether they are being discussed at a quarterly meeting, and will therefore not be able to make a decision as to whether to authorize disclosure of their medical information to the individuals responsible for making decisions about their placement on the AMP. Having the OHG provide a preliminary identification of employees who may have disability-related absence issues, and notifying the employees that there are concerns, may initiate a timely and appropriate dialogue.

Discussions between Supervisors and operators

512 Pursuant to the Guide, Supervisors play a key role in the administration of the AMP. Specifically, these Supervisors have primary responsibility for, among other things: monitoring employee attendance; and meeting with employees who exhibit excessive absenteeism, to review their attendance records, express CMBC's concerns, counsel regarding available assistance, and caution about the possible consequences of continued unacceptable absenteeism.

513 In addition, Mr. Kelly testified that the quarterly meetings are led by the Supervisor at each depot. He stated that the role of these Supervisors is extremely important, as they are the people who have direct contact with the operators. He testified that often Supervisors will be privy to particular circumstances and situations which may prevent intervention with respect to the employee by CMBC.

514 Given this framework, the information that the Supervisors have, and the use they choose to make of it, is crucially important. The evidence before me raised several concerns in this regard.

515 First, there was unchallenged evidence that, in some instances, where an employee attempted to give information to their Supervisor about the reasons for their absenteeism, the Supervisor would state that they did not want to hear that information, and that they were not the appropriate individuals to be receiving the information. Mr. Jones and Mr. MacLeod both testified that they had often had this experience when accompanying an em-

ployee to an AMP meeting with Supervisors. Further, they testified that, in some instances, the Supervisor would instruct the employee to contact the OHG if they wanted to provide such information.

516 In addition to this general evidence, there was specific evidence before me about instances where this occurred.

517 For example, Ms. Young testified that, throughout her experience on the AMP, her Supervisor was well aware that her absences were being caused by ongoing back problems, but that he seemed not to take this into account. Further, it appears that Ms. Young or the Union approached her Supervisor with respect to potential accommodations on a number of occasions, and the Supervisor simply told her to advise the OHG.

518 Mr. Da Luz testified that he informed his Supervisor, at his Level 1 meeting, that his absences were caused by his Crohn's disease. The Level 1 letter stated only .you need to contact the Occupational Health Nurse.....

519 Supervisors play a significant role in making decisions at two key points of the Program: first, in monitoring employee attendance and meeting with employees to discuss any attendance issues; and second, in attending quarterly meetings to discuss employees under their supervision. As noted above, Mr. Kelly testified that Supervisors are key because they may have information about the employee that no one else does. In my view, it is problematic for these individuals to refuse to hear or take into account relevant information. Especially in cases where an employee, who is being represented by the Union, chooses to provide medical information, the Supervisor, as a decision maker, has an obligation to receive that information and take it into account in both roles in which they are key.

520 Second, there was also evidence before me of instances where a Supervisor was proactive in seeking out the reasons for absences, and the appropriateness of placing an operator on the AMP. However, when that Supervisor sought assistance from the OHG, the information they were provided was difficult for them to decipher. In one instance, a Supervisor asked a question about employee E03590: specifically, whether the employee's chronic disability put the employee into the AMP and whether it escalated the employee through the process. The OHN responded:

> Have just received [E03590]'s Level 2 medical assessment back. [E03590] has a mild medical condition that is expected to resolve in time. [E03590] also has a chronic medical condition which is being actively treated. [E03590] is capable of unrestricted work as a Transit Operator.

521 The Supervisor forwarded this e-mail to Mr. Kelly, among others, stating:

> A couple of days ago I asked the question regarding the below e mail. The question I asked was DID [E03590]'s CHRONIC DISABILITY PUT [E03590] INTO OUR

> PROGRAM AND DID IT ESCALATE [E03590] TRHOUGH THE PROCESS. I am not clear on this answer and should I proceed further with issuing the letter 3. I think I am getting mixed messages as to what I should do.

522 Mr. Kelly agreed in cross-examination that in this circumstance there was some lack of clarity about the information that was being passed on from the OHN, but that it was unlikely that the OHN could give any more specific information.

523 The fact that the OHN cannot or will not give more specific information to the individuals who are assessing the employee's placement on the AMP is problematic, and illustrative of a systemic flaw in the type of information used when making these decisions.

524 It may be that CMBC is attempting to address this issue. In the 2006 Guide, there is a direction to Supervisors that, where they are dealing with an employee whose excessive absenteeism may be at least partly associated with a disability, they *must* refer that employee to the OHG. This, however, is only a partial answer to the problems posed by the strictures of confidentiality, as it does not address situations where the OHG has information relating to an operator's disability, but is not requested to provide it at the quarterly meeting. It also does not address situations where the OHG does not provide such information to the Supervisor who has the responsibility to monitor the attendance of employees under their supervision.

Impact of Confidentiality/Information issues: failure to consider accommodation at an early stage

525 In addition to the issues raised by the confidentiality requirements of the Collective Agreement, there are also more general problems with respect to the coordination of information between departments.

526 I note, in this regard, the evidence of Ms. Lopez with respect to the involvement of the OHG in the AMP process. Aside from providing RTW information requested for the quarterly meeting process, the OHG is next involved in organizing medical assessments at the Level 2 stage, as well as potentially being involved in discussions at the ESR stage. What is notably missing is any indication that the OHG is specifically involved in considering early accommodation options.

527 In short, at the early stages of the AMP, or prior to an employee's initiation into the AMP, the only CMBC employee with information about the employee's medical status may well be the OHN. However, because the OHN's primary involvement under the AMP comes later in the process, the identification and potential accommodation of individuals with chronic disabilities is difficult.

528 The effect of these confidentiality and information issues is that CMBC does not have the opportunity to fully consider accommodation requirements and options for operators with chronic disabilities which affect their attendance at the early stages of the AMP process. This is illustrated in a number of the individual situations before me.

529 First, with respect to Ms. Cable. Ms. Cable testified that, in 2002, she was placed on Level 1 of the AMP. She attributed the absences giving rise to this placement to two disabilities: a heart condition, and depression. She testified that, following her Level 1 meeting, she contacted the OHN asking for her support to be removed from the AMP, given her disabilities. The OHN told her that she could not provide such support until Ms. Cable reached Level 2 of the AMP and her doctor provided a medical questionnaire that indicated the presence of chronic medical conditions. Ms. Cable's evidence in this regard was not challenged on cross-examination.

530 Mr. Da Luz's circumstances provide a further example. As outlined above, Mr. Da Luz was identified as having an attendance problem. In 2001, he was placed on Level 1 of the AMP. Mr. Da Luz testified that his Supervisor was aware that he was suffering from Crohn's disease, and the Level 1 letter confirms that he raised this issue with his Supervisor during the meeting. Mr. Da Luz was advised in that letter to contact the OHN, but there is no indication that he did so.

531 Nevertheless, given Mr. Da Luz's advice to his Supervisor, and the fact that the OHG would have information regarding the reasons for at least some of Mr. Da Luz's absences, CMBC must be taken to have knowledge of Mr. Da Luz's condition at the time it placed him on Level 1 of the AMP.

532 During the following year, Mr. Da Luz's attendance improved, but was still above the average (seven occasions and 21 days of absence). He was placed at Level 2 of the AMP, and a medical assessment was sought. That medical assessment indicated that Mr. Da Luz had an ongoing medical condition which .could have attendance implications in the longer term.. Nevertheless, he was placed at Level 3 of the AMP and given a target of 20 days absence (which was only one less than his previous year's absence rate). The letter also provided:

> Simply staying within the prescribed number of days, during the assessment period, will not be acceptable if it is achieved without due regard to the frequency of your absences. Please by advised that the number of absences per year, per employee, in your group averages less than two.

533 Mr. Da Luz has a chronic medical condition which, at the time in question, led to a pattern of intermittent, short-term absences. He was placed on the AMP at a point when his absences were approximately five days over the average. He was advanced to Level 3 of the AMP at a time when his

absences were one over the average. His frequency was above average, but this frequency was consistent with his disability.

534 One of the reasons that accommodation was not considered for Mr. Da Luz at an earlier stage of the Program relates to the lack of communication between various departments responsible for the AMP. The fact that Mr. Da Luz was not accommodated at an earlier stage of the Program clearly illustrates the way in which CMBC's application of the AMP may discriminate against those with disabilities.

535 The testimony given by, and with respect to, Mr. Fernandes was also notable. Mr. Fernandes was initially placed at Level 1 of the AMP following a number of absences, which, although unknown to him at the time, were caused by diabetes. He was subsequently absent from work for an extended period while his diabetes was properly diagnosed and treated. On his return to work, he was placed on Level 2 of the AMP and asked to seek a medical assessment, which he did. He also advised his Supervisor that most of his absences were related to diabetes.

536 In cross-examination of Mr. Fernandes, CMBC suggested that it needed to understand his new diagnosis and the impact it might have on his ability to drive buses. Given that Mr. Fernandes is employed in a safety sensitive position, as a bus driver, it is clear that CMBC had the responsibility to ensure that Mr. Fernandes was safe to work in that capacity. That does not explain, however, why Mr. Fernandes had to be advanced through the AMP for this to be accomplished. CMBC has the ability to seek medical assessments of its employees outside of the AMP. Further, as noted above, Mr. Fernandes was asked to obtain the Level 2 medical assessment only after he had completed a six-month rehabilitation assignment and had been driving buses for a month. If CMBC was concerned about whether Mr. Fernandes was safe to resume his employment, it is surprising that it did not obtain such an assessment prior to allowing him to return to work as an operator.

537 Thus, the evidence before me indicates that the structure in place to protect confidentiality and information issues, in practice, leads to situations where decisions under the AMP are made with incomplete information. CMBC is not taking into account all of the information it has available to it, and its failure to do so means that any accommodation process which may be required cannot be commenced at an early stage. This, in turn, leads to employees being subjected to the stress of being placed on the AMP and advanced through it in situations where this may not be appropriate.

b. When is accommodation required?

538 In addition to CMBC failing to exchange information necessary to the consideration of possible accommodations at an early stage of the AMP (or prior to an employee being placed on the AMP), the evidence before me also indicates that CMBC's understanding of when accommodation should be considered leads to systemic problems within the AMP.

539 Specifically, even in situations where CMBC personnel are aware that an employee may suffer from a disability, and that the employee's absenteeism is related to this disability, it does not appropriately consider accommodation options at an early stage of the process.

540 In this regard, I will first examine the role of .average. absence rates in the AMP, then consider the basis on which CMBC justifies the imposition of the .average. absenteeism standard on employees with disabilities.

Role of the average attendance rate

541 Average attendance rates play an important role as a yardstick against which to measure an individual's attendance at two key stages in the AMP.

542 First, as noted above, Mr. Kelly considers the average attendance rate in compiling the lists of employees for consideration at quarterly meetings.

543 Second, the average attendance rate comes into play in setting attendance parameters for those at Level 3 of the AMP.

544 In this regard, the Level 3 letters (as outlined in the Guide, and as delivered to the witnesses who testified for the Union) state:

> Without intending to suggest that any particular rate of absenteeism is acceptable, and after reviewing the particular circumstances of your case, Coast Mountain Bus Co. expects you to maintain an attendance performance that is at least equal to the average for employees in your group. Specifically, Coast Mountain expects that you will not be absent more than __________ days per year, for a period of two years.

545 While the letters indicate that the parameters are arrived at .taking into account all of the circumstances of [the employee's] case., this assertion was not borne out in the evidence, and is not consistent with actual practice. In this regard, Mr. Kelly was asked who decides what the applicable parameters will be. He said that the parameters invariably reflect the average absenteeism rate, as that is the benchmark on which CMBC makes its assessment. Thus, once the decision is made that parameters will be imposed, there appears to be no individual assessment with respect to what those parameters will be.

546 Mr. Kelly indicated in his testimony that, where parameters are imposed and an employee is unsuccessful in meeting those parameters, consideration is given at that point to whether this failure should lead to termination (*i.e.*, prior to advancing the employee to an ESR). The fact that there may be consideration given to not enforcing the standard at a later date does

not remedy or address the problem at the stage of setting the parameters. In my view, the fact that lip service is given to an individualized assessment that never occurs at this stage reflects a further systemic problem in the application of the AMP.

Basis on which CMBC justifies imposition of .average. absenteeism standard

547 As noted above, where parameters are imposed, those parameters are invariably the .average. absenteeism rate for CMBC operators. The basis on which CMBC justifies such an imposition in all circumstances is inconsistent with human rights principles.

548 In this regard, I note the evidence led by CMBC with respect to their assessment of whether an operator is .fit to return to work. (and what such a finding means), and CMBC's assessment of the medical information it receives from an employee's physician.

549 Where an employee has been off work as a result of a disability, and is seeking to return to work, they will be asked to provide medical information with respect to their ability to return to work. Mr. Kelly testified that, .if an employee is cleared to return to work as an operator, we assume that clearance includes a medical opinion that they are capable of regular attendance.. Ms. Lopez echoed this view, testifying that, if the OHG receives medical information that an employee is fit to return to work, that means there is no need for accommodation. In my view, this assumption is not justified.

550 Where a medical opinion is provided that an employee is fit to return to work, this does not necessarily mean that the employee is no longer affected by their disability. Nor does it mean that the fact that the absence was related to their disability is irrelevant for accommodation purposes.

551 In *Morris*, the Tribunal noted that the fact that a person is able to work does not mean that they cannot remain disabled for the purpose of the *Code*:

> Following Mr. Morris' return to work, not only Ms. Deveaux, but all involved members of BCRail's management team knew, or ought to have known, that while Mr. Morris was cleared as fit to return to work, he continued to be affected by his depression. He was, as assessed by Dr. Buchanan, having difficulties with self-confidence and making decisions. Mr. Morris himself told everyone he could find that he needed to stay in the comfort of the familiar while he continued to recover. Mr. Morris' pleas in this regard were entirely disregarded by those with decision-making power. BCRail viewed the fact that Dr. Buchanan had cleared Mr. Morris as fit to return to work as giving it *carte blanche* to ignore anything which Mr. Morris might have to say about the effect his depression was having on his performance. (para. 235)

552 CMBC cannot use a doctor's report that indicates that an employee is fit to return to work as the basis for assuming that the employee is no longer

affected by their disability; for example, that they are necessarily capable of regular attendance. CMBC would require a specific basis for such a conclusion.

553 In addition, the fact that an employee is fit to return to work *after* a period of absence due to a disability does not mean that an employer can ignore the fact that an employee was absent *because of* the disability. However, on the evidence before me, it is clear that CMBC takes just this approach.

554 CMBC's approach in this regard is illustrated by their response to a grievance filed on behalf of Ms. Lieb with respect to her placement on Level 3 of the AMP. The Union argued, among other things, that CMBC failed to accommodate Ms. Lieb. CMBC replied:

> In every instance of a return-to-work following a medical leave, including her latest surgery, Ms. Lieb's healthcare providers cleared her as being fit and capable of returning to her safety-sensitive position as a transit operator. Accordingly, the Company was not under any obligation to provide an accommodation.

555 A similar approach is illustrated in the case of Mr. Minch. In that case, CMBC wrote:

> [T]he nature of your ongoing medical condition makes it unlikely that any accommodation would lead to an improvement in your attendance. Each time your ongoing condition resolves, you are cleared to return to work as a transit operator and you have not requested an accommodation.

556 Also notable is CMBC's approach to Mr. Da Luz. When Mr. Da Luz was placed at Level 3 of the AMP on January 20, 2003, Mr. Da Luz's Supervisor noted that, while the medical assessment indicated that he had an ongoing medical condition which could have attendance implications in the longer term, he was .currently. fit to perform his job duties as a transit operator and capable of attending work on a regular and consistent basis.

557 A further example is provided in the case of Mr. Prasad. Prior to January 2000, Mr. Prasad was absent for a five-month period due to surgery he required as a result of liver dysfunction. Following his return to work, Mr. Prasad was placed on parameters. The OHN's comment on his medical assessment was that he was fit to perform his duties as a transit operator and that no significant health problems were anticipated. It appears that no consideration at all was given to the reason for the absence and whether, given the nature of the absence, it was appropriate to place Mr. Prasad on parameters.

558 CMBC's approach appears to be that, once an employee has been cleared to return to work, they do not require accommodation. The fact that an employee is declared fit to return to work does not necessarily lead to the conclusion that an employer is under no obligation to accommodate that employee. An employer must take a broader view and look at any medical

conditions which the employee may have experienced or is currently experiencing, the way in which those conditions have affected past attendance, and the way they may affect attendance in the future.

559 Further, with respect to some employees with chronic disabilities leading to excessive absenteeism, the issue is not whether they can return to work, but whether they can maintain regular attendance and, if they cannot, whether they can be accommodated *vis-à-vis* attendance standard.

560 The assumption that an employee is capable of regular attendance and the imposition of the .average. parameters is more questionable where CMBC has specific information from an employee's physician that, due to the employee's disability, they may have difficulty meeting the attendance standard in question. Yet both in specific examples before me and in more general evidence, which is discussed in more detail below, it became clear that this is precisely what CMBC does.

561 This issue most frequently arises at Level 2, where the employee is asked to provide a medical assessment. The questions asked in that assessment include whether the overall condition of the employee's health is sufficient to meet the demands of their job.

562 The evidence indicates that, even where such a medical assessment states that the employee is fit to return to work but may experience higher absenteeism rates, the .average. attendance parameters are imposed on the employee, without modification.

563 This was the situation faced by Mr. Da Luz, and discussed above. It was also the situation faced by Mr. Prasad.

564 As noted above, Mr. Prasad has at least three chronic conditions. He has a long history in the AMP. He was initially progressed from Level 1 to Level 3, met the Level 3 parameters for one year, and then experienced another year of high absenteeism. He was returned to parameters for two years, and successfully completed this monitoring period. He subsequently was placed on the AMP again and, at Level 2 was asked to provide a medical report.

565 In the report, his physician indicated that Mr. Prasad .has a chronic medical condition that can fluctuate in severity. ... Fluctuations in these conditions may lead into periods of temporary disability which preclude maintaining regular attendance.. In the Level 3 letter, CMBC wrote:

> Our OHN has advised us that the medical questionnaire received from your Doctor indicates that you have three (3) medical conditions. We are further advised that all of these conditions are being regularly followed up and there is no requirement for an accommodation at this time. Given this information, you are expected, aside from an occasional flare-up of one of these conditions, to be able to attend work on a regular and consistent basis.

566 The letter continues:

> Without intending to suggest that any particular rate of absenteeism is acceptable, Coast Mountain Bus Company intends to closely monitor your attendance for the next 2 years. The Company will take into account the particular circumstances of your case and will use the current averages of 19 days on 2 occurrences per year as a guide in assessing whether or not your attendance is acceptable.

567 Thus, Mr. Prasad was placed on a two-year monitoring period, on parameters that reflected the average absence rate, and the average frequency rate, although the letter indicated that the Company would use these numbers as a .guide..

568 At the time he gave his evidence, Mr. Prasad had successfully completed his first year of monitoring, but he testified that, for fear of job-related consequences, he had delayed required surgery so he would not have additional absences that would count towards the parameters.

569 These instances are fully consistent with Mr. Kelly's evidence. Mr. Kelly testified that, where a medical assessment is received that says an employee might experience higher absenteeism rates, CMBC does not do anything except .wait and see.. Mr. Kelly stated that this means that CMBC will impose the average attendance parameters on the employee, and wait and see if they can meet the parameters. If it turns out that they cannot meet the parameters, the impact of the disability may be taken into account in deciding not to progress the employee to an ESR, or in discussions at the ESR regarding whether or not to terminate the employee's employment.

570 The employees who testified before me all indicated that being placed in the AMP was highly stressful to them, and being placed on parameters even more so. These employees were keenly aware that their employment was at risk if they exceeded the attendance parameters. They each testified that they would attempt to attend work when they were unwell, and many testified that they had postponed medical procedures for fear that such absences would cause them to exceed their parameters. They experienced acute anxiety, frustration and, in some cases, anger, at being placed in a situation where their continued employment was at risk as a result of medical conditions that were known to their employer, and that were largely beyond their control.

571 In my view, it is contrary to human rights principles to process such individuals through the AMP first, and to determine whether the employee can be accommodated later. Mr. Kelly testified that, in his view, it would be discriminatory for CMBC to assume that those with chronic conditions would have higher rates of absence. However, that is not the situation pointed to in the evidence. Rather, where CMBC has specific information from the employee's physician that the employee's condition will likely re-

sult in an above average rate of absenteeism, it is discriminatory to fail to take this information into account.

572 Assuming that if an employee is declared fit to return to work, there is no need to accommodate that employee, is a systemic issue. Ignoring medical information that indicates that an employee will likely experience elevated rates of absenteeism as a result of a disability is a systemic issue. Placing employees on parameters where CMBC has significant medical information indicating that the employee will not be able to meet those parameters, or will experience serious difficulty in meeting them, without *first* considering accommodation options, is a systemic issue. These issues, taken together, give rise to discrimination *vis-à-vis*employees with disabilities which affect their attendance.

c. Narrow view of accommodation

573 Just as the evidence before me leads to the conclusion that CMBC has taken a narrow view of when accommodation can be considered, it also indicates that CMBC has taken a somewhat narrow view of *what* accommodation may entail.

574 Mr. Kelly's testimony with respect to his understanding of the duty to accommodate employees with disabilities which affect their attendance was telling. He testified in cross-examination that he understood that CMBC had to consider the duty to accommodate to the point of undue hardship, and that the fundamental question was whether the operator could be accommodated .somewhere else.. The focus, therefore, was on another job within CMBC, rather than on the employee's own job with attendance requirements modified.

575 Ms. Lopez's testimony was consistent with Mr. Kelly's. In cross-examination, she was asked whether the OHG writes to the doctor with information about attendance rates and asks whether accommodation is required with respect to those rates. She answered that this is not the process. Rather, where it is appropriate, the OHN asks the physician if accommodation is required where an employee is unable to return to work.

576 This narrow understanding is reflected in the manner in which some of the individual situations before me were addressed. For example, Mr. Prasad's physician provided CMBC with a letter which indicated that he had a chronic medical condition:

> ... that can fluctuate in severity. When he is well, there is no restriction in participating as a transit operator. Fluctuations in these conditions may lead into periods of temporary disability which preclude maintaining regular attendance.

577 In the Level 3 letter, CMBC stated that, although his doctor had identified these medical conditions there was .no requirement for an accommoda-

tion at this time.. It may well be that there was no requirement for accommodation into an alternate position or for modification of Mr. Prasad's duties in the operator's position at the time, but the interpretation that .no accommodation. was required flies in the face of the medical information received. The letter leaves open the question of whether Mr. Prasad needs to be accommodated *vis-à-vis* attendance standard of the AMP. No real inquiry was made into this issue, and Mr. Prasad was advised that .average. attendance rates and frequencies would be used as a guide in assessing his attendance.

578 This perspective underlines a problem that runs through CMBC's application of the AMP. Both the Attendance Management Department and the OHG appear to be focussed on the accommodation of employees with attendance problems in other positions within CMBC, to the exclusion of accommodation of employees with respect to the standard outlined by the AMP.

579 This is reflected, to some extent, in statements made in the 2006 Guide, which states:

> Having a disability does not lessen the obligations on the employee to meet acceptable performance standards, including attendance, however, it may impose on CMBC a duty, to the point of undue hardship, to search for an accommodation that will enable the employee to meet acceptable standards in the performance of meaningful work.

580 What is missing from this statement is any acknowledgement that, in some cases, the .acceptable performance standards. themselves may need to be looked at. This is contrary to the approach outlined by the Supreme Court of Canada in *British Columbia (Public Service Employee Relations Commission) v. B.C.G.E.U.*, [1999] 3 S.C.R. 3 (S.C.C.) ("*Meiorin*") and *British Columbia (Superintendent of Motor Vehicles) v. British Columbia (Council of Human Rights)*, [1999] 3 S.C.R. 868 (S.C.C.) ("*Grismer*"), which will be discussed in more detail below.

581 What was striking in the evidence before me was, first, the complete lack of any acknowledgement that some operators have disabilities which simply make them more likely to have a higher rate of absenteeism; and, second, the dearth of circumstances in which CMBC has been prepared to consider relaxing the attendance parameters, or not applying them at all, in respect of absences relating to an employee's chronic or recurring disability.

582 This reluctance is inconsistent with CMBC's own policies relating to accommodation. For example, under the Accommodation of Employees with a Permanent Disability Policy, the first step which CMBC must take is to look at whether it is possible to modify an employee's own job. If the job

cannot be modified appropriately, CMBC will then look at whether the employee can be accommodated in another position.

583 On the evidence before me, CMBC considers that .modifications. to an employee's position include physical modifications to the work station and similar considerations. However, the enquiry about whether an employee's own job can be modified goes beyond a consideration of physical modifications to the workplace, or the manner of performing a task, and may include a consideration of whether policies and standards that apply to the operators, such as any attendance standards applied under the AMP, can be modified with respect to a specific employee without CMBC incurring undue hardship.

584 In all of the individual cases presented before me, there is little indication that CMBC considered how much variance from the normal attendance target would be appropriate for employees with one or more chronic or recurring disabilities. For example, in the case of Mr. Da Luz, CMBC appears never to have considered what the appropriate target was, considering his struggle with Crohn's disease. I note in this regard the comment of Mr. Da Luz's physician that .I have never considered his level of absenteeism to be inappropriately high, considering his condition..

585 In the evidence before me, there was only one example of consideration being given to formally modifying the attendance target for an employee (E04998). Further, in that case, the employee had progressed through the stages of the AMP and was at the point of an ESR before consideration was given to this alternative.

586 Similarly, there have been cases where there has been some relaxation of the parameters in respect of individuals after the Level 3 parameters were exceeded, but prior to an ESR. For example, Mr. Da Luz was not terminated despite exceeding Level 3 parameters. However, in these cases, the employees were not explicitly told that there would be an accommodation, or what the parameters of that accommodation might be. This causes the increased stress of not being able to meet parameters and worrying about termination, with the possible deleterious effects that stress may have on a recurring condition and a particularly vulnerable employee.

587 Mr. Da Luz, for example, testified that after he exceeded his Level 3 parameters and was off work as the result of a car accident, he knew that his employment was in jeopardy and experienced a great deal of stress as a result. His Crohn's disease, which is aggravated by stress, acted up and he became very ill. Other employees, including Mr. Templeman, Ms. Lieb and Mr. Fernandes, testified about postponing medical procedures, or arranging to have these procedures done during their vacation time, to avoid exceeding their parameters.

588 Even in cases, discussed above, where the medical information appears to support the argument that the employee would experience .higher than average absenteeism., no formal accommodation within the standards was provided. Mr. Kelly's response to this, that CMBC would wait and see and deal with it at the ESR, is not satisfactory, or in accordance with s. 13 of the *Code*. It fails to take into account the particular vulnerability of the affected employee, whose future employment may be at risk through no fault of their own.

589 In this regard, the statements of the Supreme Court of Canada in *Grismer* are apposite:

> Employers and others governed by human rights legislation are now required in all cases to accommodate the characteristics of affected groups within their standards, rather than maintaining discriminatory standards supplemented by accommodation for those who cannot meet them. (para 19, see also *Meiorin* at para. 68)

590 CMBC's current approach, of applying the standards and then possibly accommodating once an employee has failed to meet them does not constitute providing for accommodation within the standard itself, and is an example of the type of approach the Supreme Court of Canada found to be discriminatory in both *Meiorin* and *Grismer*.

591 What is also notable is that this issue has been known to CMBC for some period of time. It was, for example, addressed in the report prepared with respect to Ms. Cable. The findings of fact and law in the report are not binding on me. However, CMBC itself took the position that the report was binding on it, at least with respect to the circumstances involving Ms. Cable.

592 In any event it was noted in the report that the OHN told the investigator that she would not advise the AMP staff and depot manager that an employee's chronic condition would result in poor attendance until the point at which CMBC decided whether to dismiss the employee. The investigator stated:

> Failure to advise the Company that an employee requires accommodation by relaxing the attendance requirements exposes the disabled employee to invasive scrutiny due to having to justify absences beyond their control. Failure by the Occupational Health department to intervene at an early stage does not meet the Supreme Court's requirement to search for accommodation based on the unique capabilities, inherent worth and dignity of every individual employee. (p. 69)

593 I agree, and I find that CMBC focuses on accommodating disabled operators who cannot meet the attendance standards in other positions to the exclusion of considering accommodation within the standard itself.

594 In addition, to the extent that accommodation in other positions is one possible form of accommodation, the considerations which CMBC takes

into account in determining whether such an accommodation should be pursued as a possibility raise some concerns.

595 Certainly, there are some situations in which accommodation of an operator into an alternate position will be appropriate. Where CMBC has medical information that an employee is not capable of working as a transit operator, accommodation into an alternate position may be the only alternative.

596 Further, given the operational requirements of keeping the buses staffed and running, absenteeism may have a more significant impact in the operations department. There may be a desire to move operators with poor attendance into non-operational positions, where any absenteeism would not be so keenly felt, or so costly to replace.

597 However, it was clear from the evidence before me that a primary factor taken into account by CMBC in determining whether it is appropriate to accommodate an individual with an attendance issue in another position is whether that accommodation has the potential to improve the employee's attendance. For example, in addressing the possibility of accommodation with Mr. Minch, CMBC wrote that it was .unlikely that accommodation [into another position] would lead to an improvement in your attendance., and thus it was not considered to be a viable alternative.

598 Whether an accommodated position would assist in improving an employee's attendance may well be one consideration. However, CMBC does not seem to appreciate that it is not the only standard by which an accommodation should be measured.

d. Treatment of employees on GRTWs

599 A further aspect of the AMP which I have taken into account in finding the application of the AMP to be *prima facie* discriminatory involves the treatment of partial days that an employee is not able to work while on a rehabilitation or GRTW assignment as an .absence..

600 The existence of this practice was established by both the general evidence of Mr. MacLeod and the evidence of individual employees.

601 Mr. MacLeod testified that, in his experience as a Union representative, where an employee was on a GRTW, and was only cleared to work partial days, the part of the day that the employee was unable to work was considered an .absence. by CMBC for the purposes of the AMP.

602 This practice was also illustrated in the circumstances of some of the individual employees who testified at the hearing, including Ms. Young, Mr. Prasad, Mr. Templeman, Ms. Cable, Mr. Da Luz and Mr. Minch; in instances ranging in date from 2000 to 2003.

603 It may well be the case, as asserted by CMBC, that taking into account such time will not usually have a significant effect on its calculation of an employee's attendance rate. However, it is equally clear that it can.

604 For example, Mr. Da Luz testified that, while he was serving parameters in 2003, he experienced back problems which he attributed to his Crohn's disease. He worked in a temporary alternate placement as a vehicle maintenance man for a 5-6 week period on a GRTW basis. The work was performed on a GRTW basis because he was not able to work a full week at full shifts due to his medical condition. He was informed that the days that he would normally have worked but did not on the GRTW were counted as absences for the purposes of the AMP. It is not entirely clear from the evidence before me how many days this amounted to, or the way in which it impacted on Mr. Da Luz's status. However, given the length of the GRTW, it clearly had the potential for being significant.

605 The issue is illustrated even more clearly by the circumstances of Mr. Minch.

606 As noted above, Mr. Minch was advanced to Level 3 of the AMP in December 2001, and placed on parameters for a two-year period. Initially, he was advised that his parameters were 24 days. However, as Mr. Minch worked a CWW, the applicable parameters were subsequently amended to 19 CWW days per year. In the first year of monitoring, Mr. Minch was absent 23 CWW days, and thus had exceeded the parameters. However, given the confusion with respect to the appropriate parameters, CMBC simply continued Mr. Minch on parameters for a second year. With respect to Mr. Minch's status in the second year of monitoring, CMBC advised:

> Company attendance records show that since December 13, 2002, you have been absent from work for 4 complete CWW days, plus the absence-hours associated with a gradual return to work beginning on December 23, 2002. Those GRTW absence hours represent the difference between your hours worked and the 9.23 hours of a CWW day and total 142.78 absence hours, which equates to 15.2 CWW days. You resumed fulltime work on February 17, 2003, leaving you with 37.22 hours or 3.96 CWW days remaining before you would exceed the parameters set out in the December 13, 2001 letter.

607 Thus, in his second year of monitoring, Mr. Minch was on parameters of 19 CWW days, and it appears that his GRTW time accounted for 11.2 days: clearly a significant number.

608 While Mr. Minch did not exceed his parameters on that occasion, his employment was subsequently terminated under the AMP: while he was returning to work on a GRTW. It is not clear on the evidence before me whether the days he did not work while on this GRTW were taken into account in CMBC's determination that he had exceeded his parameters.

609 On the basis of the evidence before me, I conclude that CMBC does take into account the partial days that an employee does not work while on a GRTW in calculating the employee's attendance rate and number of absences. In my view, this practice is *prima facie* discriminatory. A GRTW is, in essence, an accommodation of an employee returning from time off work due to illness or injury (which may also constitute a disability). Considering the hours not at work in a GRTW as absences constitutes a penalization of employees who are seeking an accommodation. Thus, the accommodation, the GRTW, is undermined by the fact that any time not worked is counted as an absence and may, at the end of the day, be one of the factors in an employee's termination.

610 As noted above, I accept that counting partial days of absence while on a GRTW may not have a significant impact on the attendance rate of most employees. It does have the potential to do so, however, as is illustrated by the circumstances of Mr. Minch. It is also illustrative of the other concerns I have identified with the AMP, in that the AMP is not well integrated with CMBC's accommodation policies.

e. Conclusion on prima facie case

611 The Union argued that the AMP is used as an .assembly line to termination.. I cannot agree. There are several examples of discretion and accommodation that have been established in the evidence. However, the evidence also established a number of areas which, taken together, lead to the conclusion that the application of the AMP results in systemic discrimination against some employees who suffer from chronic or recurring disabilities.

612 First, there is insufficient coordination and communication between various departments involved in the AMP, including the Attendance Management Group and the OHG. These communication problems, whether caused by the Company's understanding of confidentiality requirements or simply by communication breakdowns, have a particularly harsh effect on those with chronic and recurring disabilities. With respect to these employees, the lack of communication creates an environment in which accommodation is not considered at the earlier stages of the identification of disability issues affecting attendance. This, in turn, results in individuals being placed in and processed through the AMP in situations where it may be inappropriate to do so.

613 Second, in applying the AMP, CMBC takes a narrow view of the points at which accommodation should be considered. Specifically, while CMBC has a fairly comprehensive structure in place for the accommodation of employees who are returning to work from an illness or injury (including GRTWs and returning to work in alternate positions), little consideration is

given to employees who, although they are fit to return to work in their regular position, may still require some form of accommodation, including consideration of whether attendance parameters should be waived or relaxed.

614 Third, while CMBC did put forward instances where discretion was used not to advance employees in the AMP, the evidence indicated that, where an employee was advanced to Level 3 of the AMP, and placed on parameters, those parameters invariably reflected the .average. absenteeism of the operator group. This is despite the fact that the letter outlining the parameters states that, in arriving at those parameters, CMBC takes into account the circumstances of each individual case. This occurs even in instances where CMBC has information that indicates that an employee's disability may lead to elevated absence levels.

615 Fourth, when CMBC does consider whether an employee's disability-related absenteeism can be accommodated, the focus of the accommodation search is on accommodation in another position. In addition, the consideration occurs predominantly in the later stages of the AMP. For example, there is no evidence before me that CMBC has ever considered modifying the AMP standards as a possible accommodation, *prior* to placing an employee at Level 3 of the AMP (and very few thereafter).

616 Fifth, I have found CMBC's treatment of partial day absences resulting from an employee being placed on a GRTW placement to be discriminatory. In my view, this practice is illustrative of an underlying problem, discussed in this decision, of the AMP being poorly integrated with CMBC's accommodation policies.

617 Taken together, the evidence establishes that the AMP, as applied by CMBC, results in systemic discrimination against some employees with disabilities and, in particular, employees with one or more chronic or recurring disability/ies.

2. Is the AMP nevertheless a bona fide occupational requirement?

618 Where, as here, a complainant has established a *prima facie* case of discrimination, the onus shifts to the respondent to establish, on the balance of probabilities, that its conduct was justified because it was based on a *bona fide* occupational requirement. In *Meiorin*, the Supreme Court of Canada set out three requirements that a respondent must establish to justify its conduct:

1. The standard was adopted for a purpose or goal that is rationally connected to the function being performed;
2. The standard was adopted in good faith in the belief that it is necessary for the fulfillment of the purpose or goal; and

3. The standard is reasonably necessary to accomplish its purpose or goal, in the sense that the respondent cannot accommodate persons with characteristics of the complainant without incurring undue hardship. (para. 54)

619 As noted by the Tribunal in *Radek*, the application of the *Meiorin* requirements in the context of an analysis of systemic discrimination is not without its difficulties. This is because what is in issue is not a single standard, but a complex of interrelated practices, policies and attitudes resulting in a pattern of systemic discrimination: para. 610.

620 However, as in *Radek*, the parties in this case framed their submissions in accordance with the *Meiorin* analysis, and I will employ it, with the necessary modifications applicable to this context.

a. What is the .standard. at issue?

621 The first step in applying the *Meiorin* analysis to the circumstances of any given case is identifying the .standard. which is at issue. As noted above, in a complaint alleging systemic discrimination, this step can be problematic because what is at issue is not, in fact, a single standard (for example, that an employee may not exceed the average attendance rate), but rather a complex of interrelated policies and practices.

622 In *Radek*, instead of focusing its analysis on a "standard", the Tribunal focused on "practices, policies and attitudes". Thus, the Tribunal in *Radek* asked whether these practices, policies and attitudes were rationally connected to the function being performed; whether they were adopted in good faith; and whether they were reasonably necessary to accomplish their purpose or goal.

623 In this case, I will adopt a similar approach. The focus of the enquiry in this case is the AMP, as it is implemented in practice by CMBC.

b. Rational connection

624 In *Meiorin*, the Court held that the first step in assessing whether the respondent has successfully established a BFOR defence is to identify the general purpose of the impugned standard and determine whether it is rationally connected to the performance of the job: para. 57. The initial question is what the standard in issue is generally designed to achieve.

625 CMBC asserts, and I accept, that the general purpose of the AMP is to identify and address disruptive and costly absenteeism problems.

626 The next issue is whether CMBC has demonstrated that there is a rational connection between this purpose, and the objective requirements of the job. In this case, CMBC argues that there is an obvious rational connection between a workplace rule requiring reasonable attendance and the re-

quirements of the job. CMBC argues that good attendance is critical to efforts to provide cost-effective and reliable bus service. Absences affect service delivery to the public, and are costly, amounting to tens of millions of dollars per year.

627 The Union states in its argument that it does not challenge CMBC's right to ensure that its employees attend work on a regular and consistent basis. The Union does not appear to challenge CMBC's assertion that it adopted the AMP for a purpose rationally connected to the performance of the job.

628 On the basis of the information before me, I agree with CMBC, and find that the adoption of the AMP meets the first step in the *Meiorin* analysis.

c. Honest and good faith belief

629 In *Meiorin*, the Court noted that, once the legitimacy of the employer's more general purpose is established, the employer must then demonstrate that it adopted the particular standard with an honest and good faith belief that it was necessary to the accomplishment of its purpose, with no intention of discriminating against the complainants: para. 60.

630 In this case, CMBC asserts that the AMP was adopted in an honest and good faith belief that it was necessary to identify and address unreasonable absenteeism problems.

631 On the basis of the evidence before me, I agree. The AMP was adopted as a result of the concern relating to the level of absenteeism at B.C. Transit, coupled with the Auditor General's report and recommendations. There is absolutely no evidence before me that it was adopted for any other, ulterior purpose.

d. Accommodation to the point of undue hardship

632 The real issue before the Tribunal in determining whether the AMP is a BFOR is whether CMBC has demonstrated that it is impossible to further accommodate individual employees within the AMP without experiencing undue hardship. In this regard, the Supreme Court outlined some of the important questions that may be asked in the course of this analysis. They include:

(a) Has the employer investigated alternative approaches that do not have a discriminatory effect, such as individual testing against a more individually sensitive standard?

(b) If alternative standards were investigated and found to be capable of fulfilling the employer's purpose, why were they not implemented?

(c) Is it necessary to have all employees meet the single standard for the employer to accomplish its legitimate purpose or could standards reflective of group or individual differences and capabilities be established?

(d) Is there a way to do the job that is less discriminatory while still accomplishing the employer's legitimate purpose?

(e) Is the standard properly designed to ensure that the desired qualification is met without placing an undue burden on those to whom the standard applies?

(f) Have other parties who are obliged to assist in the search for possible accommodation fulfilled their roles? ... (*Meiorin*, para. 65)

633 CMBC does not argue that accommodating those with disabilities within the AMP would create an undue hardship for it. Rather, CMBC argues that it does accommodate employees with disabilities within the AMP.

634 CMBC argues that the AMP does not set any explicit or absolute standard applicable to all employees. There is no objective attendance standard as a requirement for continued employment; nor is there a standard at which an employee will receive a warning; or at which an employee will be monitored, or reviewed. In particular, CMBC argues that the AMP does not require that disabled operators meet any average absenteeism rate except at the advanced or Level 3 stage. CMBC also states that, even at this point, many employees have had the average relaxed in some way to accommodate particular circumstances.

635 I agree that there were a number of examples given in which an employee exceeded the parameters and was not terminated. However, while the evidence indicates that there has been accommodation in individual cases, the duty to accommodate requires more than this. In this regard, the Court in *Meiorin* stated as follows:

> Employers designing workplace standards owe an obligation to be aware of both the differences between individuals, and differences that characterize groups of individuals. They must build conceptions of equality into workplace standards. .... The standard *itself* is required to provide for individual accommodation, if reasonably possible. (emphasis in original, para. 68)

636 In this regard, accommodation within an attendance standard is no different than accommodation within any other standard that is applicable in a workplace.

637 The evidence before me established that, in applying the AMP, CMBC treats individuals with chronic or recurring disabilities as "attendance problems" and forces them into the AMP process. Although they may eventually be accommodated in the later stages of the process, this approach ignores the stress and anxiety experienced by employees who are placed on

the AMP and the frustration and anger which may result when the fact that they have a disability is seemingly ignored. It imposes on an employee a standard, average attendance, which the employee may be unable to meet. As outlined above, it is not sufficient to say that, at some point in the process, there may be an accommodation reached, after the employee has exceeded the standard. In fact, such an approach is contrary to the directions of the Supreme Court of Canada in *Meiorin* and *Grismer*, which indicate that there must be accommodation within the standard, not just a standard set with the possibility of accommodation at the end stages.

638 In addition, while CMBC led evidence of the substantial cost of employee absenteeism to its operation, that evidence related to the global cost of absenteeism to its operations. There was no evidence on which I could assess the cost related specifically to those employees with chronic or recurring disabilities. Thus, there is no evidence before me on which I could find that considering accommodating those with such disabilities at an earlier stage in the Program, or expanding the possible accommodation options available in the manner outlined above, would so escalate costs to CMBC as to create an undue hardship.

639 For these reasons, I find that CMBC has failed to establish that it is not possible to further accommodate employees with chronic or recurring disabilities short of undue hardship. I therefore find that CMBC has not established that the AMP is a *bona fide* occupational requirement. Therefore, it has failed to establish a defence to the complaint of discrimination.

IV. Remedy

640 I have found that the AMP, as it is applied to operators with chronic or recurring disabilities, constitutes a form of systemic discrimination. Further, I have found that CMBC has not shown that the AMP is a *bona fide* occupational requirement, as it has not shown that it is impossible to accommodate those with chronic or recurring disabilities short of undue hardship.

641 The question which remains is, given these findings, what are the appropriate remedies.

642 Section 37 of the *Code* provides the Tribunal with broad authority to remedy discrimination. It provides, in part:

> (2) If the member or panel determines that the complaint is justified, the member or panel
>
> (a) must order the person that contravened this Code to cease the contravention and to refrain from committing the same or a similar contravention,
>
> (b) may make a declaratory order that the conduct complained of, or similar conduct, is discrimination contrary to this Code,

(c) may order the person that contravened this Code to do one or both of the following:

   (i) take steps, specified in the order, to ameliorate the effects of the discriminatory practice;

   (ii) adopt and implement an employment equity program or other special program to ameliorate the conditions of disadvantaged individuals or groups if the evidence at the hearing indicates the person has engaged in a pattern or practice that contravenes this Code, and

(d) if the person discriminated against is a party to the complaint, or is an identifiable member of a group or class on behalf of which a complaint is filed, may order the person that contravened this Code to do one or more of the following:

   (i) make available to the person discriminated against the right, opportunity or privilege that, in the opinion of the member or panel, the person was denied contrary to this Code;

   (ii) compensate the person discriminated against for all, or a part the member or panel determines, of any wages or salary lost, or expenses incurred, by the contravention;

   (iii) pay to the person discriminated against an amount that the member or panel considers appropriate to compensate that person for injury to dignity, feelings and self respect or to any of them.

(3) An order made under subsection (2) may require the person against whom the order is made to provide any person designated in the order with information respecting the implementation of the order.

643 In this case, the Union seeks that:

a) The AMP be struck down;

b) Those members of the Representative Group who have been terminated as a result of non-culpable absenteeism under the AMP from six months prior to the filing of the complaint should be reinstated and made whole; and

c) Those members of the Representative Group who have been placed at the third level of the AMP from six months prior to the filing of the complaint should be made whole by compensation for injury to dignity, feelings and self-respect.

644 CMBC did not specifically address the remedies sought by the Union, arguing instead that there was no breach of the *Code* and therefore no remedies were indicated.

A. Systemic Remedies: Should the AMP be struck down?

645 I have found, for the reasons outlined above, that the AMP is fundamentally flawed in its formulation and application, and that these flaws lead to systemic discrimination against those with chronic or recurring disabilities.

646 In *Meiorin*, the Court held that a standard (in this case a policy) which unnecessarily fails to reflect the differences among individuals (in this case, fails to consider the actual characteristics of the disabilities suffered by individuals) runs afoul of the prohibitions contained in the various human rights statutes and must be replaced: para. 68.

647 I have highlighted those aspects of the AMP that I have found to be discriminatory. In particular, it is the absence of consideration given to the circumstances of those with chronic or recurring disabilities, including the timing of considering accommodation options, the type of accommodation options considered, and the treatment of other forms of accommodation (such as GRTWs) within the Program, which is contrary to the *Code*.

648 Throughout this complaint the Union has repeated that it does not dispute the right of CMBC to have an attendance management program, and I find that CMBC does have such a right. Specifically, I have found that the operation of the AMP is not discriminatory (in the context of this complaint) as it is applied to employees whose absenteeism is not the product of chronic or recurring disabilities.

649 In these circumstances, and given the systemic issues discussed above, I am required, under s. 37(2)(a) of the *Code* to order CMBC to cease and desist in its application of the AMP to operators with chronic or recurring disabilities, where those disabilities are the cause of some or all of the absenteeism considered excessive under the AMP.

650 Clearly, this order raises questions about the status of operators with chronic or recurring disabilities who are currently involved in the AMP. In addition, the parties may not agree on which operators can be considered to have recurring or chronic disabilities. As a result, I order the parties to engage in Tribunal-assisted mediation to discuss revisions to the AMP, or its application, which would address the systemic concerns outlined in this decision, as well as the circumstances of individual operators with chronic or recurring disabilities who are currently involved in the AMP.

651 I will retain jurisdiction and, if necessary, hear evidence on the issue of systemic remedy in the event that no agreement has been reached by a date six months from the date of this decision, or such longer date as the parties and the mediator feel is necessary.

B. Individual Remedies

652 This complaint raises difficult issues regarding any individual remedies which should be awarded to members of the class. Some of these issues, relating to employees whose individual circumstances have been the subject of arbitration awards, were discussed above. Other issues arising with respect to individual remedies were addressed in the preliminary decision of

the Tribunal in *CAW No. 7*. The Tribunal noted that the bringing of a representative complaint on behalf of a class of persons does not inhibit the Tribunal's ability to award individual remedies where appropriate. In this regard, the Tribunal stated:

> The Tribunal clearly has the ability to award both individual and systemic remedies, given the appropriate evidentiary base. However, the question which remains is how these individual issues are to be dealt with in the context of a representative complaint.
>
> The Court in *Dutton* commented on this issue as well, and found that the courts retain discretion with respect to the determination of how individual issues should be addressed, once common issues have been resolved. (at para. 50) The courts must have flexibility to address these procedural complexities on a case-by-case basis, seeking a balance between efficiency and fairness. Similar concerns motivate the Tribunal.
>
> In a case such as this, evidence with respect to individual circumstances may well form part of the complainant's case: systemic discrimination may be demonstrated by a pattern of behaviour against a number of individuals. Thus, evidence of specific circumstances may well be necessary to support the argument that the AMP systemically discriminates against those with disabilities, actual or perceived. ... To the extent that evidence is presented with respect to the circumstances of individual operators that substantiates their individual claims of discrimination, as well as demonstrate a systemic pattern, the Tribunal may award individual remedies with respect to those operators. ...
>
> In my view, the resolution of the common issues should provide the parties with assistance and direction in the resolution of issues relating to all individuals who are members of the representative [class]. Should the Tribunal find in Local 111's favour on the merits, it can remain seized of the implementation, application or clarification of its award with respect to members of the representative [class] with respect to whom individual remedies were not sought at the common hearing. (para. 53-56)

653 In this case, the Union seeks individual remedies on behalf, first, of all operators terminated under the AMP; and second, all operators who have been placed at Level 3 of the AMP.

654 In my decision, outlined above, I have found that the AMP systemically discriminates against operators with chronic and recurring disabilities. Thus, any individual remedies are appropriately directed to operators who fall into this category.

1. Employees terminated under the AMP

655 Pursuant to the evidence of Mr. Kelly, at the time of the hearing of this matter, there had been eleven employees terminated under the AMP: E05299, Ms. Young, E05983, Ms. Cable, Mr. Minch, E07219, E05125, Mr. Essex, E07385, Mr. Watson, and E03647. Of these, the final six employees have been reinstated as the result of favourable arbitration decisions. One

employee, E07219, was reinstated at arbitration but is no longer employed by CMBC.

656 Of those who were terminated, and not reinstated, at least four have had their terminations confirmed at arbitration. It is not clear whether there was an arbitration with respect to employee E05299.

657 As noted above, it is not the Tribunal's role to reconsider arbitration decisions with respect to the specific outcome for the individuals in question. Those individuals have all had the specific circumstances of their terminations individually and fully considered by an arbitrator, who has rendered a decision based on all the evidence placed before him or her.

658 Thus, with respect to those operators whose employment was terminated, and whose terminations were grieved and went to arbitration, I find that it would not be appropriate for the Tribunal to provide any further remedy.

659 I come to a similar finding with respect to Mr. Essex, whose termination was grieved and who was reinstated as part of a settlement between CMBC and the Union. Given that his reinstatement was arrived at as part of an agreement between CMBC and the Union, and related specifically to the issue of his termination under the AMP, I find it would not be appropriate to grant any individual remedy.

660 With respect to employee E05299, if the issues pertaining to the termination of this employee have not been the subject of arbitration or settlement between the parties, I order the parties to engage in Tribunal-assisted mediation with respect to the circumstances of this employee. If the parties are unable to reach agreement on issues relating to this employee, I retain jurisdiction to hear evidence and argument with respect to the circumstances of this employee's situation.

2. Employees placed at Level 3 of the AMP

661 As noted above, the Level 3 stage is now referred to as the "Advanced Concern" Stage. For the purposes of this decision, I will continue to refer to the stage at which an employee is placed on attendance parameters as "Level 3".

662 There is no evidence before me with respect to the number of operators who have been placed at Level 3 of the AMP since January 1, 2003. Mr. Kelly testified that, at the June 2006 Quarterly Meetings, there were 30 employees at this Level.

663 Further, there is no evidence before me with respect to how many of the operators who have been placed on Level 3 of the AMP suffer from chronic or recurring disabilities. Such findings will be very fact specific.

664 For example, on the evidence before me, it is clear that Mr. Da Luz, Mr. Prasad, and Mr. Fernandes suffer from chronic disabilities. In addition, the series of car accidents in which Mr. Templeman was involved have led to shoulder and back complaints and which caused him to develop PTSD. I find that these conditions constitute either chronic or recurring disabilities. Similarly, Ms. Lieb suffered from a series of recurring disabilities which led to absences, including irritable larynx syndrome and gall bladder issues. Finally, when Mr. Watson was reinstated to employment with CMBC following his grievance arbitration hearing, CMBC placed him at Level 3 of the AMP. This placement could only have been the result of his past attendance record, which the arbitrator found was latterly attributable, in significant part, to two disabilities.

665 On the basis of the evidence before me, and in particular the evidence of Mr. Da Luz, Mr. Prasad, Mr. Templeman, Ms. Lieb, Mr. Fernandes, Ms. Young, Ms. Cable, and Mr. Watson, I find that employees with chronic and recurring disabilities placed at Level 3 of the AMP may suffer injury to their dignity, feelings, and self-respect.

666 Pursuant to s. 37(2)(d)(iii) of the *Code*, the Tribunal may compensate a complainant for injury to dignity, feelings and self-respect. The quantum of such an award requires an assessment of the impact of the discriminatory conduct on the complainant, and will therefore depend on the specific facts of each individual case.

667 I have the information before me to make such awards with respect to the operators who testified, and it is to a consideration of their circumstances which I now turn.

a. Sergio Da Luz

668 As outlined above, Mr. Da Luz has a chronic medical condition that leads to a pattern of intermittent, short term absences. He was placed on the AMP at a point when his absences were approximately five days over the average. He was advanced to Level 3 of the AMP at a time when his number of absences was one over the average. His frequency was above average, but this frequency was consistent with his disability.

669 Mr. Da Luz's situation is complicated by the fact that CMBC was provided information from his doctor which indicated that employment as a transit operator is not suitable for Mr. Da Luz on a long-term basis. CMBC believes that Mr. Da Luz has failed to accept reasonable accommodation into another position, as he was advised by his doctor to do.

670 There are clearly issues involved in Mr. Da Luz's situation which go beyond the impact of the AMP on him. Specifically, my decision with respect to Mr. Da Luz should not be taken as a finding that CMBC is necessa-

rily required to accommodate him as a transit operator (rather than in an alternate position).

671 However, that does not alter my finding that Mr. Da Luz has been adversely affected by the AMP process, which I have found to be systemically discriminatory in nature. Specifically, Mr. Da Luz was introduced into the AMP and advanced through the AMP in situations where CMBC should have been aware that a search for accommodation, including accommodations involving relaxed attendance standards, may have been indicated.

672 In this regard, Mr. Da Luz testified about the stress he experienced in being subjected to the AMP. He testified that it adversely affected his Crohn's disease, and that at one point he became so ill that he lost 20 pounds in three to four weeks. He testified that it was frustrating and baffling being placed on the AMP for absences that he had no real control over, when he was doing his best to try to manage his condition.

673 In all of the circumstances before me, I find that it is appropriate to award Mr. Da Luz $6,000 for injury to his dignity, feelings and self-respect.

b. Shailendra Prasad

674 Mr. Prasad's physician has informed CMBC that Mr. Prasad has three chronic medical conditions: bile duct disorder, osteoarthritis and diabetes. His physician has stated that he is capable of unrestricted work as a transit operator as long as there are no flare ups of his chronic conditions. Flare-ups in his conditions may lead to periods during which he is temporarily unable to work, and which preclude maintaining regular attendance.

675 Mr. Prasad's most recent placement on Level 3 of the AMP occurred on October 1, 2004. In the Level 3 letter, CMBC indicated that it had received the doctor's advice that he had three chronic conditions but that .there is no requirement for an accommodation at this time.. Mr. Prasad was therefore placed on Level 3 parameters of 19 days on two occurrences.

676 There was language in the Level 3 letter indicating that these requirements would be considered "aside from an occasional flare-up", and that CMBC would use the parameters while "taking into account the particular circumstances of your case" There was no formal indication that the parameters would not be applied or would be relaxed in reference to Mr. Prasad's three chronic conditions.

677 Mr. Prasad testified about his most recent experience on Level 3 of the AMP. He testified that, during his first year on monitoring, he met the parameters with 15 days of absence. He delayed knee surgery until he had enough holiday time available so that his absence would not count towards his attendance record.

678 Mr. Prasad testified that, during his time in the AMP, he has worked hard to maintain regular attendance. He testified that he has followed his medical practitioner's advice about medication, diet and exercise. He has taken vacation time off and unpaid leaves of absence to tend to his medical needs so that he could stay within the parameters.

679 Mr. Prasad testified that he has found it extremely difficult to stay off the AMP, given the three disabilities he has to live with and manage.

680 He states that he has a family that he is responsible for supporting, and that his status on the AMP jeopardizes his employment. He finds it threatening and intimidating. He testified that he is doing his best to provide his services, but he feels like a gun is being held to his head. He finds it frustrating and stressful on top of a job that has more than its fair share of stressors.

681 Given the impact of the systemically discriminatory conduct on Mr. Prasad, I find that an award of $6,000 is appropriate in all of the circumstances of the case.

c. Gary Templeman

682 Mr. Templeman had a series of accidents from February 1999 to December 2001 that caused a number of injuries to his shoulders and back, and which required a great deal of time off work and surgical intervention. He eventually returned to work as a transit operator in March 2002.

683 Immediately following his return to work, he was placed at Level 1 of the AMP. Shortly after this meeting, Mr. Templeman was diagnosed with PTSD as a result of the multiple traffic accidents. He attempted a variety of returns to work from December 2002 to August 2003, but found that the alternate placements arranged by CMBC aggravated his shoulder and back condition.

684 On October 27, 2003, Mr. Templeman had a Level 3 interview. In the letter which confirmed that interview, Mr. Templeman's Supervisor stated the following with respect to Mr. Templeman's medical assessment:

> The doctor you attended forwarded the results of your medical assessment to our Occupational Health Nurse, who, in turn, advised us that you do not have a medical condition which would prevent you from performing your job duties as a transit operator or from attending at work on a regular and consistent basis.

685 It is clear, however, that Mr. Templeman's back and shoulder condition did continue to affect him. Mr. Templeman was scheduled for shoulder surgery in June 2004, but cancelled that surgery because of his concern at being at Level 3 of the AMP.

686 Mr. Templeman also testified that he brought a letter from his surgeon to his Supervisor. He told him that he needed shoulder surgery, but he was

still on 17 day parameters. He declined the surgery because his job was in jeopardy.

687 Mr. Templeman talked about the frustration he experienced as a result of these events. He had suffered a series of injuries which required time off work. As a result of absences due to those injuries, he had been placed on the AMP. When he followed the directions of CMBC in the Level 1 letter and contacted EAP, he was booked off work. The rehabilitation placement arranged by the OHN exacerbated his physical injuries. The fitness program he had been assigned by LTD had helped his condition, but was counted against him in the AMP. He was in pain, and depressed as a result of the PTSD, and he couldn't deal with the situation. He felt that his only option was to go back, and drive his bus in pain. His condition didn't go away, it continued. He did not receive the treatment he needed because he was at work.

688 Mr. Templeman testified that his experience with the AMP caused him to lose trust in the Company: although he has been removed from Level 3 parameters he still has not scheduled needed shoulder surgery because he is very concerned that it would cause CMBC to advance him in the AMP.

689 Given the impact of the systemically discriminatory conduct on Mr. Templeman, I find that an award of $5,000 is appropriate in all of the circumstances of the case.

d. Carlos Fernandes

690 Mr. Fernandes was placed on Level 1 of the AMP in August 2000. One year later, in August 2001, he was booked off work and did not return until March 2002. He did not return to driving buses until November 2002. The bulk of his absences were caused by diabetes.

691 Shortly after his return to work as an operator, he was placed on Level 2 of the AMP, and asked to seek a medical assessment. After review of this assessment, Mr. Fernandes was placed on Level 3 of the AMP, on parameters of 20 days absent per year for a period of two years.

692 Mr. Fernandes testified that, in early 2003 he had a discussion with his Supervisor about some corrective surgery that he needed as a result of a condition arising from his diabetes. The Supervisor advised that taking the time off could result in problems under the AMP, and that the only way to safeguard his position would be to get the operation done during his vacation time, which he did.

693 Eventually, Mr. Fernandes successfully completed his monitoring period. He was formally removed from the AMP in early 2006.

694 Despite his successful removal from the AMP, Mr. Fernandes testified that the events had a negative effect on him. He felt that he should not have

been placed on the AMP as a result of complications from his diabetes. He felt humiliated that he had to have corrective surgery performed on his vacation time in order to ensure that he did not risk his employment. He was stressed, angry and felt as if it was an injustice.

695 In all of the circumstances of Mr. Fernandes' case, I find that it is appropriate to award him $5,000 as injury to his dignity, feelings and self-respect.

e. Christopher Watson

696 Mr. Watson's employment was terminated under the AMP, but he was reinstated at arbitration. In reinstating him to employment, the arbitrator found that CMBC had discriminated against him by basing his termination, in part, on his disabilities, and by failing to initiate a search for permanent accommodations. The arbitrator also stated that Mr. Watson had arrived at the ESR level on a discriminatory path and that, absent the discriminatory application of the AMP, Mr. Watson may never have found himself facing termination.

697 When CMBC reinstated Mr. Watson, it placed him at Level 3 of the AMP. In doing so, CMBC basically disregarded the arbitrator's findings that Mr. Watson had been subject to systemic discrimination. It placed him in precisely the position he had been in just prior to his termination: placed on parameters, with the real possibility of termination if he failed to meet them.

698 Mr. Watson experienced a great deal of stress as a result of his placement at Level 3 of the AMP. As noted, he had recently suffered a stroke at the time of his testimony and stated that he fully expected to be terminated again once he was able to return to work. It was clear that this belief weighed extremely heavily on him.

699 In all of the circumstances of Mr. Watson's case, I find it appropriate to award him $6,000 for injury to dignity, feelings, and self-respect.

f. Susan Lieb

700 Ms. Lieb was initially placed on the AMP after she returned from a two-year absence caused by inhaling toxic fumes on her bus. She was advanced to Level 2 after an 11-week absence for a suspected stroke. During much of this time, Ms. Lieb was placed on TBQ status by the OHN and so could not return to work until her doctors had finished their investigations into what had caused her symptoms.

701 While she was on Level 3, Ms. Lieb suffered a gall bladder attack and was advised to have surgery. However, she was worried that if she had the surgery, she would exceed the parameters. She initially delayed the surgery

until she had a further attack and was advised to have the operation immediately. Although advised to stay off work for a month, she returned after three weeks so that she would not exceed her parameters.

702 Ms. Lieb testified that she was angry and confused by her placement on the AMP. She testified that it compounded the difficulties that she was experiencing with her health.

703 Ms. Lieb also testified that her placement on the AMP has hurt her ability to advance in the Company. Specifically, she stated that she wanted to apply for a Supervisor position. When she asked her own Supervisor about this possibility, she was told that she should not apply because she was on the AMP and would therefore not be accepted.

704 In all of the circumstances of Ms. Lieb's situation, I find it appropriate to award her $5,000 for injury to her dignity, feelings, and self-respect.

g. Other operators

705 None of the other operators who testified before me who had been placed at Level 3 of the AMP during the period for which a remedy is sought by the Union (other than those operators whose employment was subsequently terminated). Mr. Mayes was at Level 1 at the time of his testimony. Ms. Welch has been placed at Level 3 in 1999, prior to the period for which a remedy is sought by the Union. She was again placed at Level 3 of the AMP on September 24, 2004. However, the Union successfully grieved this placement and Ms. Welch was returned to Level 1 in December 22, 2005.

706 With respect to other operators placed at Level 3 of the AMP during the relevant period, an award in respect of injury to dignity, feelings and self respect would require two things: First a finding by the Tribunal, or agreement between the parties, that the operators suffer from chronic or recurring disabilities and have been placed at Level 3 of the AMP at least in part because of those disabilities. Second, evidence with respect to the impact of such a placement on their dignity, feelings or self-respect.

707 In order to resolve these issues, the parties are to meet to discuss the list of operators who have been placed at Level 3 of the AMP. The parties are to identify:

a) those operators who they agree have chronic or recurring disabilities which have contributed to their placement at Level 3 of the AMP; and
b) those operators with respect to whom there is a dispute about whether they have chronic or recurring disabilities that have contributed to their placement at Level 3 of the AMP.

708 The parties will then enter into Tribunal-assisted mediation with a view to resolving the issue of the appropriate identification of and compensation payable to those operators. If the parties are unable to resolve these issues, I remain seized of the matter and will hear the evidence and argument necessary to decide the issues outlined above.

C. Summary of Remedial Orders

709 I have found the Union's complaint to be justified and, as a result, pursuant to s. 37(2)(a) of the *Code*, I order CMBC to cease the contravention and to refrain from committing the same or a similar contravention.

710 Further, pursuant to both 37(2)(a) and 37(2)(c)(i), I order that CMBC cease applying the AMP to operators who would otherwise be subject to the AMP but whose attendance is affected by chronic or recurring disabilities.

711 With respect to individual remedies I find that, to the extent that all of the individual operators terminated under the AMP have had their circumstances considered and decided through the arbitration process, or through settlement of their grievances, it would not be appropriate to make any further award.

712 With respect to those individuals who have been placed at Level 3 of the AMP since six months prior to the filing of the complaint, I order that CMBC pay the following in respect of injury to dignity feelings, and self-respect:

a) to Sergio Da Luz, the sum of $6,000;
b) to Shailendra Prasad, the sum of $6,000;
c) to Gary Templeman, the sum of $5,000;
d) to Carlos Fernandes, the sum of $5,000;
e) to Christopher Watson, the sum of $6,000; and
f) to Susan Lieb, the sum of $5,000.

713 Post-judgment interest is payable on these amounts, and I so order.

714 I order the parties to participate in Tribunal-assisted mediation to attempt to resolve the following:

a) Revisions to the AMP, or its application, which would address the systemic concerns outlined in this decision;
b) The status of individual operators with chronic or recurring disabilities who are currently involved in the AMP;
c) The appropriate compensation payable to employee E05299, if the termination of that employee's employment has not been the subject of an arbitration or settlement between the parties;

d) The appropriate identification of and compensation payable to those operators with chronic or recurring disabilities which have contributed to their advancement to Level 3 (now the advanced concern stage) of the AMP (since January 1, 2003). Prior to the mediation, the parties are to identify:

   i) those operators who they agree have chronic or recurring disabilities which have contributed to their placement on or advancement at Level 3; and

   ii) those operators with respect to whom there is a dispute about whether they have chronic or recurring disabilities that have contributed to their placement on or advancement at Level 3; and

e) any other related issues the parties and the mediator consider appropriate.

715 The Tribunal will contact the parties forthwith to make the necessary arrangements for the mediation.

716 If the parties are unable to come to a resolution within six months of the date of this decision, or such longer time as the mediator and the parties advise me is necessary, I retain jurisdiction to hear argument and, if necessary, evidence on the issue of the appropriate remedies and to make additional orders pursuant to s. 37(2).

Appendix

Glossary of Defined Terms

TERM	DEFINITION
Action Travail des Femmes	*C.N.R. v. Canada (Human Rights Commission)*, [1987] 1 S.C.R. 1114
AMP	CMBC's Attendance Management Program
ASO	Administrative services only
CAW No. 7	*CAW-Canada, Local 111 v. Coast Mountain Bus Co.*, 2005 BCHRT 478 (B.C. Human Rights Trib.)
CMBC	Coast Mountain Bus Company Ltd.
Collective Agreement	The collective agreement in place between the Union and CMBC. At the time of the hearing, the collective agreement in place was effective from April 2004 to March 2007
Company	Coast Mountain Bus Company Ltd.

TERM	DEFINITION
COPE	Canadian Office and Professional Employees Union, Local 378, the union that represents CMBC's office employees
CUPE	Canadian Union of Public Employees, Local 4500, the union that represents CMBC's front-line supervisors
CWW	Compressed work week
EAP	Employee Assistance Program
ESRC	Employment Status Review Committee
ESR	Employment Status Review
Grismer	*British Columbia (Superintendent of Motor Vehicles) v. British Columbia (Council of Human Rights)*, [1999] 3 S.C.R. 868 (S.C.C.)
GRTW	Graduated return to work
Guide	The Supervisor's Guide for Managing Employee Attendance, revised regularly. Unless otherwise indicated, references to the Guide are to the 2004 revision of the Guide.
GWL	Great West Life, the administrator of the STD and LTD plan for CMBC's employees
IBS	Irritable Bowel Syndrome
IME	Independent Medical Examination
Local 2200	National Automobile, Aerospace, Transportation and General Workers of Canada (CAW.Canada) Local 2200, the union that represents CMBC's maintenance employees
LTD	Long-term disability
Meiorin	*British Columbia (Public Service Employee Relations Commission) v. B.C.G.E.U.*, [1999] 3 S.C.R. 3 (S.C.C.)
Notice	Notice issued by CMBC to its employees about the AMP in January 2001, as result of the Policy Decision
OHG	Occupational Health Group
OHN	Occupational Health Nurse
Operations Supervisors	The direct supervisors of transit operators

TERM	DEFINITION
Policy Decision	*National Automobile, Aerospace, Transportation and General Workers of Canada (CAW.Canada) Local 111 -and- Coast Mountain Bus Company (Re: Attendance Management Policy)*, unreported award, December 13, 2000 (Dorsey)
Program	CMBC's Attendance Management Program
RTW	Return to work
STD	Short-term disability
TBQ	To be qualified status.a designation CMBC uses where an employee cannot return to work until their physician specifies that they are fit to return to work in the safety sensitive position of transit operator
T-Comm	Transit Communication
Union	National Automobile, Aerospace, Transportation and General Workers of Canada (CAW-Canada) Local 111, the union that represents CMBC's transit operators. Includes its predecessor, ICTU, Local 11.
WCB	Workers' Compensation benefits

Keays v. Honda Canada Inc.

2008 CarswellOnt 3743, 2008 SCC 39 (S.C.C.)

Bastarache J.

1. Overview

1 On March 29, 2000, after 14 years of employment, the respondent, Kevin Keays, was terminated from his employment at Honda Canada Inc. ("Honda"). Keays sued for wrongful dismissal. The trial judge found that Keays was entitled to a notice period of 15 months. He then considered additional damages dependent on the manner of dismissal (the so-called "*Wallace* damages") and increased the notice period to 24 months. In addition, the trial judge awarded punitive damages against Honda in the amount of $500,000, plus costs on a substantial indemnity scale with a 25 percent premium. The Court of Appeal unanimously upheld the finding of wrongful termination as well as the regular damages and the damages for manner of dismissal (*Wallace* damages). It also ordered that the costs premium be reduced. A majority (Goudge J.A. dissenting) ordered that the quantum of punitive damages be reduced from $500,000 to $100,000.

2 I would allow the appeal in part. The regular damages award should be maintained. The Court of Appeal erred however in maintaining the damages for manner of dismissal (*Wallace* damages) and simply reducing the quantum of punitive damages. These awards, as well as the costs premium, must thus be set aside. I would deny the cross-appeal dealing with the reduction of the award of punitive damages.

3 Keays started working for Honda in 1986, first on the assembly line and later in data entry. In 1997, his diagnosis of chronic fatigue syndrome ("CFS") was confirmed by a doctor from the Sleep Disorder Clinic in Toronto, Dr. Moldofsky. He ceased work and received disability insurance benefits through an independent insurance provider, London Life Insurance Co., until 1998 when his benefits were discontinued based on the insurer's evaluation that Keays could return to work full-time. Keays' appeal to the insurer on this evaluation was denied. Honda had no part in the decision to terminate Keays' benefits.

4 Although London Life's decision was based on medical opinion that Keays could return to work without restrictions, Keays continued to absent himself. He was placed in the Honda Disability Program, which permits disabled employees to take absences without the invocation of Honda's attendance policy by confirming that the absence from work is related to the disability. However, Keays missed more work than his diagnosing physi-

cian, Dr. Morris, had predicted, and the notes he offered to explain his absences changed in tone leaving the employer to believe that the doctor did not independently evaluate whether he missed work due to disability.

5 In late 1999, Honda's administrative coordinator, Susan Selby arranged for Keays to see Dr. Lester Affoo, an independent physician hired by Honda, because of the increasing frequency of absences. In January and February 2000, Keays again experienced increased absences (14 days in total). This prompted Betty Magill, Keays' manager, to raise the issue with Selby. They met on March 3 and decided to ask Keays to meet with Dr. Brennan, an occupational medicine specialist, in order to determine how his disability could be accommodated. After this meeting, but before Honda had a chance to meet with Keays, Keays decided to retain counsel to attempt to mediate his concern that he would ultimately be terminated. On March 17, Honda received a letter from Keays' counsel outlining his concerns and offering to work towards a resolution. Honda did not respond.

6 On March 21, Magill and Selby met with Keays to explain their concerns about the deficiencies in the doctors' notes, described as "cryptic" by Dr. Reinders, and asked him to meet with Dr. Brennan to determine what could be done to support him at his work. They also discussed the letter they had received from Keays' lawyer a few days earlier and explained that they had not responded to the lawyer because they had a practice of dealing with associates directly, not with third party advocates. At this meeting, Keays agreed to meet with Dr. Brennan. However, the next day he told Honda that, on the advice of counsel, he would not meet with Dr. Brennan without explanation of the purpose, methodology and parameters of the consultation. Keays did not come to work for a week following this incident. Upon his return to work, on March 28, 2000, Selby gave Keays a letter ("March 28 letter") which I think it is useful to reproduce in its entirety.

> As you know, Betty Magill and I met with you on March 21, 2000, to discuss your current employment situation at Honda. After you left the meeting, you returned for some clarification and we had another detailed discussion.
>
> The following is a summary of the matters we discussed:
>
> 1. You were told that we have been reviewing your absenteeism as well as the doctor's notes that you had been providing to cover those absences. We discussed your situation with Dr. Affoo who is familiar with your case. In addition, we had Dr. Brennan (a new physician) review your completed medical file. Both doctors advised us that they could find no diagnosis indicating that you are disabled from working.
> 2. The doctor's notes that you have been providing to cover your absences have provided limited information. The notes were merely repeating what you were telling the doctor. There was no independent diagnosis or prognosis.
> 3. It was our intention to meet with you following the March break, to discuss our expectations. Before we had a chance to do so, we received a letter from your

lawyer dated March 17, 2000. In that letter, your lawyer was asking that you no longer be required to bring notes to support your absences.

4. When we met on March 21, 2000, we advised you that we would no longer accept that you have a disability requiring you to be absent. Dr. Brennan and Dr. Affoo both believe that you should be attending work on a regular basis. In order for Dr. Brennan to get to know you and understand completely your condition, we advised that we would arrange for Dr. Brennan to meet with you. The plan was that Dr. Brennan would then communicate directly with your doctor to effectively manage your condition.
5. Before the meeting ended, you were agreeable to meeting with Dr. Brennan and I was to proceed to schedule the appointment.

The next day, (March 22, 2000) you submitted a letter declining to meet with Dr. Brennan. You requested clarification on the "purpose, the methodology and the parameters of the assessment." Since that date, you have called in sick with return to work date unknown. You returned to work today.

Our position remains as we explained it to you on March 21, 2000. Kevin, we do not accept the need for your recent absence nor do we intend to elaborate further on the purpose of your meeting with Dr. Brennan. This was all explained to you carefully on March 21, 2000. Our position remains the same. We expect you to meet with Dr. Brennan and, we expect you to come to work.

Kevin, we sincerely hope that you will co-operate with our efforts. As you have admitted, your condition has not improved over the past three years and you would do anything to get better and come to work on a regular basis. We are committed to supporting you in a full return to work. We sincerely hope that you will co-operate with us.

Kevin, you must understand that the current situation is unacceptable. If you do not agree to meet with Dr. Brennan, we will have no alternative but to terminate your employment.

7 Later the same day, Selby telephoned Keays to urge him to reread the letter and re-consider. Keays remained unwilling to meet Dr. Brennan. In accordance with its warning, Honda terminated his employment.

2. Decisions Below

2.1 Ontario Superior Court of Justice (2005), 40 C.C.E.L. (3d) 258 (Ont. S.C.J.)

8 McIsaac J. concluded that Honda bore the burden to show just cause for termination and that it had failed to carry that burden. McIsaac J. found that Honda's direction to meet with Dr. Brennan was not reasonable under the circumstances, and that Keays had a reasonable excuse for resisting that direction. The termination was not proportional to his refusal. The trial judge then concluded that Keays was entitled to 15 months' notice based on the principles of *Bardal v. Globe & Mail Ltd.* (1960), 24 D.L.R. (2d) 140 (Ont. H.C.). Moreover, McIsaac J. decided that, given the "egregious bad faith displayed by Honda in the manner of this termination and the medical

consequences flowing therefrom", that notice period should be extended to 24 months (para. 48). Since he had increased the notice period, McIsaac J. did not consider it appropriate to offer Keays an additional award on the basis of intentional infliction of nervous shock/emotional distress.

9 McIsaac J. determined that the court was without jurisdiction to consider a tort based on whether Honda breached his rights under the Ontario *Human Rights Code*, R.S.O. 1990, c. H.19. He accepted, however, that such complaints could constitute "independent actionable wrongs" such as to trigger an award of punitive damages, assuming they also merit punishment (para. 50).

10 McIsaac J. denied Keays' claim for compensation based on "lost" disability benefits that would have been available from the insurer based on his total disability caused by the wrongful termination. Such relief was unavailable, the trial judge explained, because Keays did not plead aggravated damages. I take it that the trial judge meant by this that Keays had not argued that there was an independent cause of action to support his further claim for true aggravated damages as defined in *Wallace v. United Grain Growers Ltd.*, [1997] 3 S.C.R. 701 (S.C.C.).

11 McIsaac J. noted that punitive damages are exceptional but he had "no difficulty in finding that the plaintiff has proved that Honda committed a litany of acts of discrimination and harassment in relation to his attempts to resolve his accommodation difficulties" (para. 57). McIsaac J. attributed to Honda a "conspiracy to insinuate Dr. Brennan into the plaintiff's long-established medical relationship with his own doctors and, hopefully, to exclude them from any participation in advocating for his patient's rights" (para. 60). In light of all the circumstances, the trial judge awarded $500,000 in punitive damages.

12 McIsaac J. awarded costs to Keays on a substantial indemnity basis adding a 25 percent premium which together totalled $610,000.

2.2 Court of Appeal for Ontario (Rosenberg, Feldman and Goudge (dissenting in part) JJ.A.) (2006), 82 O.R. (3d) 161 (Ont. C.A.)

13 The Ontario Court of Appeal dismissed the appeal. Goudge J.A., writing for the court, except with respect to the quantum of punitive damages, noted that heavily fact-laden conclusions by the trial judge were entitled to substantial deference. In particular, Goudge J.A. perceived no reason to interfere with the trial judge's conclusions that the order to see Dr. Brennan was unreasonable, that Keays had a reasonable excuse for not complying with the order, and that the dismissal of Keays was a disproportionate response to his alleged insubordination and therefore was done without just cause.

Goudge J.A. also upheld the trial judge's conclusions regarding the appropriate notice period required.

14 Goudge J.A. wrote for the court regarding the availability of punitive damages. He cited *McKinley v. BC Tel*, [2001] 2 S.C.R. 161, 2001 SCC 38 (S.C.C.), for the proposition that acts of discrimination in breach of human rights legislation may serve as a separate actionable wrong so as to give rise to a punitive damages award in a wrongful dismissal case. Goudge J.A. rejected Honda's argument that the Ontario *Human Rights Code* offers a complete remedial scheme that permits punitive damages only in the event of prosecution with the written consent of the Attorney General and only to a maximum fine of $25,000. Goudge J.A. thus upheld the trial judge's finding of an independent actionable wrong. Given Honda's conduct, an award of punitive damages was a rational response on the part of the trial judge.

15 With respect to the quantum of punitive damages, Goudge J.A. wrote for himself alone. He noted that an appellate court should review the quantum awarded by asking whether the amount was rationally required in all the circumstances to punish the defendant's misconduct. Goudge J.A. concluded that $500,000 in punitive damages did not exceed what was rationally required to punish Honda.

16 Once again writing for the court, Goudge J.A. discussed Honda's argument that the trial judge created a reasonable apprehension of bias, requiring a new trial. He acknowledged that the trial judge used "several colourful metaphors" but rejected allegations that this reflected a want of fairness or impartiality (para. 75).

17 With regard to costs, Goudge J.A. noted that he would reduce the premium to $77,500 from $155,000. He dismissed the cross-appeal.

18 Rosenberg J.A. wrote for the majority on the question of the quantum of punitive damages, which he reduced to $100,000. He did so because he believed that the trial judge had relied on findings of fact not supported by the evidence and because the award failed to accord with the fundamental principle of proportionality. In particular, Rosenberg J.A. found no evidence of a protracted corporate conspiracy. The trial judge also referred to "five years" of outrageous conduct whereas the case involved a mere seven-month period. According to Rosenberg J.A., a punitive damage award on the scale imposed by the trial judge in this case could be justified only by extraordinary circumstances. He used *Whiten v. Pilot Insurance Co.*, [2002] 1 S.C.R. 595, 2002 SCC 18 (S.C.C.), as a comparison and noted (at para. 110) that a comment from that case regarding the fact that "it takes a large whack to wake up a wealthy and powerful defendant to its responsibilities" had been taken by the trial judge out of context. Rearing in mind the trial judge's findings that were supported by the evidence, and especially evi-

dence pointing to conduct by Honda suggesting planned and deliberate attempts to intimidate and then dismiss a vulnerable employee, Rosenberg J.A. concluded that an award in excess of those awarded in other wrongful dismissal cases was appropriate. He saw an award of no more than $100,000 as justified. He reduced the punitive damages award accordingly. In all other respects, Rosenberg J.A. concurred with Goudge J.A.

3. Analysis

19 This appeal raises a number of important issues related to the proper allocation of damages in wrongful dismissal cases. Before assessing the validity of the separate heads of damages awarded by the trial judge and the Court of Appeal, it is essential to point out, as will be later demonstrated, that the trial judge made a number of palpable and overriding errors, some of which are mentioned by Rosenberg J.A: Two errors in particular have, in my view, coloured the trial judge's judgment, making other findings and inferences suspect. The trial judge first found that Honda's "misconduct" was "planned and deliberate and formed a protracted corporate conspiracy" (para. 60). As concluded by the Court of Appeal, and as will be further discussed below, there is simply no evidence to support the trial judge's allegation of a conspiracy. Secondly, the trial judge insisted that the "outrageous conduct" had continued for five years when in fact the problem period was no more than seven months. He therefore was considering the wrong period when dealing with Keays' conduct; this error was seemingly attributable to the fact that he considered the cancellation of Keays' long-term benefits by London Life to be a relevant factor in assessing the conduct of Honda, while all evidence points to the fact that the decision was entirely independent of Honda.

20 The remaining analysis will reveal more palpable and overriding errors of fact. However, the above examples alone would suffice to question carefully the factual basis for the trial judge's conclusions. I am therefore compelled to review the record in some detail in my analysis.

21 Beyond creating the need to address the many overriding and palpable errors of the trial judge, this appeal presents the Court with the opportunity to clarify and redefine some aspects of the law of damages in the context of employment.

22 First, I would like to clarify what factors should be considered when allocating compensatory damages in lieu of notice for wrongful dismissal.

23 Second, a review of the basis for and calculation of damages for conduct in dismissal must be undertaken.

24 Third, in considering the allocation of punitive damages in this case, I conclude that it is not necessary to reconsider whether breaches of the On-

tario *Human Rights Code* are independent actionable wrongs for the purposes of punitive damages. I will however discuss the need to avoid overlap of damages for conduct in dismissal and punitive damage awards.

3.1 General Damages: The 15-Month Notice Period

25 After finding that Keays had been wrongfully dismissed, the trial judge determined that he was entitled to an award of damages reflecting the need for 15 months' notice. In doing so, he followed *Bardal* and *Minott v. O'Shanter Development Co.* (1999), 168 D.L.R. (4th) 270 (Ont. C.A.), at p. 293, wherein it was held that an appropriate notice period is to be determined in consideration of factors including, but not limited to, the character of the employment, length of service, the age of the employee and the availability of other employment. In arriving at 15 months, McIsaac J. pointed to: Honda's "flat" (i.e., egalitarian) management structure as limiting the effect of Keays' lower position in Honda's hierarchy; the fact that Keays had specialized training to compensate for his lack of formal education; his long service; and the lack of comparable employment in Alliston. The Court of Appeal agreed with this assessment.

26 On appeal before this Court, Honda did not contest the finding of wrongful dismissal. However, Honda argued that the 15-month notice period allocated by the trial judge was excessive because he failed to conduct a proper analysis of Keays' job functions. Specifically, Honda claimed that an analysis of Keays' job functions shows that his responsibilities were minimal and that he spent a large percentage of his time on data entry. According to Honda, in view of Keays' 14 years of service, his little formal education and the character of his employment, 8 to 10 months would have been appropriate. The fact that Keays' had no management function was crucial.

27 It is true that Honda's "flat management structure" did not truly illuminate the character of Keays' employment and that this label should not matter: what matters is experience, qualifications and other factors mentioned in *Bardal.*

28 In determining what constitutes reasonable notice of termination, the courts have generally applied the principles articulated by McRuer C.J.H.C. in *Bardal*, at p. 145:

> There can be no catalogue laid down as to what is reasonable notice in particular classes of cases. The reasonableness of the notice must be decided with reference to each particular case, having regard to the character of the employment, the length of service of the servant, the age of the servant and the availability of similar employment, having regard to the experience, training and qualifications of the servant.

29 These four factors were adopted by this Court in *Machtinger v. HOJ Industries Ltd.*, [1992] 1 S.C.R. 986 (S.C.C.). They can only be determined on a case-by-case basis.

30 It is true that there has been some suggestion that a person's position in the hierarchy should be irrelevant to assessing damages for wrongful dismissal (see *Bramble v. Medis Health & Pharmaceutical Services Inc.* (1999), 214 N.B.R. (2d) 111 (N.B. C.A.), and *Byers v. Prince George (City) Downtown Parking Commission* (1998), 53 B.C.L.R. (3d) 345 (B.C. C.A.). The traditional assumptions about the relevance of a person's position in the hierarchy was not directly challenged in this case. It will therefore suffice to say here that Honda's management structure has no part to play in determining reasonable notice in this case. The "flat management structure" said nothing of Keays' employment. It does not describe the responsibilities and skills of that worker, nor the character of the lost employment. The particular circumstances of the individual should be the concern of the courts in determining the appropriate period of reasonable notice. Traditional presumptions about the role that managerial level plays in reasonable notice can always be rebutted by evidence.

31 This position is consistent with the original formulation of the *Bardal* test where McRuer C.J.H.C. stated:

> There can be no catalogue laid down as to what is reasonable notice in particular classes of cases. [Emphasis added; p. 145.]

32 No one *Bardal* factor should be given disproportionate weight. In the present case, the trial judge erred in applying one of the factors, alluding to the flat management structure, rather than examining the actual functions of Keays. Despite this error, the 15-month notice period is entitled to deference since, on the entirety of the circumstances here, there is no basis to interfere with the conclusions of the trial judge. Keays was one of the first employees hired at Honda's plant. He spent his entire adult working life with Honda. He did not have any formal education and suffered from an illness which greatly incapacitated him. All these factors will substantially reduce his chances of re-employment and justify an assessment of 15 months' notice.

3.2 Damages for Conduct in Dismissal

33 In applying *Wallace*, the trial judge concluded that Honda's manner of dismissing Keays was an egregious display of bad faith that warranted an extension of the notice period to 24 months. He made the following findings of fact in support of his award:

- In the letter dated March 28, Honda deliberately misrepresented the views of its doctors.
- Keays was being "set up" when asked to see Dr. Brennan.

- Keays' condition worsened after the dismissal: he became depressed, developed an adjustment disorder for 3-4 months, and has been unable to work since then.
- Honda's decision to cancel the "accommodation" was a form of reprisal for Keays' retaining legal counsel.

34 The Court of Appeal concluded that given the factual nature of determining whether Honda acted in bad faith, Honda had to demonstrate that the trial judge committed a palpable and overriding error. It concluded that Honda had failed to demonstrate this and that the trial judge's decision was sufficiently supported in the evidence. I cannot agree with this conclusion. A proper reading of the record shows that Honda's conduct in dismissing Keays was in no way an egregious display of bad faith justifying an award of damages for conduct in dismissal.

35 As earlier mentioned, it is my view that the trial judge made a number of significant overriding and palpable factual errors that relate directly to the factual matrix that justified, according to him, an award of damages for manner of dismissal (*Wallace* damages). For that reason alone, the decision cannot stand. I will elaborate on this. I note, however, that this case sheds light on the legal problems associated with the allocation of these damages. It is therefore appropriate for this Court to reconsider the *Wallace* approach and make some adjustments.

3.2.1 The Factual Analysis

36 None of the four foundations accepted by the trial judge for his "Wallace award" of damages is valid. I will examine them individually.

3.2.1.1 The March 28 Letter

37 In its submissions to this Court, Honda points out that the trial judge had no basis for concluding that the March 28 letter (set out in para. 6 above) was callous and insensitive. In reviewing the facts and reading the letter, it is clear that Honda was relying on expert advice and simply conveying the information obtained from experts to Keays. The following two paragraphs were the most "contentious" of the letter:

> 1. You were told that we have been reviewing your absenteeism as well as the doctor's notes that you had been providing to cover those absences. We discussed your situation with Dr. Affoo who is familiar with your case. In addition, we had Dr. Brennan (a new physician) review your complete medical file. <u>Both doctors advised us that they could find no diagnosis indicating that you are disabled from working.</u>
>
> 4. When we met on March 21, 2000, we advised you that we would no longer accept that you have a disability requiring you to be absent. <u>Dr. Brennan and Dr. Affoo both believe that you should be attending work on a regular basis.</u> In

> order for Dr. Brennan to get to know you and understand completely your condition, we advised that we would arrange for Dr. Brennan to meet with you. The plan was that Dr. Brennan would then communicate directly with your doctor to effectively manage your condition. [Emphasis added.]

38 The trial judge accepted Keays' submission that Honda deliberately misrepresented the positions of both physicians for the purpose of intimidation, excluding his own doctors, and forcing him to meet with Dr. Brennan. The evidence contradicts this finding.

39 First, Dr. Affoo concluded that Keays was able to work and should try to work as much as possible. He communicated this information to Selby. Dr. Affoo's testimony is clear on this point:

> Q. ... did you have any conversation with anyone at Honda about Mr. Keays?
>
> A. Subsequently I reported back to Associate Services, Susan Selby, as to our meeting. I explained to her that Mr. Keays had been diagnosed with a diagnosis of chronic fatigue syndrome, as he assured me he had. We talked about him missing a lot of time off work, and I explained to her that from Mr. Keays' point of view he didn't feel that-he felt that, that he was doing his best and that we could expect him to be off work as he has been in the past.
>
> Q. Any other conversation that you recall?
>
> A. Probably within those terms.
>
> Q. Do you recall if you made any suggestion as to whether or not Mr. Keays' condition, as you understood it, warranted absenteeism?
>
> A. Well, I felt that he was coping quite well at Honda. You know, I discussed-I told her the fact that, that he was at a desk and so on and so forth, and he seemed to be coping quite well at his work place. I felt that, that in my experience with chronic fatigue one, you know, one wants him to come to work, and, and we would try and get him to work as, as, as much as we can. And certainly, I didn't think he needed to be off work the kind of pattern he had in the past. I felt that, you know, that he could be off-I felt that he probably would be off work maybe three or four times a month, possibly, from his condition, but with a regimented lifestyle, and you know, with the things that he's being, that he's being treated with my his own physician, that he should be able to do well. [Emphasis added.]

40 Second, Dr. Brennan communicated to Honda that he was *unable* to diagnose Keays with CFS without meeting with him first. During his examination, Dr. Brennan stated the following:

> I did not accept the diagnosis of chronic fatigue syndrome, largely because I didn't feel that I had all the information. [Emphasis added.]

There is nothing misleading or false with Honda's assertion that both doctors advised that they could find no diagnosis that would bar Keays from working. Dr. Affoo clearly stated that he thought it would be good for Keays to work, and Dr. Brennan clearly could find no diagnosis of CFS without first meeting Keays. Honda was simply relaying the information it received from its experts to Keays. Given this evidence, I do not see how the trial judge could have concluded that Honda was trying to intimidate Keays by twisting the positions of the physicians. The physicians' positions were clear, and Honda had no reason not to accept the expert advice it was receiving. The trial judge made an overriding and palpable error in faulting Honda for relying on the advice of its medical experts.

41 The trial judge stated, at para. 43 of his decision:

> Although parts of the letter may have been accurate in isolation, when considered in its entirety, it presented a "twisted" view of his condition.

42 The trial judge gave no reason to explain why, in its "entirety", the letter presents such a view. For a written document to have a certain flavour or sense "in its entirety", there must be indicators that create such a flavour within that document. In this case, the letter contains no such clues. "[I]n its entirety", the March 28 letter simply conveyed to Keays that Honda wanted him to meet with Dr. Brennan because their experts had advised them that his condition did not preclude him from working. The whole context is one in which Honda recognizes that Keays has a disability and that it has to be dealt with; this is an important consideration in determining good faith on the part of Honda.

3.2.1.2 No "Set-Up"; No "Hardball"

43 The trial judge concluded, at para. 45 of his judgment, that Keays was being "set up" for failure because Dr. Brennan had already made up his mind that his condition was bogus. First, I think it is important to note that there is no evidence that Dr. Brennan took on a "hardball" attitude. A careful analysis of the record reveals that Dr. Brennan simply could not, with the information that was provided to him, accept a diagnosis of CFS without first meeting Keays.

44 The trial judge stated, at para. 45, that a note written by Dr. Brennan to Honda on December 3, 2000 reveals that Dr. Brennan "referenced the fact that the diagnosis of CFS carries 'considerable controversy' and that 'many physicians' do not believe it should be taken as a 'stand alone' diagnosis" and that "[h]e himself was of the view that it 'may well be a bona fide medical condition', but only in certain 'very limited circumstances'". These assertions alone should not lead one to believe that Dr. Brennan was taking a "hardball" approach to workplace absences. But there is more that has to be taken into account here. After stating that he believed that chronic fatigue syndrome is a *bona fide* medical condition under very limited circumstances, he continued to say:

> Those circumstances are those as outlined by the Centre for Disease Control (CDC) in Atlanta. The CDC has developed some strict diagnostic criteria for Chronic Fatigue Syndrome (CFS) to aid in its diagnosis and differentiation from depression, fatigue of chronic illness, malingering, multiple rheumatic diseases etc.

45 Dr. Brennan was thus simply espousing the prevalent approach adopted by the CDC. I do not see how this can be qualified as "hardball", as he was reiterating the information at his disposal. However, even if one were to conclude that Dr. Brennan was taking a somewhat "hardball" approach to workplace absences, Honda cannot be faulted for accepting his expert advice unless a conspiracy exists. As concluded by the Court of Appeal, there simply was no conspiracy to terminate Keays. Rosenberg J.A. correctly stated at paras. 91 and 93 of his reasons that:

> There is no evidence to support the finding of a protracted corporate conspiracy. The appellant accommodated the respondent's increasingly more serious disability over several years. The fact that the company ran a lean operation in which it was difficult to accommodate prolonged absences was not proof of a conspiracy.
>
> . . . . .
>
> ... There is no evidence to support this conspiracy to interfere with the respondent's relationship with his own physician. In fact, the trial judge's finding on this issue is inconsistent with his broad finding that the appellant intended to dismiss the respondent. There would be no need to 'insinuate" Dr. Brennan into the relationship if the company's intent all along was to terminate the employment.

46 As such, it was not open to the Court of Appeal to accept the trial judge's finding that Keays was being set up when asked to meet with Dr. Brennan. Honda was merely listening to expert advice that can hardly be qualified as "hardball". There is no rational way to justify the conclusion that the request for a meeting between Keays and Dr. Brennan was not perfectly normal in the circumstances.

3.2.1.3 No Reprisal

47 The trial judge committed another overriding and palpable error in concluding that Honda's decision to cancel its accommodation was a form of reprisal for Keays' decision to retain legal counsel. The decision to stop accepting doctors' notes was not reprisal for Keays seeking legal counsel. Rather, as concluded by Rosenberg J.A. in Court of Appeal, at para. 98, Honda was simply seeking to confirm Keays' disability. Here again, it is important to note that Honda does not deny that there is a problem that has to be dealt with in a professional and fair way. As earlier mentioned, the notes had changed in character and were "cryptic" (para. 6 above). Moreover, as stated in para. 5 above, Shelby and Magill met to address the deficiencies in Keays' doctors notes and Keays' absences well before Keays' lawyer sent his letter.

3.2.1.4 Keays' Condition Worsened

48 The trial judge committed an overriding and palpable error in considering Keays' disability subsequent to termination; this was not compensable

under the *Wallace* umbrella because there was no evidence that the disability was caused by the manner of termination.

3.2.2 The Legal Analysis

49 The trial judge's decision in this case highlights the problems we face in dealing with damages for conduct in the context of termination of employment. In particular, it raises questions about the propriety of damages for manner of dismissal, whereby damages are awarded by extending the notice period (*Wallace* damages). This re-evaluation is mandated particularly by this Court's recent decision in *Fidler v. Sun Life Assurance Co. of Canada*, [2006] 2 S.C.R. 3, 2006 SCC 30 (S.C.C.).

3.2.2.1 Current State of the Law

50 An action for wrongful dismissal is based on an implied obligation in the employment contract to give reasonable notice of an intention to terminate the relationship in the absence of just cause. Thus, if an employer fails to provide reasonable notice of termination, the employee can bring an action for breach of the implied term (*Wallace*, at para. 115). The general rule, which stems from the British case of *Addis v. Gramophone Co.*, [1909] A.C. 488 (Eng. H.L.), is that damages allocated in such actions are confined to the loss suffered as a result of the employer's failure to give proper notice and that no damages are available to the employee for the actual loss of his of her job and/or pain and distress that may have been suffered as a consequence of being terminated. This Court affirmed this rule in *Peso Silver Mines Ltd. v. Cropper*, [1966] S.C.R. 673 (S.C.C.), at p. 684:

> [T]he damages cannot be increased by reason of the circumstances of dismissal whether in respect of the [employee's] wounded feelings or the prejudicial effect upon his reputation and chances of finding other employment.

51 Later in *Vorvis v. Insurance Corp. of British Columbia*, [1989] 1 S.C.R. 1085 (S.C.C.), McIntyre J. stated at p. 1103:

> I would conclude that while aggravated damages may be awarded in actions for breach of contract in appropriate cases, this is not a case where they should be given. The rule long established in the *Addis* and *Peso Silver Mines* cases has generally been applied to deny such damages, and the employer/employee relationship (in the absence of collective agreements which involve consideration of the modern labour law régime) has always been one where either party could terminate the contract of employment by due notice, and therefore the only damage which could arise would result from a failure to give such notice.

52 The Court in *Vorvis* nevertheless left open the possibility of allocating aggravated damages in wrongful dismissal cases where the acts complained of were also independently actionable. McIntyre J. stated at p. 1103:

> I would not wish to be taken as saying that aggravated damages could never be awarded in a case of wrongful dismissal, particularly where the acts complained of were also independently actionable, a factor not present here. [Emphasis added.]

53 In *Wallace*, Iacobucci J. endorsed a strict interpretation of the *Vorvis* "independently actionable wrong" approach, rejecting both an implied contractual duty of good faith and a tort of bad faith discharge. At para. 73, he said:

> Relying upon the principles enunciated in *Vorvis*, *supra*, the Court of Appeal held that any award of damages beyond compensation for breach of contract for failure to give reasonable notice of termination "must be founded on a separately actionable course of conduct" (p. 184). Although there has been criticism of *Vorvis*... this is an accurate statement of the law....An employment contract is not one in which peace of mind is the very matter contracted for (see e.g. *Jarvis v. Swan Tours Ltd.*, [1973] 1 Q.B. 233 (C.A.)) and so, absent an independently actionable wrong, the foreseeability of mental distress or the fact that the parties contemplated its occurrence is of no consequence.
>
> [Emphasis added.]

54 This brings us to *Fidler*, where the Court, *per* McLachlin CJ. and Abella J., concluded that it was no longer necessary that there be an independent actionable wrong before damages for mental distress can be awarded for breach of contract, whether or not it is a "peace of mind"contract. It stated at para. 49:

> We conclude that the "peace of mind"class of cases should not be viewed as an exception to the general rule of the non-availability of damages for mental distress in contract law, but rather as an application of the reasonable contemplation or foreseeability principle that applies generally to determine the availability of damages for breach of contract.

This conclusion was based on the principle, articulated in *Hadley v. Baxendale* (1854), 9 Exch. 341, 156 E.R. 145 (Eng. Ex. Div.), that damages are recoverable for a contractual breach if the damages are "such as may fairly and reasonably be considered either arising naturally... from such breach of contract itself, or such as may reasonably be supposed to have been in the contemplation of both parties"(p. 151). The court in *Hadley* explained the principle of reasonable expectation as follows:

> Now, if the special circumstances under which the contract was actually made were communicated by the plaintiffs to the defendants, and thus known to both parties, the damages resulting from the breach of such a contract, which they would reasonably contemplate, would be the amount of injury which would ordinarily follow from a breach of contract under these special circumstances so known and communicated. But, on the other hand, if these special circumstances were wholly unknown to the party breaking the contract, he, at the most, could only be supposed to have had in

> his contemplation the amount of injury which would arise generally, and in the great multitude of cases not affected by any special circumstances, from such a breach of contract. [p. 151]

55 Thus, in cases where parties have contemplated at the time of the contract that a breach in certain circumstances would cause the plaintiff mental distress, the plaintiff is entitled to recover (para. 42 *of Fidler*; p. 1102 of *Vorvis)*. This principle was reaffirmed in para. 54 of *Fidler*, where the Court recognized that the *Hadley* rule explains the extended notice period in *Wallace*.

> It follows that there is only one rule by which compensatory damages for breach of contract should be assessed: the rule in *Hadley v. Baxendale*. The *Hadley* test unites all forms of contractual damages under a single principle. It explains why damages may be awarded where an object of the contract is to secure a psychological benefit, just as they may be awarded where an object of the contract is to secure a material one. It also explains why an extended period of notice may have been awarded upon wrongful dismissal in employment law: see *Wallace v. United Grain Growers Ltd.*, [1997] 3 S.C.R. 701. In all cases, these results are based on what was in the reasonable contemplation of the parties at the time of contract formation. [Emphasis deleted.]

56 We must therefore begin by asking what was contemplated by the parties at the time of the formation of the contract, or, as stated in para. 44 of *Fidler*: "what did the contract promise?"The contract of employment is, by its very terms, subject to cancellation on notice or subject to payment of damages in lieu of notice without regard to the ordinary psychological impact of that decision. At the time the contract was formed, there would not ordinarily be contemplation of psychological damage resulting from the dismissal since the dismissal is a clear legal possibility. The normal distress and hurt feelings resulting from dismissal are not compensable.

57 Damages resulting from the manner of dismissal must then be available only if they result from the circumstances described in *Wallace*, namely where the employer engages in conduct during the course of dismissal that is "unfair or is in bad faith by being, for example, untruthful, misleading or unduly insensitive"(para. 98).

58 The application of *Fidler* makes it unnecessary to pursue an extended analysis of the scope of any implied duty of good faith in an employment contract. *Fidler* provides that "as long as the promise in relation to state of mind is a part of the bargain in the reasonable contemplation of the contracting parties, mental distress damages arising from its breach are recoverable"(para. 48). In *Wallace*, the Court held employers "to an obligation of good faith and fair dealing in the manner of dismissal"(para. 95) and created the expectation that, in the course of dismissal, employers would be "candid, reasonable, honest and forthright with their employees"(para. 98). At least since that time, then, there has been expectation by both parties to

the contract that employers will act in good faith in the manner of dismissal. Failure to do so can lead to foreseeable, compensable damages. As aforementioned, this Court recognized as much in *Fidler* itself, where we noted that the principle in *Hadley* "explains why an extended period of notice may have been awarded upon wrongful dismissal in employment law"(para. 54).

59 To be perfectly clear, I will conclude this analysis of our jurisprudence by saying that there is no reason to retain the distinction between "true aggravated damages"resulting from a separate cause of action and moral damages resulting from conduct in the manner of termination. Damages attributable to conduct in the manner of dismissal are always to be awarded under the *Hadley* principle. Moreover, in cases where damages are awarded, no extension of the notice period is to be used to determine the proper amount to be paid. The amount is to be fixed according to the same principles and in the same way as in all other cases dealing with moral damages. Thus, if the employee can prove that the manner of dismissal caused mental distress that was in the contemplation of the parties, those damages will be awarded not through an arbitrary extension of the notice period, but through an award that reflects the actual damages. Examples of conduct in dismissal resulting in compensable damages are attacking the employee's reputation by declarations made at the time of dismissal, misrepresentation regarding the reason for the decision, or dismissal meant to deprive the employee of a pension benefit or other right, permanent status for instance (see also the examples in *Wallace*, at paras. 99-100).

60 In light of the above discussion, the confusion between damages for conduct in dismissal and punitive damages is unsurprising, given that both have to do with conduct at the time of dismissal. It is important to emphasize here that the fundamental nature of damages for conduct in dismissal must be retained. This means that the award of damages for psychological injury in this context is still intended to be compensatory. The Court must avoid the pitfall of double-compensation or double-punishment that has been exemplified by this case.

3.2.2.2 Application of the Revised Test to this Case

61 I have reviewed the major overriding and palpable errors which undermine the trial judge's finding that Honda acted in "bad faith"when terminating Keays. There was, in my opinion, no such breach and no justification for an award of damages for conduct in dismissal.

3.3 Punitive Damages

62 In *Vorvis*, McIntyre J., for the majority, held that punitive damages are recoverable provided the defendant's conduct said to give rise to the claim is itself "an actionable wrong". This position stood until 2002 when my colleague Binnie J., writing for the majority, dealt comprehensively with the issue of punitive damages in the context of the *Whiten* case. He specified that an "actionable wrong"within the *Vorvis* rule does not require an independent tort and that a breach of the contractual duty of good faith can qualify as an independent wrong. Binnie J. concluded, at para. 82, that "[a]n independent actionable wrong is required, but it can be found in breach of a distinct and separate contractual provision or other duty such as a fiduciary obligation". In the case at hand, the trial judge and the Court of Appeal concluded that Honda's "discriminatory conduct"amounted to an independent actionable wrong for the purposes of allocating punitive damages. This being said, there is no need to discuss the concept of "actionable wrong"here; this was done in *Whiten*. What matters here is that there was no basis for the judge's decision on the facts. I will therefore examine the facts and determine why punitive damages were not well justified according to the criteria in *Whiten*. I will also discuss the need to avoid duplication in damage awards. Damages for conduct in the manner of dismissal are compensatory; punitive damages are restricted to advertent wrongful acts that are so malicious and outrageous that they are deserving of punishment on their own. This distinction must guide judges in their analysis.

63 In this case, the trial judge awarded punitive damages on the basis of discriminatory conduct by Honda. Honda argues that discrimination is precluded as an independent cause of action under *Bhadauria v. Seneca College of Applied Arts & Technology*, [1981] 2 S.C.R. 181 (S.C.C.). In that case, this Court clearly articulated that a plaintiff is precluded from pursuing a common law remedy when human rights legislation contains a comprehensive enforcement scheme for violations of its substantive terms. The reasoning behind this conclusion is that the purpose of the Ontario *Human Rights Code* is to remedy the effects of discrimination; if breaches to the Code were actionable in common law courts, it would encourage litigants to use the Code for a purpose the legislature did not intend-namely, to punish employers who discriminate against their employees. Thus, a person who alleges a breach of the provisions of the Code must seek a remedy within the statutory scheme set out in the Code itself. Moreover, the recent amendments to the Code (which would allow a plaintiff to advance a breach of the Code as a cause of action in connection with another wrong) restrict monetary compensation to loss arising out of the infringement, including any injuries to dignity, feelings and self-respect. In this respect, they confirm the Code's remedial thrust.

64 The Court of Appeal, relying on *Mckinley*, concluded that *Bhadauria* only precludes a civil action based directly on a breach of the Code-but does not preclude finding an independent actionable wrong for the purpose of allocating punitive damages. It is my view that the Code provides a comprehensive scheme for the treatment of claims of discrimination and *Bhadauria* established that a breach of the Code cannot constitute an actionable wrong; the legal requirement is not met.

65 Keays argued in cross-appeal before this Court that the decision in *Bhadauria* should be set aside and that a separate tort of discrimination should be recognized. In *Bhadauria*, Laskin C.J., writing for the Court, held that the plaintiff was precluded from pursuing a common law remedy because the applicable human rights legislation (the Code) contained a comprehensive enforcement scheme for violations of its substantive terms. The subtext of the *Bhadauria* decision is a concern that the broad, unfettered tort of discrimination created by the Court of Appeal would lead to indeterminate liability. Laskin C.J. wrote, at p. 189:

> It is one thing to apply a common law duty of care to standards of behaviour under a statute; that is simply to apply the law of negligence in the recognition of so-called statutory torts. It is quite a different thing to create by judicial fiat an obligation-one in no sense analogous to a duty of care in the law of negligence-to confer an economic benefit upon certain persons, with whom the alleged obligor has no connection ....

The concern that a tort of discrimination does not contain an effective limiting device was raised by interveners in this appeal. Moreover, as noted by the intervener Manitoba Human Rights Commission, jurisdictions outside Ontario have human rights legislation that vests jurisdiction exclusively with the provincial/territorial human rights tribunal. Accordingly, the concern in *Bhadauria* that recognition of a tort of discrimination would be inconsistent with legislative intent is still real.

66 The Council of Canadians with Disabilities, another intervener, raised the concern that recognition of a tort of discrimination may undermine the statutory regime which, for many victims of discrimination, is a more accessible and effective means by which to seek redress.

67 This said, there is no need to reconsider the position in *Bhadauria* in this case and deal with Keays' request for recognition of a distinct tort of discrimination. There was no evidence of discrimination to support a claim under s. 5 of the Ontario *Human Rights Code*, therefore no breach of human rights legislation serving as an actionable wrong, as required by Goudge J.A. Furthermore, there was no evidence of conduct meeting the strict requirements in *Whiten*. The trial judge concluded that the accommodation provided by admission to the disability program was itself discriminatory because Keays "had to "earn' each dispensation from being "coached' for

any absences by presenting a "note' from his doctor like some child who is suspected of "playing hooky' from school"(para. 53). The trial judge then added that it made little sense to have a disability program and then deter its use by asking for doctors' notes. The association of coaching and the requirement of notes made by the trial judge here is puzzling. The requirement of notes was in effect part of the accommodation because it permitted absences without the possibility of the same leading to disciplinary action for failing to meet work requirements. There was no detriment in being part of the disability program and being treated differently from persons with "mainstream illnesses". The differential treatment was meant to accommodate the particular circumstances of persons with a particular type of disability and to provide a benefit to them. It is indeed apparent from the record that the program was designed to establish a continuous relation between management and treating physicians and monitor absences in order to establish in particular an expected rate of absences which would not give rise to disciplinary action. The suggestion that the program itself was discriminatory is not supported by the facts.

68 Even if I were to give deference to the trial judge on this issue, this Court has stated that punitive damages should "receive the most careful consideration and the discretion to award them should be most cautiously exercised"(*Vorvis*, at pp. 1104-5). Courts should only resort to punitive damages in exceptional cases (*Whiten*, at para. 69). The independent actionable wrong requirement is but one of many factors that merit careful consideration by the courts in allocating punitive damages. Another important thing to be considered is that conduct meriting punitive damages awards must be "harsh, vindictive, reprehensible and malicious", as well as "extreme in its nature and such that by any reasonable standard it is deserving of full condemnation and punishment"(*Vorvis*, at p. 1108). The facts of this case demonstrate no such conduct. Creating a disability program such as the one under review in this case cannot be equated with a malicious intent to discriminate against persons with a particular affliction.

69 The majority of the Court of Appeal upheld the award of punitive damages, but reduced the quantum to $100,000. The findings supporting this decision are demonstrably wrong and, in some cases, contradict the Court of Appeal's own findings. Before delving into the factual analysis, however, it is worth mentioning that even if the facts had justified an award of punitive damages, the lower courts should have been alert to the fact that compensatory damages were already awarded, and that under the old test, they carried an element of deterrence. This stems from the important principle that courts, when allocating punitive damages, must focus on the defendant's misconduct, not on the plaintiff's loss (*Whiten*, at para. 73). In this case, the same conduct underlays the awards of damages for conduct in dis-

missal and punitive damages. The lower courts erred by not questioning whether the allocation of punitive damages was necessary for the purposes of denunciation, deterrence and retribution, once the damages for conduct in dismissal were awarded. Be that as it may, we now have a clearer foundation to distinguish between damages for conduct in dismissal and punitive damages.

70 As earlier mentioned, there was considerable duplication in the award of damages for conduct in dismissal and punitive damages in this case. The discussion of punitive damages must nevertheless begin with a consideration of the conduct attributed to Honda that justified the award.

71 As earlier mentioned, the main allegation was that Honda discriminated by requiring Keays to bring in a doctor's note to justify each absence when employees with "mainstream illnesses"did not have to do so. The trial judge also found that this requirement had the effect of lengthening absences, ignoring the evidence of Ms. Selby who testified that Honda did not require the employee to produce a doctor's note as a precondition to returning to work. As discussed earlier, employees outside the disability program did not require notes for absences of less than five days but were subject to discipline for excessive absences (A.R., at pp. 282-83), whereas employees in the program were allowed regular absences without discipline beyond the usual attendance requirement under a system of supervision based on regular contacts with doctors. The object of the disability program is to maintain regular contact with the family doctor in order to support treatment. It allows for disability-related absences, a form of accommodation determined in consultation with doctors. The program requires that medical notes be provided to establish that absences are in fact related to the disability. There is no stereotyping or arbitrariness here (*Syndicat des employés de l'Hôpital général de Montréal c. Sexton*, [2007] 1 S.C.R. 161, 2007 SCC 4 (S.C.C.) at para. 49). In addition, I accept that the need to monitor the absences of employees who are regularly absent from work is a *bona fide* work requirement in light of the very nature of the employment contract and responsibility of the employer for the management of its workforce.

72 The trial judge also found the refusal to remove the "coaching"record from Keays' file to be discriminatory, even if there was no evidence of any adverse consequences to the existence of a coaching file. The evidence was that coaching is not a disciplinary procedure and would simply permit entry into the disability program allowing absences without disciplinary consequences (A.R., at pp. 306-14).

73 The trial judge also based his decision on harassment; he seemed to relate this entirely to a suggestion made by Dr. Affoo that Keays consider taking a position with a light physical component (trial judgment, at para.

55). It is certainly difficult to see a course of conduct in a single incident. Moreover, this was a single suggestion made by an independent expert, never acted upon. I have already dealt with this argument at para. 43 when discussing the damages for conduct in dismissal.

74 A final basis for the finding that punitive damages were justified is that Honda had "retaliated"against Keays. I have dealt with this at para. 47.

75 The Court of Appeal pointed to the finding that Honda knew that Keays valued his employment and was dependent upon it for disability benefits. It is no doubt true that Keays valued his job and that he was dependent upon that employment for his disability benefits. However, knowledge of this cannot justify an award of punitive damages. All employees value their jobs. What matters is Honda's conduct with regards to Keays' need for medical attention and special accommodation. In this respect, it was wrong to blame Honda for Keays' loss of disability benefits. London Life's decision to cut off Keays' long-term disability benefits had nothing to do with Honda. It was therefore erroneous to attribute the insurer's decision to Honda and allow for punitive damages on such grounds.

76 The Court of Appeal found that Honda knew Keays was particularly vulnerable because of his medical condition. However, according to the Court of Appeal's own findings, Honda did not know about the seriousness or true nature of Keays' medical condition because Keays would not facilitate an exchange of information about it. Honda was sceptical about Keays' disability and was taking steps to confirm it. His medical file did not disclose a definitive diagnosis of CFS and Keays refused to meet with Dr. Brennan despite repeated assurances that the meeting was only a "get to know you"session, to be followed by contacts with Keays' personal physician.

77 Finally, the Court of Appeal pointed to Honda's refusal to deal with Keays' counsel. There is no legal obligation on the part of any party to deal with an employee's counsel while he or she continues with his or her employer. Parties are always entitled to deal with each other directly. What was egregious was the fact that Honda told Keays that hiring outside counsel was a mistake and that it would make things worse. This was surely a way of undermining the advice of the lawyer. This conduct was ill-advised and unnecessarily harsh, but it does not provide justification for an award of punitive damages.

78 The evidence and the Court of Appeal's own findings lead me to conclude that Honda's conduct was not sufficiently egregious or outrageous to warrant an award of punitive damages under the *Whiten* criteria. The Court of Appeal's award must thus be overturned.

4. The Cost Premium

79 The final issue that must be addressed relates to the cost premium. In *Walker v. Ritchie*, [2006] 2 S.C.R. 428, 2006 SCC 45 (S.C.C.), this Court found that the risk of non-payment of lawyer's fees is not a relevant factor under the Ontario *Rules of Civil Procedure* (Rule 57.01). This decision, which was released after the cost premium was awarded in this case, and Honda's success on this appeal are determinative. Thus, the cost premium should be set aside.

5. Conclusion

80 The appeal is allowed in part and the cross-appeal is dismissed. The damages for conduct in dismissal and punitive damages awards are set aside. Costs on this appeal and cross-appeal are awarded to Honda. At other levels, costs should be at a partial indemnity scale and the cost premium set aside.

LeBel J.

81 I have read the reasons of my colleague Justice Bastarache. I agree with him that there was no basis for the claim for punitive damages and that it overlaps with the award of what were formerly known as "*Wallace* damages". I also agree with him that there is a need to review the categories of damages for dismissal. But any revision must reflect the view accepted by this Court that the contract of employment is a good faith contract that is informed by the values protected by and recognized in the human rights codes and the *Canadian Charter of Rights and Freedoms*, particularly in respect of discrimination. As the Court found in *Wallace v. United Grain Growers Ltd.*, [1997] 3 S.C.R. 701 (S.C.C.), the contract of employment often reflects substantial power imbalances. As a result, it must be performed and terminated in good faith, and fairly.

82 With respect, I believe that on the facts of this case, the award of additional damages for manner of dismissal (formerly "Wallace damages") should stand. The trial judge committed no overriding errors in this respect ((2005), 40 C.C.E.L. (3d) 258 (Ont. S.C.J.)). Although his review of the facts may not have been flawless, there was a sufficient basis for the findings of bad faith and discrimination in the manner in which the employment of the respondent, Kevin Keays, was terminated by Honda.

83 After discussing this, I will add a few comments on this Court's judgment in *Bhadauria v. Seneca College of Applied Arts & Technology*, [1981] 2 S.C.R. 181 (S.C.C.), and on its impact on the development of the law of torts.

I. Appellate Review and the Findings of Bad Faith

84 This Court's jurisprudence has had a significant impact on the review of facts by appellate courts. Indeed, the Court recognizes that it too is bound by the principle of deference to the findings of a trier of fact (*St-Jean c. Mercier*, [2002] 1 S.C.R. 491, 2002 SCC 15 (S.C.C.), at paras. 37 and 46, *per* Gonthier J.). The trial in the Superior Court of Justice lasted 30 days. The trial judge heard extensive, and often conflicting, evidence about which he made numerous findings of fact. Despite some flaws in his review of the facts, his findings of bad faith and discrimination had an adequate factual foundation. Given the way the issues were addressed in this Court, I will discuss the errors allegedly committed by the trial judge in some detail in order to show that the factual foundation for those findings was adequate.

85 I have reviewed the errors identified by the majority of the Court of Appeal, as well as those identified by Justice Bastarache to support his conclusion that *Wallace*, or manner of dismissal, damages were not warranted in this case. In my view, several of the findings the majority of the Court of Appeal identified as errors were in fact supported by the evidence. The findings my colleague identifies as errors are also, in my opinion, generally supported by the evidence. I will review each alleged error in turn below.

86 I agree that the trial judge wrongly associated the termination of Mr. Keays' long-term disability insurance with Honda. The majority of the Court of Appeal properly rejected this finding, as there was no evidence that Honda was involved in the cancellation or in Mr. Keays' failed appeal. The majority of the Court of Appeal also identified the following findings as errors:

1. The appellant's misconduct was "planned and deliberate and formed a protracted corporate conspiracy". The majority found that this was not supported by the evidence.
2. The appellant conspired to interfere with the respondent's relationship with his own physician. The majority found that this contradicted the trial judge's finding that the appellant intended to dismiss the respondent. If it intended to dismiss him, there was no need to introduce Dr. Brennan into the relationship between Mr. Keays and his own physician.
3. The appellant benefited from its misconduct because it rid itself of a "problem associate". The majority could find no evidence to support this conclusion.
4. The appellant's in-house counsel breached the Rules of Professional Conduct of the Law Society of Upper Canada. The majority

> concluded that at most the behaviour was technical misconduct and that it provided no basis for increasing the punitive damages.
>
> ((2006), 82 O.R. (3d) 161 (Ont. C.A.), at paras. 91, 93, 96 at 100-101)

87 In the case of the first finding, it may be that the trial judge exaggerated the extent of Honda's misconduct. However, the evidence supports the trial judge's view that Honda was unfairly skeptical of Mr. Keays' condition and was seeking to justify its skepticism. It should be kept in mind that Honda's intention in seeking to justify its skepticism was clearly: (1) to preclude Mr. Keays from using his condition to justify absences from work and thereby avoiding disciplinary action; and/or (2) to justify the termination of Mr. Keays for any continued absences. In either case, Honda's conduct was to Mr. Keays' detriment.

88 The second finding, that of interference with the respondent's relationship with his doctor, was also reasonable. As I will explain below with respect to Dr. Brennan's "hardball"approach, the gist of this approach was that Dr. Brennan would be brought in to "second-guess"the opinion of an employee's treating physician. Further, there was a clear conflict between Dr. Brennan's objective-to maximize employee productivity-and the objective of an employee's treating physician-to maximize the individual's well-being. Such a conflict may not always play out. In this case, however, a high potential for conflict arose out of the controversial nature of chronic fatigue syndrome ("CFS") and the difficulty of making a diagnosis.

89 In my view, it was fair for the trial judge to characterize Honda's conduct as interference with Mr. Keays' relationship with his treating physician. Honda did not accept the diagnosis and the assessments of Mr. Keays' treating physician. Yet, it gave no basis for its skepticism. The characterization of the notes of Mr. Keays' doctor as "cryptic"and as merely "parroting"his complaints is unfair because of the self-reporting nature of his condition. As the trial judge pointed out, if Honda was skeptical, the first logical step "was to determine if there had been, at any time, any form of legitimate diagnosis for the claim of CFS"(para. 18).

90 Further, this finding does not contradict the trial judge's conclusion that Honda had intended to terminate Mr. Keays. I do not read the trial judge's reasons as suggesting that Honda intended to terminate Mr. Keays from the outset. Rather, the trial judge refers to Honda's intent to "deprive him of the accommodation he had already earned"(para. 60). That was the primary objective. According to the trial judge, Honda went about this by means of a course of conduct whose purpose was to discourage absences (through intimidation and through the requirement that he provide a doctor's note before returning), and which ultimately resulted in termination when Mr.

Keays refused to go along. The implication of the facts as found by the trial judge is that Honda wanted to introduce Dr. Brennan into the process in order to legitimize its conduct. Either Mr. Keays would meet with Dr. Brennan, who would justify Honda's skepticism and avert any further absences, or he would be fired for insubordination (or for continued illegitimate absences) and any need to accommodate him would disappear.

91 I will now turn to the third finding. If it is accepted that Honda intended to deprive Mr. Keays of any accommodation, then Honda clearly succeeded in this objective by terminating him. It is logical to assume that if Honda intended to deprive him of accommodation, it would in some way benefit from doing so. The facts include concerns about workplace morale and Mr. Keays' ability to perform the duties of his job in accordance with the requirements of Honda's "lean"operation policy. To the extent that Mr. Keays impeded efficiency goals, Honda clearly benefited from his termination.

92 As regards the fourth finding, I agree after reviewing the record that the trial judge mischaracterized the situation, at least according to the other two Honda employees who testified (Susan Selby and Betty Magill). They stated that they had met with Mr. Keays to discuss the proposed meeting with Dr. Brennan. After Mr. Keays left the room, Ms. Selby and Ms. Magill were paged by Honda's in-house counsel, who wanted to meet with them about an unrelated matter. Counsel came to the room they were in, and Mr. Keays re-entered the room after counsel had arrived. Some discussion about Mr. Keays' situation ensued, although it appears to have been minimal.

93 In summary, it is my view that the Court of Appeal correctly identified three errors made by the trial judge: (1) his association of Honda with the cancellation of Mr. Keays' long-term disability insurance; (2) his conclusion, based on the date the insurance was terminated, that Honda's course of conduct had lasted five years; and (3) his characterization of the incident involving Honda's in-house counsel as a breach of the Rules of Professional Conduct. However, I disagree with the majority's conclusions in respect of the other alleged errors. These "errors"relate to some extent to the error identified by Justice Bastarache regarding the March 28 letter, which I will now discuss.

A. The March 28 Letter

94 At paras. 37-42 of his reasons, Justice Bastarache explains his conclusion that the trial judge erred in finding that Honda had deliberately misrepresented the positions of Dr. Affoo and Dr. Brennan in its March 28 letter for the purpose of intimidation. He states, at para. 40, that there was "nothing misleading"about the letter. He concludes, at para. 42, that the "letter simply conveyed to Keays that Honda wanted him to meet with Dr. Bren-

nan because their experts had advised them that his condition did not preclude him from working."

95 However, there was evidence on which the trial judge could conclude that the letter was misleading. The letter contained the following statement: "Both doctors advised us that they could find no diagnosis indicating that you are disabled from working."The following comment was also made: "we advised you that we would no longer accept that you have a disability requiring you to be absent". Yet, as the trial judge pointed out, Dr. Brennan testified that "he never told Honda that Mr. Keays did not have a disability, only that he was unable to "verify' one"(para. 43). The trial judge also mentioned the testimony of Dr. Affoo, who agreed with the plaintiff's suggestion that absences of four per month was in the "ball-park' for an individual who suffered [from] CFS"(para. 43). Moreover, it should be noted that although Dr. Affoo testified, on the basis of his experience with other CFS patients, that four CFS-related absences a month would not be unreasonable, he also said that he could not recall precisely what he told Ms. Selby regarding the rate of absence that could be expected from Mr. Keays. Dr. Affoo merely recalled confirming that "he may be off due to his condition"(A.R., at p. 572).

96 The trial judge concluded that "the clear implication of this communication was that his condition was "bogus' and that he was able to attend work without absences"(para. 43). While it is arguable whether the letter implied that Mr. Keays' condition was bogus, it clearly did imply that his condition did not require him to miss work. I am unable to find any evidence that either doctor advised Honda that he believed Mr. Keays' condition was bogus or that Mr. Keays was able to attend work without any CFS-related absences. To the contrary, Dr. Affoo testified that he had informed Honda that some absences were to be expected. It was therefore open to the trial judge to conclude that the letter was a "misrepresentation of the medical information available to Honda at the time"(para. 43).

B. Allegations of a "Set-up"and a "Hardball"Approach

97 At paras. 43-46, Justice Bastarache rejects the trial judge's finding that Mr. Keays was being "set up"by Honda when it insisted that he meet with Dr. Brennan, as well as his finding that Dr. Brennan took a "hardball"approach to workplace absences. My colleague's bases for rejecting these findings are; (1) that Dr. Brennan was merely relying on the criteria for diagnosing CFS developed by the "Centre for Disease Control ("CDC"); and (2) that Honda cannot be faulted for taking its expert's advice unless a conspiracy existed (and none did). Justice Bastarache concludes that Honda's request that Mr. Keays meet with Dr. Brennan was "perfectly normal in the circumstances"(para. 46). After reviewing the record, in my opin-

ion, the trial judge could reasonably conclude that Dr. Brennan took a "hardball"approach and that Mr. Keays was, at least to a certain extent, being "set up"for failure by Honda's request that he meet with Dr. Brennan.

98 First, I must point out that Justice Bastarache erroneously associates the trial judge's reference to Dr. Brennan's "hardball"attitude with Dr. Brennan's approach to CFS. In refuting the trial judge's view that Dr. Brennan took a "hardball"approach, my colleague reviews Dr. Brennan's opinion on CFS in order to demonstrate that Dr. Brennan was "simply espousing the prevalent approach adopted by the CDC"(para. 45). However, what the trial judge actually stated was that "the record establishes beyond any debate that Dr. Brennan is of the "hardball' approach *to workplace absences associated with illnesses or injuries*"(para. 45 (emphasis added)). Dr. Brennan's opinion concerning CFS is a separate issue. Although Justice Bastarache makes reference to Dr. Brennan's "'hardball' approach to workplace absences"(at paras. 44 and 45), his only discussion of that approach relates to Dr. Brennan's views on CFS.

99 Several excerpts from Dr. Brennan's testimony are indicative of a "hardball"approach toward absences, and toward accommodating disabilities generally. In describing his approach to accommodation, Dr. Brennan stated that "the gold standard for accommodating somebody, in fact, *is to not to have to accommodate them*, meaning that their impairment is not of a nature that would stop them from doing their regular work"(A.R., at p. 618 (emphasis added)). He then went on to describe a process whereby disabled workers are "matched"with duties they can perform despite their impairments. Later in his testimony, Dr. Brennan acknowledged that some people have issues with an "accommodation"that involves being moved to another job they view as less "prestigious"(A.R., at p. 662). He added that this does not affect his recommendation as to the appropriate "accommodation", stating that "... my opinion is based on [a] medical approach or a functional approach. Prestige isn't a medical issue."

100 These excerpts are troubling. The implication is that Dr. Brennan's objective is to recommend the "accommodation"that is best for Honda, not the one that is best for the employee. Although he suggests that he is only giving a "medical"opinion, his opinion is focussed on maximizing an employee's productivity for Honda in light of the employee's condition. His goal is clearly not to find ways for Honda to make it easier for the disabled employee to do his or her current job. Certainly, disabilities may make it impossible for individuals to continue in their current positions. But if accommodation is truly a cooperative and collaborative process, it requires give and take on both sides. Dr. Brennan's approach suggests that rather than assisting disabled employees to continue in their current roles, employers can simply place disabled employees in other roles that do not require

any true accommodation on the employers' part. This approach makes the disability the employee's problem, not a problem shared with the employer. This is of concern from an equality perspective because it limits the employment options available to disabled persons.

101 Generally, Dr. Brennan appeared to be of the view that only he can truly ascertain whether an employee has an impairment. He showed skepticism toward the opinions of other doctors and indicated that he would insist on meeting with an employee no matter what was in the employee's medical records, because he needed to assess the person himself in order to assess the employee's "impairment"and determine the appropriate "accommodation". As a doctor, he was able to give a "medical"opinion both about what an individual was capable of doing and about what would be "best"for the individual from a medical perspective. This could easily lead to a situation in which Dr. Brennan's opinion conflicts with the opinion of the employee's treating physician. His objective is not to provide medical care for the individual employee but, as I mentioned above, to maximize productivity. In my view, the above passages provide ample support for the trial judge's view that Dr. Brennan took a "hardball"approach to absences, and to accommodation generally.

102 It was argued that regardless of Dr. Brennan's approach, Honda cannot be faulted for taking its expert's advice unless a conspiracy existed. The "advice"referred to is purportedly that Dr. Brennan needed to meet with Mr. Keays face to face in order to accept the diagnosis of CFS. However, the trial judge expressly rejected the argument that it was necessary for Dr. Brennan to meet with Mr. Keays. This was a critical finding in the trial judge's analysis of the wrongful dismissal claim. The trial judge found that, given the numerous references to CFS in Mr. Keays' medical file as well as his lengthy period of CFS-related disability, there was no need for Mr. Keays to meet with Dr. Brennan "to resolve [his] attendance defaults"(para. 18).

103 Mr. Keays was concerned about meeting with Dr. Brennan because of his previous experience with his insurer. The insurer had required him to meet with its doctor for an assessment, after which his long-term disability insurance was terminated even though his own physician was still of the view that he was not able to return to work. Mr. Keays feared that a similar situation would occur in which Dr. Brennan would not accept that he had to miss work due to his CFS, and that this would have negative implications for his continued employment at Honda. It appears that the trial judge referred to Dr. Brennan's "hardball"approach in order to validate Mr. Keays' concern that Dr. Brennan would not accept his need for CFS-related absences. There was some evidence that Honda knew (and approved) of Dr. Brennan's approach. Ms. Selby testified that Dr. Brennan "had a very good

reputation, from what I was told, in terms of dealing with workplace absences and a fresh approach, fresh start"(A.R., at p. 449).

104 The trial judge's main point appears to be that Honda was relying on Dr. Brennan and his approach to "deal with"Mr. Keays and his absences. In other words, Honda was relying on Dr. Brennan to legitimize its view that the absences were not warranted. In light of the evidence, this conclusion was not unreasonable.

105 In regard to the issue of whether Mr. Keays was being "set up", Dr. Brennan testified that he was asked by Susan Selby to review Mr. Keays' file and "provide an opinion as to whether there was a proven impairment and whether he should be attending work"(A.R., at p. 624). This suggests that before involving Dr. Brennan in the case, Honda already harboured suspicions about the legitimacy of Mr. Keays' condition. Further, Honda cancelled its accommodation of Mr. Keays' condition at the same time as it urged Mr. Keays to meet with Dr. Brennan (the trial judge referred specifically to this fact at para. 29). It was therefore not unreasonable for the trial judge to conclude that the purpose of the meeting was to confirm Honda's view that the absences were not justified. I will discuss this further below with respect to reprisal.

106 Finally, although it was suggested that Dr. Brennan was consulted in order to confirm the diagnosis of Mr. Keays' condition, the testimony of Ms. Magill and Ms. Selby is unclear in this regard. At several points, they suggested that Dr. Brennan was consulted in order to obtain his opinion on whether Mr. Keays was able to work on a more regular basis (i.e. without CFS-related absences), not on whether Mr. Keays had a *bona fide* medical condition. Ms. Magill testified that the purposes of having Mr. Keays meet with Dr. Brennan were threefold: first, simply to review Mr. Keays' medical file with him in person and to discuss his condition, his symptoms and their impact on his work; second, to develop a treatment plan that was to be coordinated with Mr. Keays' own physician; and third, to review and assess any restrictions on Mr. Keays' ability to work and to consider alternative roles for him at Honda (A.R., at pp. 402-3). Ms. Magill stated that Dr. Brennan had not reached a conclusion on Mr. Keays' condition, but had simply reached one about his ability to work (A.R., at p. 406).

107 Ms. Selby denied that one of the purposes of the meeting was to develop a treatment plan for Mr. Keays that Dr. Brennan was to coordinate with Mr. Keays' physician (A.R., at p. 506). However, she did testify that one of the purposes of the proposed meeting, in addition to sharing information, was to see whether "there was something that Dr. Brennan could do to help support [Mr. Keays] in the future"(A.R., at p. 457). Ms. Selby also testified that Mr. Keays "didn't have restrictions to assess"and therefore de-

nied that one of the purposes of the meeting was to assess any restrictions in order to consider an alternative role for Mr. Keays at Honda (A.R., at p. 507).

108 Ms. Selby testified that she had originally spoken to Dr. Brennan regarding Mr. Keays in order to get his opinion on whether it was "fair to expect Kevin to provide regular attendance"(A.R., at p. 449). However, Dr. Brennan testified that Ms. Selby had asked him to review Mr. Keays' record in order to "provide an opinion as to whether there was a proven impairment and whether he should be attending work"(A.R., at p. 624). Dr. Brennan added that he had proposed to Ms. Selby that he meet with Mr. Keays in order to go over his medical history (A.R., at pp. 667-68). Both Ms. Magill and Ms. Selby stated that Mr. Keays was told that the purpose of the meeting was to review his file and share information (A.R., pp. 341 and 503).

109 I raise the purpose of the meeting as a concern in relation to the set-up issue, because the record shows an apparent lack of candour in what Mr. Keays was told about the purpose of the meeting. The testimony of Ms. Magill, Ms. Selby and Dr. Brennan is somewhat conflicting, so the precise purpose of the meeting remains unclear. Dr. Brennan's testimony suggests that the meeting was held in response to Ms. Selby's request to verify whether there was a "proven impairment"and whether Mr. Keays' absences were justified. Yet, this does not seem to be what Mr. Keays was told. Although Ms. Magill mentioned some other purposes, none of these were communicated to Mr. Keays either. If there was a lack of candour, this might support the trial judge's view that Mr. Keays was being "set up."

C. Reprisal

110 At para. 47, Justice Bastarache rejects the trial judge's finding that Honda had cancelled Mr. Keays' accommodation as a reprisal for his having retained legal counsel. Justice Bastarache suggests that "Honda was simply seeking to confirm Keays' disability". He also notes that Mr. Keays' superiors had met to address the deficiencies in his doctors' notes "well before Keays' lawyer sent his letter."

111 In my view, the timing of the cancellation and of the insistence that Mr. Keays meet with Dr. Brennan is suspect. The letter from Mr. Keays' counsel was dated March 16. In it, counsel requested that Mr. Keays be exempted from providing a doctor's note for each absence before returning to work. This was a request for a more appropriate accommodation of Mr. Keays' disability. Honda's response to Mr. Keays' request that he be exempted from providing doctors' notes was to preclude him from claiming *any* disability-related absences. It was at a meeting on March 21 that Honda

told Mr. Keays that it would no longer accept that he had a disability requiring him to be absent and that he would have to meet with Dr. Brennan in order to "manage"his condition.

112 I disagree that it was a palpable and overriding error for the trial judge to conclude that the cancellation was, at least in part, a reprisal for Mr. Keays' attempt to assert his right to proper accommodation under the Ontario *Human Rights Code*, R.S.O. 1990, c. H.19. Instead of considering Mr. Keays' position, Honda denied any need for his continued absences. I do not see how this could be seen as an attempt by Honda "to confirm Keays' disability". Honda stated expressly in the March 28 letter that it no longer accepted that he had a disability requiring absences. Further, even if Honda was suspicious of Mr. Keays' condition, the fact that such concerns had been raised prior to the March 21 meeting does not, in my view, explain or justify the unilateral cancellation, on such short notice, of the minimal accommodation that had been provided.

D. Keays' Worsened Condition

113 Justice Bastarache also rejects the trial judge's consideration of Mr. Keays' worsened condition because he rejects the conclusion that Honda acted in bad faith. As I explained above, I question the reasoning that leads him to reject the trial judge's findings of fact. In my view, the impugned findings of fact were supported by the evidence. Given my view that Honda did act in bad faith, Mr. Keays' worsened condition following his termination is relevant to the assessment of *Wallace* damages.

II. Reconsidering the Issue of Wallace Damages

114 In his reasons, Justice Bastarache clarifies the proper approach to assessing *Wallace* damages in a wrongful dismissal action. As I mentioned above, his review is a necessary and welcome restatement of the law on damages for wrongful dismissal. Justice Bastarache explains that *Wallace* damages will be available where "the manner of dismissal caused mental distress that was in the contemplation of the parties"(para. 59). But because this Court held in *Wallace* that employers have an obligation of good faith and fair dealing when dismissing employees "and created the expectation that, in the course of dismissal, employers would be "candid, reasonable, honest and forthright with their employees'"(para. 58), an employer's failure to properly discharge that obligation makes it foreseeable that a dismissal might cause mental distress. A failure to show good faith may therefore justify an award of compensatory damages. The instant case is a case in point.

115 There is ample evidence to support the trial judge's conclusion that Honda acted in bad faith. Several aspects of Honda's conduct are particularly persuasive in this regard. Most notable is the misleading nature of the March 28 letter, which indicated that, according to Dr. Affoo and Dr. Brennan, Mr. Keays did not have a disability requiring him to be absent from work. The clear implication was that Mr. Keays' recent absences were unrelated to his disability or, at the very least, that they were medically unnecessary. A further implication, one that was expressly spelled out later in the letter, was that any CFS-related absences from work by Mr. Keays in excess of the normal allowances would result in disciplinary action. In other words, he was no longer eligible to participate in the disability program. The justification given for this decision was the opinion of Honda's medical experts, yet neither doctor had recommended that Mr. Keays be removed from the disability program, nor had they claimed that any CFS-related absences were unjustified.

116 A further concern is the apparent lack of candour on Honda's part in regard to the purpose of the proposed meeting between Mr. Keays and Dr. Brennan. Neither Ms. Magill nor Ms. Selby provided any justification for their refusal to explain the purpose of the meeting to Mr. Keays other than to say that the purpose had already been explained to him in person. Yet, as I mentioned above, there was conflicting testimony about the purpose of this meeting. Given the confusion among Honda's own employees, it is understandable that Mr. Keays was still unclear about the purpose and that he sought further clarification. In addition, the failure to provide clarification in writing is somewhat suspicious. Further, given that Mr. Keays was willing to meet with Dr. Brennan if clarification was provided and that Mr. Keays' refusal to meet with Dr. Brennan without such clarification resulted in his dismissal, the refusal to provide it seems unduly harsh.

117 The nature of the events leading up to Mr. Keays' termination makes it reasonable to conclude that the conduct of Honda surrounding his termination, and not the fact of termination alone, led to his worsened state. Accordingly, an award of damages can be justified in this case on the basis of Honda's conduct and of the harm Mr. Keays suffered as a result. Although, as Justice Bastarache explains, *Wallace* damages are intended to be compensatory, given the lack of evidence on the precise loss Mr. Keays suffered as a result of Honda's conduct, I would uphold the compensation the trial judge granted over and above the 15-month notice period. The quantum of the damages appears reasonable and would give Mr. Keays adequate compensation.

III. Bhadauria and Tort Law

118 I agree that it is not necessary to reconsider *Bhadauria* in the present appeal. But in my opinion Laskin C.J. went further than was strictly necessary in *Bhadauria*. The main thrust of the decision was that Ms. Bhadauria did not have a legally protected interest at common law that had been harmed by the defendant's allegedly discriminatory conduct (pp. 191-92). However, rather than stop there, Laskin C.J. went on to hold that *The Ontario Human Rights Code* "foreclose[s] any civil action based directly upon a breach thereof [and] also excludes any common law action based on an invocation of the public policy expressed in the Code"(p. 195). These conclusions imply (and have been interpreted to mean) that any allegations resembling the type of conduct that is prohibited by the Code cannot be litigated at common law. The Code covers a broad range of conduct in promoting the goal of equality. Yet the conduct at issue in *Bhadauria* was limited to the facts of that case. It would have been sufficient to simply conclude that the interest advanced by Ms. Bhadauria was not protected at common law. It was not necessary for this Court to preclude all common law actions based on all forms of discriminatory conduct.

119 The development of tort law ought not to be frozen forever on the basis of this *obiter dictum*. The legal landscape has changed. The strong prohibitions of human rights codes and of the *Charter* have informed many aspects of the development of the common law.

120 On the facts of this appeal, discrimination was a troubling aspect of the decision to terminate Mr. Keays. The presence of this discrimination aspect taints the process and has an impact on the issue of whether the employment relationship was terminated in good faith. Justice Bastarache notes that Mr. Keays suffered no detriment in being treated differently from employees with "mainstream"illnesses, because the differential treatment was intended to accommodate him and he is thus implicitly compared with that category of employees (para. 67). However, Justice Bastarache does not inquire into whether this method of accommodation was appropriate and whether it addressed the difference of the employee, namely his particular disability.

121 The National ME/FM Action Network, an intervener in this appeal, explained why the accommodation provided by Honda was not appropriate:

> ME/CFS is as yet poorly understood. Those who suffer from it may have highly variable symptoms. There is no laboratory test that can be used to confirm a diagnosis. In this context, attributing undue significance to matters such as doctors' notes which are based upon the patient's own reporting of symptoms, the treating doctor's lack of precision in forecasting absences, and the inability of doctors employed or retained by an employer to "verify"a diagnosis of CFS or to accept CFS as justifying

> absences, will likely be inimical to the accommodation required under human rights codes.
>
> (Factum, at para. 14)

Although I agree with Justice Bastarache that employers are justified in monitoring the absences of employees, particularly those who are regularly absent from work (at para. 71), he did not consider whether Honda's method of monitoring absences was appropriate (i.e. non-discriminatory). Honda's assertion that its disability program and its treatment of Mr. Keays under that program were non-discriminatory cannot simply be taken at face value.

122 Mr. Keays had requested to be exempted from the requirement to provide a doctor's note for each CFS-related absence. Honda refused to consider this request, despite the assertion by Mr. Keays' attorney that Mr. Keays was concerned that the note requirement created a barrier to his speedy return to work. Regardless of whether or not the notes created a barrier, it is clear that Honda was skeptical of Mr. Keays' condition because of the "cryptic"nature of his doctors' notes and because his absences had become more frequent than originally predicted. Yet if variable self-reporting conditions are characteristic of Mr. Keays' disability, it is arguable that Honda acted in a discriminatory manner in subjecting him to the kind of scrutiny he underwent and, in fact, denying him accommodation for his disability.

123 While monitoring employee absences certainly remains a valid objective, this can be done in a variety of ways. Requiring a doctor's note for each absence is only one alternative. Others include seeking semi-regular updates from an employee's physician regarding the nature of the condition and the course of treatment, checking in with the employee directly, or requiring doctors' notes only when the number of absences exceeds the expected number within a given time frame. Not all monitoring methods may be considered non-discriminatory in every context. As stated by the Ontario Network of Injured Workers' Groups, another intervener in this appeal, "[individualized accommodation is at the heart of the duty to accommodate and is instrumental in creating a discrimination free workplace"(Factum, at para. 17). In my view, the employer must, in monitoring absences, remain mindful of all the circumstances, which include the nature of the employee's condition. It should not be assumed that all monitoring methods are acceptable and non-discriminatory.

124 For these reasons, I would allow the appeal in part by setting aside the award of punitive damages and the costs premium. The cross-appeal should be dismissed. Given the outcome and the circumstances of the case, I would award costs to the respondent.

Appeal allowed in part.
Pourvoi accueilli en partie.

Parisien v. Ottawa-Carleton Regional Transit Commission

2003 CarswellNat 3230, 2003 CHRT 10 (C.H.R.T.)

Hadjis Member:

1 The Complainant worked as a bus operator for the Respondent. Throughout the course of his employment, he was absent from work for a significant number of days, mainly on account of illness. Eighteen years after he was hired, the Respondent dismissed the Complainant due to his "chronic absenteeism". As a result, the Complainant filed the present complaint in which he alleges that the Respondent discriminated against him by refusing to accommodate him and by refusing to continue to employ him because of his disability, contrary to s. 7 of the *Canadian Human Rights Act* ("*Act*"). The disability consists principally of post-traumatic stress disorder (also known as "*PTSD*") and ailments related thereto.

2 The Complainant's employer at the time of his termination in 1996 was the "Ottawa-Carleton Regional Transit Commission", which operated Ottawa's public transit system (otherwise known as "*OC Transpo*"). His complaint was filed several months later and the same organization was named as the Respondent. In 2001, pursuant to s. 9 of the *City of Ottawa Act, 1999*, OC Transpo's operations, including all its assets and liabilities, were transferred to the amalgamated City of Ottawa.[47] Ms. Lois Emburg, a manager with the City of Ottawa, stated during her testimony that the City of Ottawa is accepting any liability to be attributed to the Respondent in the present case. In light of her representations, the Ottawa-Carleton Regional Transit Commission shall continue to be treated as the Respondent in this case. It should be noted, though, that according to the abovementioned legislative provision, the Respondent was dissolved on January 1, 2001.

I. Facts

3 Most of the facts are not in dispute. All of the parties agree that during his employment with the Respondent (a total of about 18 years and 2 months), the Complainant was absent for about 1664 full days and 33 partial days. His absences were mostly related to illness. The Respondent does not call into question the genuineness of these illnesses.

---

[47] S.O. 1999, c. 14.

A. The Complainant's Employment History with the Respondent

4 The Complainant was hired by the Respondent as a bus operator in November 1977. His employment was subject to an initial probationary period. The Respondent's records demonstrate that from the outset, the Respondent was concerned with the Complainant's level of absenteeism, so much so that the probationary period was extended by three months in January of 1979. In the month of September 1979, he was even suspended for several days because of his absenteeism, in accordance with the Respondent's policy in place at that time. No evidence was led as to the nature of the illnesses or other causes that resulted in the Complainant's absences during this early period. The Complainant acknowledges that he was made aware early on that excessive absenteeism within the OC Transpo workforce was an ongoing cause of concern for the employer.

5 In his testimony, the Complainant brought up some of the events in his life that he feels may have contributed to the onset years later of post-traumatic stress disorder. In 1979, his relationship with a woman to whom he was engaged to be married suddenly ended. This break-up was "devastating" for him but it did not lead to his being absent from work. In October of 1980, the Complainant's mother died of cancer. He also describes this loss as devastating, noting that he had maintained a very close relationship with her. He took three days off work on bereavement leave, as permitted under the collective agreement.

6 Only a couple of months later, in December 1980, the Complainant was the victim of a violent assault while he was driving his bus. A passenger wearing army fatigues and a balaclava over his head entered the bus and without any warning hit the Complainant on the side of his face, knocking him unconscious. The Complainant was treated at the hospital and released the same day. He did not return to his job until one week later.

7 No evidence was led detailing the Complainant's attendance during the early 1980's other than an acknowledgement by him and the Commission that he worked "on and off". However, his attendance sheets for the years 1984 and following were produced. In 1984, the Complainant was absent for the entire period from March to early September. The attendance sheet indicates that he was in receipt of worker's compensation benefits during this period but no explanation was provided at the hearing as to the nature or cause of his illness or disability. In 1985, the Complaint was absent due to illness for thirteen full days and four partial days. In 1986, he was absent for thirty full days and one partial day.

8 In 1987, the Complainant's father suddenly died. The Complainant testified that this was also a significant and disturbing loss for him. He took the permitted bereavement leave of three days. During 1987, he was absent 42

full days and another 4 partial days, due to illness. The Complainant was on sick leave for 28 full days and seven partial days in 1988.

9 On March 7, 1989, the Complainant was interviewed by management regarding his level of absenteeism. As luck would have it, only two weeks later, another unsettling incident occurred while he was at work. A male passenger entered his bus and began yelling at him. The passenger eventually got off the bus, but just two days later, he confronted the Complainant again. The Complainant was standing outside his bus, at the starting point of his bus route, when the individual approached him. The man had his hand in his pocket and began telling the Complainant that he was going to kill him. Two other bus operators happened to witness the incident and one called over a supervisor. The supervisor reacted by assisting the individual onto another bus, but he did not make a report nor call the police. The Complainant claims that he was genuinely scared of the passenger and that he felt "very unprotected and unsafe" as a result of the manner in which his employer had dealt with the threat.

10 Although he did not miss any work at the time of these incidents, in the weeks and months that followed, the number of absences due to illness increased significantly. On July 18, 1989, the employer interviewed him regarding his absenteeism. The Complainant recalls that following the March incidents, he began getting "pains in [his] stomach" and was feeling "quite sick". He went off work from December 1989 until February 1990, his medical certificates indicating that he was suffering primarily from gastrointestinal problems. He returned to his job in early March 1990 but ceased working on March 21, 1990. This leave of absence ended up lasting for 199 working days. During this period, he was compensated by the Workers' Compensation Board, as his disability was deemed to be related to the trauma associated with the death threat made against him. The medical certificates issued by the Complainant's family physician during this period refer to his "anxiety state", "job tension" and "adjustment reaction".

11 While the Complainant was on leave in 1990, OC Transpo's Occupational Health Unit ("*Health Unit*") communicated regularly with him to follow up on his status and his expected date of return to work. According to the evidence adduced by the Respondent, the Health Unit had a mandate that included gathering information regarding the condition of employees on sick leave and advising the divisions where they worked (their "*employing divisions*") when and if they were ready to return to work. The Health Unit would also assess whether a non-occupational disability claim was well founded, based on the medical information available. It was composed of several nurses who were employed full time as well as one medical doctor who was not an employee of the Respondent but who would be asked occasionally to provide an opinion. The Health Unit's activities were inte-

gral to the program that the Respondent had established to manage the attendance of its employees ("*Attendance Management Program*"). One of the main reasons for the existence of this separate unit was to protect the confidentiality of the employees' medical information. As such, the Health Unit never disclosed to management the details of an employee's condition. It would only provide to employing divisions general conclusions and opinions as to an employee's preparedness to return to work.

12 On December 14, 1990, based on the medical information collected from the Complainant and his physician, the Health Unit determined that commencing January 2, 1991, he would be able to resume regular job duties, provided that he be initially assigned to work four hours per day instead of eight. This type of transitional activity was referred to as a process of "work hardening". The Complainant performed these modified duties until February 25, 1991, when he went on sick leave, suffering from back pain and abdominal pain, according to the medical certificates submitted to the Respondent at the time.

13 By April 1991, the Complainant's family physician had come to the realization that the Complainant was "preoccupied with being assaulted" on his job, "to the point of almost paranoid feelings". The family physician apparently concluded that the Complainant was suffering from post-traumatic stress disorder. The physician therefore informed the Respondent that the Complainant could not yet return to work. He referred the Complainant to the Royal Ottawa Hospital for a psychiatric assessment. Dr. Hamilton Sequeira, M.D., a psychiatrist, examined the Complainant on May 17, 1991, and made a provisional diagnosis of "post-traumatic stress disorder of longstanding with anxiety, depressive, somatic manifestations". In presenting his diagnosis, Dr. Sequiera referred in his report to the 1980 assault and the 1989 threat as well as the sudden deaths of the Complainant's parents. The Complainant's family physician issued an updated medical certificate declaring that the Complainant would be unable to return to work for an indefinite period. The Complainant received workers' compensation benefits while on this extended medical leave.

14 Dr. Sequiera recommended a therapeutic approach for the Complainant that included medications as well as cognitive behavioural therapy to "desensitize him from his trauma related negative constructs and feelings". For this latter purpose, Dr. Sequiera sought the assistance of Dr. David Erickson, PhD, R. Psych., who was at that time doing his internship to become a clinical psychologist, a recognition that he achieved in 1994. Dr. Erickson testified that cognitive behavioural therapy involves two components: the behavioural aspect encompasses the breaking down of a person's fear into small manageable steps. The cognitive aspect is conducted once some success has been achieved with respect to the behavioural element, and con-

sists of the individual attempting to imagine in advance, doing the activities which are at the source of his anxiety.

15 Dr. Erickson began treating the Complainant on November 4, 1991. He determined that the Complainant was a good candidate for cognitive behavioural therapy. Between November 1991 and August 1992, Dr. Erickson met the Complainant weekly. He kept the Health Unit abreast of the Complainant's progress. He states in the expert's report that accompanied his testimony in this case, that by July 1992, after eight months of cognitive behavioural therapy combined with medication, the Complainant's state was "dramatically improved" and "ready for a graduated return to work". As part of this transition to full-time work it was agreed between the Health Unit and Drs. Sequeira and Erickson that the Complainant begin this process by driving what was known as the "DERC shuttle bus". DERC is the acronym for the Disabled Employees Review Committee, made up of OC Transpo employee and management representatives. The DERC was established by the Respondent in order to assist in the reintegration of disabled employees into the workforce. The DERC shuttle bus was in fact a mini bus in which operators were driven to various locations to take over runs from other drivers. The only passengers on this bus were other OC Transpo employees.

16 The Complainant drove this vehicle from mid-July to mid-September 1992, following which he was assigned to modified duties (four hours per day) driving regular OC Transpo passenger buses. According to Dr. Erickson, by mid-October 1992, the Complainant was "symptom-free and back to his normal level functioning". The Health Unit accordingly recommended to the Complainant's employing division that he could return to full time regular job duties beginning October 14, 1992.

17 Between December 7, 1992 and January 14, 1993, the Complainant booked off sick for a total of thirteen full days and two partial days, suffering from blurred vision, dizziness, insomnia and gastroenteritis. Dr. Erickson noted, after speaking with the Complainant on December 14, 1992, that his anxiety problems had returned, in part as a result of driving on some of the routes that he most feared prior to his treatment. Medication was prescribed for him by Dr. Sequeira and regular visits were scheduled with Dr. Erickson.

18 Unfortunately, on January 15, 1993, a bus that the Complainant was driving was hit from the rear by another vehicle, as a result of which he suffered a whiplash injury (cervical neck strain). According to his family physician, the injury was such that he could not return to work until May 1993. Dr. Erickson notes in his expert's report that the Complainant experienced great frustration at being prevented from working as a result of the

accident, and some gastro-intestinal problems and headaches that he suffered over this period were likely related to this distress. However, Dr. Erickson points to the absence at that time of any anxiety, mood problems or sleep disturbance that would indicate residual post-traumatic stress disorder.

19 After being on leave due to the work-related whiplash injury for a total of 92 working days, the Complainant returned to his regular job duties at the beginning of June 1993. In August 1993, he went on sick leave for a total of six days and one partial day. According to the medical certificate that he submitted, he was suffering from "acute anxiety". By October 1993, the Complainant had developed a major sleep disturbance and had to take another leave of absence that was to extend until June 1994.

20 His sleep had been reduced to two to three hours per night. Dr. Sequeira transferred the Complainant to the care of another psychiatrist with a specialty in sleep disorders. His treatment included prescribing medication to help the Complainant sleep and to prevent the occurrence of periodic partial leg movements that were awakening him during his sleep. By May 1994, this psychiatrist deemed the sleep problems to be "now under control" and believed that the Complainant was ready to return to work.

21 On May 27, 1994, the Health Unit sent a memo to the Complainant's employing division stating that his prognosis was now for "regular attendance at work". The memo referred to an unnamed treating physician of the Complainant who had declared that his medical problem had been resolved and that it "should not cause him any future problem". In addition, the Complainant was examined by the external medical practitioner of the Health Unit and the memo notes his observation that the Complainant's attitude was very positive, more so than in earlier assessments conducted by the same doctor in 1992 and 1993.

22 The Complainant therefore returned to his regular job duties on June 2, 1994. Shortly after returning to work, he was confronted by several teenagers while driving his bus, in a manner that he perceived as threatening. He felt scared and vulnerable, as if someone was always out to get him. He found himself unable to sleep again so he took a higher dose of his sleep medication. This resulted in drowsiness that rendered him unable to perform his work properly. On June 5, 1994, the Superintendent of Operational Personnel, Mr. Ron Mooney, having observed the Complainant's reduced faculties, instructed him to cease operating a bus. The superintendent sent a memo several days later to the Health Unit asking that the Complainant be reassessed to determine if he was capable of returning to regular full time employment.

23 By July, 1994, Dr. Sequeira had resumed all of the Complainant's psychiatric care. The Complainant also recommenced receiving treatment from

Dr. Erickson. Within weeks, Dr. Sequeira observed that the Complainant had become so depressed, anxious and sleep-deprived that it became necessary to admit him into the Mood Disorders Unit of the Royal Ottawa Hospital. He was diagnosed with major depression, sleep disorder and generalized anxiety disorder. He was discharged from the hospital on September 20, 1994. The depression and sleep troubles were resolved by June 1995.

24 As these problems diminished, though, the presence of post-traumatic stress disorder symptoms became apparent again. His "avoidance pattern" was consistent with a fear of being assaulted, combined with regular daytime flashbacks. Dr. Erickson implemented another program of cognitive behavioural therapy for the Complainant. According to Dr. Erickson, as part of the therapy, the Complainant exerted great effort as he relived the fear of being assaulted on a daily basis. In Dr. Erickson's opinion, the therapy proved effective and by February 1996, (the month in which the Complainant was dismissed) the post-traumatic stress disorder had been "vanquished".

B. Events in the Months Leading up to the Complainant's Dismissal

25 On October 26, 1995, the Health Unit interviewed the Complainant, in accordance with a policy that required such meetings periodically with employees who were in receipt of long-term disability benefits. It determined, based on the Complainant's comments as well as information obtained from his physicians, that he hoped to return to his regular occupation as a bus operator. According to a memo prepared by the Health Unit after the meeting, the Complainant was advised that his job with the Respondent was only protected for a period of 24 months following the date when he began receiving long term disability benefits. This period was to come to an end on February 2, 1996. If by that time he did not return to his own job or to some other job within OC Transpo, the Respondent would make a decision as to his "continuing status" and would "in all likelihood [...] medically terminate" him.

26 On December 13, 1995, Dr. Sequeira filled out a form for the Ontario Ministry of Transport. The Complainant's "C" Class driver's licence, which permitted him to operate buses, had been downgraded because he was disabled on a long-term basis. The application for regaining the permit required that a physician report on the driver's medical condition. Dr. Sequeira stated on the form that the Complainant was ready to regain his licence as he was "much improved of the symptomatology of fear-anxiety-avoidance-depression that was part of his post-traumatic stress disorder".

27 On January 31, 1996, Dr. Sequeira and Dr. Erickson signed a letter that they had jointly prepared, addressed to the Health Unit of OC Transpo, in which they stated the following:

> Alain is now in the final stages. Within a few weeks, the [cognitive behavioural therapy] regarding the post-traumatic anxiety will be sufficiently advanced to allow a safe return to work. The feared stimuli, i.e. clothing worn by his assailant, will no longer prompt incapacitating anxiety. Rather, Alain will experience only mild tremulousness.
>
> His sleep disturbance is similarly well controlled. While he continues to have anxiety-related nightmares, they are no longer severe enough to disrupt his sleep. He does continue to have difficulty waking in the morning, however: once he has had time to gradually adjust to a structured daily routine, this problem will return to normal limits.
>
> Finally, Alain's depressed mood is no longer an issue. In the past month, he has experienced mild dysphoria an average of 2-3 times per week, where each occasion lasts 1-2 hours. No period of severe or sustained depressed mood has occurred in the past month. Thus, Alain's mood is clearly within normal limits.

Drs. Sequiera and Erickson then went on to describe the Complainant's medications, noting that they would not interfere with his ability to operate an OC Transpo bus. It was also pointed out that the Complainant would continue to see both specialists over the following several months, just to deal with any remaining anxieties and to monitor the medications. The following conclusions were made towards the end of their letter:

> During this time, Alain's health will be best served by beginning with part-time duties, and gradually building up to full-time duties. In the initial period of readjustment, extreme hours are contraindicated because of their potential for sleep disturbance. We would greatly appreciate being consulted in preparing increases in Alain's scope of duties, as experience from his past has shown that it is possible to do too much too soon.
>
> In sum, the prognosis is very good. Alain has worked hard to regain positive and constructive moods, such that he is now well within normal limits. The PTSD-related anxiety is much diminished, and will not interfere with his performance as an operator.
>
> (My emphasis)

28 The Complainant contacted the head nurse of the Health Unit to discuss his coming back to work, several days in advance of the February 2, 1996 deadline that the Respondent had set for his return. She advised him to simply show up at work on that designated day and speak to Mr. Mooney, the Superintendent of Operational Personnel. The Complainant did so, and when he met with Mr. Mooney, he explained that he was ready to work, requesting only that some adjustments be made to ease his transition back, in accordance with the recommendations of his psychiatrist and psychologist. Mr. Mooney informed the Complainant that no such work-hardening adjustments would be made available to him and, according to the Com-

plainant, when he asked if he could be assigned to work at some other job at OC Transpo, he was told "there was nothing". Instead, Mr. Mooney said that the Complainant's file was under investigation and that the Complainant would be informed of the outcome two weeks later. The Complainant's testimony regarding these meetings was not contradicted and neither the head nurse nor Mr. Mooney testified in this case.

29 On February 6, 1996, Mr. Mooney wrote to the Health Unit asking if the Complainant's present condition, for which he had just received treatment, was the same as the condition for which there had been a prognosis of regular attendance back in May 1994. He also asked if the Health Unit was convinced, based on the medical information, that the Complainant should return to work as a bus operator when his licence was reinstated. In the Health Unit's reply, dated February 9, 1996, specific reference was made to the recently obtained opinions of Drs. Sequiera and Erickson to the effect that the Complainant could begin with part-time duties and gradually build up to full time duties. The Health Unit, however, concluded as follows:

> Taking into consideration the medical information on file at present, the fact that Mr. Parisien does not hold a class "C" licence at present, as well as his past record of attendance, the Health Unit is not fully convinced at this time that Mr. Parisien will be able to perform his duties as a bus operator on a regular basis.
>
> If the Transportation Division [the Complainant's employing division] is able and prepared to offer Mr. Parisien alternate employment, we will contact his medical advisors to quantify his restrictions and to obtain a more complete prognosis. Please advise us as to your decision.
>
> (My emphasis)

30 Mr. Mooney met with the Complainant about a week later, on February 15, 1996, and advised him that his employment was terminated. In a follow-up letter addressed to the Complainant on February 19, 1996, Mr. Mooney stated:

> This letter is to confirm our meeting held on February 15, 1996 to clarify your employment status with the Commission.
>
> Based on the information presented at our meeting we find it necessary to terminate your employment with the Commission due to chronic innocent absenteeism effective February 15, 1996.

31 The Complainant claims that he pleaded with Mr. Mooney to allow him to return to work for OC Transpo but he was told that the decision to terminate would stand. He contends that at the time of his termination he was feeling "quite good" and wanted to get back right away to his ordinary duties as a bus operator. He acknowledges that he was not yet "one hundred per-cent" and that he could not have immediately returned to regular full-time bus driving duties. He would, however, have been able to perform modified job duties during a period of transition, as Drs. Sequiera and Erickson had recommended.

C. Events Subsequent to the Complainant's Termination

32 The Complainant filed a grievance against his dismissal several days later. The grievance passed through the required stages in the grievance process and was ultimately ruled upon through an expedited arbitration process on December 4, 1998. The labour arbitrator decided that there was just cause for the Complainant's termination and dismissed the grievance. He found that the Respondent "reasonably concluded, on the evidence before it" that the Complainant "would not be able to perform his duties as a bus operator on a regular basis".

33 In a preliminary motion presented to the Tribunal prior to the hearing on the merits of the present case, the Respondent submitted that the subject matter of the Complainant's human rights complaint fell within the exclusive jurisdiction of the labour arbitrator and that the doctrines of issue estoppel and cause of action estoppel deprived the Tribunal of jurisdiction to hear the matter. The motion was dismissed by Tribunal Chairperson Anne L. Mactavish on July 15, 2002.[48] In her ruling, the Chairperson found that the issue before the arbitrator was whether the Complainant's termination was unjust and not whether he had been a victim of a discriminatory practice within the meaning of the *Act*.

D. The Evidence of the Experts

34 The Commission called Dr. Erickson and Dr. Sequeira to testify as experts at the hearing. They were qualified as persons who have acquired special or peculiar knowledge through study, education and experience with the Complainant, such that they could assist the Tribunal with respect to their interactions with him and their respective fields generally (psychology for Dr. Erickson and psychiatry for Dr. Sequeira).

35 In Dr. Erickson's opinion, between 1989 and 1996 inclusively, the Complainant experienced two distinct episodes of post-traumatic stress disorder, one at the beginning of this period (from the threat to his life in 1989 until his return to work in September, 1992) and another towards the end (from June 1994 until February 1996). Between these "bookends", the Complainant also passed through an episode of "severe sleep, mood and generalized anxiety", from about October 1993 until June 1995, overlapping onto the final PTSD bookend. Dr. Erickson believes that this episode was "likely related — in an indirect way" to the Complainant's initial bout with PTSD.

---

[48] *Parisien v. Ottawa-Carleton*, [2002] C.H.R.D. No. 23 (Can. Human Rights Trib.).

36 Dr. Erickson finds that the Complainant exhibited all of the classic elements of post-traumatic stress disorder, including:

- experiencing a traumatic event,
- intrusive daytime reliving of that event, as well as recurring nightmares,
- avoiding certain behaviours that he used to enjoy in the past, and
- being in a state of persistent hyper-arousal.

37 For his part, Dr. Sequeira agrees that the initial diagnosis of PTSD was "well-substantiated" and that the PTSD had fully developed by 1989. In his opinion, the second episode, in 1994-95, was a re-emergence of the PTSD and not so much a bookend. With respect to some of the other illnesses that caused the Complainant to be absent from work, Dr. Sequeira points out that it is not uncommon for persons suffering from PTSD to also experience generalized anxiety disorder, phobia, major depression and sleep disorder. According to Dr. Sequeira, a connection may even exist between PTSD and some of the other ailments from which the Complainant suffered, including diarrhea and muscle spasms, although it is also possible that these symptoms were unrelated.

II. Legal Framework and Analysis

A. The Law

38 Section 7 of the *Act* declares that it is a discriminatory practice to refuse to continue to employ an individual, or to treat an employee in an adverse differential manner, on the basis of a prohibited ground of discrimination. Disability is included amongst the list of prohibited grounds of discrimination set out in s. 3 of the *Act*. According to s. 25, "disability", for the purposes of the *Act*, means "any previous or existing mental or physical disability and includes disfigurement and previous or existing dependence on alcohol or a drug".

39 Section 15 (a), as it was designated prior to the 1998 amendments to the *Act*,[49] provides that it is not a discriminatory practice if the differential treatment exercised by the employer is based on a *bona fide* occupational requirement ("*BFOR*"). In 1999, the Supreme Court of Canada, in what are

[49]This provision is now designated as S. 15 (1)(a). See An Act to amend the Canada Evidence Act and the Criminal Code in respect of persons with disabilities, to amend the Canadian Human Rights Act in respect of persons with disabilities and other matters and to make consequential amendments to other Acts, S.C. 1998, c.9, s. 10.

generally referred to as the *Meiorin*[50] and *Grismer*[51] cases, had the occasion to restate the approach to be followed whenever such a defence is invoked. The Court reaffirmed that a complainant bears the initial burden of establishing that the standard or policy adopted by the employer-respondent is *prima facie* discriminatory.

40 Once a *prima facie* case of discrimination has been established, the employer-respondent may justify the impugned standard by establishing on the balance of probabilities:

1. that the employer adopted the standard for a purpose rationally connected to the performance of the job;
2. that the employer adopted the particular standard in an honest and good faith belief that it was necessary to the fulfilment of that legitimate work-related purpose;
3. that the standard is reasonably necessary to the accomplishment of that legitimate work-related purpose. To show that the standard is reasonably necessary, it must be demonstrated that it is impossible to accommodate individual employees sharing the characteristics of the claimant without imposing undue hardship upon the employer.[52]

B. The Prima Facie Case

41 The Commission submits that one need only look at the Respondent's Statement of Particulars, which was prepared prior to the hearing in accordance with the Tribunal's *Interim Rules of Procedure*, to conclude that a *prima facie* case has been established. Amongst the items detailed in the document are the material facts that the Respondent seeks to prove in support of its case (Interim Rule 6(1)(a)). The Respondent declares, as a material fact, that the Complainant's absences from work were the result of illnesses, some of which were diagnosed as being PTSD and chronic sleep disorder. After detailing the number of days that the Complainant was absent from work, the Respondent states that on February 15, 1996, the Complainant was dismissed due to chronic absenteeism, "as there was no prospect of regular or reliable attendance at work".

---

[50] *British Columbia (Public Service Employee Relations Commission) v. B.C.G.E.U.*, [1999] 3 S.C.R. 3 (S.C.C.) ("Meiorin").

[51] *British Columbia (Superintendent of Motor Vehicles) v. British Columbia (Council of Human Rights)*, [1999] 3 S.C.R. 868 (S.C.C.) ("Grismer").

[52] Supra, note 4 at 32-33.

42 In a subsequent letter from Respondent counsel to the Commission, it was clarified that at the time of the dismissal, the Respondent considered the Complainant fit to return to full and regular duties as a bus operator. However, the Respondent did not accept that the medical report from Dr. Sequeira and Dr. Erickson dated January 31, 1996, provided any prognosis of regular attendance in respect of the performance of these duties, and the Complainant was consequently dismissed.

43 Two former managers at OC Transpo, Mr. Ron Marcotte and Mr. Gerald Timlin, testified that amongst the factors considered by the Health Unit, when assessing whether an employee has any prognosis of regular attendance, is his or her previous attendance record. Unquestionably, the Complainant's attendance record was poor, but the Commission points out that this came as a result of the Complainant's illnesses, principally PTSD, a "mental" disability falling within the definition of "disability" as set out in s. 25 of the *Act*.

44 Thus, it is argued, all of the elements of the *prima facie* case have been made out. The Complainant, who suffered from a disability, was dismissed from his employment by the Respondent, at least in part, because of his record of absenteeism. The primary cause of the absenteeism was his disability. Therefore, one of the factors in the Respondent's decision to dismiss the Complainant was his disability, which constitutes one of the proscribed grounds of discrimination under the *Act*. For a complaint to be substantiated, discrimination need only be one of the factors underlying a respondent's conduct.[53] Accordingly, submits the Commission, the Respondent in the present case is *prima facie* in breach of the *Act*.

45 The Respondent disagrees, arguing that in order for a *prima facie* case to be established, it must be demonstrated that the Complainant has actually been discriminated against. It is not sufficient to contend that merely because a disabled person has been dismissed, discrimination has taken place. It must be shown that the individual was dismissed *because* of the disability. The Respondent points out that it did not disagree with the opinion of the medical experts to the effect that the Complainant was able to return to work as a bus operator. Counsel for the Respondent reiterated, in his final submissions, the position that he had adopted in his pre-hearing correspon-

---

[53] *Singh v. Canada (Statistics Canada)* (1998), 34 C.H.R.R. D/203 (Can. Human Rights Trib.) at para. 174; aff'd *Canada (Attorney General) v. Singh* [2000 CarswellNat 588 (Fed. T.D.)] (April 14, 2000) T-2116-98; *McAvinn v. Strait Crossing Bridge Ltd.*, [2001] C.H.R.D. No. 36 (Can. Human Rights Trib.) at para. 102; *Holden v. Canadian National Railway* (1990), 14 C.H.R.R. D/12 (Fed. C.A.) at para. 7; *Pitawanakwat v. Canada (Secretary of State)* (1992), 19 C.H.R.R. D/110 (Can. Human Rights Trib.) at para. 85.

dence with the Commission: that is, when the Complainant was dismissed in February 1996, the Respondent considered him fit to return to full and regular duties as a bus operator. The Respondent argues that the decision to dismiss the Complainant, therefore, was not based on any assumption that he was disabled. In the absence of this element, the Commission cannot claim that the Complainant was subject to discriminatory treatment on the basis of a disability. The Complainant was simply let go because of the poor prognosis of his regular and reliable attendance, not his ability to perform the work whenever he would attend. The Respondent's treatment of the Complainant, pursuant to its policy on innocent absenteeism, was no different than that afforded any worker, whether disabled or not, who failed to have a good attendance record and whose predicted attendance in the future was equally unsatisfactory.

46 I find that the facts do not support this argument. The Respondent's decision to dismiss the Complainant was clearly influenced by the Complainant's medical condition, as appears from the evidence of Mr. Timlin, who was then Director of Occupational Health, Safety and Benefits at OC Transpo. He participated in the management process that led to the decision to dismiss the Complainant. Mr. Timlin testified that in deciding to fire the Complainant, OC Transpo relied heavily on the opinion of its Health Unit. The memo that the Health Unit sent to management regarding the Complainant's prognosis could not have been any more clear, stating that its finding took into consideration "the medical information on file" and the Complainant's "past record of attendance". The Respondent cannot now suggest that the Complainant's medical condition was not at least one of the factors that lead to its conclusion to dismiss him. As I indicated earlier, it is not necessary for a proscribed ground to be the only factor underlying a respondent's conduct for there to be a finding of discrimination. I would also add that Mr. Timlin testified that OC Transpo's decision to terminate the Complainant was not influenced at all by the other consideration stated in the Health Unit's memo, that of his lacking a Class C driver's licence. Mr. Timlin explained that the Respondent regularly assists employees, whose permits have been downgraded while on leave, to reacquire the required certification.

47 As an indication that the decision to dismiss the Complainant was not influenced by his medical condition, the Respondent refers to the Complainant's poor overall attendance record, dating back to the 1970's, and well before his affliction with PTSD. It is therefore suggested that the Complainant was simply someone who could not maintain regular and reliable attendance. An employer that suffers the consequences of an employee's failure to fulfill his work obligations should be justified at some point to consider the employment contract as having come to an end. But this argu-

ment does not truly reflect the facts of this case either. As I have already stated, the Health Unit's memo, upon which the Respondent's decision to dismiss was based, unquestionably concerned the Complainant's medical condition. Furthermore, although some of the Complainant's absences were not related to PTSD, the largest portion of them was, and, moreover, I accept the evidence of the Commission's experts that some of his other illnesses may have been related to the PTSD. In any event, even if the absenteeism prior to the PTSD was the only factor in his dismissal, why was the Complainant not dismissed before the onset of the disability? It is noteworthy that in the period leading up to his dismissal, the Complainant's longest continuous absence from work occurred while he was recovering from PTSD and other illnesses that may be related to this disorder.

48 I do not accept the Respondent's further submission that the treatment of the Complainant should only be compared to that of other OC Transpo employees with poor non-culpable absenteeism records. The Complainant's attendance record was inextricably linked to his disability. The Respondent concedes that as of the date of the Complainant's dismissal, he was considered fit to return to work. Yet the employer expected him to produce medical or other evidence to demonstrate that he would be able to maintain regular and reliable attendance in the long term, defined by Mr. Timlin to mean as many as twenty years into the future. Other OC Transpo employees who were healthier than the Complainant were able to maintain good attendance records in the past because they lacked his distinguishing characteristic, a disability. It was not suggested that those employees were expected to provide evidence demonstrating a 20-year prognosis of regular and reliable attendance. In this sense, the Complainant, a person who had suffered from a disability, was treated differently than employees who were not disabled.

49 I find that the Respondent's prediction that the Complainant's attendance in the future would be poor was based on the likelihood that he would suffer some form of relapse. When Mr. Mooney, the Superintendent of Operational Personnel, sought the Health Unit's opinion prior to dismissing the Complainant, he was interested in knowing whether the Complainant's condition, at that time, was any different from that for which there had been a prognosis of regular attendance, in 1994, after the Complainant's recovery from the sleep disorder. According to Mr. Timlin's testimony, the employer was in effect seeking some additional guarantee that the Complainant's attendance would improve.

50 I am convinced that underlying the Respondent's decision to dismiss the Complainant was an assumption that he would likely suffer from some sort of recurrence of prior illnesses, which would in turn result in additional absences from work. Conduct that is based on an actual or perceived possibility that an individual may develop a disability in the future constitutes dis-

crimination on the basis of disability, according to the Supreme Court of Canada, in *Québec (Commission des droits de la personne & des droits de la jeunesse) c. Montréal (Ville)* ("*Montreal*").[54] Although that case dealt with the Quebec *Charter of Human Rights and Freedoms*,[55] which prohibits discrimination based on a person's "handicap", as opposed to his "disability", the Court stressed that the objectives of human rights statutes throughout Canada do not vary because of such differences in terminology.[56]

51 The Respondent argues that its motive at all times was to manage the attendance within its workforce. Labour relations law recognizes the right of an employer to dismiss an employee due to excessive innocent absenteeism, provided the employer satisfies the test of demonstrating that the employee has a record of undue absenteeism in the past and that he or she is incapable of regular attendance in the future.[57] However, any discussion relating to the Respondent's motives is irrelevant to the issue before this Tribunal. It is trite law that an intention to discriminate is not a necessary element to proving discrimination under Canadian human rights legislation.[58] If the application of a labour relations policy has as an unintended effect, the adverse differential treatment of an individual based on a proscribed ground of discrimination, there may still be a finding of discrimination against the employer who is implementing the policy.

52 The Respondent is concerned that if this approach is followed, the logical outcome will be that an employer will never be permitted to dismiss an employee whose level of disability-related absenteeism is unacceptably high. In effect, the employer will be compelled to keep an employee who is unable to fulfill his end of the employment bargain, that is, the performance of his work. Counsel for the Respondent directed me to the labour arbitration decision in *AirBC Ltd. v. C.A.L.D.A.*,[59] wherein the arbitrator rejected such a suggestion and noted that the existence of human rights legislation does not result in the eradication of the labour relations doctrine of non-culpable absenteeism.

---

[54][2000] 1 S.C.R. 665 (S.C.C.), at 700.

[55]R.S.Q., c. C-12.

[56]Supra, note 8 at 689.

[57]See *AirBC Ltd. v. C.A.L.D.A.* (1995), 50 L.A.C. (4th) 93 (Can. Arb. Bd.).

[58]*O'Malley v. Simpsons-Sears Ltd.*, [1985] 2 S.C.R. 536 (S.C.C.), at 547; *Robichaud v. Brennan*, [1987] 2 S.C.R. 84 (S.C.C.) at para. 10.

[59]Supra, note 11.

53 The conclusions of the labour arbitrator in that case, though, serve to demonstrate that the Respondent's concerns are, in fact, unwarranted. As is pointed out in the decision, there are two issues to be considered in such cases: first, did the employer meet the tests set out in labour relations jurisprudence to establish a case of non-culpable absenteeism, and then, second, whether the employer's conduct contravenes the applicable human rights legislation. This latter issue is resolved by conducting a BFOR analysis, the approach for which was most recently set out in *Meiorin*. It is the third step of the *Meiorin* test that maintains an employer's right to dismiss an employee in such cases, provided the employer demonstrates that it cannot accommodate the employee without imposing undue hardship on itself. Where an employer is able to establish these elements, its decision to dismiss an employee due to his or her non-culpable absenteeism will be justified.

54 When measured against the labour relations test, there is no doubt that the Complainant's record of innocent absenteeism was very high. There is some issue as to what the prognosis for regular attendance was. The medical experts' letter of January 31, 1996 stated that his prognosis was "very good", yet in their respective testimonies, they were both forthright in their explanations that this prediction was limited to the short term. It would have been irresponsible of them to have attempted to foretell the state of the Complainant's health to any greater extent. Counsel for the Respondent suggests that I am in some way bound by the findings of fact of the labour arbitrator who, in his ruling regarding the Complainant's grievance, stated that the prognosis for his regular attendance was indeed poor. However, I do not see the necessity to follow this course, considering that the medical evidence of the Commission's experts does not contradict the position of the Respondent that at the time of the dismissal, the prognosis beyond the short term was at the very least uncertain.

55 The point to be made here is that even if the Respondent was correct in its assessment of the Complainant's condition and its decision satisfied the non-culpable absenteeism test formulated in labour relations law jurisprudence, the matter before this human rights tribunal remains undecided. One must still proceed through the BFOR analysis articulated by the Supreme Court of Canada in *Meiorin*.

56 To summarize on this point, I find that a *prima facie* case of discrimination has been established. The decision by the Respondent to dismiss the Complainant, in furtherance of its program to manage and improve attendance within its workforce, was based, at least in part, on the Complainant's disability. It is therefore now incumbent upon the Respondent to demonstrate that its decision was based on a *bona fide* occupational requirement.

C. Meiorin Test

(i) Steps 1 & 2

57 The first element of the *Meiorin* test requires the employer to demonstrate that the standard in issue was adopted for a purpose rationally connected to the performance of the job. A document describing OC Transpo's Attendance Management Program was entered into evidence. Mr. Marcotte testified that the principles set out therein reflect the policy that was in place when the Complainant was dismissed in 1996, although the document itself may have been drafted some months thereafter. According to this text, the stated purpose of the Attendance Management Program was as follows:

> [...] to reduce the high cost of absenteeism in a way that is consistent and fair to all employees. Employees have an obligation to maintain regular attendance; OC Transpo has a responsibility to; [*sic*] create working conditions conducive to good attendance, monitor attendance, and to work with employees who are experiencing extraordinary levels of absenteeism.

As the Canadian Human Rights Tribunal concluded in *Eyerley v. Seaspan International Ltd.*,[60] there is an obvious rational connection between a rule designed to maintain reasonable levels of attendance on the job and the requirements of that job. In any event, the Commission did not argue that Step 1 was not satisfied in the present case.

58 It is similarly not in dispute that the Respondent adopted the Attendance Management Program in an honest and good faith belief that it was necessary for the fulfilment of this stated purpose.

(ii) Step 3

59 In order for the Respondent to show that its program regarding innocent absenteeism was reasonably necessary for the accomplishment of its stated purpose of maintaining reasonable levels of attendance, it must be demonstrated that it was impossible to accommodate the Complainant or other employees sharing his characteristics, without imposing undue hardship upon the Respondent.

60 When the *Act* was amended in 1998, Section 15(2) was added to provide that health, safety and cost are the factors to be considered in determining whether accommodating a person's needs would impose undue hardship on an employer. However, the facts giving rise to the present complaint occurred prior to the passage of this amendment, and, as was pointed out in *Desormeaux v. Ottawa-Carleton Regional Transit Commission*[61], my con-

---

[60] [2001] C.H.R.D. No. 45 (Can. Human Rights Trib.) at para. 139.

[61] 2003 CHRT 2 (Can. Human Rights Trib.)

sideration of the accommodation issue is therefore governed by the principles articulated by the Supreme Court in *Central Alberta Dairy Pool v. Alberta (Human Rights Commission)*[62] and several subsequent cases. Some of these principles have been summarized in *Eyerley*:[63]

> In *Central Okanagan School District No. 23 v. Renaud*,[64] Sopinka, J. noted that undue implies that some hardship is acceptable; it is only undue hardship that satisfies this test. In *Central Dairy Pool v. Alberta (Human Rights Commission)*,[65] other relevant factors considered by the Supreme Court include, financial cost, interchangeability of the workforce and facilities, the provisions of the collective agreement, substantial interference with the rights and morale of other employees, and employee safety. Excessive cost may justify a refusal to accommodate those with disabilities, but there must not be too low a value put on accommodating disability. Otherwise it would be too easy to use increased cost as a reason for refusing to accord the disabled equal treatment.[66] The provisions of a collective agreement cannot absolve the employer of its duty to accommodate, although substantial departure from its terms is a factor to be considered for undue hardship.[67]

61 The Respondent contends that in cases involving innocent absenteeism releases, the accommodation aspect of the analysis may not be necessary. When assessing an employee's prognosis for regular and reliable attendance, an employer implicitly takes into consideration whether that employee could be accommodated to the point of undue hardship. As Counsel for the Respondent noted, there is "nothing incompatible with innocent absenteeism releases and human rights considerations flowing through each other". In such cases, therefore, there no longer remains any need to proceed through the third step in the *Meiorin* analysis.

62 I respectfully disagree. As the arbitral decision in *Air B.C.* illustrates, there are two stages involved in reviewing innocent absenteeism dismissals. The first is conducted in accordance with labour relations law and the second in accordance with human rights law. I fail to see how one can assume that once an employer properly concludes that an employee's prognosis for attendance is poor, the employer's duty to accommodate under human rights law is satisfied. A review of the labour arbitration ruling regarding the Complainant's grievance supports this point. OC Transpo's decision to dismiss the Complainant was held to be just, even though the arbitrator did

---

62[1990] 2 S.C.R. 489 (S.C.C.), at 520-21

63Supra, note 14 at para. 141.

64[1992] 2 S.C.R. 970 at 984.

65[1990] 2 S.C.R. 489 at 520-21.

66Grismer, supra, note 4 at para. 41; *Eldridge v. British Columbia (Attorney General)*, [1997] 3 S.C.R. 624 at paras. 87-94.

67Renaud, supra, note 18 at 587.

not examine whether the employer had accommodated the employee to the point of undue hardship, in accordance with the human rights principles referred to above. The Arbitrator's comments on the issue were limited to a blanket statement that the Complainant had been "amply accommodated in the past to no avail" and that therefore, it was "not a case where the employer has failed to accommodate a disability". The notion of "undue hardship" was never even discussed.

63 The Respondent goes on, however, to provide a second reason for not proceeding through an accommodation analysis. Based on the medical opinion of Drs. Sequeira and Erickson, OC Transpo viewed the Complainant as being fit to work as a bus operator at the time of his dismissal. Consequently, there remained no disability for the employer to accommodate. Having come to the conclusion that the Complainant's prognosis for regular and reliable attendance in the long term was poor, the only possible form of accommodation would have been for OC Transpo to "tolerate" the Complainant's predicted high level of absenteeism. This, argues the Respondent, is not an acceptable form of accommodation.

64 Counsel for the Respondent directed me to the 1992 case of the Ontario Board of Inquiry in *Bonner v. Ontario (Minister of Health)*,[68] which related to a complainant who suffered from periodic bouts of depression. The Board mentioned in its ruling that "a person who by reason of handicap cannot work competently on a regular basis is incapable of satisfying the requirements of the position regardless of how he or she might perform when unaffected by that handicap".[69] The Board went on to reject the premise that someone with such a disability should be accommodated in the sense of being tolerated.

65 I find this decision of limited relevance to the present case. First of all, these references constitute *obiter dicta*, as the principal finding of the Board was that the complainant in that case would not have performed satisfactorily, irrespective of his handicap. Furthermore, the Board did not consider differential treatment of someone who may possibly develop a disability in the future, as being a form of discrimination. This finding is incompatible with the subsequent judgment of the Supreme Court in the *Montreal* case. Overall, the Board took a narrow view regarding accommodation and undue hardship. The Board asserted that the principle of undue hardship does not require an employer to hire or retain employees who, because of a handicap, are always or occasionally incapable of doing the work, simply because the

---

[68](1992), 16 C.H.R.R. D/485 (Ont. Bd. of Inquiry)

[69]*Ibid.* at para. 82.

employer has the resources to tolerate "actually deficient work".[70] The law has moved well beyond such an interpretation, as evidenced by the statement of the Supreme Court of Canada, in *Meiorin*, that the employer bears the burden, under the third step of the analysis, of demonstrating that it is *impossible* to accommodate individual employees sharing the characteristics of the complainant without imposing undue hardship on the employer.[71]

66 Besides, I fail to see how "tolerating" absenteeism cannot constitute an acceptable type of accommodation. Certainly, all employers must be prepared to accept some level of absenteeism from all employees as it is inevitable that they will be unable to attend their work, from time to time. The issue to be decided is whether this "tolerance" of a certain level of absenteeism would impose undue hardship on the employer, taking into consideration all the appropriate factors. In the recent Alberta Court of Queen's Bench case of *U.N.A., Local 115 v. Calgary Health Authority*,[72] one of the issues to be decided was whether an employer is obliged to hire a qualified woman who is pregnant, for a term position, if it is known from the outset that she cannot complete the entire term due to the impending birth of her child. The Court found that it would be erroneous to assume that accommodating this sort of availability issue would inevitably result in undue hardship. The Court saw no distinction between the duty to accommodate such absenteeism from the duty in cases such as *Central Alberta Dairy Pool* and *Simpsons-Sears*,[73] where the employers were obliged to accommodate employees who would be absent on a regular basis, to the point of undue hardship. I do not, therefore, accept the Respondent's suggestion that the third step in the *Meiorin* analysis has no application in this case.

67 One of the reasons why the Respondent considered that the only form of accommodation available would be to tolerate absenteeism was because it assumed that the Complainant could only and would only work as a bus operator. Yet, the evidence shows otherwise. To begin with, the Health Unit memo, which OC Transpo management relied upon in deciding to terminate the Complainant's employment, suggested in its second paragraph that the Health Unit was willing to contact his medical advisors regarding "alternate employment", if his employing division was "able and prepared to offer the Complainant" such employment. The Health Unit, therefore, had not re-

---

70 *Ibid.* at para. 83.

71 *Supra*, note 4 at 40.

72 *U.N.A., Local 115 v. Calgary Health Authority*, 2002 ABQB 859 (Alta. Q.B.).

73 *Supra*, note 12.

jected the possibility of his being able to perform satisfactorily in another job.

68 In addition, the Complainant testified that when he was told that he would not be allowed to return to his job, he asked Mr. Mooney to let him take on some other duties within OC Transpo. Mr. Mooney refused and informed him that no form of "rehabilitation" would be provided. I found the Complainant's entire testimony forthright and credible and no evidence was led to contradict his recollection of this conversation. Even if the OC Transpo managers who decided to dismiss the Complainant (including Mr. Mooney and Mr. Timlin) thought that the only employment option available in his case was to keep him as a bus operator, the information before them clearly suggested that other options should have been examined.

69 This raises another important failure on the part of the Respondent in dealing with the Complainant. In *Meiorin*, the Court alluded to the practical usefulness, in conducting the accommodation analysis, of considering separately:

a) the appropriateness of the *procedure* that the employer adopted to assess the issue of accommodation, and

b) the *substantive content* of the accommodating standard that was offered to the employee, if any.[74]

The Commission submits that, with respect to the Complainant's disability, the Respondent failed to even observe the policies outlined in its own Attendance Management Program, and, as such, neglected to accommodate him procedurally. For instance, the Attendance Management Program provided that all reasonable efforts must be taken to try to rehabilitate or accommodate an employee who is found to be innocently absent from work because of a disability, if this can be done without undue hardship. These accommodation mechanisms included the options offered by the DERC, such as the shuttle bus to which the Complainant had been assigned in 1992.

70 The Attendance Management Program goes on to declare that an employee can only be "medically terminated" once "every reasonable effort has been made to accommodate the employee within the work place". The Commission argues that the Complainant was terminated before any such effort was made. Indeed, I find that the Respondent, on whom rests the burden to demonstrate that the employee could not be accommodated, did not present evidence that any such attempts were made. To the contrary, it appears that the Respondent, having concluded that the Complainant was al-

---

[74] *Supra*, note 4 at 37.

ready fit, proceeded with the dismissal without considering any other options. Yet, as I have already explained, OC Transpo's decision was tainted with an assumption that the Complainant would not be able to regularly attend work, on account of a possible occurrence of illness in the future.

71 There was some suggestion in the medical experts' letter of a process of work hardening that would assist in the Complainant's "readjustment". In addition, the Complainant's past experience demonstrated that his recoveries were undermined when confronted with stressful situations, such as driving on routes on which he had been attacked in the past. Ensuring that the Complainant avoided such circumstances may have assisted in preventing any recurrence of his disabilities. The Respondent argues that the Complainant's medical advisors never suggested that he needed to do another job, but that he was ready to return to his duties as a bus driver. I do not find this argument convincing. There is no evidence that any question about alternate employment was ever asked of the experts. Dr. Sequeira and Dr. Erickson certainly were prepared, as indicated in their January 31, 1996 letter, to be consulted by the employer regarding the assignment of duties, presumably as a bus driver. Considering the Respondent's concern that the Complainant would be unable to maintain regular attendance as a bus operator, nothing prevented the Respondent, at this point, from requesting that the Complainant's experts provide their opinion regarding alternate employment. There is no evidence that any such request was made.

72 Do employers have the obligation to make such an enquiry? The Respondent suggests not, citing as authority for its position the recent judgment of the British Columbia Court of Appeal in *Oak Bay Marina Ltd. v. British Columbia (Human Rights Commission)* ("*Oak Bay*").[75] The Court found that the employer in that case was entitled to rely on its own experience with the complainant in assessing his ability to perform the job, and was not required to investigate any further into his mental disability by, for instance, obtaining additional expert opinions. However, the findings in this decision are clearly fact-specific. The job in question was that of a guide working on small fishing boats travelling over what were described as among the deadliest waters in British Columbia. The lives of the employer's clients rested in the hands of the guide and it is evident that the Court believed that in the interests of their safety, the employer was entitled to rely on its own empirical knowledge regarding the complainant's capacity to function under these circumstances. In the present case, the Respondent does not question the Complainant's ability to perform his duties well,

[75] 2002 BCCA 495 (B.C. C.A.).

when he is working. The issue for the Respondent is the Complainant's level of absenteeism.

73 The Court also suggested that the scope of the duty to investigate could vary depending on the nature and size of the employer. The Court distinguished the small business of the employer in that case from, as an example, the operations of a government "with entire departments and volumes of information available to it".[76] OC Transpo certainly is more reflective of the latter example. Finally, regarding this question of the duty to investigate, I am guided yet again by the findings in *Meiorin*. The Court identifies some of the important questions to be asked in the course of the Step 3 analysis, including whether the employer investigated alternative approaches that do not have a discriminatory effect. Implicit in this finding is the duty upon an employer to conduct such an investigation. Without question, there also exists a duty upon the employee to cooperate with the employer in such a process but, as I discussed earlier, I am convinced that the Complainant and his medical advisors were willing and prepared to cooperate in finding a way to rehabilitate him and assure his full reintegration back into the OC Transpo workforce.

74 Assuming the only available accommodation, as suggested by the Respondent, was to tolerate the Complainant's absenteeism in the future, what evidence was presented to demonstrate that this would impose undue hardship on the employer?

75 The work schedule for bus operators was typically established on the basis of four or five booking periods per year. In advance of each period, drivers were permitted to select their routes and dates of work, based on their seniority. One of the options available to them was to work on the "spare board". The spare board consisted of a number of drivers (the evidence suggests between 30 and 50 persons) who were available to replace absent workers, as the need arose. These absences were typically unexpected in nature, such as when an operator overslept, was snowed in or fell sick. Spare board drivers received their full salary, whether they were assigned to replace another operator or not.

76 In the event that the number of absentees exceeded the number of drivers on the spare board, OC Transpo was obliged to ask other drivers to fill in, who were then paid on an overtime basis. On occasion, enough overtime operators could not be found, in which case buses did not go out and service to the public was affected. Dissatisfied transit users were known to com-

---

[76] *Ibid.* at para 26.

plain about service interruptions to their local politicians who in turn conveyed these concerns to the OC Transpo management.

77 Mr. Marcotte has served as Manager of Staff Relations and Employee Relations at OC Transpo. He testified as to the complexity associated with attempting to predict how many individuals would be absent on a given day and accordingly, estimating the number of operators to put on the spare board.

78 In the case of longer term absences, where it was known in advance of a booking period that an employee would be unavailable for the entire term, the operator was not permitted to book any shifts. It is my understanding, based on the somewhat sketchy evidence on this issue, that because such absentees had no scheduled shifts, they were not replaced with drivers on the spare board. On the other hand, if it was uncertain whether the duration of the absence would cover an entire booking period, the employee was permitted to book work dates. If he or she was ultimately unable to come in on those days, a spare board driver would have to fill in.

79 To summarize, the hardship that the Complainant's potential future absenteeism may have imposed is the following:

- a spare driver, who would receive a salary whether the driver was assigned to a bus route or not, would have to replace him;
- between 30 and 50 drivers were assigned to the spare board on any given day. If an insufficient number of spare drivers were available, another operator would have to be paid overtime wages to fill in;
- if an overtime employee could not be found, the bus service on that run would be interrupted;
- affected transit users could complain to their local politicians who would pass on the complaints to OC Transpo management.

80 I do not find that this evidence demonstrates that accommodating the Complainant's possible absenteeism would impose undue hardship on the Respondent.

81 To begin with, this evidence, introduced through the testimonies of Mr. Timlin and Mr. Marcotte, was basically anecdotal in nature. Mr. Timlin prefaced some of his comments with a warning that his expertise related to the payment of employee benefits, not the work scheduling process. Neither he nor Mr. Marcotte provided any details whatsoever as to the actual financial cost of running the spare board or paying the overtime wages when the spare board was depleted, particularly in comparison to OC Transpo's overall expenditures. No evidence was led as to how frequently the spare

board was depleted nor how often transit service to the public was interrupted due to absenteeism.

82 The Complainant had received disability benefits during many of his absences. No evidence was led by the Respondent to indicate the related costs, if any, and the level of hardship to the Respondent arising therefrom.

83 Mr. Marcotte confirmed that a bus operator's absence did not put anyone's health at risk. He also acknowledged that it would be a "stretch" to contend that excess overtime imposed so much stress on the replacing employees that safety concerns were raised. In fact, the Respondent did not demonstrate what hardship would be imposed on the workforce at large. Most of the alleged hardship relates to the spare board process. Yet the evidence regarding the Complainant shows that during many of these absences, especially while he was being treated for PTSD, he was placed on long-term disability leave. Thus, over a period of nine months in 1992 and for the last eleven months leading up to his dismissal, the Complainant had not booked any shifts. Spare board employees should therefore not have been called upon to replace him in these periods. If the Complainant was likely to be innocently absent in the future, as the Respondent had predicted, it is certainly possible that these absences would have resembled the past incidents and resulted in his being disabled over a long term. The spare board would consequently have been unaffected.

84 Respondent counsel referred me to the recent judgment of the Ontario Divisional Court in *Ontario (Human Rights Commission) v. Ford Motor Co. of Canada* [hereinafter *Roosma*],[77] which affirmed a decision of the Ontario Board of Inquiry. The case concerned two employees at the Ford automobile plant in Oakville who for religious reasons could not work from sunset on Friday until sunset on Saturday. They sought to be permanently excused from working Friday evenings. The Ontario Human Rights Commission led evidence that the cost to Ford of replacing the employees on those shifts was negligible. The Board of Inquiry disagreed with this assessment by extending the notion of cost to include the real cost of resulting declines in both quality and production, which while difficult to measure were nonetheless deemed real. The Board concluded that accommodating these employees, by arranging for the swapping of shifts or the hiring of part-time or student workers, would impose undue hardship on Ford.

85 The circumstances regarding the *Roosma* case differ significantly from those of the present case. First of all, the Court did not necessarily adopt the reasons of the Board of Inquiry; it simply concluded that the board's find-

---

[77] [2002] O.J. No. 3688 (Ont. Div. Ct.), leave to appeal to F.C.A. refused.

ings met the "reasonableness" standard of judicial review. The Court noted that the Board was presented with extensive detailed and uncontradicted evidence from Ford, regarding the consequences of accommodating the complainants. Moreover, amongst the factors that influenced the Board's findings was not only the financial cost to Ford but also the interchangeability of its operations, the importance of having the regular operator on each job, the impact of the collective agreement, safety considerations and the substantial effect of accommodation on other workers.[78]

86 As I have already indicated, I have no evidence before me of the actual financial cost regarding the Respondent's measures for accommodating or "tolerating" absenteeism. Safety issues do not arise and evidence was not introduced regarding the impact of the collective agreement. Aside from the mention of the possible, though unlikely, additional stress on overtime employees, I was not provided with any insight as to how accommodating the Complainant's potential future absenteeism would affect other employees. In addition, contrary to the evidence raised in *Roosma* with respect to Ford's automobile assembly line workers, the evidence before me suggests that the functions of a bus operator are highly interchangeable. I thus find that *Roosma* can be distinguished from the present case.

87 The Respondent has failed to establish that accommodating the potential innocent absenteeism of the Complainant after his return to work in February 1996 would have imposed undue hardship on OC Transpo.

88 The complaint is therefore substantiated.

III. Remedy

A. Reinstatement

89 In human rights cases, where a complaint of discrimination is found to be substantiated, it is the duty of the Tribunal to attempt to restore a complainant to the position that he or she would have been in, but for the discrimination.[79] The Commission accordingly submits that the Complainant should be reinstated to the position of bus operator or such other suitable occupation as the Tribunal may determine.

90 Respondent counsel argued that reinstatement is inappropriate in the present circumstances. In the seven years since his dismissal, the prognosis for the Complainant's attendance has remained unchanged. Once he is reinstated, and provided the employer's predictions hold true, the parties will

---

[78] *Ibid.* at para. 158.

[79] *McAvinn, supra*, note 7 at para. 189; *Morgan v. Canada (Armed Forces)* (1991), [1992] 2 F.C. 401 (Fed. C.A.), at 414-15.

again find themselves in the difficult situation of having to deal with the Complainant's excessive absenteeism. This argument appears to me to be predicated on an assumption that is itself related to the Complainant's disability. I have already held that such an assumption is discriminatory and it can therefore play no role in the fashioning of the remedy.

91 I am satisfied that the appropriate remedy would be for the Complainant to be reinstated as a bus operator. I therefore order the Respondent to reinstate the Complainant to the position of bus operator, together with the commensurate seniority and benefits of a full-time permanent employee, the whole with retroactive effect to the date of his dismissal.

92 According to the evidence, the Respondent ordinarily assists employees returning from extended leave in their reintegration into the workforce. This assistance includes the provision of training as well as aid in the reacquisition of any necessary driving permits from the appropriate authorities. The Respondent must provide this assistance to the Complainant.

B. Damages for Lost Income

93 The Respondent is ordered to pay to the Complainant damages for his lost wages from February 2, 1996, until the date of his return to full time employment, taking into account other income, statutory deductions and gross-up for the purposes of the *Income Tax Act*. All of his benefits should also be adjusted accordingly.

94 I do not accept the Respondent's suggestion that the damages for lost wages should only run from the date of the labour arbitrator's decision that the Complainant was justly terminated. The Respondent's liability flows from its decision to end the Complainant's employment, based in part on a discriminatory ground, irrespective of whether the labour arbitrator deemed the dismissal just.

95 Instead of presenting evidence or submissions at the hearing with respect to the calculation of these damages, the parties agreed to work together to determine these amounts. As I explain below, I will retain jurisdiction in case these discussions do not prove fruitful.

C. Hurt Feelings

96 The facts giving rise to the complaint precede the 1998 amendments to the *Act*. Section 53(3) stated, at that time, that the Tribunal could order a respondent to pay up to $5,000 in compensation to a victim of discrimination who had suffered in respect of feelings or self-respect. I am in agree-

ment with the findings of the Tribunal, in *Premakumar v. Air Canada*[80] and *Desormeaux*[81], that the $5,000 maximum award must be reserved for the very worst cases that fall within the range of cases in which such awards are warranted.

97 The Complainant testified as to the effect that the termination had on his life. He felt a loss of dignity and feared for his family's economic well-being. The financial impact was so great that it became difficult for him to purchase appropriate food for his family. The evidence does suggest, though, the dismissal did not lead to a recurrence of PTSD and that to the contrary, Dr. Erickson having noted that the Complainant was "taking it extremely well".

98 Taking into account these and all of the other circumstances in this case, I order the Respondent to pay to the Complainant the sum of $3,500 as special compensation.

D. Policy Review

99 The Commission seeks an order that the Respondent's policy regarding the accommodation of employees with disabilities be reviewed and revised. Over seven years have passed since the Complainant was dismissed. The evidence is that since that time, the employer has changed (to the City of Ottawa) and the accommodation policies and attendance management programs have gone through several modifications and updates. The newest attendance management program that is now being implemented extends to all the employees of the City of Ottawa, not just those working within OC Transpo. Furthermore, the liability in the present case stems in part from the Respondent's failure to apply the program that was in place at the time of the Complainant's dismissal, and was not necessarily the result of a particular defect in the program itself. The Commission's request is consequently denied.

E. Interest

100 Interest is payable regarding all of the monetary awards made pursuant to this decision. The interest shall be simple interest calculated on a yearly basis, at a rate equivalent to the Bank Rate (Monthly Series) set by the Bank of Canada. With respect to compensation for hurt feelings, the interest shall accrue from the date of dismissal until the final payment of the award. Interest on the lost wages shall also run from the date of dismissal until the

---

[80](2002), 42 C.H.R.R. D/63 (Can. Human Rights Trib.) at para. 107.

[81]*Supra* note 15 at para 128.

final payment of the award, but shall be calculated as the wages would have become payable to the Complainant.

F. Retention of Jurisdiction

101 In the event that any difficulties arise in the implementation of these remedies, including a failure by the parties to reach an agreement regarding the damages for lost wages, I retain jurisdiction to receive evidence, hear further submissions and make further orders.

Complaint upheld.

Syndicat des employés de l'Hôpital général de Montréal c. Sexton

2007 CarswellQue 110, 2007 SCC 4 (S.C.C.)

Deschamps J.:

1 This appeal concerns the interaction between labour law and the right of a person to be absent from work owing to an illness or disability. More specifically, what is in issue is the role of a collective agreement in the assessment of an employer's duty to accommodate an employee who is absent for an indeterminate period owing to personal health problems. For the reasons that follow, I find that the collective agreement plays an important role in determining the scope of the employer's duty to accommodate and that, in the case at bar, the three-year period provided for in the collective agreement represents a reasonable accommodation.

I. Facts and Judicial History

2 On March 24, 2000, on account of a nervous breakdown, Alice Brady took a leave of absence from her job as a medical secretary for the appellant, McGill University Health Centre (Montreal General Hospital) ("Hospital"), a position she had held since 1985. Between June 26, 2000 and February 28, 2001, on her doctor's orders, she attempted a gradual return to work. Her workload was accordingly reduced to three days a week. No other less demanding work was available. Since the collective agreement in force provided for a maximum period of six months for rehabilitation and no progress had been noted in an evaluation dated February 28, 2001, the Hospital notified Ms. Brady that she would have to stay home until she was able to work full time. On March 14, the rehabilitation period was extended until September 17, 2001 following negotiations with the respondent Syndicat des employés de l'Hôpital Général de Montréal ("Union"), which represented Ms. Brady. On September 14, her return to full-time work was postponed to October 21, 2001, and it was subsequently postponed again to November 23, 2001. However, on November 1, 2001, Ms. Brady's supervisor asked her to go home because she was disorganized and behaving inappropriately. Her supervisor suggested that she see her doctor. The doctor recommended that a new gradual return to work be attempted beginning March 11, 2002, but the Hospital, relying on the lack of progress observed during the previous rehabilitation periods, rejected this recommendation. A return to full-time work was accordingly scheduled for September 2002, but Ms. Brady had an automobile accident on July 28, 2002.

3 The collective agreement provided that rehabilitation periods did not interrupt the disability period. On March 12, 2003, the Hospital notified Ms. Brady that her employment would be terminated on April 3, 2003. It cited her prolonged absence as the reason for its decision. The Union filed a grievance in which it contested the decision of March 12, 2003 and asked the Hospital to negotiate a reasonable accommodation with Ms. Brady.

4 On November 5, 2003, the final day of the grievance hearing, Ms. Brady was still receiving total disability benefits from the Société de l'assurance automobile du Québec and was waiting for a shoulder operation. According to the medical reports in the record, the date of her return to work was undetermined.

5 The arbitrator dismissed the grievance (SOQUIJ AZ-50227506). He found a number of clauses in the collective agreement to be relevant, including one concerning the protection of employees from discrimination and another providing for loss of employment in the event of an absence owing to illness. The clauses quoted by the arbitrator are reproduced in the appendix to these reasons. The arbitrator pointed out that the Hospital had already accommodated Ms. Brady by granting her rehabilitation periods more generous than those provided for in the collective agreement, and that Ms. Brady was still unfit for work at the end of the three-year period provided for in the agreement. He considered the facts subsequent to the termination of the employment to be relevant, since they were [TRANSLATION] "clearly interrelated facts on a continuum, with Ms. Brady still being, as of the final hearing day, totally [incapable] of performing the usual duties of her position or of any other comparable position for medical reasons" (p. 17). In the arbitrator's view, "it is difficult to imagine an ... additional duty to accommodate an employee whose attending physician considers her to be totally disabled" (p. 20). After thus finding that the Hospital had discharged its duty to accommodate, the arbitrator concluded "that the employer has treated Ms. Brady in a way that was just and non-discriminatory in correctly applying an express rule set out in the collective agreement" (p. 21). The Union applied for judicial review of the arbitrator's decision.

6 The Superior Court judge who heard the application noted that Ms. Brady's illness, which was the cause of her loss of employment, was a handicap within the meaning of the *Charter*:

> [TRANSLATION] There is no question in the case at bar that Ms. Brady's illness, which is the cause of the loss of her employment, is a handicap within the meaning of the Charter, and "it is of little relevance whether the arbitrator found that there was direct discrimination (handicap) or adverse effect discrimination (because the employee did not meet the availability requirements)". How it is characterized is unimportant, since, in either case, the Supreme Court, in BCGSEU, requires the em-

> ployer to accommodate the employee in a manner that is not excessive, and to take reasonable measures.
>
> ([2004] Q.J. No. 7555 (QL), at para. 37)

She summed up the arbitrator's conclusions as follows:

> [TRANSLATION] It appears from his decision that the arbitrator found it difficult to imagine a duty to accommodate Ms. Brady, since she was disabled. For him, this in itself constituted undue hardship, as an employer does not have a duty to keep on employees who are incapable of performing their duties. [para. 41]

7 The judge found that these observations were based on a correct and reasonable interpretation of the evidence and that, even though the arbitrator had not expressly mentioned the principles set out in *British Columbia (Public Service Employee Relations Commission) v. B.C.G.E.U.*, [1999] 3 S.C.R. 3 (S.C.C.) ("*Meiorin*"), and *British Columbia (Superintendent of Motor Vehicles) v. British Columbia (Council of Human Rights)*, [1999] 3 S.C.R. 868 (S.C.C.), he had applied them correctly. She dismissed the application for judicial review. The Union appealed her decision.

8 In the Court of Appeal, the Union argued that the Hospital had [TRANSLATION] "failed to take reasonable measures to accommodate the plaintiff" ([2005] R.J.D.T. 693, 2005 QCCA 277 (Que. C.A.), at para. 9). The Court of Appeal concluded that the arbitrator had not assessed the reasonable accommodation issue on an individualized basis but had instead merely applied the provision of the collective agreement mechanically. The Court of Appeal reversed the judgment of the Superior Court and remitted the case to the arbitrator for a ruling on this duty and, if applicable, on the appropriate compensation.

9 The Hospital was granted leave to appeal to this Court on the issue of the scope of the duty to accommodate and on the possibility of agreeing on it in advance in the context of a collective agreement. The Hospital submits that the clause in dispute is generous and meets the test in *Meiorin*. It claims to have discharged its duty, explaining that it was impossible to further accommodate Ms. Brady, since she was totally disabled and since no date for her return to work was scheduled. The Union, however, considers it contradictory to argue, on the one hand, that accommodation must be individualized and, on the other, that the duty of accommodation can be discharged by mechanically applying a general clause.

10 The rules governing reasonable accommodation in the workplace are well established. The parties do not dispute these principles. The issue here is how they apply to a termination of employment clause.

II. Duty to Accommodate and Collective Labour Relations

11 The duty to accommodate in the workplace arises when an employer seeks to apply a standard that is prejudicial to an employee on the basis of specific characteristics that are protected by human rights legislation. This can occur in the context of a sick employee's right to be absent from work, as in the case at bar, or of a similarly protected right, such as a woman's right to be absent from work owing to pregnancy.

12 As can be seen from the many cases in this area, collective agreements often contain clauses providing for termination of the employment relationship after an absence for a specified period of time. Such clauses are clearly aimed at ill or disabled persons. The clause in issue in the instant case reads as follows:

> [TRANSLATION] **12.11** An employee shall lose his or her seniority rights and his or her employment in the following cases:
>
> . . . . .
>
> 5 - absence by reason of illness or of an accident other than an industrial accident or occupational disease (see above), after the thirty-sixth (36th) month of absence.

13 It is well established that the employer must justify the standard it seeks to apply by establishing:

(1) that the employer adopted the standard for a purpose rationally connected to the performance of the job;

(2) that the employer adopted the particular standard in an honest and good faith belief that it was necessary to the fulfilment of that legitimate work-related purpose; and

(3) that the standard is reasonably necessary to the accomplishment of that legitimate work-related purpose. To show that the standard is reasonably necessary, it must be demonstrated that it is impossible to accommodate individual employees sharing the characteristics of the claimant without imposing undue hardship upon the employer.

(*Meiorin*, at para. 54)

14 The first and second steps enable the court to assess the legitimacy of, respectively, the standard's general purpose and the employer's intent in adopting it. They thus guarantee that the standard, whether viewed objectively or subjectively, does not have a discriminatory foundation. The third step is a test of rationality whose purpose is to determine whether the standard is *necessary* in order to accomplish a legitimate purpose. The employer must demonstrate that it cannot accommodate the complainant without suffering undue hardship.

15 The factors that will support a finding of undue hardship are not entrenched and must be applied with common sense and flexibility (*Meiorin*, at para. 63; *Chambly (Commission scolaire régionale) c. Bergevin*, [1994] 2 S.C.R. 525 (S.C.C.), at p. 546; and *Central Alberta Dairy Pool v. Alberta (Human Rights Commission)*, [1990] 2 S.C.R. 489 (S.C.C.), at pp. 520-21). For example, the cost of the possible accommodation method, employee morale and mobility, the interchangeability of facilities, and the prospect of interference with other employees' rights or of disruption of the collective agreement may be taken into consideration. Since the right to accommodation is not absolute, consideration of all relevant factors can lead to the conclusion that the impact of the application of a prejudicial standard is legitimate.

16 The parties' positions can be summed up succinctly. The Hospital submits that a collective agreement may, in advance, establish the scope of the duty to accommodate and provide for a maximum period of time beyond which any absence would constitute undue hardship. The Union counters that the Hospital cannot rely on employee benefits granted under a collective agreement as a substitute for the duty to accommodate. In the Union's view, this duty arises when the period provided for in the collective agreement expires.

17 It is quite true that employee benefits cannot be invoked as a substitute for the duty to accommodate. But the Hospital is not saying that they can.

18 Insofar as the operation of an enterprise relies on its workforce, there is no doubt that an employer may establish *bona fide* measures to ensure employees' regular attendance. For example, an employer's right to require that employees work on certain days of the week was recognized in *O'Malley v. Simpsons-Sears Ltd.*, [1985] 2 S.C.R. 536 (S.C.C.) ("*O'Malley*"), at pp. 555-56, and in *Central Alberta Dairy Pool*, at p. 520. Similarly, it must be recognized that parties to a collective agreement have a right to negotiate clauses to ensure that sick employees return to work within a reasonable period of time. If this valid objective is recognized, the establishment of a maximum period of time for absences is thus a form of negotiated accommodation.

19 The fact that such a period of time has been negotiated and included in the collective agreement indicates that the employer and the union considered the characteristics of the enterprise and agreed that, beyond this period, the employer would be entitled to terminate the sick person's employment. The consensus that has been reached is significant, because it was reached by the people who are most familiar with the particular circumstances of the enterprise, and also because these people were representing different interests. It can therefore be assumed that the clause has been negotiated in the

mutual interest of the employer and the employees. The three-year period is not, therefore, a monetary benefit included in the remuneration of employees in the same way as health insurance or disability benefits. Rather, it is the maximum period that an employee can be absent before the employment relationship will be terminated. Considered from the perspective of the duty to accommodate, this clause, like the right to return to work part time, is among the measures implemented in the enterprise to enable a sick employee to be accommodated.

20 The period negotiated by the parties is therefore a factor to consider when assessing the duty of reasonable accommodation. Such clauses do not definitively determine the specific accommodation measure to which an employee is entitled, since each case must be evaluated on the basis of its particular circumstances. In *Chambly (Commission scolaire régionale) c. Bergevin*, Cory J. wrote the following:

> The provisions of a collective bargaining agreement cannot absolve either the employer or the union from the duty to accommodate. Yet, the terms of the agreement are relevant in assessing the degree of hardship which may be occasioned by interference with its terms. Thus, as pointed out in *Renaud, supra*, at p. 987, a substantial departure from the normal operation of the conditions or terms of employment set out in the collective agreement may constitute undue interference in the operation of the employer's business. [p. 551]

Neither the employer nor the union may impose a period shorter than the one to which a sick person is entitled under human rights legislation in light of the facts of and criteria applicable to his or her particular case. A clause purporting to do so would have no effect against an employee who is entitled to a longer period. Since the right to equality is a fundamental right, the parties to a collective agreement cannot agree to a level of protection that is lower than the one to which employees are entitled under human rights legislation, nor can they definitively establish the length of the period in advance, since the specific circumstances of a given case will not be known until they occur, that is, after the collective agreement has been signed.

21 It has long been recognized that the parties to a contract cannot agree to limit a person's fundamental rights: *Ontario (Human Rights Commission) v. Etobicoke (Borough)*, [1982] 1 S.C.R. 202 (S.C.C.), at p. 213. This principle was reaffirmed in the context of management rights in *Parry Sound (District) Welfare Administration Board v. O.P.S.E.U., Local 324*, [2003] 2 S.C.R. 157, 2003 SCC 42 (S.C.C.):

> Under a collective agreement, the broad rights of an employer to manage the enterprise and direct the work force are subject not only to the express provisions of the collective agreement, but also to statutory provisions of the *Human Rights Code* and other employment-related statutes. [para. 23]

Thus, a clause that meets minimum employment standards is *a priori* not suspect. The parties may refer to it to determine the individual accommodation to which an employee is entitled in a given situation.

22 The importance of the individualized nature of the accommodation process cannot be minimized. The scope of the duty to accommodate varies according to the characteristics of each enterprise, the specific needs of each employee and the specific circumstances in which the decision is to be made. Throughout the employment relationship, the employer must make an effort to accommodate the employee. However, this does not mean that accommodation is necessarily a one-way street. In *O'Malley* (at p. 555) and *Renaud v. Central Okanagan School District No. 23*, [1992] 2 S.C.R. 970 (S.C.C.), the Court recognized that, when an employer makes a proposal that is reasonable, it is incumbent on the employee to facilitate its implementation. If the accommodation process fails because the employee does not co-operate, his or her complaint may be dismissed. As Sopinka J. wrote in *Central Okanagan*, "[t]he complainant cannot expect a perfect solution" (p. 995). The obligation of the employer, the union and the employee is to come to a reasonable compromise. Reasonable accommodation is thus incompatible with the mechanical application of a general standard. In this sense, the Union is correct in saying that the accommodation measure cannot be decided on by blindly applying a clause of the collective agreement. The arbitrator can review the standard provided for in the collective agreement to ensure that applying it would be consistent with the employer's duty to accommodate.

23 A number of termination of employment clauses have been considered judicially. In *S.P.G.Q. c. Lavoie*, [2005] R.J.Q. 944, 2005 QCCA 311 (Que. C.A.), the Quebec Court of Appeal ruled on an application for review of an arbitration award dismissing the grievance of an employee whose employment had been terminated after over two years' absence owing to illness. The Court of Appeal criticized the arbitrator for applying the clause mechanically and remitted the case to him to assess the duty to accommodate on an individualized basis. However, Thibault J.A. noted that the employer would be entitled to dismiss a complainant at the end of the period provided for in the collective agreement if the employee could not establish that she would be able to work within a reasonable period of time:

> [TRANSLATION] As drafted, clause 3-1.18 of the collective agreement does not authorize the employer to automatically dismiss an employee at the end of the salary insurance period, although the employer may do so if the employee cannot establish that he or she will be able to work within a reasonable period of time. [para. 76]

24 In Ontario too, courts and tribunals have refused to find that a termination of employment clause authorizes an employer to dismiss an employee without considering the employee's specific circumstances: *Maple Leaf*

Meats Inc. v. U.F.C.W., Locals 175 & 633 (2001), 149 O.A.C. 295 (Ont. Div. Ct.), and *Bowmanville Memorial Hospital v. O.N.A.* (1993), 35 L.A.C. (4th) 401 (Ont. Arb. Bd.).

25 To sum up, the conclusion to be drawn from the case law is that a termination of employment clause will be applicable only if it meets the requirements that apply with respect to reasonable accommodation, in particular the requirement that the measure be adapted to the individual circumstances of the specific case. If the period provided for in the termination of employment clause is less generous than the one to which the employee is entitled under the principles applicable to the exercise of human rights, the clause will have no effect against the employee and the employer will have to propose further measures to accommodate him or her. The period provided for in a clause such as this is not meant to be a threshold representing the minimum period to which an employee is entitled. On the contrary, the clause should provide for a generous accommodation likely to meet the needs of as many employees as possible. In providing for the most demanding of circumstances, the employer grants employees whose needs are less acute a period more generous than would be required by human rights legislation. Unions can therefore play an important role, where such clauses are concerned, in the course of the collective bargaining process.

26 The three-year period provided for in the agreement between the Hospital and the Union in the case at bar is longer than those provided for in a number of statutes and collective agreements that have already been considered on judicial review (see: *Canada Labour Code*, R.S.C. 1985, c. L-2, s. 239; *Act respecting labour standards*, R.S.Q., c. N-1.1, s. 79.1; *Employment Standards Act*, S.N.B. 1982, c. E-7.2, s. 44.021; *Labour Standards Act*, R.S.N.L. 1990, c. L-2, s. 43.11; *Labour Standards Act*, R.S.S. 1978, c. L-1, s. 44.2).

27 Thus, although a clause providing for termination of the employment relationship after a specified period is not determinative, it does give a clear indication of the parties' intention with respect to reasonable accommodation. It is accordingly a significant factor that an arbitrator must take into account in considering a grievance. In these circumstances, and depending on the duration of the authorized period of absence, such a clause can serve as evidence of the maximum period beyond which the employer will face undue hardship. This evidence may prove very useful, especially in the case of a large organization, where proving undue hardship resulting from an employee's absence could be complex.

28 In short, it cannot be concluded that the accommodation provided for in the collective agreement is a complete answer to the complaint of an employee claiming a more generous accommodation measure. But it is no

more appropriate to say that the benefit incorporated into the collective agreement should not be taken into account in the overall assessment of the accommodation granted by the employer.

III. Did the Arbitrator Err in the Case at Bar?

29 The Court of Appeal faulted the arbitrator for failing to assess on an individualized basis the accommodation to which Ms. Brady was entitled:

> [TRANSLATION] The arbitrator could not simply apply the provisions of the collective agreement and state that it is not discriminatory to refuse to extend the employment of an individual who is not physically capable of performing the duties of the position. He should have considered whether the employer had discharged its burden of proof with regard to the submission that the requested accommodation measure was unreasonable because the additional time the employee would have before returning to work would cause it undue hardship. [para. 32]

30 The analysis the arbitrator had to make concerned the reasonableness of the accommodation requested by Ms. Brady. Did the arbitrator fail to discharge his duty? In my view, the Superior Court's interpretation captures the spirit of the arbitrator's analysis better than that of the Court of Appeal. The arbitrator did indeed conclude that the clause in the collective agreement applied to Ms. Brady, but he did so only after having reviewed and analysed the evidence.

31 The arbitrator started by quoting the clauses of the collective agreement that incorporate the employer's quasi-constitutional obligations relating to the right to equality. He then also quoted the clauses concerning rehabilitation measures and, finally, the one that sets out the circumstances that will result in termination of the employment relationship. If he had felt that only the latter clause was relevant and had simply applied it blindly, he would probably have quoted only it.

32 The arbitrator also related the facts and stated that he had to rule on the applicability of the clause [TRANSLATION] "in the context of the duty to accommodate imposed on the employer" (p. 20). He noted that the employer had discharged its duty to accommodate by granting rehabilitation periods that were longer than the ones provided for in the collective agreement. He concluded with a comment that was determinative in the circumstances that had been presented to him, namely that he found it [TRANSLATION] "difficult to imagine an ... additional duty to accommodate an employee whose attending physician considers her to be totally disabled" (p. 20).

33 The Court of Appeal appears to have held that the duty to accommodate must be assessed as of the time the employee was effectively denied an additional measure (para. 31). In my view, this approach is based on a compartmentalization of the employee's various health problems. Undue hard-

ship resulting from the employee's absence must be assessed globally starting from the beginning of the absence, not from the expiry of the three-year period.

34 The arbitrator was correct to assess the circumstances in light of all the events leading up to the termination of the employment relationship. What is more, when he ruled on the Union's objection to the introduction in evidence of facts subsequent to the filing of the grievance, he made it clear that the employee's overall state of health was relevant:

> [TRANSLATION] Certain facts arising after the filing of the grievance designated as Exhibit S-2 are relevant to this case and must be considered, since they help to explain the situation that existed at the time the grievance arose. These facts are clearly, from the perspective of the instant case, complementary facts, are intimately related to the original events and make it possible to ascertain the actual situation at the time the grievance was filed. They are clearly interrelated facts on a continuum, with Ms. Brady still being, as of the final hearing day, totally [incapable] of performing the usual duties of her position or of any other comparable position for medical reasons.
>
> [Emphasis added; p. 17]

35 The arbitrator took into account not only the accommodation measures granted by the Hospital, which had agreed to rehabilitation periods longer than those provided for in the collective agreement, but also the dynamics leading to the failure of the attempt to return to work before the expiry of the three-year period and, finally, the state of Ms. Brady's health after the employer's decision.

36 The arbitrator thus did not limit himself to automatically applying a clause of the collective agreement. He was aware of the scope of the employer's duty to accommodate but could not anticipate that the employee would be returning to work in the foreseeable future. He therefore correctly concluded that the employer could not continue to employ someone who had been declared to be disabled for an indeterminate period.

37 The arbitrator took into account the clause of the collective agreement that authorized the employer to terminate Ms. Brady's employment, which was an important piece of evidence. This clause was not considered in a factual vacuum. Rather, it acquired particular significance for the purpose of demonstrating the Hospital's willingness to accommodate Ms. Brady during the rehabilitation periods despite the absence of evidence that she would be able to return to work in the foreseeable future.

38 The duty to accommodate is neither absolute nor unlimited. The employee has a role to play in the attempt to arrive at a reasonable compromise. If in Ms. Brady's view the accommodation provided for in the collective agreement in the instant case was insufficient, and if she felt that she would be able to return to work within a reasonable period of time, she had

to provide the arbitrator with evidence on the basis of which he could find in her favour.

IV. Conclusion

39 For these reasons, it is my view that the Superior Court did not err in dismissing the application for judicial review. I would accordingly allow the appeal and set aside the Court of Appeal's decision with costs in both courts.

Abella J.

40 An employer has a duty to provide a discrimination-free workplace. It is important, therefore, to be clear about what discrimination is-and what it is not-so that employers know their duties and employees know their rights.

41 The grievor, Alice Brady, asked that "By virtue of the collective agreement ... the employer arrive at a reasonable accommodation with myself." Notably, Ms. Brady did not claim that the automatic termination clause of the collective agreement pursuant to which her employment was terminated, was discriminatory. Nor did the union allege a breach of the collective agreement.

42 Both Jean Sexton, the arbitrator, and Poulin J. found no discrimination on the part of the employer in refusing to continue to employ someone who, after three years of absence due to illness, is still deemed to be incapable of returning to work by her own doctor. I agree.

43 One preliminary matter. Ms. Brady did in fact return to work intermittently on a part-time basis during her absence of more than 36 months. The arbitrator held that these periods of rehabilitation did not interrupt her absence from work under the collective agreement. He reasoned that "absence"-an undefined term in the agreement-should be construed with reference to the definition of "period of disability". The latter provided for continued sick-leave benefits if an employee returned for less than 15 days of full-time work *or if the employee could show that a completely unrelated accident or illness had caused any subsequent periods of disability*. This is important because it would appear that Ms. Brady was injured in a car accident less than two months before she was scheduled to return to work on a full-time basis. Clearly, the injuries she sustained from the car accident were unrelated to her previous illness. Ms. Brady, however, declined to argue the applicability of the sick-leave benefits clause on this appeal, and I would not interfere with the arbitrator's decision on this issue. It appears that it was not clearly established whether Ms. Brady would have been available for work had it not been for the car accident.

44 The central issue is whether Ms. Brady has established *prima facie* discrimination, shifting the onus to the employer to justify its workplace standard or conduct. I accept that a collective agreement does not necessarily immunize an employer from a transcendent duty not to discriminate (see *Parry Sound (District) Welfare Administration Board v. O.P.S.E.U., Local 324*, [2003] 2 S.C.R. 157, 2003 SCC 42 (S.C.C.)), and that this may involve accommodating an employee to the point where it would impose undue hardship on the employer (*British Columbia (Public Service Employee Relations Commission) v. B.C.G.E.U.*, [1999] 3 S.C.R. 3 (S.C.C.) ("*Meiorin*")). But this is different from creating a legal paradigm that *even if* the employer's conduct is not discriminatory, there is a legal duty to justify all distinctions.

45 Section 10 of the Quebec *Charter of Human rights and freedoms*, R.S.Q., c. C-12 ("*Quebec Charter*"), explains discrimination as follows:

> **10.** Every persons has a right to full and equal recognition and exercise of his human rights and freedoms, without distinction, exclusion or preference based on race, colour, sex, pregnancy, sexual orientation, civil status, age except as provided by law, religion, political convictions, language, ethnic or national origin, social condition, a handicap or the use of any means to palliate a handicap.
>
> Discrimination exists where such a distinction, exclusion or preference has the effect of nullifying or impairing such right.

46 Establishing discrimination under s. 10 of the *Quebec Charter* requires a three-step analysis. A plaintiff must demonstrate:

(1) that there is a 'distinction, exclusion or preference';

(2) that the 'distinction, exclusion or preference' is based on one of the grounds listed in the first paragraph of s. 10 of the Quebec *Charter*; and

(3) that the 'distinction, exclusion or preference has the effect of nullifying or impairing' the 'right to full and equal recognition and exercise of a human right or freedom'.

(*Chambly (Commission scolaire régionale) c. Bergevin*, [1994] 2 S.C.R. 525 (S.C.C.), at p. 538)

47 McIntyre J. defined discrimination in *Andrews v. Law Society (British Columbia)*, [1989] 1 S.C.R. 143 (S.C.C.), in similar terms:

> I would say then that discrimination may be described as a distinction, whether intentional or not but based on grounds relating to personal characteristics of the individual or group, which has the effect of imposing burdens, obligations, or disadvantages on such individual or group not imposed upon others, or which withholds or limits access to opportunities, benefits, and advantages available to other members of society. Distinctions based on personal characteristics attributed to an individual solely on the basis of association with a group will rarely escape the charge of discrimination, while those based on an individual's merits and capacities will rarely be so classed." [pp. 174-75]

48 At the heart of these definitions is the understanding that a workplace practice, standard, or requirement cannot disadvantage an individual by attributing stereotypical or arbitrary characteristics. The goal of preventing discriminatory barriers is inclusion. It is achieved by preventing the exclusion of individuals from opportunities and amenities that are based not on their actual abilities, but on attributed ones. The essence of discrimination is in the arbitrariness of its negative impact, that is, the arbitrariness of the barriers imposed, whether intentionally or unwittingly.

49 What flows from this is that there is a difference between discrimination and a distinction. Not every distinction is discriminatory. It is not enough to impugn an employer's conduct on the basis that what was done had a negative impact on an individual in a protected group. Such membership alone does not, without more, guarantee access to a human rights remedy. It is the link between that group membership and the arbitrariness of the disadvantaging criterion or conduct, either on its face or in its impact, that triggers the possibility of a remedy. And it is the claimant who bears this threshold burden.

50 If such a link is made, a *prima facie* case of discrimination has been shown. It is at this stage that the *Meiorin* test is engaged and the onus shifts to the employer to justify the *prima facie* discriminatory conduct. If the conduct is justified, there is no discrimination.

51 To justify it, an employer must show that the conduct was reasonably necessary to accomplish a legitimate workplace purpose. Part of proving reasonable necessity, as McLachlin J. explained in *Meiorin* at para. 54, is demonstrating that "it is impossible to accommodate individual employees sharing the characteristics of the claimant without imposing undue hardship upon the employer". This is where we examine whether the employer has reasonably accommodated an individual whose group identity has resulted in an arbitrary workplace disadvantage.

52 *Meiorin* defines the applicable evidentiary burden on an employer for justifying discriminatory conduct, that is, for demonstrating that such conduct is brought "within an exception to the general prohibition of discrimination": para. 67. It is an onerous burden, and properly so. It reinforces the primacy of human rights principles in a workplace and tells employers that they can only justify such conduct towards a particular employee if the employee cannot reasonably be accommodated. If they can justify the conduct, there is no discrimination. It is part of the justification defence, not a stand-alone legal duty: if the conduct or standard is not discriminatory, on its face or in effect, no such burden of justification falls on the employer.

53 There is no need to justify what is not, *prima facie*, discriminatory. Unlike Deschamps J., then, the issue for me is not whether the employer has

made out the justification defence of having reasonably accommodated the claimant, but whether the claimant has satisfied the threshold onus of demonstrating that there is *prima facie* discrimination, namely, that she has been disadvantaged by the employer's conduct based on stereotypical or arbitrary assumptions about persons with disabilities, thereby shifting the onus to the employer to justify the conduct.

54 I cannot accept the conclusions of the majority that "automatic" termination clauses automatically represent *prima facie* discrimination. This renders presumptively vulnerable, no matter the reasonableness of their length, all time-limited legislated employment protections for absences due, for example, to illness, disability, or pregnancy. It is hard to see how three years of job protection for a disabled employee-a significantly longer period than the 26 weeks in a 12-month period required by Quebec's *Act respecting labour standards*, R.S.Q., c. N-1.1, s.79.1-constitutes an arbitrary disadvantage merely because it is finite.

55 Moreover, from a policy perspective, designating such clauses as presumptively discriminatory removes the incentive to negotiate mutually acceptable absences. It suggests that, regardless of the reasonableness of the duration of the protection, an employee can still, by bringing a grievance, render the clause's term meaningless, shifting the burden to the employer to explain why it was reasonable to terminate a particular employee.

56 This would leave disabled employees without the lengthy guarantee of job and seniority protection such clauses offer. It is true that they are finite, and therefore, in a technical sense, arbitrary. But they are not arbitrary in the way we understand arbitrariness in the human rights context, that is, they do not unfairly disadvantage disabled employees because of stereotypical attributions of their ability. Instead, these clauses acknowledge that employees should not be at unpredictable risk of losing their jobs when they are absent from work due to disability.

57 Generally, automatic termination clauses of reasonable length represent a trade off *for employees* between their right to be dismissed for just and sufficient cause (which entails that their employment will not be terminated unless there is no prospect that they may return to work in a reasonable period), and the certainty that the employment relationship will be maintained for a fixed period. There is nothing inherently discriminatory in such a trade-off, especially if the resulting protection is significantly longer than the applicable employment standards legislation.

58 Whether *prima facie* discrimination is established, shifting the obligation of justification on the employer, depends on the facts of the particular case, including the negotiated terms of any contract. In *Meiorin*, *prima facie* discrimination was established by the fact that the requirement at issue had the

practical effect of excluding most women from employment as firefighters. This was sufficient to require that the employer justify the requirement.

59 Arbitrators seized with a case such as this must determine, on a case-by-case basis, whether the particular agreement negotiated by the parties is *prima facie* discriminatory. A very short period of leave for disability or illness will raise more concerns than a longer one. The length of time provided by the negotiated clause must be assessed in the context of the nature of the employment and other relevant factors, to determine whether a *prima facie* case of discrimination is established.

60 In this case, the arbitrator, albeit in the context of discussing reasonable accommodation, concluded that the three-year leave period provided by the collective agreement-refusing to maintain the employment of someone who has been "totally incapable" of performing the job for three years and who, after three years, continues to be "totally incapable" of doing so-did not raise a *prima facie* case of discrimination. He stated: [TRANSLATION] "it seems clear that clause 12.11.5 of the collective agreement in no way infringes sections 10 and 16 of the *Charter of human rights and freedoms*" (SOQUIJ AZ-50227506, at p. 21). In the Superior Court, Poulin J. endorsed the arbitrator's conclusion ([2004] J.Q. No. 7555 (Que. S.C.)(at paras. 31-42). I see no reason to interfere with the arbitrator's conclusion on this point.

61 Far from representing discrimination on the basis of disability, the length of this termination clause represents, in purpose and effect, extensive protection from job loss caused by disability. Through clause 12.11.5 of the collective agreement, the union has negotiated exemplary protection for employees who are absent due to illness or accident unrelated to work (work-related accidents or illnesses are covered by a different provision). For 36 months, the employee's job and seniority are protected. According to the definition of "disability" in clause 23.03 of the collective agreement, employees can lose their jobs only if, at the end of the three years, they are [TRANSLATION] "totally incapable of the usual duties of his or her job or of any other comparable, similarly compensated job".

62 Non-culpable absenteeism, including the failure to achieve a reasonable degree of attendance because of illness, is accepted in arbitral jurisprudence as a just cause for dismissal. The absence of a protection such as the one found in clause 12.11.5 leaves an employee vulnerable to the unpredictable judgment of an employer as to whether his or her "innocent absenteeism" for illness is excessive and therefore justifies dismissal. Here, just cause is only presumed after three years of absence. The clause replaces the uncertainty with a guarantee of job protection for three years. It is common sense that the union and employer would make the trade-offs necessary to avoid

an individualized, case-by-case approach to undefined periods of absence and, instead, try to delineate a universal, generous period of job protection for disabled employees beyond which the mutual rights and obligations end.

63 This does not target individuals arbitrarily and unfairly because they are disabled; it balances an employer's legitimate expectation that employees will perform the work they are paid to do with the legitimate expectations of employees with disabilities that those disabilities will not cause arbitrary disadvantage. If the employee is able to return to work, the same or an analogous job remains available. If not, he or she lacks, and has lacked for three years, the ability to perform the job. This, it seems to me, is precisely what is protected by s. 20 of the *Quebec Charter* which states, in part, that "[a] distinction, exclusion or preference based on the aptitudes or qualifications required for an employment ... is deemed non-discriminatory".

64 On the facts and the findings of the arbitrator, the claimant did not establish *prima facie* discrimination. Absent this, the employer is not called upon to justify the standard or its conduct.

65 For these reasons, I agree with the conclusion of Deschamps J. that the appeal should be allowed.

Appendix

Collective Agreement

[TRANSLATION] *3.01* The employer shall treat its employees fairly, and the union shall encourage them to do their work properly.

. . . . .

3.03 For the purposes of this collective agreement, neither management, nor the union, nor their respective representatives shall make threats, exercise coercion or discriminate against an employee because of the employee's race, colour, nationality, social origin, language, sex, pregnancy, sexual orientation, marital status, age, religious beliefs or lack thereof, political opinions, disability, kinship, parental situation or exercise of a right conferred on the employee by this agreement or by law.

Discrimination exists where such a distinction, exclusion or preference has the effect of nullifying, impairing or restricting a right conferred by this agreement or by law for one of the reasons set out above.

Notwithstanding the above, a distinction, exclusion or preference based on the aptitudes or qualifications required to perform the duties of a position is deemed non-discriminatory.

. . . . .

5.03 No special agreement between an employee and the employer respecting working conditions that differ from those provided for in this agreement or that are not provided for in this agreement shall be valid without the written approval of the union.

. . . . .

12.11 An employee shall lose his or her seniority rights and his or her employment in the following cases:

1 - voluntary termination of his or her employment;

2 - in the case of a student, a return to full-time studies constitutes voluntary termination of employment. This paragraph applies only to students hired as replacements for the annual leave (vacation) period;

3 - dismissal;

4 - lay-off for a period exceeding twelve (12) months, except in the case of an employee to whom clause 15.03 applies;

5 - absence by reason of illness or of an accident other than an industrial accident or occupational disease (see above), after the thirty-sixth (36th) month of absence.

. . . . .

23.03 Definition of disability

Disability means a state of incapacity resulting from an illness-including an accident, a pregnancy complication, a tubal ligation, vasectomy or similar case related to family planning, or an organ donation-that requires medical care and renders the employee totally incapable of performing the usual duties of his or her job or of any other comparable, similarly compensated job offered to the employee by the employer.

23.04 A period of disability is any continuous period of disability or a succession of periods separated by fewer than fifteen (15) days of full-time work or availability for full-time work, unless the employee demonstrates to the satisfaction of the employer or the employer's representative that a subsequent period is attributable to an illness or accident that is totally unrelated to the cause of the earlier disability.

23.17

(c) From the eighth (8th) week of disability within the meaning of clause 23.03, an employee holding a position and receiving salary insurance benefits may, at the employee's request and upon the recommendation of the employee's attending physician, benefit from one or more periods of job rehabilitation within a period not exceeding three (3) consecutive months. This job rehabilitation must be agreed to by the employer and must allow the employee to perform all the usual duties of the position. During any rehabilitation period, the salary insurance plan shall continue to apply to the employee.

At the end of the period of three (3) months, the employer and the employee may, on the recommendation of the attending physician, agree to extend this period for up to three (3) consecutive months.

The employee may terminate the period of rehabilitation before the end of the period agreed upon by submitting a medical certificate from the employee's attending physician.

During the rehabilitation period, the employee is entitled to receive both his or her salary for the proportion of the time worked and the benefits for which he or she is eligible for the proportion of the time not worked.

No period of rehabilitation shall have the effect of interrupting the disability period or extending the period of payment of full or partial salary insurance benefits beyond one hundred and four (104) weeks of benefits for the disability.

At the end of a rehabilitation period, the employee may return to his or her position if he or she is no longer disabled. If the disability persists, the employee shall continue to receive benefits as long as he or she is eligible therefor.

Appeal allowed with costs.

INDEX

A